SUMMER THUNDER

One final but very important comment: of the 4.1 million who wore the blue and the gray from 1861 to 1865, over 600,000 gave their lives in a war that determined what the United States would become. What our country is today is because of their commitments and sacrifices.

Those veterans who survived the war have passed on. The generation that followed them, who personally knew them, has also gone. The personal contact that later generations had to these veterans and their war is now gone forever. The only contact we and future generations have are the writings, the artifacts, and the ground upon which they stood, fought, and died. The most direct contact we can have with those veterans and the Civil War is the battlefields themselves. One of the reasons this and other guidebooks are written is to provide that connection with past events on the actual spots where they happened.

Fortunately national, state, and local governments have preserved some of this ground. However, a crisis in battlefield preservation is upon us. Urban development in our country is growing at an exponential rate. In the past, where we may have had a generation or a decade to protect battlefields, we now have only a few years, or in some very threatened places only a few months. If you believe in saving this vital part of our heritage, I encourage you to become active in battlefield preservation.

One of the most successful organizations in preserving battlefields is the nonprofit Civil War Preservation Trust (CWPT). I strongly urge you to become a member of the CWPT and leave a legacy that will be passed to future generations of your family. The CWPT can be contacted by writing: Civil War Preservation Trust, 1331 H Street NW, Suite 1001, Washington, DC, 20005, by calling 202-367-1861, or via the Internet at www.civilwar.org.

Matt Spruill
Littleton, Colorado

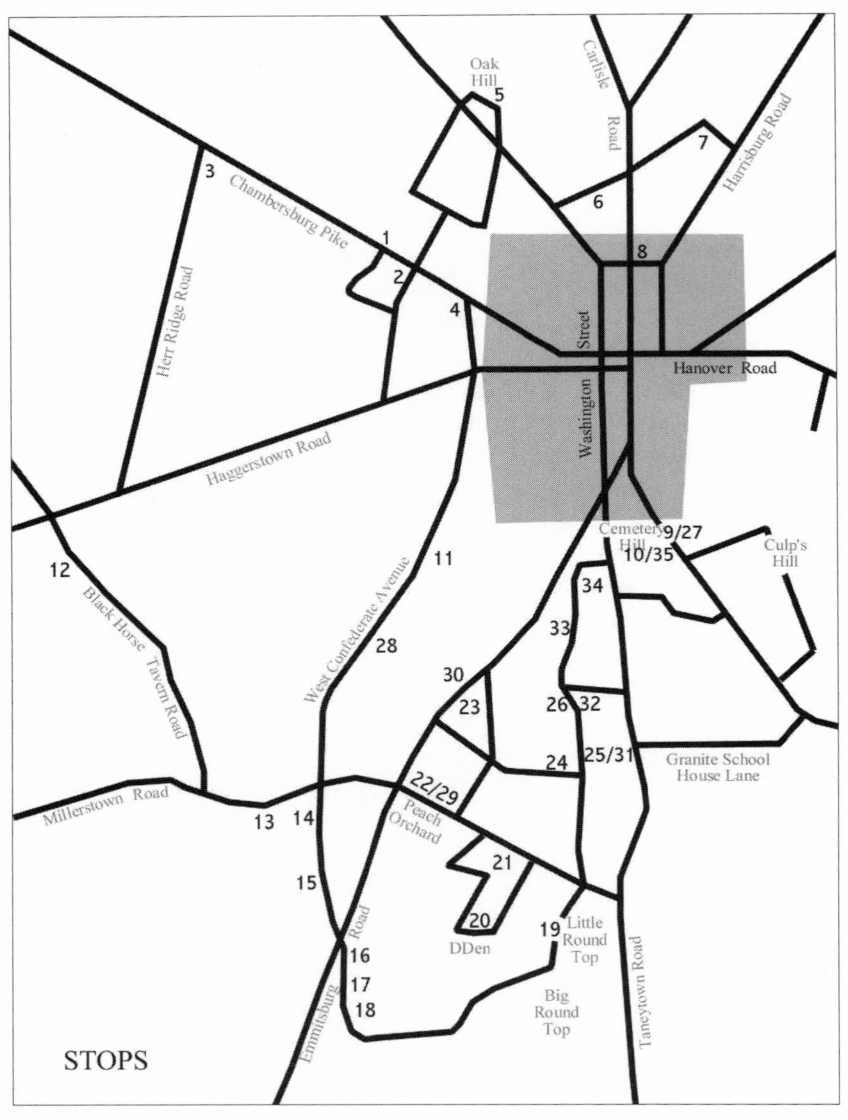

Oak Hill
Carlisle Road
Harrisburg Road
Chambersburg Pike
Herr Ridge Road
Washington Street
Hanover Road
Haggerstown Road
Cemetery Hill
Culp's Hill
West Confederate Avenue
Black Horse Tavern Road
Millerstown Road
Peach Orchard
Granite School House Lane
Little Round Top
DDen
Big Round Top
Emmitsburg Road
Taneytown Road
1
2
3
4
5
6
7
8
9/27
10/35
11
12
13
14
15
16
17
18
19
20
21
22/29
23
24
25/31
26
28
30
32
33
34
STOPS

Chapter 1

PRELUDE

The artillery of the Army of the Potomac and the Army of Northern Virginia that fought at Gettysburg had progressed a long way in organization, weapons, and efficiency since the commencement of the war twenty-seven months before.

Although there were artillery regiments in the U.S. Army and some Union state militias, they were essentially paper organizations. The battery, organized with four to six guns each, was the true basic artillery combat unit. Depending on what was available, initially there were a variety of weapons in each battery. As the war progressed, an effort was made in the Army of the Potomac to standardize with six guns per battery. However, this goal was not always met, and, as late as July 1863, there were batteries in Meade's army with four guns.

Early in the war most batteries were attached to an infantry brigade. This made for almost immediate fire support at the brigade level but was a determent to concentrating batteries for massed fire against a specific target. As the war went into its second year, artillery batteries were removed from the brigades and assigned to each infantry division, but there were occasions when batteries still continued to be attached to the infantry brigades.

The number assigned varied but was usually three or four. In the Army of the Potomac, the senior battery commander, usually a captain, of the assigned batteries was designated as the chief of artillery for the division. In addition to commanding his battery, he was also responsible for deploying the other batteries. This was some improvement in organization but had many drawbacks that prevented full utilization of the artillery. By the time of the Peninsula Campaign, the Army of the Potomac had an army level artillery reserve. Colonel Henry J. Hunt was placed in command of this reserve artillery, which consisted of seventeen batteries organized into five brigades (battalions). However, there still was not a chief of artillery for the army with overall tactical command or centralized command and control of the army's artillery. Subsequently the ability to mass guns consistently and rapidly against a specific target was still lacking.

Hunt was promoted to brigadier general on September 5, 1862, and made the army's chief of artillery, but he had no specific tactical command authority over the army's artillery. Batteries continued to be grouped together in a tactical arrangement at divisional level, and there was an artillery reserve at army level. However, the large reserve with seventeen batteries organized into five brigades was soon disbanded. At the Battle of Antietam, the artillery reserve was a small force of only seven batteries, it was increased to nine batteries at the time of the Battle of Fredericksburg, and, by the time of the Battle of Chancellorsville, it had increased in size to twelve batteries. This twelve-battery reserve with no intermediate command organization such as brigades or battalions proved too large a span of control for the commander of the reserve to command or control effectively or tactically.

There were several offensive and defensive examples in 1862 and early 1863 that should have pointed the direction for artillery organization. An offensive example occurred on April 6, 1862, at the Battle of Shiloh when Brigadier General *Daniel Ruggles* concentrated fifty guns under his command to place concentrated fire on the Union defensive position at the Hornet's Nest.

A defensive example occurred on January 2, 1863, at the Battle of Stones River. Captain John Mendenhall, the chief of artillery for the Left Wing of the Army of the Cumberland, brought together twelve batteries, fifty-seven guns, in the vicinity of McFadden's Ford on the Stones River to halt and drive back what to that point had been a successful attack by a four-brigade infantry division, supported by artillery, of the Confederate Army of Tennessee.

Within the Army of the Potomac, there was a glaring example of concentrated artillery under central control during a defense. On July 1, 1862, during the last of the Seven Days Battles, at Malvern Hill the Union artillery on the forward defensive line was placed under the command of Brigadier General Charles Griffin, a prewar regular army artillery officer. Supported by Hunt's artillery reserve, Griffin delivered concentrated artillery fire that defeated two Confederate attempts to establish artillery positions in support of their infantry. Devastating artillery fire into *Lee's* attacking infantry followed this.

All three of these actions showed the value of having artillery under a central control at division, corps, and army level that gave a senior commander the capability to deploy or maneuver his artillery to the decisive position within his tactical area of responsibility. Such an organization would also allow the next senior commander to reinforce his subordinate with artillery in a timely manner and with sufficient firepower to influence the battle. Only in the Army of Northern Virginia were these lessons partially applied, while in the Army of the Potomac, artillery organization took backwards steps at Antietam, Fredericksburg, and Chancellorsville.

After the disastrous use of artillery at Chancellorsville, Hunt was able to convince the army commander, Major General Joseph Hooker, that a major reorganization was required. He then proceeded to revamp the artillery, creating the centralized, responsive, and flexible organization that fought at Gettysburg.

On May 12, 1863, Army of the Potomac Special Order 129 organized all of the artillery batteries into fourteen artillery brigades. Each brigade was under the command of an artillery officer, assisted by a staff. The seven infantry corps were each assigned an artillery brigade, and the cavalry corps received two artillery brigades. The artillery brigade commanders reported directly to and were responsive to their corps commanders. The remaining five brigades were grouped together into an army level artillery reserve that was commanded by Brigadier General Robert O. Tyler, who reported directly to Hunt. The reserve brigades could be temporarily assigned to an infantry corps or deployed independently wherever they where needed.

The brigade strengths varied. Of the seven brigades assigned to the infantry corps, one had four batteries, five had five batteries, and one had eight batteries. Guns per brigade ranged from a low of twenty to a high of forty-eight, with a average of twenty-six to twenty-eight. The cavalry's two brigades had six and four batteries with thirty and twenty-two guns, respectively. Four of the reserve artillery's brigades had four batteries, with twenty-two to twenty four guns in each brigade. A fifth brigade had five batteries for a total of twenty-eight guns.

Hunt's reorganization also reduced a supply problem. Previously the ammunition supply trains for the artillery were mixed in with the infantry divisions' supply trains. Many times when a resupply of ammunition was needed, battery personnel could not find their wagons. When the artillery brigade system was instituted, each brigade was provided with its own separate ammunition supply train that moved under the control of the brigade commander. In addition there was also a reserve ammunition train under the control of the artillery reserve commander. With direct control of his ammunition train, a brigade commander could have his batteries resupplied, refitted, and back into action at a much faster rate than before. At Gettysburg this capability played a significant role in the effectiveness of the Army of the Potomac's artillery.

The acceptance and implementation of Hunt's reforms in the month prior to the campaign created a highly responsive and flexible artillery organization. This timely reorganization provided Meade and his corps commanders a powerful and efficient artillery organization to support the infantry and had a decisive effect on the battle.

The Army of the Potomac began the war with a variety of artillery pieces, but by early 1862 steps were taken to establish a degree of standardization as to the types of guns that would be used. In the summer of 1863 seven types of guns composed the army's artillery. Three types of guns were 94 percent of the artillery issued to the army. They were the 3-inch Ordnance rifle, the 12-pound Napoleon, and the 10-pound Parrott rifle. The first two weapons accounted for 40 percent and 38 percent (total of 78 percent) of the artillery, and the third type accounted for 16 percent. The remaining four types of guns, the 20-pound Parrott rifle, 12-pound howitzer, James rifle, and 4.5-inch rifle made up only 6 percent of the artillery. Of the army's sixty-eight batteries, only one, the Second Connecticut of the Second Volunteer Artillery Brigade, had two different types of guns.

Types and number of guns in the Army of the Potomac on July 1, 1863 were:

3-inch Ordnance rifle	152
12-pound Napoleon	142
10-pound Parrott	60
20-pound Parrott	6
12-pound howitzer	2
James rifle	4
4.5-inch rifle	12
TOTAL	378

A distribution of artillery by type and artillery brigade is at appendix III.

With only three types of guns making up 94 percent of the total guns, there was a requirement to carry fewer different calibers of ammunition. This provided two logistical advantages. First, there was a high probability that the ammunition supply train of one artillery unit could also resupply other batteries. This provided a logistical flexibility that could result in rapid resupply of batteries and a culmination of more guns in action over a period of time. Second, with a commonality of ammunition among batteries, it was possible for ammunition to be cross-leveled between batteries if supply trains were not close at hand.

The organizational development of the Army of Northern Virginia's artillery followed a pattern similar to the Army of the Potomac. However, the advantage of creating artillery battalions was recognized and acted upon earlier in the Confederate army.

When the war began in the southern states there was no formal tactical organization of artillery above the battery level, except for a few actual battalions. Batteries were organized with four to six guns each with a variety of weapons in each battery. The Army of Northern Virginia attempted to standardize at four guns per battery, but in July 1863 some batteries in *Lee's* army had more than four guns and some fewer.

In what would become the Army of Northern Virginia, the initial practice was also to attach batteries to infantry brigades. Again, as the war went into its second year, artillery was assigned to each infantry division. The difference from the Union practice was the designation of a major, lieutenant colonel, or colonel to be the division's chief of artillery. These officers had tactical command of the division's artillery batteries except when they were attached to an infantry brigade, a practice that continued in 1862.

In the Army of Northern Virginia, the artillery organization continued to develop with the formation of an army level artillery reserve commanded by Brigadier General *William N. Pendleton.* This reserve artillery consisted of fifteen batteries formed into five battalions. In addition *Pendleton* was also the army's chief of artillery, which made him responsible for all of the army's artillery. This gave *Lee* an artillery organization that was semicentralized at division level with a centralized reserve at army level. With this organization *Lee* had the capability (not always used), through *Pendleton,* to influence a battle directly by the deployment of a significant amount of artillery to a specific area.

By the time of the Second Battle of Bull Run, *Lee's* artillery had taken another step forward in organizational development. In *Longstreet's* Command (soon to be designated a corps), there was an artillery reserve of two battalions under command of a corps chief of artillery. This organization provided the corps commander the capability of shifting artillery to influence a battle without removing batteries from the various infantry divisions' artillery. *Jackson's* Command, also later a corps, because of almost continuous combat operations, was unable to organize an artillery reserve and continued to operate with all batteries grouped with the infantry divisions. After the Battle of Antietam, *Jackson* was able to reorganize his artillery so that he had a one-battalion artillery reserve. With these artillery organizations *Longstreet* and *Jackson* fought the Battle of Fredericksburg.

In early 1863 *Lee's* army was organized into two infantry corps—commanded by Lieutenant Generals *James Longstreet* and *Thomas "Stonewall" Jackson*—a division of cavalry commanded by Major General *J. E. B. Stuart* and an artillery reserve commanded by Brigadier General *William N. Pendleton.* Except for the cavalry's artillery, all of the batteries were organized into fourteen battalions. Each infantry division was assigned a battalion composed of four to six batteries. Each corps had one or two artillery battalions in reserve, while six batteries formed into two battalions constituted the army's artillery reserve. This reorganization gave *Lee* the capability to influence a battle by maneuvering artillery, through *Pendleton,* to critical points on the battlefield. The corps commanders also had the same reserve artillery capability within their corps, while the divisional artillery normally was deployed under command of a division's chief of artillery. It was this artillery organization, minus the two battalions with *Longstreet* in southeastern Virginia, which fought at the Battle of Chancellorsville.

In the winter of 1862–63, *Lee* considered reorganizing his army. He believed that *Longstreet's* and *Jackson's* corps, with five divisions and four divisions, respectively, were too large, especially in wooded terrain, to be effectively maneuvered. However, he had not taken the steps necessary to reorganize.

After *Jackson's* wounding at Chancellorsville and death on May 10, *Lee* proceeded with a reorganization of his army. On May 30, 1863, Special Order 146 reorganized the army from two to three infantry corps, with each corps having three infantry divisions. *Lee* also reorganized the artillery. The artillery batteries, except the cavalry's, were redistributed to form fifteen battalions. With some exceptions, each battalion was organized with four batteries of four guns each, for a total of sixteen guns. Each infantry corps was assigned five artillery battalions that were under the tactical control of each corps commander and his corps chief of artillery. Of these five battalions each of the three infantry divisions had one artillery battalion attached for fire support, while the other two battalions were kept as a corps artillery reserve. This organization was flexible enough to allow corps commanders to shift battalions around to concentrate firepower or meet special circumstances. In this reorganization all of the battalions of the army artillery reserve were reassigned to the corps artillery, and the army artillery reserve ceased to exist. While this reorganization provided more artillery to each corps commander, it left *Lee* with no army level artillery he could directly employ to influence a battle. Having no central reserve of artillery to command, *Pendleton* as the army's chief of artillery concentrated on administrative duties.

Lee's army also began the war with a wide variety of guns. However, unlike their Union counterparts, the artillery was unable to reach the same level of standardization. In July 1863 *Lee's* artillery was composed of ten types of weapons. Five types of guns made up 95 percent of the artillery. They were the 3-inch Ordnance rifle (29 percent), the 12-pound Napoleon (36 percent), the 10-pound Parrott (15 percent), the 20-pound Parrott (4 percent), and the 12-pound howitzer (11 percent). The remaining five types of artillery composed 5 percent of the artillery. These guns were the 24-pound howitzer (1.4 percent), 6-pound gun (0.3 percent), 3-inch naval rifle (1.4 percent), the Whitworth rifle (0.7 percent), and the Blakely rifle (1.2 percent).

Types and number of guns in the Army of Northern Virginia on July 1, 1863 were

3-inch Ordnance rifle	78
12-pound Napoleon	98
10-pound Parrott	44
20-pound Parrott	10
12-pound howitzer	33
24-pound howitzer	4
6-pound gun	1
3-inch naval rifle	4
Whitworth rifle	2
Blakely rifle	3
TOTAL	277

A distribution of artillery by type and artillery battalion can be found in appendix IV.

A majority of the seventy batteries that were the Army of Northern Virginia's artillery were composed of a mixture of guns. Thirty-seven batteries were equipped with two types of guns, seven were equipped with three or four types of guns, while just twenty-six had only one type of gun. Among *Lee's* major maneuver units, the number of the types of guns per battery was

	2 Types of Guns	3 or 4 Types of Guns	1 Type of Gun
Longstreet's Corps	11	3	8
Ewell's Corps	8	1	11
Hill's Corps	13	3	4
Cavalry	5	0	3
Total	37 (52.8%)	7 (10%)	26 (37.2%)

The actual number of guns in each battery also varied significantly. The organizational goal was to equip each battery with four guns, preferably all of the same type. Fifty-five of the seventy batteries were equipped with four guns. Of these, twenty-three batteries had four guns of the same type, twenty-eight had two types of guns, and four had three types of guns. Among the remaining fifteen batteries, the number of guns ranged from one gun to six guns each.

The number of guns per battery in the major maneuver units was

	1 Gun	2 Guns	3 Guns	4 Guns (Same)	4 Guns (2 types)	4 Guns (3 types)	5 Guns	6 Guns
Longstreet's Corps	1	0	3	6	8	1	1	2
Ewell's Corps	0	0	1	11	7	1	0	0
Hill's Corps	0	0	1	4	10	2	1	2
Cavalry	0	1	1	2	3	0	1	0
Total	1 (1.5%)	1 (1.5%)	6 (8%)	23 (33%)	28 (40%)	4 (5%)	3 (4%)	4 (5%)

Batteries that were equipped with smooth-bore and rifled guns possessed the capability of close-in defense with the smooth bore's canister and long-range precision with the rifled guns. However, to concentrate either smooth-bore or rifled guns for a particular mission required the grouping of many batteries and in some cases, with rifled guns concentrated, leaving the smooth-bore weapons in the rear. In addition each battery had to carry two or more calibers of ammunition. This added to the logistical burden at the battery level, which was compounded at the battalion level, where ammunition for up to four different types of guns, and in one battalion five different types, was required. The large variety of ammunition at battalion level particular to that battalion's guns degraded the capability for the ammunition supply train of one battalion to resupply another and brought a degree of inflexibility to the artillery's logistics.

His army's reorganization completed, in the early days of June *Lee* began positioning the Army of Northern Virginia for his Summer Campaign of 1863. *Ewell's* and *Longstreet's* Corps were moved west, away from Fredericksburg, Virginia, while *Hill's* Corps was left in position to observe the Army of the Potomac on the other side of the Rappahannock River. On June 10 *Lee* sent *Ewell* into the Shenandoah Valley with orders to march north and clear the valley of Union presence. *Ewell* accomplished this when he arrived at Winchester on June 13 and defeated Union forces in that vicinity. On June 15 *Longstreet* began advancing north along the east side of the Blue Ridge Mountains, while *Hill* began moving his corps west from Fredericksburg, and then entered the Shenandoah Valley on June 19 and 20 and marched north. *Longstreet* in the meantime occupied the upper gaps in the Blue Ridge Mountains, and *Ewell* marched into Maryland. On June 22 the lead elements of *Ewell's* Corps crossed into Pennsylvania and three days later was in the vicinity of Chambersburg. On June 24 *Hill's* and *Longstreet's* Corps continued moving north and by the twenty-seventh had reached Chambersburg. Meanwhile on June 24 two of *Ewell's* Divisions (*Rodes's* and *Johnson's*) continued marching northward and arrived at Carlisle on the twenty-seventh. *Ewell's* other division (*Early's*) had been sent east through a gap in South Mountain, marched through and north of Gettysburg, and on June 28 occupied York with a brigade father east along the Susquehanna River at Wrightsville. Up to this point in the campaign, except for the fighting in the vicinity of Winchester, Virginia, the artillery had not played a significant role. This was about to change.

In the first days of June, the Army of the Potomac was positioned north of the Rappahannock River in the vicinity of Fredericksburg. By June 12 its commander, Major General Joseph Hooker, had received sufficient intelligence on *Lee's* movements that he began to shift the army northward. This and all subsequent moves were to comply with its prime directive to maintain the Army of the Potomac between *Lee's* army and Washington, D.C. By June 14 Hooker's army had left the vicinity of Fredericksburg and was moving north to and beyond Manassas. During June 17–24 the army occupied positions from the Potomac River south to the east-west Manassas Gap Railroad. In this location it formed a protective arc to the west and northwest of Washington and was between the capital and *Lee's* army. While in these locations, the Union and Confederate cavalry battled each other for control of the upper gaps through the Blue Ridge Mountains (June 19–21). On June 25 Hooker's army began moving north again, crossed the Potomac River, entered into Maryland, and by the twenty-eighth was concentrated around Frederick, Maryland. Hooker was relieved of command of the army on June 28, and Major General George G. Meade replaced him. Meade ordered the army north into Pennsylvania on June 29.

The last days of June saw both armies moving toward each other. *Lee's* army approached from the west and north, while Meade's army came up from the south. The night of June 28, *Lee* received intelligence that the Union army was across the Potomac River in Maryland and was moving northward. *Lee* responded to this intelligence by ordering his army to concentrate in the Cashtown-Gettysburg area. By the night of June 30 the corps with their artillery had marched to locations that would allow the army to concentrate the next day. *Hill's* corps had advanced from the area of Chambersburg east through a gap in South Mountain and was concentrating in the vicinity of Cashtown. Up to this point each of his three infantry divisions had been marching with an artillery battalion attached, while the other two battalions were maintained as a corps reserve. On the night of June 30, the three artillery battalions were detached from the infantry divisions and placed

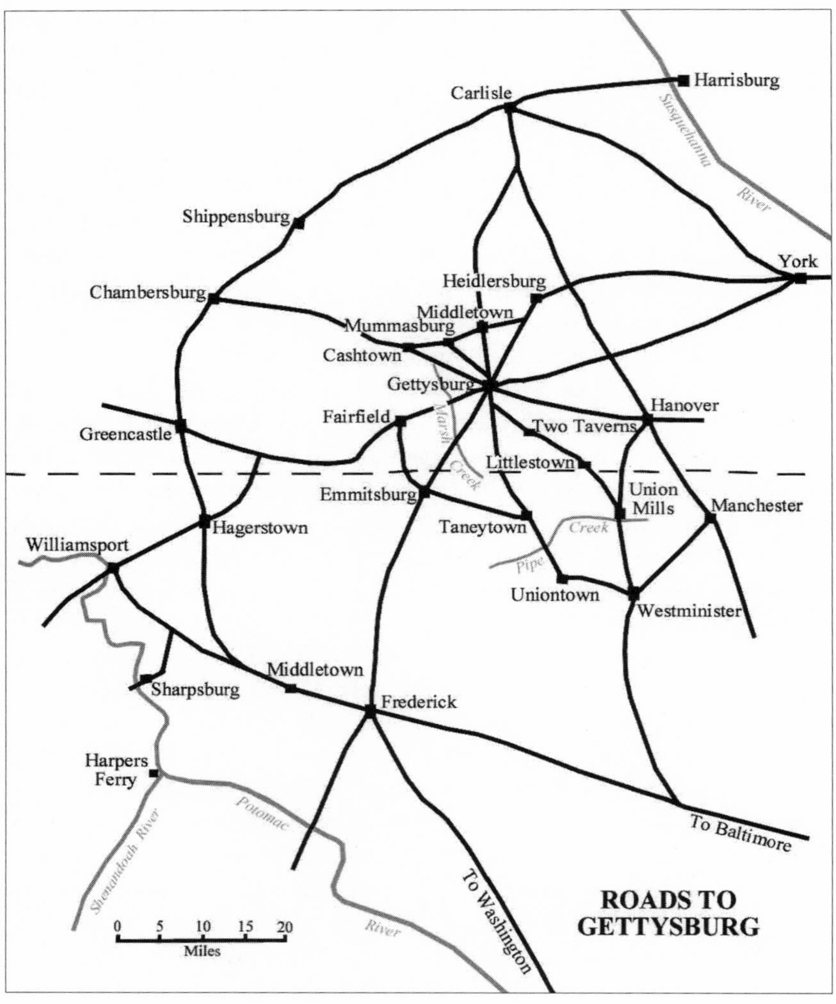

with the other two in the artillery reserve and under a central command. The next morning two battalions moved east to support *Heth's* and *Pender's* march toward Gettysburg, while the other three were kept in reserve. Two divisions of *Longstreet's* Corps (*McLaws's* and *Hood's*) had been following *Hill's* Corps and spent the night at the western base of South Mountain, while one division (*Pickett's*) remained at Chambersburg.

Ewell's Corps had the farthest to travel and marched by multiple routes. *Early's* Division with *Jones's* Artillery Battalion departed York on the morning of the thirtieth and bivouacked that night near Heidlersburg. On the same day *Rodes's* Division with *Carter's* Artillery Battalion marched south from Carlisle to Heidlersburg, where they remained over night. The next morning both divisions resumed their marches and approached Gettysburg from the north and northeast. *Ewell's* other division, *Johnson's,* and the corps artillery reserve traveled the longest distance. *Johnson's* Division accompanied by *Andrew's* Artillery Battalion departed Carlisle and headed back toward Chambersburg. The next day, turning east, *Johnson's* Division marched through the gap in South Mountain and rejoined the remainder of *Ewell's* Corps late in the afternoon, too late to participate in that day's fighting. The Corps Artillery Reserve (*Dance's* and *Nelson's* Battalions) marched with *Johnson's* Division and did not reach the battlefield in time to participate in the July 1 fighting.

On the last day of June, Meade's army was moving north searching for *Lee's.* Two of Meade's cavalry divisions, operating in front of the army, had reached Gettysburg and Hanover. Four of the infantry corps with their artillery brigades had entered or were about to enter Pennsylvania. The First Corps and its artillery brigade were just south of Marsh Creek. The Eleventh and Third Corps, and their artillery brigades in the vicinity of Emmitsburg, were just south the First Corps. Twenty miles to the east the Twelfth Corps accompanied by its artillery brigade had reached Littlestown. Behind these advance corps were the remaining three corps and their artillery. The Second was at Uniontown, the Fifth at Union Mills, and the Sixth at Manchester. The army's Artillery Reserve was concentrated at Taneytown.

The next day elements of Meade's army began marching. Early on reports came from Brigadier General John Buford that he was engaging Confederate infantry west of Gettysburg, and Union infantry was ordered to march to his support. Events of the next ten hours brought more and more units from each army into the fight. The night of July 1 and the morning of July 2 brought the rest of each army to Gettysburg.

In the summer of 1863 the Blue and Grey cannoneers brought a terrible man-made thunder and lightning to the peaceful fields and wooded lots around a small crossroads town. The test of the men, weapons, organization, and command and control of both armies' artillery had begun.

Chapter 2

WEDNESDAY, JULY 1, 1863

Begin your tour at the Visitor Center. There is an access road through the Visitor Center facility that connects the parking lots to the Baltimore Pike to the east and the Taneytown Road to the west. From any of the parking lots, drive west to the Taneytown Road.

As you reach the Taneytown Road, the small house several hundred yards to your right front, on the other side of the road, is the Leister House. This is where Meade established his headquarters.

Turn right on to the Taneytown Road and drive north for 0.5 mile to the intersection with Steinwehr Avenue (U.S. Business 15). The National Cemetery will be on your right as you drive on the Taneytown Road. At the intersection with Steinwehr Avenue, there is a stoplight. Steinwehr Avenue goes to your right. Continue straight on through the intersection and on to Washington Street. Drive on Washington Street for 0.6 mile to the intersection with Chambersburg Street. As you travel along Washington Street and out to Seminary Ridge and McPherson's Ridge, you will be following the route Brigadier General John Buford's cavalry division used as it went through Gettysburg on June 30. Continue to drive north on Washington Street. In 0.4 mile you will see a yellow two-story building to your right, on the corner of Washington Street and High Street. This was the original home of the Lutheran Seminary. The seminary was begun here in 1826 and in 1832 moved to its present location on the ridge just west of town. In two more blocks you will come to the intersection with Chambersburg Street. There is a stoplight at this intersection.

On the northeast corner of the intersection of Washington Street and Chambersburg Street, there is a small parking lot and a store. In 1863 this was the location of the Eagle Hotel. Buford established his headquarters there on the night of June 30.

Turn left on to Chambersburg Street, also named U.S. Highway 30 West. Drive west on this road. In 0.1 mile, at the stoplight, take the right fork and follow Highway 30. Continue to drive for another 0.9 mile. You will pass beyond the town and through a traffic light where Reynolds Avenue (a park road) intersects with Highway 30. At the first park road after the traffic light and just short of a small stone building, turn left and drive for 40 yards to a small parking area in the trees on your right behind the small stone building. Turn into the parking area and park. Leave your car, and walk back toward the Chambersburg Pike. Just before you reach the pike, turn right, stay off the road, and walk 25 yards to the monument and cannon marking the position of Battery A, Second U.S. Artillery. Turn around, stand next to the cannon, and look west, which is the direction you were driving on the Chambersburg Pike.

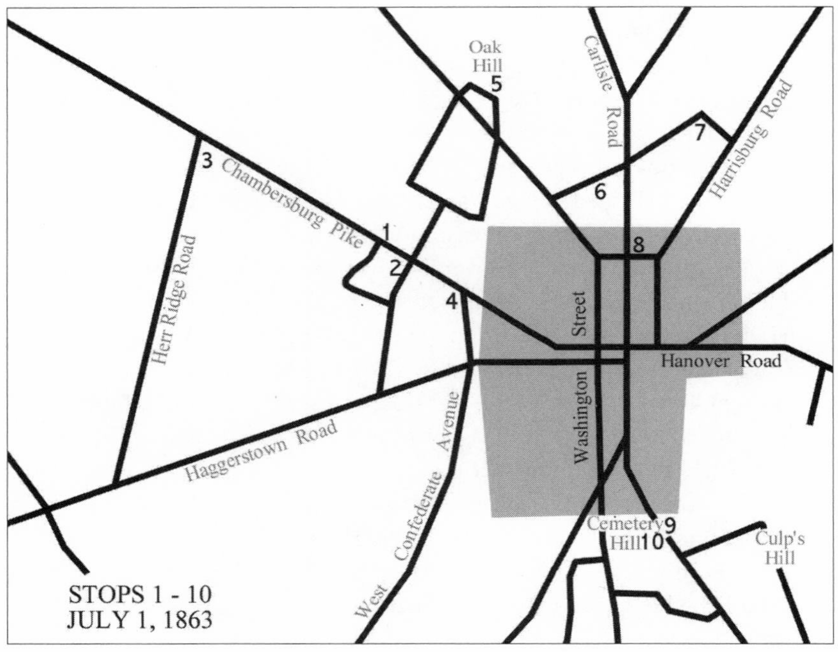

Stop 1, Position A—Horse Artillery in Action

You are standing on the western edge of McPherson's Ridge. The Chambersburg Pike, also called the Cashtown Road, is to your right. In 1,100 yards the pike crosses Herr Ridge. Six miles from where you are, the road passes by Cashtown. From there it continues over South Mountain to Chambersburg. Herbst Wood is to your left and three-fourths of a mile farther left is the Hagerstown (Fairfield) Road. The barn to your left rear was part of the farm owned by the McPherson family in 1863. The house was in the lower ground on the other side of the barn. It burned in 1896. Beyond the barn at a greater distance to the east, where the white spire rises above the trees, you can see the Lutheran Seminary. Behind you (east) is Seminary Ridge. To your right rear on the other side of the railroad is Oak Ridge. One mile to your right (north) is Oak Hill. Brigadier General Henry J. Hunt provided a good description of how this area appeared in 1863.

Report of Brig. Gen. Henry J. Hunt, USA, Chief of Artillery, Army of the Potomac

On the west of Gettysburg, about a third of a mile distant, there is a ridge running nearly north and south, parallel to the Emmitsburg pike. This ridge, on which the seminary is situated, is crossed by the Cashtown [Chambersburg] pike about 100 or 150 yards north of the seminary, and some 50 yards farther on it is cut by a railroad. On the west of the seminary is a grove of large trees, and the summit of the ridge and the upper part of both its slopes are more or less covered with open woods through its entire length. The ground slopes gradually to the west, and again rising, forms a second ridge [McPherson's Ridge], parallel to and about 500 yards distant from the Seminary

Brigadier General Henry J. Hunt, USA. Library of Congress.

Ridge. This second ridge is wider and smoother than that upon which the seminary stands, and terminates about 200 yards north of the point at which the Cashtown road crosses it. Near this point, and to the south of it, are a house and barn, with some five or six acres of orchard and wooded grounds, the rest of the ridge being cleared. [*OR* 27, Part 1, pp. 228–29]

Brigadier General John Buford's cavalry division was conducting reconnaissance to the left and left front of the Army of the Potomac as it marched north. Discovering that *Lee's* Army of Northern Virginia was apparently concentrating in the Gettysburg-Cashtown area, he communicated this intelligence to Major General John F. Reynolds. Reynolds, normally the First Corps Commander, was temporarily commanding the army's Left Wing. In this position he had under his tactical command the First, Third and Eleventh Corps. On the morning of July 1, these corps were marching north toward Gettysburg. Buford decided to conduct a delaying action to buy time for the marching infantry to reach his position.

You are in the center of the position occupied by Brigadier General John Buford's cavalry division on the morning of July 1. His First Brigade, commanded by Colonel William Gamble, was deployed along McPherson's Ridge from the railroad cut, on your right, south through your location, through the woods to your left, and on south almost to the Hagerstown Road. Colonel Thomas C. Devin's Second Brigade was deployed north of the railroad cut. Devin's line went north from the railroad cut for 1,200 yards to the Mummasburg Road. Using outposts, Devin extended his line east of Seminary Ridge and north of Gettysburg, thereby covering any Confederate approach from the north.

Report of Brig. Gen. John Buford, USA, Commanding First Cavalry Division, Cavalry Corps, Army of the Potomac

By daylight on July 1, I had gained positive information of the enemy's position and movements, and my arrangements were made for entertaining him until General Reynolds could reach the scene.

On July 1, between 8 and 9 a.m., reports came in from the First Brigade (Colonel Gamble's) that the enemy was coming down from toward Cashtown in force. Colonel Gamble made an admirable line of battle, and moved off proudly to meet him. The two lines soon became hotly engaged, we having the advantage of position, he of numbers. The First Brigade held its own for more than two hours, and had to be literally dragged back a few hundred yards to a position more secure and better sheltered. Tidball's battery, commanded by Lieutenant Calef, Second U.S. Artillery, fought on this occasion as is seldom witnessed. At one time the enemy had a concentric fire upon this battery from twelve guns, all at short range. Calef held his own gloriously, worked his guns deliberately with great judgment and skill, and with wonderful effect upon the enemy. [*OR* 27, pt. 1, p. 927]

The artillery supporting the cavalry was Battery A, Second U.S. Artillery. The battery was equipped with six 3-inch rifles, which had a maximum effective range of approximately 1,830 yards. Four guns of the battery were deployed at this position, a section (two guns each) on either side of the pike. A third section was positioned south of the woods to your left. Across the pike at the base of Buford's statue are four gun barrels mounted in stone. Gun number 233 from Battery A (see plate on the barrel when you go to Position B) was the first artillery piece fired in the Battle of Gettysburg.

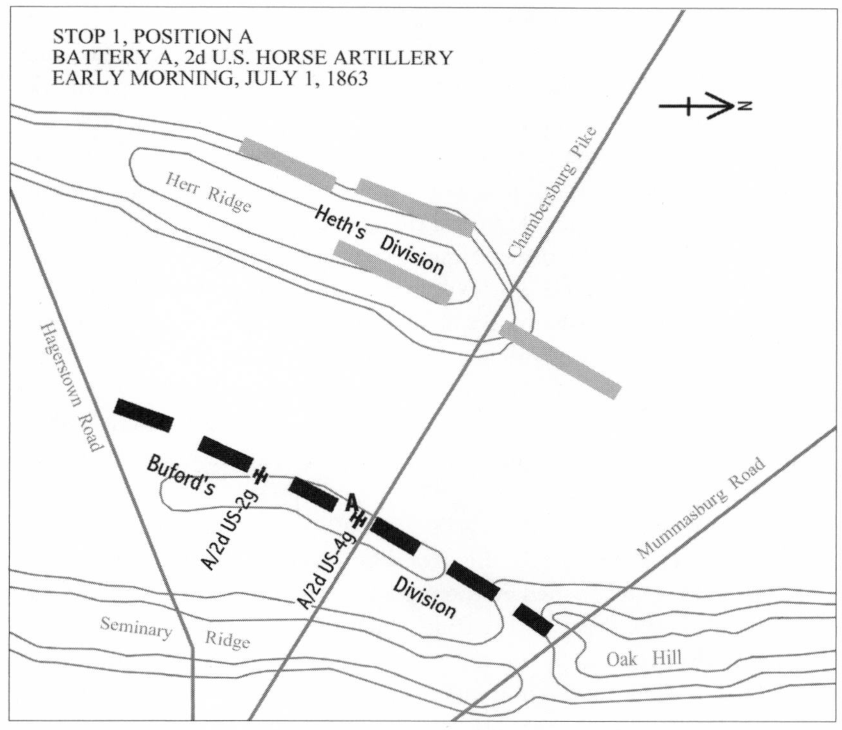

Report of Lieut. John H. Calef, USA, Commanding Battery A, Second U.S. Artillery, Second Brigade, Horse Artillery, Cavalry Corps, Army of the Potomac

Enemy reported to be advancing in heavy columns on [Chambersburg] pike, and preparations were immediately made to receive them. This was about 8 a.m. Colonel Gamble, commanding the brigade of cavalry to which my battery was attached, requested me to select my own position. I accordingly selected a position about 600 yards in front of the one held during the night. As soon as the pioneer party had leveled the intervening fences, as well as the one in front of my position, I moved forward and took up the advanced position [to the right of the Chambersburg Pike]. No sooner was this accomplished than General Buford sent for me, and told me he wished one section [two guns] on the left of the road [where you are] and one still farther to the left [on the other side of the woods]. I accordingly placed First Sergeant Newman, commanding left section, on immediate left of road, and Sergeant Pergel, commanding center section, still farther to the left. No sooner was the latter placed in position than I heard the enemy's skirmishers open upon our pickets, who were retiring.

Lieutenant Roder now fired the first gun (which opened the sanguinary battle of Gettysburg) on the head of a column of rebel [infantry] advancing on the right of the road. Two of the enemy's batteries, one on each side of the road [on Herr Ridge], now opened on my guns near the road. The number of guns in each battery, as near as I could judge, was four so that they outnumbered mine just two to one. The enemy's infantry advanced rapidly, and the musketry and artillery fire soon became extremely warm. We, however, held our position until the arrival of the First Corps. At this juncture, General Buford ordered me to withdraw my guns in each section by piece, which was accordingly executed in good order. Sergeant Newman having four horses killed and disabled at his left piece, I immediately sent back for a limber from one of the caissons, but before it could be gotten up, Sergeant Newman, by strenuous exertions, drew off the piece with one team. The enemy's infantry was so close that it was impossible to take off all the harness; two sets out of the four were, however, afterward recovered by Sergeant Newman.

Riding over to Sergeant Pergel's section, I found that the enemy had advanced out of the woods in his front, and were making rapidly for his guns. He had already opened on them, and, by well-directed shots, had succeeded in checking them for the time. Having but a small cavalry support, and the woods occupied by the enemy extending up within 200 yards of the right of the section, I thought it unadvisable to wait till they arrived within canister range, and therefore withdrew the section, and took it, with the remainder of the battery, which had by this time withdrawn, to a point indicated by Colonel Gamble, and awaited orders. While there, I had the ammunition chests replenished, which was no sooner accomplished than General Buford sent for a piece to enfilade a ditch [the railroad cut] occupied by the enemy. Lieutenant Roder took his right piece to the spot, and opened with canister, which had the effect of driving the enemy in great confusion. As he was bringing the piece into battery, the enemy, seeing it, rushed forward and exclaimed, "There is a piece—let's take it!" As soon as the piece was unlimbered, Corporal [Robert S.] Watrous, chief of piece, in bringing up a round of canister, was shot in the leg by a Minie bullet, and dropped. Private [Thomas] Slattery, with commendable presence of mind, took the round from his hands, and carried it to the piece. The effect of that round probably saved the piece. [*OR* 27, pt. 1, pp. 1030–31]

Lieutenant John H. Calef, USA. U.S. Army Military Institute.

Buford had Calef deploy his guns, by sections, across a broad front. One section was north, one section was south of the Chambersburg Pike, and a third section was south of Herbst Woods. This tactic gave the impression of there being more artillery than there actually was. It also allowed the battery to fire on a wider front as the Confederates deployed and advanced.

When ordered to withdraw his battery, Calef retired by sections—one gun at a time within each section. This technique allowed his battery to maintain a sustained fire at the Confederates even while he was withdrawing from action.

Buford's cavalry had been in contact with the lead element of Lieutenant General *Ambrose P. Hill's* corps as it marched east on the Chambersburg Pike. Major General *Henry Heth's* division was *Hill's* leading element. *Heth's* Division was supported by *Pegram's* Battalion, which was composed of five batteries.

Report of Lieut. Gen. *Ambrose P. Hill,* CSA, Commanding *Hill's* Corps, Army of Northern Virginia

On July 1, at 5 a.m., *Heth* took up the line of march, with *Pegram's* battalion of artillery, followed by *Pender,* with *McIntosh's* battalion of artillery, Colonel [*R. Lindsay*] *Walker* [Corps' chief of artillery] with the remainder of the artillery being with General *Anderson.* About 3 miles from Gettysburg, *Heth's* advance brigade (*Archer's*) encountered the advance of the enemy. *Archer* and *Davis* were thrown into line, and, with some pieces of artillery from *Pegram,* the enemy were steadily driven back to the wooded hills this side of Gettysburg, where their principal force (since ascertained to be the First and Eleventh Corps) were disposed to dispute our farther advance.

Heth's whole division was now thrown into line; *Davis* on the left [north] of the road, *Archer, Pettigrew,* and *Brockenbrough* on the right [south], and *Pender's* [Division] formed in his rear; *Thomas* on the left, and *Lane, Scales,* and *Perrin* on the right. *Pegram's* and *McIntosh's* battalions of artillery were put in position on the crest of a hill [Herr Ridge] overlooking the town of Gettysburg. *Heth's* division drove the enemy, encountering a determined resistance. [*OR* 27, pt. 2, p. 607]

Face right, be extremely careful of traffic, and cross to the north side of the Chambersburg Pike. Stand where the guns representing Hall's Second Maine Battery are and face west. As you are facing west, Seminary Ridge and Gettysburg will be behind you, and the Chambersburg Pike will be to your left.

Position B—Reinforcements Arrive

As you look west, you can see a red roof building and a brick building on Herr Ridge. The red roof building is the historic Herr Tavern, which was there at the time of the battle. *Hill's* artillery began deploying in that vicinity. The woods in the low ground between you and Herr Ridge were not there in 1863. The first Union infantry to arrive was Brigadier General James S. Wadsworth's First Division of the First Corps. Arriving with Wadsworth's division was the Second Maine Battery. Armed with six 3-inch rifles, the battery was initially deployed facing west between the Chambersburg Pike, to your left, and the railroad cut, to your right.

The battery was in the center of Brigadier General Lysander Cutler's Second Brigade. To the battery's left were the Eighty-fourth New York (Fourteenth Brooklyn) and Ninety-fifth New York Infantry Regiments. To the battery's right, in the field on the other side of the railroad cut, was the 147th New York Infantry Regiment. To the right and rear of the 147th New York were the Fifty-sixth Pennsylvania and Seventy-sixth New York Infantry Regiments.

Attacking from the west were two infantry brigades of *Heth's* Division. Brigadier General *James J. Archer's* brigade was south, and Brigadier General *Joseph R. Davis's* brigade was north of the pike.

Report of Brig. Gen. Henry J. Hunt, USA—continued

About 10.15 a.m. Hall's battery (Second Maine, six 3-inch) was ordered into action by General Reynolds on the right of the Cashtown road, on the second ridge, and some 500 yards beyond the seminary. The enemy had previously opened fire from a battery of six guns at a distance of about 1,300 yards, and directly in front of this position, on Reynolds' troops, and Hall,

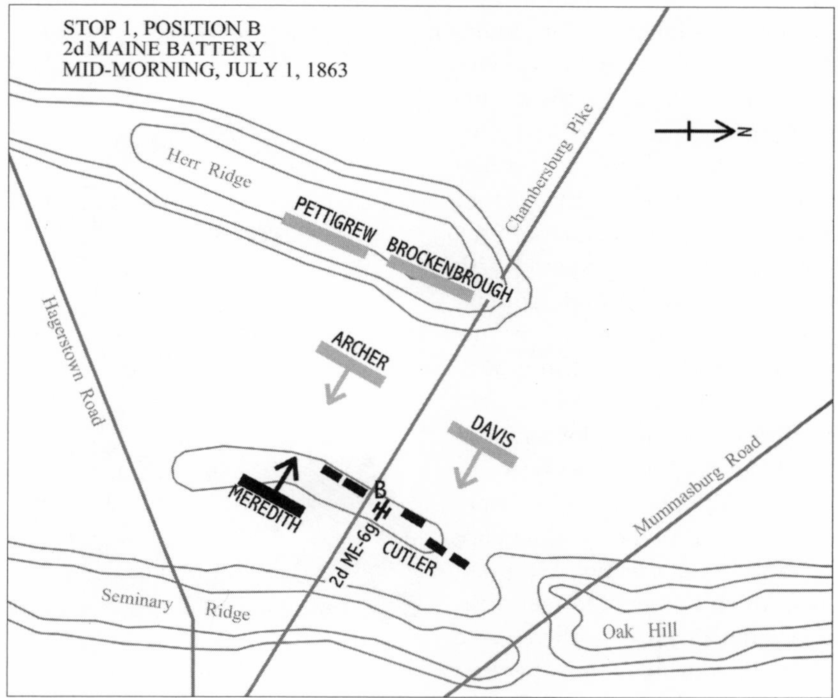

on coming into action, replied with effect. In the course of half an hour, a body of the enemy's infantry approached the right of Hall's battery under cover of a ravine, and opened upon him at a distance of 60 or 80 yards, killing and wounding a number of his men and horses. The right and center sections replied with canister, while the left section continued its fire on the enemy's battery. [*OR* 27, pt. 1, p. 229]

Report of Capt. James A. Hall, USA, Commanding Second Maine Battery, Artillery Brigade, First Corps, Army of the Potomac

We were ordered into position by General Reynolds on the right of the Cashtown road, some 400 yards beyond Seminary [Ridge]. The enemy had previously opened a battery of six guns directly in our front at 1,300 yards distance, which they concentrated upon me as I went into position, but with very little effect.

We opened upon this battery with shot and shell at 10.45 a.m., our first six shots causing the enemy to change the position of two of his guns and place them under cover behind a barn. In twenty-five minutes from the time we opened fire, a column of the enemy's infantry charged up a ravine on our right flank within 60 yards of my right piece, when they commenced shooting down my horses and wounding my men. I ordered the right and center sections to open upon this column with canister, and kept the left firing upon the enemy's artillery. This canister fire was very effective, and broke the charge of the enemy, when, just at this moment, to my surprise I saw my support [147th New York] falling back without any order having been given me to retire. Feeling that if the position was too advanced for infantry it was equally so for artillery, I ordered the battery to retire by sections, although having no order to do so. The support falling back rapidly, the right section of the battery, which I ordered to take position some 75 yards to the rear, to cover the retiring of the other four pieces, was charged upon by the

Captain James A. Hall, USA. Roger D. Hunt and Jack R. Brown, *Brevet Brigadier Generals in Blue*.

enemy's skirmishers and 4 of the horses from one of the guns shot. The men of the section dragged this gun off by hand.

As the last piece of the battery was coming away, all its horses were shot, and I was about to return for it myself, when General Wadsworth gave me a peremptory order to lose no time, but get my battery in position near the town, on the heights, to cover the retiring of the troops.

I sent a sergeant with 5 men after the piece, all of whom were wounded or taken prisoners. I had got near to the position I had been ordered to take, when I received another order from General Wadsworth to bring my guns immediately back; the officer bringing the order saying he would show me the road to take, which was the railroad grading leading out from town, which was swept at the time by two of the enemy's guns from the hills beyond, through the excavations at Seminary [Ridge]. [*OR* 27, pt. 1, pp. 359–60]

The Confederate infantry that Captain Hall mentions as being on his flank and charging up a draw was the Forty-second Mississippi of *Davis's* Brigade. The 147th New York was outflanked on the north by the rest of *Davis's* Brigade and fell back out of the field to Hall's right. This in turn caused Hall to order his guns to fall back. The report of the First Division commander provides an overall picture of the battle swirling around Hall's battery.

Report of Brig. Gen. James S. Wadsworth, USA, Commanding First Division, First Corps, Army of the Potomac

On the morning of July l, at 8 a.m., the division moved from Marsh Creek on Gettysburg, under the immediate direction of our deeply lamented commander, Major-General Reynolds. I understand that the general received information when we were within about a mile of the town that the enemy were approaching from the direction of Cashtown. He immediately turned the head of the column to the left, across the fields, and struck the Cashtown [Chambersburg] road about three-quarters of a mile west of Gettysburg at about 10 a.m. The Second Brigade, Brigadier-General Cutler, led the column, followed by the Second Maine Battery, Captain Hall, the First Brigade [the Iron Brigade], Brigadier-General Meredith, bringing up the rear. Here we met the advance guard of the enemy. Three regiments of the Second Brigade were ordered to deploy on the right of the road, the battery was placed in position near the road, and the balance of the division ordered up to the left of the road.

The right became sharply engaged before the line was formed, and at this time (about 10.15 a.m.) our gallant leader [Major General John F. Reynolds] fell, mortally wounded. The right encountered a heavy force, were outnumbered, outflanked, and after a resolute contest, bravely conducted by Brigadier-General Cutler, fell back in good order to Seminary Ridge, near the town, and a portion of the command to a point still nearer the town. As they fell back, followed by the enemy, the Fourteenth New York State Militia [Eighty-fourth New York], Colonel Fowler; Sixth Wisconsin Volunteers, Lieutenant-Colonel Dawes, and Ninety-fifth New York Volunteers, Colonel Biddle, gallantly charged [in a northward direction] on the advance of the enemy, and captured a large number of prisoners [in the railroad cut], including two entire regiments with their flags. The other regiments of the First Brigade [the Iron Brigade] advanced farther on the left, and captured several hundred prisoners, including Brigadier-General *Archer.* The enemy fell back. I reformed the line, the Second Brigade on the right, on a ridge [McPherson's Ridge], the First [Brigade] in a piece of woodland [Herbst Wood] on the left. The battery [Hall's] had fallen to the rear, disabled by the loss of horses. I found [Calef's] battery on Seminary Ridge, and advanced it to the front line, where it engaged a battery of the enemy in front of us. Major-General Doubleday, commanding the corps at that time, arrived on the ground about the time, or very soon after, General Reynolds fell, with the Second and Third Divisions.

The enemy advanced in heavy force on our right, and placed a battery in position to enfilade the line, and I was obliged to order the right to fall back to Seminary Ridge, forming the line northwesterly and diagonal to the Cashtown road. Two brigades of the Second Division were sent to our right, and gallantly held the enemy in check for an hour, capturing a large number of prisoners. I received orders direct from Major-General Howard to hold Seminary Ridge as long as possible. [*OR* 27, pt. 1, pp. 265–66]

Report of Brig. Gen. Henry J. Hunt, USA—Continued

Soon after, the Third Division (Rowley's), First Corps, occupied the open ground on this ridge with Cooper's battery (B, First Pennsylvania, four 3-inch) which took post in an oat-field, about 380 yards south of the Cashtown road.

The Second Division (Robinson's) occupied a road on the west slope of the Seminary Ridge, north of the railroad, and the Eleventh Corps came into position on the flat ground farther northeast, and in a position nearly perpendicular to that of the First Corps. [*OR* 27, pt. 1, p. 229]

The counterattack by the two New York regiments and the Sixth Wisconsin against the Confederate infantry in the railroad cut reestablished the Union line on the north side of the road. This allowed Calef's battery to return to this location and resume firing.

Report of Lieut. John H. Calef, USA—Continued

Captain Hall's [Second Maine] battery, belonging to the First Corps, occupied the first position on the right of the road held by Lieutenant Roder's section after the latter had withdrawn. In about half an hour this battery was disabled, and, leaving two pieces on the field, withdrew. The left and center sections of my battery were then ordered up again by General Wadsworth to reoccupy the ground just abandoned by Captain Hall, which was done under a heavy fire of musketry. As soon as the first gun was fired from my battery, three four-gun rebel batteries opened from the front and right of my position.

In this spot I had most men wounded, and by musketry. After occupying the ground about fifteen minutes, the rebel battery on my right and front moved off still more to the right, under cover of the woods, and took up a position so as to nearly enfilade my guns. I held this position as long as possible, but, the enemy having a crossfire with several batteries, I was forced to withdraw. I then took up a position [on Seminary Ridge] nearly on a line with my former one, but better covered by a corner of woods from the batteries in front, and remained in that position until relieved by a battery of the First Corps; then took up a position in a wheat-field about 500 yards to the rear and left of former position.

In this engagement, which was a very severe one, the battery lost 12 men badly wounded and 13 horses killed. [*OR* 27, pt. 1, pp. 1031–32]

Return to your car for the drive to Stop 2. Be extremely careful of traffic as you walk across the Chambersburg Pike.

Depart the parking lot, turn right, and follow the park road through Herbst Woods for 0.4 mile where you will come to a T intersection with Reynolds Avenue. This is the wood held by First Brigade (Iron Brigade), First Division, First Corps. At the T intersection you can see the Lutheran Seminary directly in front of you. Sergeant Pergel's section from Calef's battery was deployed 150 yards to your right. Turn left onto Reynolds Avenue, drive north for 125 yards to Battery L, First New York Artillery's monument, and stop on the right side of the road. Get out of your car and face left, west.

Stop 2—First Corps Artillery in Action

You are standing in the center of the position occupied by the First and Third Divisions of the Army of the Potomac's First Corps. The park road that goes to your left and right, south and north, indicates the general location of their battle line. To your left front is the wood you just drove through. About 50 yards to your left front, along the edge of the wood, is a small monument on a mound. This marks the location where Major General John Reynolds was killed while he urged on the Second Wisconsin of the Iron Brigade in its counterattack against *Archer's* Brigade. In front of you at a distance, you can see portions of Herr Ridge, which was a significant Confederate artillery position. To your right front is the McPherson barn and beyond that Stop 1. The Chambersburg Pike is to your right, and the railroad cut is just beyond the pike. To your right rear, the terrain on the other side of the railroad cut, with a long line of trees that stretches north, is Oak Ridge. Farther on, one mile from your location, you can see a tall white monument. This marks Oak Hill. It was a major Confederate artillery position and will be visited later. Directly behind you are the Lutheran Seminary and a portion of the ridge that acquired its name from the seminary. The Hagerstown (Fairfield) Road is 880 yards to your left.

At Stop 1 you studied the cavalry-delaying action followed by the arrival of the first infantry units. This was Cutler's Second Brigade from Wadsworth's division. Wadsworth's other brigade, the Iron Brigade, soon joined Cutler's and deployed into the woods to your left front. The next First Corps division to arrive was the Third Division. Its two brigades, Stone's and Biddle's, went into positions on either side of Herbst Wood. Colonel Roy Stone's brigade occupied the ground directly in front of you between the wood and the pike. Cutler's brigade was generally on Stone's right and right rear. Meredith's Iron Brigade was in the wood on Stone's left. To the left, south, of the wood was Colonel Chapman Biddle's brigade.

When Brigadier General John C. Robinson's division arrived it initially occupied a reserve position near the Seminary, then was sent north and occupied a position on Cutler's right in the wood line on Oak Ridge.

The Confederate forces initially in contact with Buford's cavalry and then Wadsworth's infantry were two brigades of *Heth's* Division. *Archer's* Brigade advanced toward you on the south side of the pike, while *Davis's* Brigade advanced on the north side. Part of *Davis's* Brigade swung south and attacked toward you. This attack was stopped at the railroad cut by a Union counterattack. This counterattack started in the fields in front of and behind you and moved north. After this counterattack and the Iron Brigade's attack into Herbst Wood, both *Archer's* and *Davis's* Brigades were withdrawn a short distance and additional Confederate forces brought up.

Report of Lieut. Gen. *Ambrose P. Hill,* CSA—Continued

Heth's whole division was now thrown into line; *Davis* on the left of the road, *Archer, Pettigrew,* and *Brockenbrough* on the right, and *Pender's* [Division] formed in his rear; *Thomas* on the left, and *Lane, Scales,* and *Perrin* on the right. *Pegram's* and *McIntosh's* battalions of artillery were put in position on the crest of a hill [Herr Ridge] overlooking the town of Gettysburg. *Heth's* division drove the enemy, encountering a determined resistance. [*OR* 27, pt. 2, p. 607]

With the arrival of the First Corps infantry also came its artillery brigade. The brigade was composed of five batteries, one of which, Hall's, had already been engaged. Colonel Charles S. Wainwright commanded the artillery brigade, and upon his arrival on the field he began to position the other four batteries.

Report of Col. Charles S. Wainwright, USA, Commanding Artillery Brigade, First Corps, Army of the Potomac

Gettysburg [Lutheran] Seminary is situated on a ridge about a quarter of a mile from the town, the ridge running nearly north and south and parallel with the Emmitsburg pike. It is crossed by the Cashtown [Chambersburg] pike about 100 yards north of the seminary, and cut through by the railroad some 40 yards farther on. The west front of the seminary is shaded by a grove of large trees, and the whole top of the ridge on both sides is more or less crowned with open woods through its entire length. Beyond this ridge the ground falls gradually to the west, and rises again into a parallel ridge at a distance of about 400 yards. This second ridge [McPherson's Ridge] is wider and smoother than that on which the seminary stands, but ends about 200 yards north of where the Cashtown pike crosses it.

On the south side of this point is a house and large barn [McPherson's Barn], with an apple orchard and some 5 acres of wood [Herbst Wood] to the south of it; the rest of the ridge is cleared. It was around this house and wood that the first skirmish, in which General Reynolds fell, took place.

Having massed the batteries immediately in rear of the first ridge [Seminary Ridge], I rode forward to examine the ground in front, and was met by a member of General Doubleday's staff, with an order to post a battery on the outer ridge [McPherson's Ridge], if possible. Directing Captain Reynolds to move his battery [L, First New York] forward, I rode up on to the ridge, but finding that the battery would be exposed and totally without support, I withdrew it before it reached the crest. Soon afterward the Third Division, with Cooper's Battery B, First Pennsylvania, arrived and took position along the open part of the crest, the battery being posted in an oat-field some [500] yards south of the Cashtown road. [The monument marking Cooper's position is 450 yards to your left.] One brigade of the First Division had meantime reoccupied the wood where the first engagement took place, and General Wadsworth [the division commander] sent to ask for a battery, but as there was no infantry to protect its right flank, and Captain Hall had previously come so near to losing his battery in the same position, I did not consider it safe to place a battery in that position until our Second Division, which was just arriving, had taken position and I had examined the ground on the flank, the enemy being quiet at this time.

Colonel Charles S. Wainwright, USA. U.S. Army Military Institute.

Finding General Robinson's division and the Second Brigade of the First Division occupying a wood on the west slope of Seminary Ridge north of the railroad, and the Eleventh Corps coming into position across the flat at right angles to our front, I returned to the Cashtown road, and directed Lieutenant Stewart to report to General Robinson with his battery [B, Fourth U.S. Artillery], which had previously been posted some 200 yards south of the seminary, but not engaged.

Meantime General Wadsworth had ordered [Calef's] horse battery into position on the right of his First [Iron] Brigade, where Captain Hall's battery had been, and it had just commenced a sharp engagement with the enemy's battery directly in front. As soon as possible, I moved Reynolds' battery up to relieve [Calef's], but it had not fairly gotten into position [about where you are] before the enemy opened a severe fire from a second battery immediately on our right. By this cross-fire both batteries were obliged to withdraw, Reynolds taking position again at right angles to the ridge [and facing north], so that his left was covered by [Herbst] woods. While removing his battery, Captain Reynolds received a severe wound in the right eye, but refused for some time to leave the field. The enemy's battery soon after ceased firing. Receiving another request from General Wadsworth for some guns on his front, I posted Lieutenant Wilber, with a section of [Battery] L, First New York, in the orchard on the south side

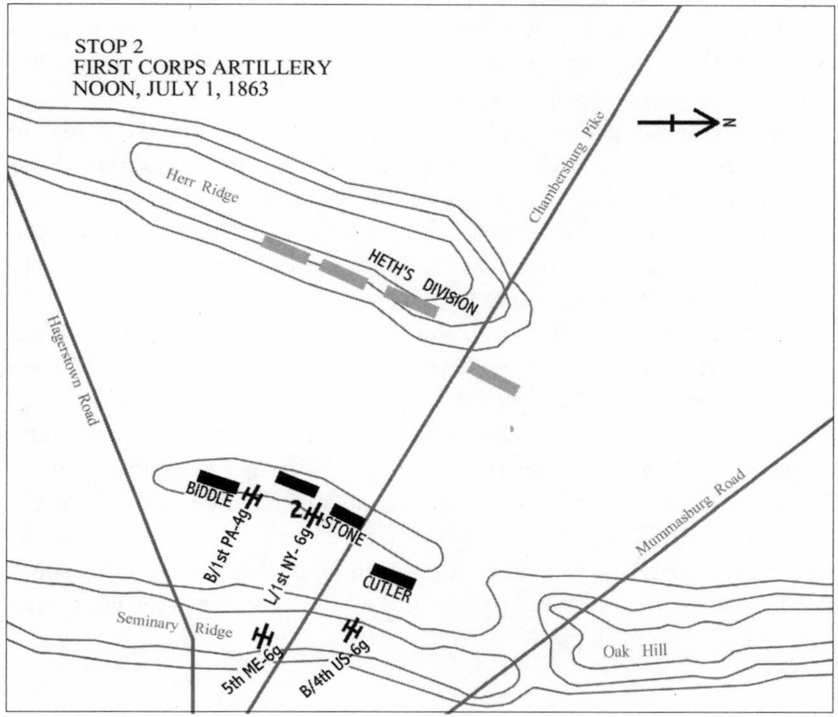

of the Cashtown road, where he was sheltered from the fire of the enemy's battery on his right flank by the intervening house and [McPherson's] barn, and moved the remaining four pieces around to the south side of the wood on the open crest. [*OR* 27, pt. 1, pp. 355–56]

Under Wainwright's supervision Captain Gilbert H. Reynolds led the six 3-inch rifles of his battery into action. When Reynolds was wounded, Lieutenant George Breck assumed command of the battery.

Report of Lieut. George Breck, USA, Commanding Battery L, First New York Artillery, Artillery Brigade, First Corps, Army of the Potomac

About 1 p.m. the battery was ordered by Col. C. S. Wainwright to advance to the support of [Calef's] battery, which occupied a knoll across a road to the front [Stop 1] and extreme left of our line as then engaged. One section of the battery had hardly come into position [where you are] when, in addition to the galling fire in front, an enfilading fire was opened from the [right], which completely swept the position and forced both batteries to retire. At this point, Captain Reynolds was severely wounded, and the command of the battery devolved upon me.

I brought the pieces again into position about 500 yards in rear of the first position, and in a line nearly west of the brick seminary. After an engagement of nearly an hour's duration in the last-named position, I moved my battery to the crest of a hill [McPherson's Ridge] to the left and front, and fired about 6 rounds at the lines of the enemy, which were very steadily extended around our left.

The right section of the battery, under command of Lieut. B. W. Wilber, was ordered to go still farther to the [right], where a few rounds only were fired, when the section was forced to retire with our troops, who were rapidly falling back, closely pressed by the enemy. The other four pieces, under command of Lieut. William H. Bower and the immediate supervision of Colonel Wainwright, returned to the second position above named. As the infantry were falling back close upon the guns, no fire was opened, and the four pieces again retired, and took position upon the ridge running south from the brick seminary and in rear of the belt of timber to the left of that building. [*OR* 27, pt. 1, pp. 362–63]

The Confederate battery on the right flank that Wainwright, Breck, and Cooper wrote about was part of the artillery battalion supporting *Rodes's* Division of *Ewell's* Corps. This battery was located on Oak Hill, one mile north, where the tall white monument is.

Wainwright fought on this line with two batteries, Reynolds's Battery L, First New York, with six 3-inch rifles, in the vicinity of where you are and Cooper's Battery B, First Pennsylvania, with four 3-inch rifles, 450 yards to your left. At various time these two batteries were position to fire west and north.

Report of Capt. James H. Cooper, USA, Commanding Battery B, First Pennsylvania Artillery, Artillery Brigade, First Corps, Army of the Potomac

On the morning of the 1st of July, the battery marched from camp near Emmitsburg, Md., to the vicinity of Gettysburg, Pa. Here it was placed in position by Colonel Wainwright, about 12 m, on the left of the Third Division, First Army Corps, and fired about twenty-five shots at a battery in front, which was firing upon the infantry of the corps and Captain Hall's battery. This battery soon ceased firing, and another directly on the right opened, when we changed front to the right, by order of Colonel Wainwright, and engaged it for a few minutes, when the colonel ordered the battery to be placed in position near the Gettysburg Seminary. [*OR* 27, pt. 1, p. 364]

Return to your car for the drive to Stop 3.

Drive north on Reynolds Avenue for 0.1 mile to the intersection with the Chambersburg Pike, where the stoplight is. Turn left on to the Chambersburg Pike, and drive west for 0.8 mile to Herr Ridge. At the red building, Herr Tavern, turn left onto Herr Ridge Road. Drive for 0.1 mile, find a safe place to park, and park alongside the road. Be careful of traffic, leave your car, and find a position where you can look east back toward Stops 1 and 2. All of this land is private. Do not trespass.

Stop 3—Confederate Artillery Joins the Fight

Left and right of where you are was the position where two battalions of Confederate artillery deployed to support *Hill's* Corps as it came into action against the Union defenses on McPherson's Ridge. Major *David G. McIntosh's* four-battery battalion with sixteen guns was deployed to your right. Major *William J. Pegram's* five-battery battalion with twenty guns was deployed to your left. *Pegram's* Battalion, marching with *Heth's* Division, was the first to deploy. Four of the five batteries took up firing positions. Captain *Edward A. Marye's* Fredericksburg (Virginia) Artillery Battery with two 3-inch rifles and two Napoleons deployed, to your left, astride the Chambersburg Pike. To *Marye's* left, north, was Captain *Joseph McGraw's* Purcell (Virginia) Artillery Battery with four Napoleons, then the four 3-inch rifles of Lieutenant *William E. Zimmerman's* Pee Dee (South Carolina) Artillery Battery. Farther north and forward was Captain *Thomas A. Brander's* Letcher (Virginia) Artillery Battery with two 10-pound Parrotts and two Napoleons. The range from the artillery on Herr Ridge to targets on McPherson's ridge was 1,400 yards, well with in the maximum effective range of the smooth-bore and rifled guns.

Report of Capt. *Ervin B. Brunson,* CSA, Commanding *Pegram's* Artillery Battalion, *Hill's* Corps, Army of Northern Virginia

On the morning of July 1, we moved forward on the [Chambersburg] pike, in rear of General *Heth's* division. When within 2 miles of Gettysburg, Captain *E. A. Marye's* section of rifled guns was run forward, unlimbered in the road, and opened on a piece of woods to the left of the pike, where was stationed a reconnoitering party of the enemy. [This is west of your present location.]

After firing some eight or ten rounds, the pieces were limbered up, and the battalion moved forward to a commanding position on the right and left of the pike. [This is where you are.]

Here we found the enemy's batteries in position, and partially concealed from view behind the crest of a hill. We opened upon them with [eight] Napoleons and seven rifled guns (the two 12-pounder howitzers were not brought into position, and one of Lieutenant *W. E. Zimmerman's* rifles was disabled while being brought rapidly into action), and forced them to limber up and retire their pieces three distinct times.

They were brought back twice under shelter of the hills, in order to support their advancing infantry, whose lines our guns played upon as they advanced, with telling effect.

During the day, Captain *T. A. Brander's* [Letcher] battery was ordered to report to Brigadier-General *Davis,* whose line was on the left of the pike, and considerably in advance of our position. Captain *Brander* was ordered to post his battery [two 10-pound Parrotts and two Napoleons] upon a hill immediately in rear of General *Davis'* skirmishers, about 500 yards from the enemy's batteries, and to open upon their infantry, which he did in handsome style, suffering considerably from the enemy's canister.

Our casualties in this battle were very small, considering the heavy fire to which the battalion was exposed for a greater portion of the day. They consisted of 2 men killed and 8 wounded also 6 horses killed. [*OR* 27, pt. 2, pp. 677–78]

The Union batteries Captain *Brunson* mentions departing under fire and returning are Calef's and Hall's.

Moving forward to support *Pegram's* Battalion and deploying where you are and to your right was *McIntosh's* Battalion. The guns deployed where you are were the four Napoleons of Captain *R. Sidney Rice's* Danville (Virginia) Artillery Battery and two Whitworth rifles from Captain *William B. Hurt's* Hardaway (Alabama) Artillery Battery. To your right were the two 3-inch rifles and two Napoleons of Lieutenant *Samuel Wallace's* Second Rockbridge (Virginia) Artillery Battery. Farther to your right were four 3-inch rifles of Captain *Marmaduke Johnson's* Virginia Battery and *Hurt's* two 3-inch rifles.

Report of Maj. *David G. McIntosh,* CSA, Commanding *McIntosh's* Artillery Battalion, *Hill's* Corps, Army of Northern Virginia

On the morning of Wednesday, July 1, [the battalion] moved with General *Pender's* division into the line of battle. One battery of Napoleons (Captain *R. S. Rice*) and a section of Whitworth [rifles] were placed first in position a short distance to the right of the turnpike, by the side of a portion of Major *Pegram's* battalion, and fire was opened slowly upon the enemy wherever they brought into view considerable bodies of troops, and occasionally upon their batteries. The Whitworth guns were used to shell the woods to the right of the town.

After a short interval, Captain *Johnson's* battery and the remaining section of Captain *W. B. Hurt's* were placed on a commanding hill some distance

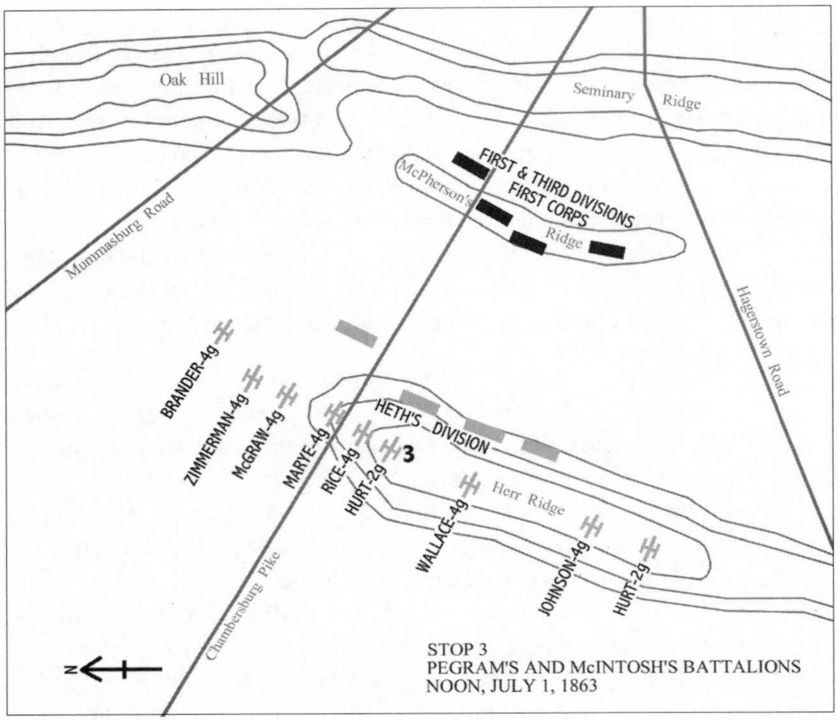

to the right [out of your sight], near the Fairfield [Hagerstown] road, at or near which point they remained during the first day's action without any occasion for an active participation, though frequently under fire. The remaining battery of the command, under Lieutenant *Samuel Wallace,* was also placed in position near the Cashtown [Chambersburg] pike, and contributed its portion of work.

Major *David G. McIntosh,* CSA. Jennings C. Wise, *The Long Arm of Lee* (1915).

The artillery fire on both sides was occasionally brisk, but deliberate on our part. At the time General *Ewell's* [Corps] batteries occupied the enemy's attention, I opened on them a flank fire, which caused them to leave the position in haste. A fine opportunity was also afforded at this time of enfilading a heavy column of the enemy's infantry, formed in the railroad cut and along a line of fence, which was employed to advantage by my batteries in connection with Major *Pegram's,* and the enemy, entirely discomfited, disappeared from the field. Previous to this time, I had advanced two of my batteries to the intervening hollow, and followed close upon the enemy as he left the hills.

No further movements were made during the day, the casualties being 1 man killed of Captain *Johnson's* and 1 wounded of Captain *Rice's* by premature explosion, and several horses disabled. [*OR* 27, pt. 2, pp. 674–75]

By mid-afternoon *Heth* had brought forward his other two brigades and deployed them just forward of Herr Ridge. From that location, supported by *Pegram's* and *McIntosh's* Battalions, he attacked the Union defenders on McPherson's Ridge.

Report of Maj. Gen. *Henry Heth,* CSA, Commanding *Heth's* Division, *Hill's* Corps, Army of Northern Virginia

The enemy had now been felt, and found to be in heavy force in and around Gettysburg. The division now formed in line of battle on the right of the road, the several brigades posted as follows: *Archer's* brigade (Col. *B. D. Fry,* Thirteenth Alabama Regiment, commanding) on the right, *Pettigrew* in the center, and *Brockenbrough* on the left [in front of where you are]. *Davis'* brigade was kept on the left of the road, that it might collect its stragglers, and from its shattered condition it was not deemed advisable to bring it again into action on that day. It, however, did participate in the action later in the day. After resting in line of battle for one hour or more, orders were received to attack the enemy in my front, with the notification that General *Pender's* division would support me.

The division had not advanced more than 100 yards before it became hotly engaged. The enemy was steadily driven before it at all points, excepting on the left, where *Brockenbrough* was held in check for a short time, but finally succeeded in driving the enemy in confusion before him.

Pettigrew's brigade encountered the enemy in heavy force, and broke through his first, second, and third lines. The Eleventh North Carolina Regiment, Colonel *Leventhorpe* commanding, and the Twenty-sixth North Carolina Regiment, Colonel *Burgwyn,* commanding, displayed conspicuous gallantry, of which I was an eye-witness. The Twenty-sixth North Carolina Regiment lost in this action more than half its numbers in killed and wounded, among whom were Colonel *Burgwyn* killed and Lieutenant-Colonel *Lane* severely wounded. Colonel *Leventhorpe,* of the Eleventh North Carolina Regiment, was wounded, and Major *Ross* killed. The Fifty-second and Forty-seventh North Carolina Regiments, on the right of the center, were subjected to a heavy artillery fire, but suffered much less than the Eleventh and Twenty-sixth North Carolina Regiments.

Archer's brigade, on the right (Col. *B. D. Fry* commanding), after advancing a short distance, discovered a large body of cavalry on its right flank. Colonel *Fry* judiciously changed his front, thus protecting the right flank of the division during the engagement. [This cavalry was Gamble's brigade of Buford's division, which after the arrival of the infantry had redeployed to and was protecting the First Corps left flank.]

After breaking through the first and second lines of the enemy, and several of the regiments being out of ammunition, General *Pender's* division relieved my own, and continued the [attack].

At the same time that it would afford me much gratification, I would be doing but justice to the several batteries of *Pegram's* battalion in mentioning the assistance they rendered during this battle. [*OR* 27, pt. 2 pp. 638–39]

The Union forces facing this attack were the four infantry brigades of the First and Third Division of the First Corps and four batteries of the corps artillery brigade. This force was deployed generally along McPherson's Ridge. Directly in front of you on McPherson's Ridge between the Chambersburg Pike and Herbst Wood was Colonel Roy Stone's Second Brigade of the Third Division. To Stones left, your right, in Herbst Wood was Colonel Solomon Meredith's First (Iron) Brigade of the First Division. To Meredith's left, your right, was the First Brigade of the Third Division commanded by Colonel Chapman Biddle. On Stone's right, your left, and north of the Chambersburg Pike was Brigadier General Lysander Cutler's Second Brigade of the First Division. These units were under almost continuous artillery fire from the Herr Ridge position and from Confederate artillery on Oak Ridge.

Return to your car for the drive to Stop 4.

Drive back to the Chambersburg Pike. Turn right onto the pike and drive east for 1 mile to a small parking area on the left, north, side of the road. The parking area is just over 0.1 mile past the stoplight at the intersection of the pike with Reynolds Avenue. Make a left turn into the parking area, park, and get out of your car. Be extremely careful of traffic and cross to the south side of the Chambersburg Pike. Once across the pike, continue walking south into the field for 50 yards, stop, and face right, west, so you are looking back toward McPherson's Ridge.

Stop 4, Position A—Seminary Ridge

You are on the western slope of Seminary Ridge. The Chambersburg Pike is to your right. The railroad—in 1863 the railroad cut—is farther to your right. On the north side of the pike is a stone building, the Thompson House, which was there in 1863. The stone part of the white house behind you, on the crest of the ridge, was there in 1863 as was the brick building to its southeast. Farther south, the next building with the tall steeple was not there, but the next one with the small copula was. In 1863 this was the tallest building on the ridge and was used as an observation post by Buford during his July 1 morning fight. All of the other buildings that are now on the west side of the ridge were not there in 1863. The area where you are was an orchard. Two hundred yards to your left was an open wood. Union infantry and artillery deployed on Seminary Ridge had clear fields of fire and observation all the way to McPherson's Ridge. The range from the defensive positions on Seminary Ridge to McPherson's Ridge was 500 yards.

Because of the action on their right flank, which you will visit later, and the continued attacks of *Heth's* Division, the four brigades and artillery of the Union First Corps were forced to fall back and occupy positions along this portion of Seminary Ridge. You are currently in the right center of the Union final position on this part of the ridge.

The Sixth Wisconsin Infantry of the Iron Brigade was in position on the other side, or north, of the railroad cut. To their right was Cutler's brigade. To the left of the Sixth Wisconsin was Stone's brigade, now commanded by Colonel Edmund L. Dana. The brigade's battle line began where the railroad cut is and went south across the pike, passed through where you are, and continued south for 75 yards. On their left the other four regiments of the Iron Brigade extended the line another 200 yards. Farther left, south, Biddle's brigade extended the line to within 200 yards of the Hagerstown Road. The next unit was an artillery battery just this side of the Hagerstown Road. Gamble's cavalry brigade was deployed south of the Hagerstown Road. The gap between Biddle's left and the artillery and Gamble was significant in the fight for this part of Seminary Ridge.

Four of the five batteries of the First Corps's artillery brigade were deployed behind you along Seminary Ridge in support of the infantry. Lieutenant James Stewart's Battery B, Fourth U.S. Artillery, with six Napoleons, was on either side of the railroad cut. Just this side of the Chambersburg Pike was a section, two 3-inch rifles, of Battery L, First New York Artillery under the command of Lieutenant Benjamin W. Wilbur. In the area behind where you are was Captain Greenleaf Stevens's Fifth Maine Battery with six Napoleons. To your left, in front of the old seminary building were the four 3-inch rifles of Captain James Cooper's Battery B, First Pennsylvania Artillery. Battery L (minus Wilbur's section), First New York Artillery, now commanded by Lieutenant George Breck, supported the left flank. Breck's four 3-inch rifles were in position just this side of the Hagerstown Road. All of the artillery was positioned on the crest of Seminary Ridge and at times fired over the heads of the defending infantry.

The report of Colonel Charles Wainwright gives a good overview of the movements and fighting of these batteries during the Confederate attack.

Report of Col. Charles S. Wainwright, USA, Commanding Artillery Brigade, First Corps, Army of the Potomac

I directed Captain Cooper to take a good position in front of the professor's house on [Seminary] ridge, and sent an order to Captain Stevens, of the Fifth Maine Battery, to occupy the position first assigned to Lieutenant Stewart. Soon after this, the enemy filed in two strong columns out of the woods, about 500 yards to our front, and marched steadily down to our left until they outflanked us nearly a third of a mile. They then formed in double line of battle, and came directly up the crest. During this movement, Battery L opened on the columns, but the firing of Lieutenant Breck's four guns was much interfered with by our own infantry moving in front of his pieces. As we had no regular line of battle on this crest, and the enemy outnumbered us five to one, I withdrew Lieutenant Breck's two sections when their first line was within about 200 yards, and ordered him behind a strong stonewall on the seminary crest.

Meantime General Doubleday had removed Captain Stevens' battery to the right of Captain Cooper's, and Lieutenant Wilber's section falling back with its support came into position at the same point, thus concentrating twelve guns in so small a space that they were hardly 5 yards apart. Lieutenant Stewart's battery was also in position on the same line, half the battery between the [Chambersburg] pike and the railroad, the other half across the railroad in the corner of a wood.

The enemy's lines continued to advance steadily across the space between the two crests, but when the first line was within about 100 yards of the seminary, Lieutenant Davison, commanding the left half of Stewart's battery, swung his guns around on the Cashtown [Chambersburg] pike, so as to enfilade the whole line. This, with the fire of the other batteries, checked them for a moment at this point, but it was only for a moment, as their second line did not halt, but pushed on, strongly reenforced by a

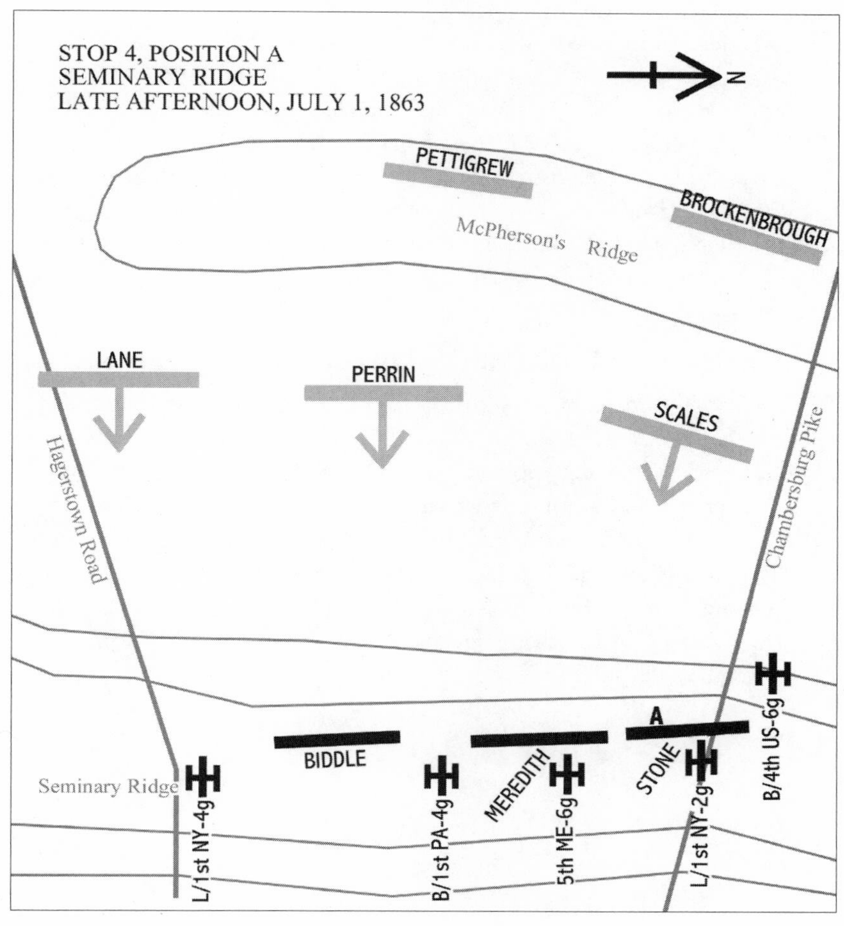

third column deploying from the [Chambersburg] road. [*OR* 27, pt. 1, pp. 356–57]

The Confederate forces attacking this part of Seminary Ridge were three brigades of Major General *William D. Pender's* division. *Pender's* Division had followed *Heth's* Division on the Chambersburg Pike. *Pender* deployed his division in a supporting line as *Heth* attacked the Union defenders on McPherson's Ridge. Once McPherson's Ridge was captured *Pender's* Division moved forward, passed through *Heth's* Division, and attacked the defenders on Seminary Ridge. Brigadier General *Alfred M. Scales's* brigade was *Pender's* left, or north, brigade. As you view it *Scales's* Brigade's battle line went from the Chambersburg Pike south, to your left, for 400 yards across the open ground in front of you. *McGowan's* Brigade, commanded by Colonel *Abner Perrin's,* was next. *Perrin's* battle line occupied the ground from *Scales's* right, your left, for 500 yards to the Hagerstown Road. Astride the Hagerstown Road Brigadier General *James H. Lane's* brigade formed the right of the battle line. *Pender's* fourth brigade, Brigadier General *Edward I. Thomas's* brigade, was held in reserve.

Face left, walk south for 50 yards, stop, and face right. Again you are looking toward McPherson's Ridge.

Position B—Direct Fire

You are just forward of the position of the Fifth Maine Battery, commanded by Captain Greenleaf Stevens. Stevens's battery was equipped with six Napoleons. These large-bore weapons, firing canister, were ideal for defense against an infantry attack. Stevens was wounded on July 2, and command of his battery passed to Lieutenant Edward Whittier, who also wrote the report of action. Coming directly toward the battery and the remnants of Stone's (Dana's) and Meredith's brigades were the regiments of *Scales's* Brigade.

Report of Lieut. Edward N. Whittier, USA, Commanding Fifth Maine Battery, Artillery Brigade, First Corps, Army of the Potomac

At a few minutes past 2, July 1, the battery being in position on the left of the seminary, orders were received by Captain Stevens to relieve Stewart's battery, and we took position on his left, one piece thrown forward to the front of the building, and opened with spherical case and shell on the enemy, rapidly advancing on our direct front.

After they were repulsed, when within range of our canister, the guns were turned to the right on the columns advancing across the turnpike, marching to our left, using solid shot and canister. When the enemy had driven our infantry from the woods protecting our left flank, by order of

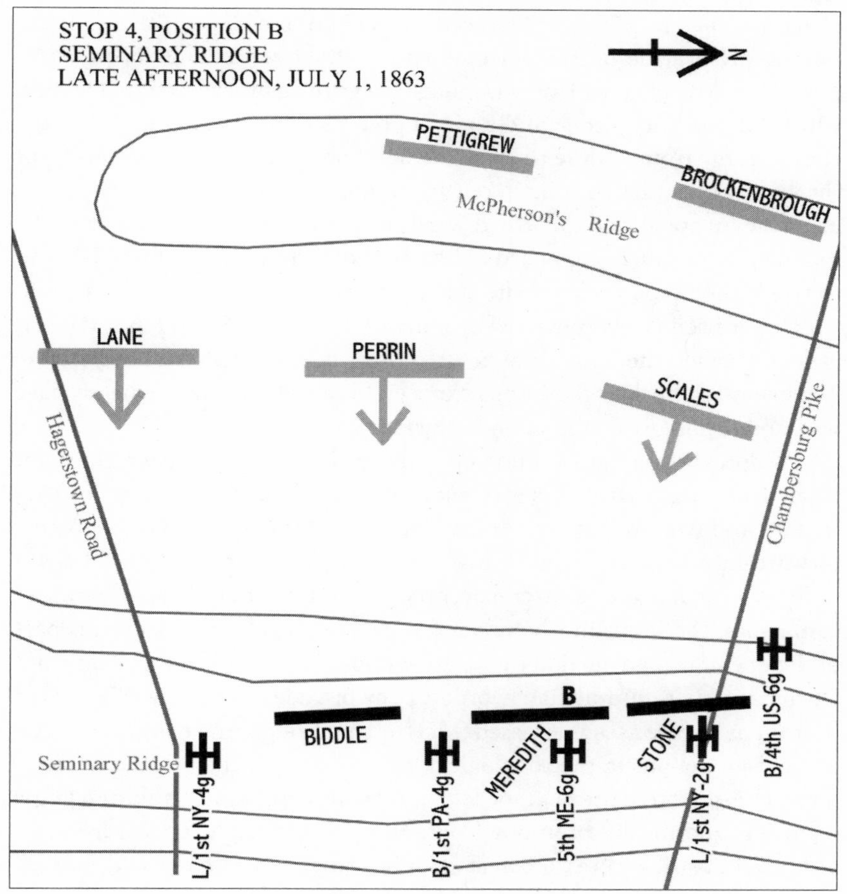

General Wadsworth, commanding First Division, the battery was limbered up and passed through the town, and was placed in position on the knoll to the right and rear of Cemetery Hill. [*OR* 27, pt. 1, pp. 360–61]

Scales's report attests to the deadliness of the defenders' artillery and rifle fire.

Report of Brig. Gen. *Alfred M. Scales,* CSA, Commanding *Scales's* Brigade, *Pender's* Division, *Hill's* Corps, Army of Northern Virginia

After marching about a quarter of a mile without any casualty, we were halted, and put in rear of the artillery belonging to *A. P. Hill's* corps. Here General *Lane's* brigade was changed to the extreme right of the division, leaving my brigade on the extreme left, without any change of position. After the lapse of some thirty minutes, we were again ordered to advance, which I did in good order, and under a pretty severe artillery fire from the enemy in my front. While thus advancing, I observed a regiment or two of the enemy about half a mile in our front, marching in line of battle parallel to the turnpike, and directly toward the road. They very soon engaged a regiment of our men (supposed to be a part of General *Davis'* brigade), who were advancing on the opposite side of the road. A heavy fight ensued, in which our friends, overpowered by numbers, gave way. Seeing this, the brigade quickened their step, and pressed on with a shout to their assistance. The enemy, with their flank thus exposed to our charge, immediately gave way, and fled in great confusion to the rear.

We pressed on until coming up with the line in our front, which was at a halt and lying down. [This was a part of *Heth's* division.] I received orders to halt, and wait for this line to advance. This they soon did, and pressed forward in quick time. That I might keep in supporting distance, I again ordered an advance, and, after marching one-fourth of a mile or more, again came upon the front line, halted and lying down. The officers on this part of the line informed me that they were without ammunition, and would not advance farther. I immediately ordered my brigade to advance. We passed over them, up the ascent, crossed [McPherson's] ridge, and commenced the descent just opposite the theological seminary. Here the brigade encountered a most terrific fire of grape [canister] and shell on our flank, and grape [canister] and musketry in our front. Every discharge made sad havoc in our line, but still we pressed on at a double-quick until we reached the bottom, a distance of about [200] yards from the ridge we had just crossed, and about the same distance from the college, in our front. Here I received a painful wound from a piece of shell, and was disabled. Our line had been broken up, and now only a squad here and there marked the place where regiments had rested.

Every field officer of the brigade save one had been disabled, and the following list of casualties will attest sufficiently the terrible ordeal through which the brigade passed:

Officers and men	Killed	Wounded	Missing	Total
Officers	9	45	1	55
Enlisted men.	39	336	115	490
Total	48	381	116	545

Some few of the missing have returned. Others, no doubt, straggled and were made prisoners, while not a few, I have no doubt, were left dead or wounded on the field. [*OR* 27, pt. 2, pp. 669–70]

Again face left, walk south for 75 yards, stop, and face right so that you are looking at McPherson's Ridge.

Position C—The Defense Collapses

Behind you on the higher part of the ridge was Captain James Cooper's Battery B, First Pennsylvania Artillery's four 3-inch rifles. Deployed with them were the remnants of the Iron Brigade, except for the Sixth Wisconsin. Farther to the left were Biddle's brigade and four guns of Battery L, First New York Artillery. This position was under attack by the right of *Scales's* Brigade and the left of *Perrin's* Brigade. Cooper's battery had been in action earlier on McPherson's Ridge at Stop 2. His report continues the action at this location.

Report of Capt. James H. Cooper, USA, Commanding Battery B, First Pennsylvania Artillery, Artillery Brigade, First Corps, Army of the Potomac

The colonel [Wainwright] ordered the battery to be placed in position near the [Lutheran] Seminary. Here it remained unengaged for a few minutes, when a battery in front again opened and fired a few minutes, when the enemy's infantry made its appearance along the woods and crest in our front. The fire of the battery was then concentrated upon them, case shot and shell being used until canister range was obtained, and this, with the assistance of Lieutenant Stewart's and Captain Stevens' batteries, reduced the enemy's lines very much. At about 5 p.m., all infantry support having been driven back, the battery was compelled to retire through Gettysburg to Cemetery Hill.

In this day's engagement about 400 rounds of ammunition were expended. [*OR* 27, pt. 1, pp. 364–65]

Biddle's brigade was to the left of Cooper's battery and the Iron Brigade. The 151st Pennsylvania was the right flank regiment. Its commander tells of the collapse of the Union defenses in this location.

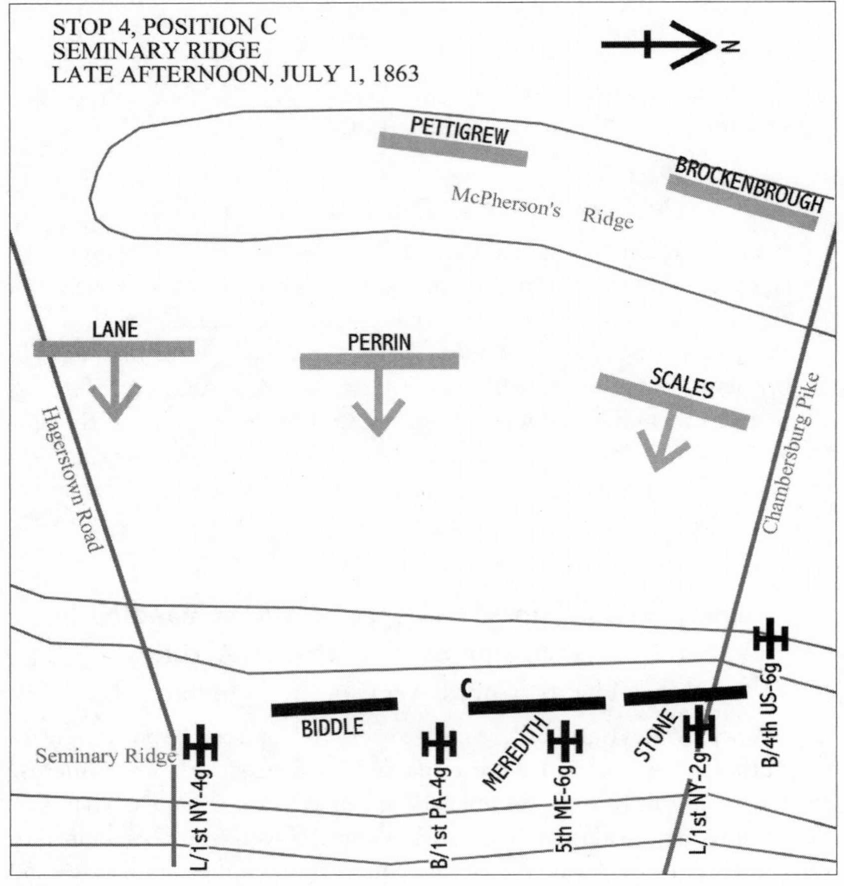

Report of Lieut. Col. George F. McFarland, USA, Commanding, 151st Pennsylvania, First Brigade, Third Division, First Corps, Army of the Potomac

I ordered the regiment to fall back [from McPherson's Ridge to Seminary Ridge], which it did in good order, to the temporary breastwork from which it had advanced, the enemy following closely, but cautiously. Here I halted, with fragments of Meredith's [Iron] brigade on my right and portions of the Twentieth New York State Militia, One hundred and twenty-first Pennsylvania Volunteers, and One hundred and forty-second Pennsylvania Volunteers, on my left.

We now quickly checked the advance of the enemy. In fact, having the advantage of breastworks and woods, our fire was so destructive that the enemy's lines in front were broken, and his first attempt to flank us greeted with such an accurate oblique fire that it failed. But in a second attempt, made soon after, he gained our left flank, moving in single file and at double-quick. Up to this time the officers and men under my command had fought with the determined courage of veterans, and an effectiveness which the enemy himself respected and afterward acknowledged (to me in conversation while a prisoner in their hands). Not a man had left the ranks, even to carry a wounded comrade to the rear. But the regiment had lost terribly, and now did not number one-fourth of what it did two hours earlier in the day. The enemy, on the contrary, had increased, and was now rapidly forming on my left. All support had left both flanks and were already well to the rear. Hence I ordered the shattered remnants of as brave a regiment as ever entered the field to fall back. [*OR* 27, pt. 1, p. 328]

The Confederate force attacking the southern part of the Union defensive position on Seminary Ridge was *McGowan's* (*Perrin's*) Brigade.

Report of Col. *Abner Perrin*, CSA, Commanding *McGowan's* Brigade, *Pender's* Division, *Hill's* Corps, Army of Northern Virginia

[About] 4 o'clock, I was ordered by General *Pender* to advance, and to pass General *Heth's* division should I come up with it at a halt, and to engage the enemy as circumstances might warrant. I soon came up with and passed Brigadier-General *Pettigrew's* brigade, the men of which seemed much exhausted by several hours hard fighting. Here I availed myself of a ravine, which sheltered us from the enemy's artillery, to reform my line, and instructed regimental commanders when the advance was resumed not to allow a gun to be fired at the enemy until they received orders to do so.

We now moved forward, preserving an alignment with General *Scales,* and, as soon as the brigade commenced ascending the hill in front, we were met by a furious storm of musketry and shells from the enemy's batteries to the left of the road near Gettysburg; but the instructions I had given were scrupulously observed—not a gun was fired. The brigade received the enemy's fire without faltering; rushed up the hill at a charge, driving the enemy without difficulty to their last position [on Seminary Ridge].

We continued the charge without opposition, excepting from artillery, which maintained a constant and most galling fire upon us, until we got within 200 yards of their last position, about the theological college. Some lines of infantry had shown themselves across the field, but disappeared as we got within range of them. While crossing the last fence, about 200 yards from a grove near the college, the brigade received the most destructive fire of musketry I have ever been exposed to. We continued to press forward, however, without firing, until we reached the edge of the grove. Here the Fourteenth [South Carolina] Regiment was staggered for a moment by the severity and destructiveness of the enemy's musketry. It looked to us as though this regiment was entirely destroyed.

I here found myself without support either on the right or left. General *Scales'* brigade had halted to return the enemy's fire, near the fence, about 200 yards distance from the enemy. General *Lane's* brigade did not move upon my right at all, and was not at this time in sight of me. This gave the enemy an enfilading fire upon the Fourteenth. This regiment, under the lead of Lieutenant-Colonel *Brown* and Major *Croft,* most gallantly stood its ground. I now directed the First [South Carolina] Regiment, under Major *McCreary,* to oblique to the right, to avoid a breastwork of rails behind, where I discovered the enemy was posted, and then to change front to the left, and attack in his flank. This was done most effectually, under the lead of this gallant officer. The enemy were here completely routed. This caused the whole of their artillery on our left, at least thirty pieces [actually eighteen], to be limbered up and moved to the rear. Much of their artillery would have been captured, but the First and Fourteenth in their pursuit again met a force of the enemy's infantry, strongly posted behind a stonewall, near and to the left of the college. It was the work of a few moments, however, to dislodge them.

While the First and Fourteenth Regiments were assailing the enemy and driving him from his breastwork near the college, I ordered the Twelfth [South Carolina] Regiment, under Colonel *Miller,* and the Thirteenth [South

Carolina], under Lieutenant-Colonel *Brockman,* to oblique to the right, and charge the enemy, strongly posted behind a stone fence, to the right of the college, from which position he had kept up a constant and withering fire of musketry upon the front and right flank of the brigade. [This was Gamble's cavalry brigade on the other side of the Hagerstown Road.] These two regiments had necessarily to change direction to the right somewhat, so as to meet the enemy full in front. This movement was most brilliantly performed by these two regiments, and was most skillfully managed by the officers I have mentioned. They rushed up to the crest of the hill and the stone fence, driving everything before them, the Twelfth gaining the stone fence, and pouring an enfilading fire upon the enemy's right flank. The Thirteenth now coming up, made it an easy task to drive the enemy down the opposite slope and across the open field west of Gettysburg.

After penetrating the enemy's lines near the college, the change of direction of the First and Fourteenth to attack the enemy in flank to the left, and the oblique movement and change of direction of the Twelfth and Thirteenth to attack the enemy in flank to the right, necessarily separated the brigade into two parts. As soon as I knew the enemy had been routed on the right, I ordered the Twelfth and Thirteenth to unite again with the First and Fourteenth, who were now pursuing the fleeing force through the town.

Finding the two last-named regiments now reduced to less than half the number with which they entered the battle, and the men much exhausted, I ordered them back from the town, to await the Twelfth and Thirteenth, and sent a small detachment through the town to take such prisoners as the enemy had left in the retreat. It was after the recall of these two regiments that the brigade of Brigadier-General *Ramseur* filed through Gettysburg from the direction of my left.

The loss of the brigade in killed and wounded did not fall short of 500. [*OR* 27, pt. 2, pp. 661–63]

Depart from your present location, and retrace your route back north to the Chambersburg Pike. Be careful of traffic and cross the pike. Walk to where your car is parked in the small parking area. From your car walk to your left front for 40 yards to the monument for Battery B, Fourth U.S. Artillery, stop, and face left. You should be looking west. The Chambersburg Pike is to your left, and the railroad is to your right.

Position D—Flanking Fire

You are in the left half of the position occupied by Stewart's Battery B, Fourth U.S. Artillery. The battery was deployed astride the railroad, half on this side and the remainder on the other side. In this position Stewart had excellent fields of fire and could support the left of Cutler's brigade or the right of Stone's (Dana's) brigade. He could control the railroad cut by firing down it to prevent it from being a protected avenue of approach into the Union defenses or fire directly ahead and cover the ground on both side of the railroad. In addition his guns could be turned 45 degrees to the right or left and fire into the flank of any force attacking Cutler's or Stone's (Dana's) brigades. This is exactly what the right half of Stewart's battery did as *Scales's* Brigade crossed McPherson's Ridge and attacked through the open ground to your left front. Armed with the larger-bore Napoleons and firing canister Stewart's six guns were a key part of the defense on this section of the ridge.

Narrative of Lieut. James Stewart, USA, Commanding, Battery B, Fourth U.S. Artillery, Artillery Brigade, First Corps, Army of the Potomac

I rode over to General Wadsworth and told him that the enemy was preparing to advance in his front, and to assist him I would place three guns [next to] the pike and place the other three on the other side of the railroad cut. The general said he would be much obliged if I would do so. I had sent the bugler to Lieutenant Davidson to bring up the battery. As soon as the battery arrived, I placed three guns [next to] the pike under Lieutenant Davidson. I then placed the others on the other side of the railroad cut about three hundred yards in advance of the left half in echelon. My right half battery was under cover, being in a piece of woods.

After placing the right half of the battery in position, I galloped over to Davidson to await developments. I had not long to wait, as we could see the bayonets of the [Confederate] infantry coming over the rising ground, the distance being about six hundred yards. They came on in fine style. Our men did not fire a musket until they came within a distance of about four hundred yards. Davidson had his guns double-shotted with canister, but he held his fire until the enemy had reached what we thought was about three hundred yards, when he opened. It was more than they could stand. They broke to the rear, where they halted, faced about and advanced again, but

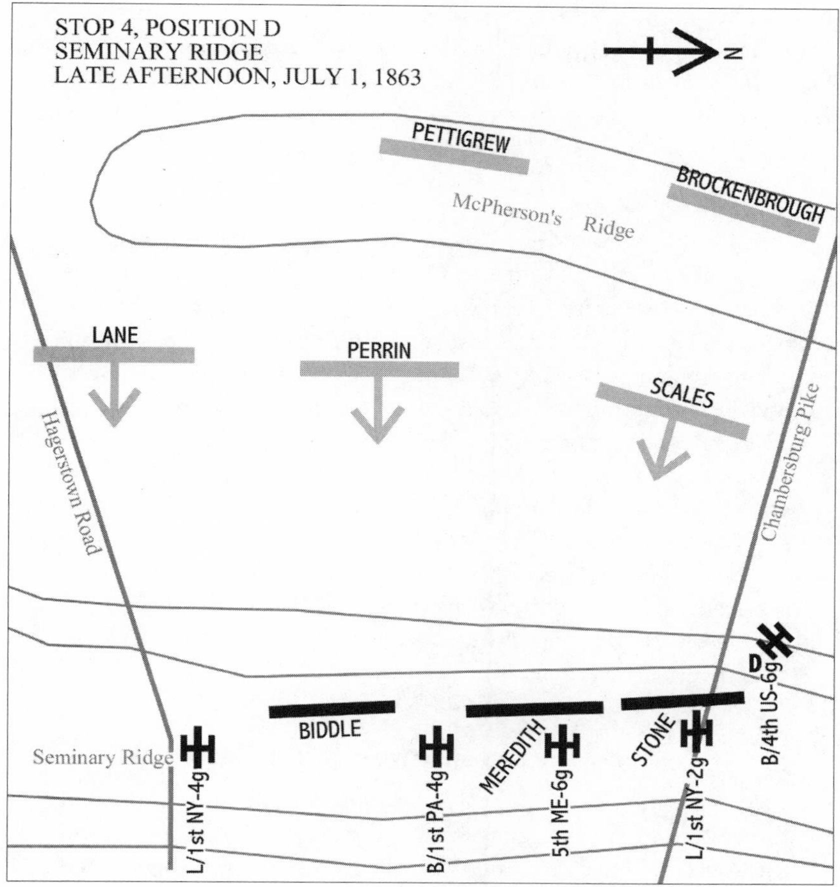

meeting such a storm of lead and iron they broke and ran over the rising ground entirely out of sight.

We were congratulating ourselves upon what we had done and with such little loss, when, after some time, an aide rode up and informed the general that the enemy were again advancing. I told Davidson that if they came on his front to use the same tactics, and that I would give it to him on his left flank. I had not very long to wait when we saw them coming. I galloped over to my half battery [on the other side of the railroad cut] and gave the command to change forward on the left piece, at the same time keeping as much under cover as I could. I then had the canister brought up and the guns double-shotted and waited for them. The enemy were not aware of us being on the other side of the railroad cut, for as they advanced they exposed their left flank, and I opened fire. This so confused them that they did not know what to do. [James Stewart, "Battery B, Fourth United States Artillery at Gettysburg," in *Sketches of War History, 1861–1865: Papers Prepared for the Ohio Commandery of the Military Order of the Loyal Legion*, vol. 4 (Cincinnati: The Robert Clarke Company, 1896), 184–86. Hereafter cited as Stewart, "Battery B," followed by page numbers.]

A canister round for the Napoleon contained twenty-seven one-and-one-half-inch-diameter iron balls. When a gun was double shotted, it fired fifty-four of these balls. The rate of fire was two or three times per minute. During each minute this was kept up, a single Napoleon was discharging between 108 to 162 iron balls. Stewart's six guns were firing between 648 to 972 iron balls into *Scales's* Brigade for every minute it was in the open ground between McPherson's and Seminary Ridges. This is the "terrific fire of grape and shell on our flank and grape and musketry in our front" that *Scales* wrote about.

Walk forward, west, for 60 yards, where you will find a gravel service road. Turn right on this road, and walk north so that you are close to, but not on, the railroad tracks. BE EXTREMELY CAREFUL: this is an active railroad.

Position E—Stewart's Retreat

You are in the center of Stewart's position. The railroad cut divided the battery with three guns on the north side and three guns on the south side. In 1863 there were no railroad tracks here. The tracks came into Gettysburg from the east and stopped. Work was being done on the roadbed west of town, but the tracks had not been put down at the time of the battle. Look west, and you can see the cuts made for the tracks through the rolling terrain. You can also gain an appreciation of how one gun firing shot, shell, or especially canister could prevent the cut from being a protected avenue of approach for Confederate infantry. East of your location there were rocks piled up along the railroad bed that presented a considerable obstacle to the withdrawal of the guns and limbers of Stewart's right half-battery.

Although Lieutenant Stewart and his battery, as well as other Union artillery and infantry units on Seminary Ridge, held tenaciously to their positions, inflicting heavy casualties on the attackers, they were eventually forced to retreat from the ridge.

Narrative of Lieut. James Stewart, USA—continued

An aide of General Robinson rode up with the order for me to fall back to the town as rapidly as possible, saying the general had forgotten I was on his left flank. I inquired how far the division [Second Division, First Corps] was from me, and he said probably about half a mile [to the rear]. As I gave the command to limber to the rear, I could not bring my wounded with me, and the beseeching looks that these men gave me quite unnerved me, and I was sorry indeed to leave them to their fate.

I moved down through the timber, running a short distance parallel with the railroad cut, and then attempted to cross. I did not know at the time that the cut was full of large rocks. However, the men got the first two pieces over, but in getting over the third, a pintle hook broke and the trail fell to the ground. As this happened, a party of rebels came running out of the timber shouting: "Halt that piece!" We were all completely surprised, but one of the men was fully equal to the occasion, and shouted back: "Don't you see that the piece is halted?" I had the leading pieces brought back upon the road and opened upon them, when they took cover very quickly. In the meantime, the men were taking the prolong off the trail and tying up the gun to the limber. When the pintle hook broke, I felt that we would never be able to get the gun out of the cut, as it took a long time to disengage the prolong from the trail; then we had to get the limber out of the cut, then the gun; then we had to tie the trail to the rear of the limber; and during all this time the enemy were firing upon us at not more than one hundred yards; and just as we got the gun out of the cut, the enemy made a dash, this time getting within fifty or sixty yards, killing one driver (the driver of the swing team), and seriously wounding the wheel driver and two horses, which again caused delay. But the two pieces kept firing at them all the time, and I will say right here that if ever men stayed by their guns, it certainly was them. After we got well on the road, I told the sergeant to move to the town and I would go back and see what Davidson was doing, as I could not believe he would have left without informing me of the fact. I started in the direction of the Thompson House, but on getting pretty near there, I saw the place was occupied by the enemy. [The Thompson House is the stone building just east of where you are.] On seeing me they shouted, "Surrender!" but as I had not gone there for that purpose, I wheeled my horse and started him off as fast as he could go.

It was my intention to catch up with my sergeant, but I found I could not reach the road as it was occupied by the enemy—in fact the enemy was closing in on all sides. On seeing that I could not make my way to where my half battery had gone, I started across the field, when the first thing I observed in front of me was a high fence, and as I could not go either to the right or left without being made a prisoner, I headed my horse for it, and he took the leap in splendid style. As he was making the jump I was struck on the thigh with a piece of shell. A short distance further, I found one of my men bursting the cartridges that were on one of the caissons. The rear axel of that caisson was broken and four of the horses had been killed. I inquired if any one had ordered him to remain and destroy the ammunition, and he said, "No, but the Rebs are following us up pretty hard, and if the caisson fell into their hands they would use the ammunition upon us." I remained with him until he had destroyed the last round and then told him to keep with me.

On reaching the courthouse, I found all my battery except the caisson. I was also told that Lieutenant Davidson had been seriously wounded. [Stewart, "Battery B," 186–89]

Retrace your path, and return to where your car is parked.

Position F—The First Corps Artillery Retreats

After rejoining his battery Stewart move it south of the town and took up a position on Cemetery Hill. With the infantry all along Seminary Ridge falling back and Confederate forces closing in on the flanks, Colonel Wainwright began to withdraw the remainder of his artillery.

Report of Col. Charles S. Wainwright, USA, Commanding Artillery Brigade, First Corps, Army of the Potomac

An order was now received by Captain Stevens from General Wadsworth to withdraw his battery. Not knowing that he had received such an order, and still under the false impression as to the importance attached to holding Seminary [Ridge], I directed all the batteries to remain in position. A few minutes, however, showed me our infantry rapidly retreating to the town. All the batteries were at once limbered to the rear, and moved at a walk down the [Chambersburg] pike until the infantry had all left it and passed under cover of the railroad embankment. By this time the enemy's skirmishers had lapped our retreating columns and opened a severe fire from behind a paling fence running parallel to and within 50 yards of the road. The pike being clear, the batteries now broke into a trot, but it was too late to save everything. Lieutenant Wilber's (Battery L, First New York) last piece had the off wheel-horse shot, and just as he had disengaged it, 3 more of the horses were shot down and his own horse killed, so that it was impossible for him to bring it off. It affords me pleasure to say that not the slightest blame can be attributed to Lieutenant Wilber in the loss of this gun.

The loss of the batteries during the day's engagement was heavy, amounting in all to 83 officers and men [out of 619] and about 80 horses. A large proportion of the last were hit while passing over the short open space between Seminary Ridge and the town, the enemy having at that time a fire upon us from three sides, and our infantry not replying.

The batteries passed immediately through the town along with the other troops, and were placed in position on reaching Cemetery Hill along with several of the Eleventh Corps batteries, so as to command the town and the approach from the northwest in case the enemy should attempt to follow us through the town. [*OR* 27, pt. 1, p. 357]

Return to your car for the drive to Stop 5.

Depart the parking area and turn right, west, on to the Chambersburg Pike. Drive for just over 0.1 mile the intersection of Reynolds Avenue, where the stoplight is, turn right on to Reynolds Avenue, and drive 0.2 mile to the T intersection with Buford Avenue. You will drive over the road bridge that goes over the railroad tracks. Turn left and follow Buford Avenue west then north for 0.7 mile, to the parking lot for the Eternal Peace Light Memorial. Park, leave your car, and walk toward the Eternal Peace Light Memorial. Follow the path to the left of the memorial for 50 yards, and walk to the second set of guns. Walk to the rear of these guns, and look back south.

Stop 5, Position A—A New Type of Gun

Before you look at the action from this location, take a few minutes to examine the pair of guns in front of you. You will notice they are different from any other guns on the battlefield. They are 12-pounder Whitworth breech-loading rifles. At the rear of the barrel, the breech, there is a screw type of arrangement. This allowed these guns to be loaded from the breech rather than from the front of the barrel, the muzzle. These guns could fire a 2.75-inch-diameter round over 5,000 yards, far beyond the fire control capability of Civil War field artillery. The Withworth was one of the immediate predecessors of twentieth-century artillery. The major difference between the Whitworth and modern artillery is the absence of a hydraulic recoil system and a sighting system for indirect fire. These are the only two guns like this on the battlefield. They were not at this location on July 1 but were deployed on Herr Ridge, Stop 3, as part of *McIntosh's* Battalion.

Walk to the front of the memorial. Walk up on the base of the memorial, and stand so that the tall shaft is behind you and you are looking south.

Position B—Confederate Artillery Arrives From The North

You are on Oak Hill. As you look south, you can see at a distance of 1 mile the McPherson Barn and the area of Stops 1 and 2. To your right front at a distance of 1.1 mile, 1,940 yards, is Herr Tavern at the intersection of the Chambersburg Pike and Herr Ridge. The center of the firing positions occupied by *Pegram's* and *McIntosh's* Artillery Battalions was in that general location. From your location it is easy to visualize the artillery crossfire that can be brought from this location and Herr Ridge upon the Union defenders between the McPherson Barn and the railroad cut.

The Confederate infantry and artillery arriving on and in close proximity to this location was Major General *Robert E. Rodes's* infantry division consisting of five brigades and Lieutenant Colonel *Thomas H. Carter's* supporting artillery battalion of four batteries with sixteen guns. This force along with another division had been approaching Gettysburg from the north and northeast.

Report of Maj. Gen. *Robert E. Rodes,* CSA, Commanding *Rodes's* Division, *Ewell's* Corps, Army of Northern Virginia

On July 1, in pursuance of the order to rejoin the army, the division resumed its march, but upon arriving at Middletown [today's Biglerville and five miles north of you], and hearing that Lieutenant-General *Hill's* corps was moving upon Gettysburg, by order of General *Ewell,* the head of the column was turned in that direction. When within 4 miles of the town, to my surprise, the presence of the enemy there in force was announced by the sound of a sharp cannonade, and instant preparations for battle were made.

On arriving on the field, I found that by keeping along the wooded ridge, on the left side of which the town of Gettysburg is situated, I could strike the force of the enemy with which General *Hill's* troops were engaged upon the flank, and that, besides moving under cover, whenever we struck the enemy we could engage him with the advantage in ground.

The division was, therefore, moved along the summit of the ridge, with only one brigade deployed at first, and finally, as the enemy's cavalry had discovered us and the ground was of such character as to admit of cover for a large opposing force, with three brigades deployed; *Doles* on the left, *O'Neal,* in the center, and *Iverson* on the right, the artillery and the other two brigades moved up closely to the line of battle. The division had to move nearly a mile before coming in view of the enemy's forces, excepting a few mounted men, and finally arrived at a point—a prominent hill on the ridge [where you are]—whence the whole of that portion of the force opposing General *Hill's* troops could be seen. To get at these troops properly, which were still over half a mile from us, it was necessary to move the whole of my command by the right flank, and to change direction to the right.

While this was being done, *Carter's* battalion was ordered forward, and soon opened fire upon the enemy, who at this moment, as far as I could see, had no troops facing me at all. [*OR* 27, pt. 2, p. 552]

As *Rodes* came near the edge of the wood and looked south, as you are, this is what he saw: directly in front, at a distance, is the Chambersburg Pike, McPherson's Barn, and Herbst Wood. On the edge of the wood and around the barn *Rodes* could see Union forces. To the left of the barn, where the north-south park road is today, he could see a Union battle line. Along the continuation of the park road north of the Chambersburg Pike and the railroad cut, marked by a bridge, were additional Union forces. In the long tree line that begins to the left (east) of the bridge over the railroad cut, comes north toward you, and ends 500 yards to your left front, *Rodes* saw more Union troops. All of these troops were from the First Corps. Farther to his left in the lower open ground east of the ridge, he saw the Eleventh Corps deploying.

Rodes believed the First Corps defensive position ended in the northern edge of the tree line that is 500 yards to your left front. If you look closely to the left of the edge of the trees, you will see a rock wall and monuments that go from south to north. Union infantry regiments were at that location, but, because of the rock wall and the manner that the ground falls off behind the wall, they could not be seen. Believing that he was in position to strike the right of the Union defenses facing west, the First Corps, and with his artillery already firing, *Rodes* ordered an attack.

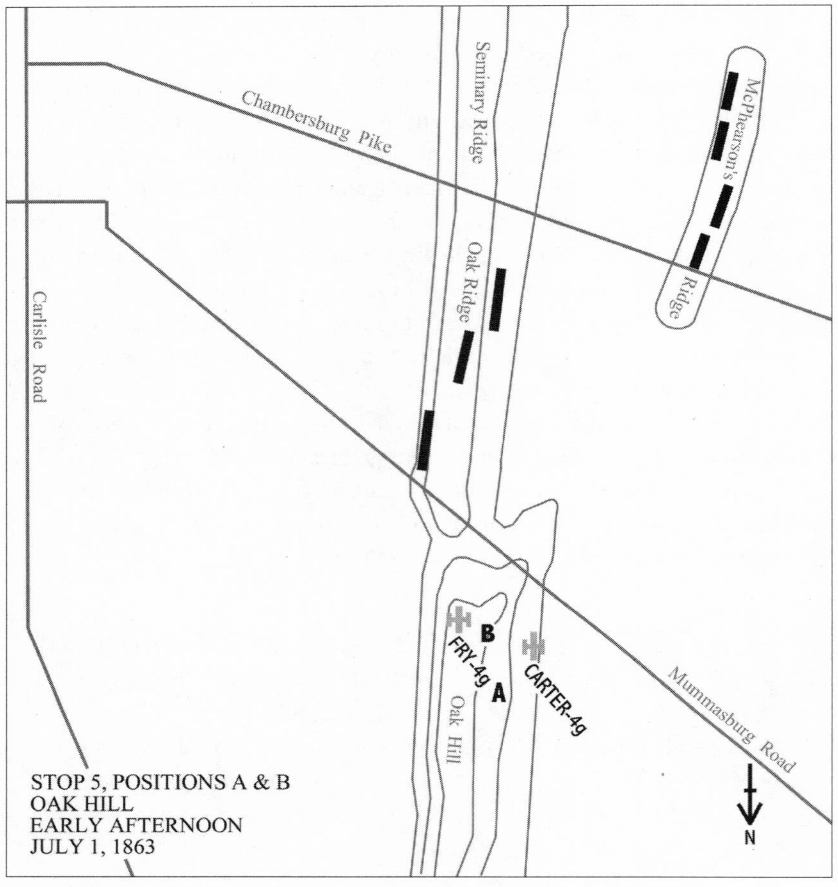

Report of Lieut. Col. *Thomas H. Carter,* CSA, Commanding *Carter's* Artillery Battalion, *Ewell's* Corps, Army of Northern Virginia

On reaching the field, July 1, the enemy was found to be in possession of a high ridge west of Gettysburg. Their advance line occupied a small crest still farther west, and was engaged with *A. P. Hill's* corps when we arrived. *Rodes'* division was deployed in two lines, at right angles to the high crest and to the enemy's lines of battle. The batteries of Captain *W. P. Carter* [King William (Virginia) Artillery Battery, two 10-pound Parrotts and two Napoleons, deployed to your right] and Captain *C. W. Fry* [Orange (Virginia) Artillery Battery, two 3-inch rifles and two 10-pound Parrotts, deployed to your left] were ordered to a high point in front of *Rodes'* lines, near the [Mummasburg] road, to enfilade the enemy's lines and batteries, which stretched along the small crest [McPherson's Ridge] to the railroad cut. The batteries fired with very decided effect, compelling the infantry to take shelter in the railroad cut, and causing them to change front on their right. The enemy's guns replied slowly. Owing to the exposed position of Captain *Carter's* battery, which was unavoidable, it suffered much at this point, having 4 men killed outright and 7 more or less severely wounded. [*OR* 27, pt. 2, p. 602]

Lieutenant Colonel *Thomas H. Carter*, CSA. Jennings C. Wise, *The Long Arm of Lee* (1915).

It was the fire of these two batteries that was reported by Captain Cooper, Stop 2, as causing his battery to change front to the right, north. It also caused some of the infantry regiments near the McPherson Barn to change their position and face north. However, this exposed them to an enfilading fire from the Confederate artillery on Herr Ridge.

Rodes's brigades attacked across the open ground in front of you and were repulsed by the Union force along the railroad cut and hit hard in the flank by the defenders behind the stone wall to your left front. The Eleventh Corps, east of this location, caused *Rodes* to extend his line across the low ground east of Oak Hill and to deploy his two other artillery batteries on the east slope of the ridge.

Walk forward from the Eternal Peace Light Memorial to the parking area. Turn left in the parking area, and follow the park road east for 150 yards. Walk off the left side of the road for a few yards so that you can see the markers and guns just below you. The markers and guns indicated the approximate position of *Carter's* two other batteries. They are Captain *Richard C. M. Page's* Morris (Virginia) Artillery Battery and Captain *William J. Reese's* Jeff. Davis (Alabama) Artillery Battery. *Reese's* Battery was actually deployed 400 yards to the left of *Page's* battery, but, as this location is not on park property and not easily accessible, the marker has been placed where you can see it. Look east and southeast across the open fields below you.

Position C—Arrival of the Union Eleventh Corps

You are looking over the fields that were the scene of bloody fighting between the Union Eleventh Corps and *Ewell's* Corps.

To your right, on the other side of the Mummasburg Road, is Oak Ridge. From here you can see how the drop of the ground on the eastern side effectively hid Union troops from view at your last position. The buildings that are the northern edge of Gettysburg are part of Gettysburg College. The college was there in 1863, but the northern edge was two blocks south of where it is today. Find the college building with a tall brick spire. Look to the right of that building, and at a long distance you will see a hill with trees and a U.S. flag on it. This is Cemetery Hill. It is one of the most tactically important pieces of ground on the battlefield and was constantly occupying *Robert E. Lee's* thoughts. It is an ideal position for infantry and artillery and controls the roads leading south from Gettysburg toward Baltimore and Washington. To the left of Cemetery Hill is Culp's Hill. This hill became the right anchor of the Union line. Cemetery Hill and the other hills and ridges around it became Meade's strong defensive position from the night of July 1 onward. Buford's cavalry and the First and Eleventh Corps fought along McPherson's Ridge and Seminary Ridge and in the area north of Gettysburg. This combat bought time for the rest of the Army of the Potomac to march and join them on this key terrain.

Now look a little closer in. When the Eleventh Corps marched through Gettysburg, it left one division with a supporting artillery battery on Cemetery Hill. The other two divisions marched through the town. The leading division was headed for the ridge where you are. However, upon coming out of the town, it discovered *Rodes* already occupied this ground. This division was forced to deploy on the open ground in front of you. If you look carefully, you can see a park road and a series of monuments that go across the field from your right, near the Mummasburg Road, to your left. This line of monument goes to the north-south Carlisle Road. Halfway along this line, you can see some artillery. These Union batteries aggressively engaged the Confederate artillery where you are. This was important, for, as you can see, artillery up here can dominate the lower open ground in front of you.

From the Carlisle Road the Eleventh Corps line went east to the small hill or knoll that has a few trees and a monument on it. This is Barlow's Knoll. Brigadier General Francis C. Barlow's division occupied the far end of the Eleventh Corps position. They would have been better off to have stayed along the northern edge of Gettysburg. However, they moved forward because the knoll is an excellent artillery position that provided a tactical advantage to whoever was there. Unfortunately for Barlow, his division's right flank barely extended beyond the knoll and was exposed.

View from *Page's* Battery (Stop 5C) on Oak Hill to the Eleventh Corps position. Battery I, 1st Ohio Artillery's position (Stop 6B) is over the white farm house and on the far side of the field.

Report of Maj. Gen. Oliver O. Howard, USA, Commanding Eleventh Corps, Army of the Potomac

At 8 a.m. [July 1] orders were received from [Major General Reynolds] directing the corps to march to Gettysburg. The column was at once set in motion, my First Division, General Barlow commanding, following the First Corps by the direct route; my Third, General Schurz, and my Second, General Steinwehr, in the order named, taking the route by Horner's Mill. One battery accompanied the First Division; the remainder of the artillery (four batteries), under command of Major Osborn, accompanied the other two divisions. The distance by the direct route was between 10 and 11 miles, and by the other about 13. As soon as the corps was set in motion, I pushed on with my staff by the direct road, and when within 2 miles of Gettysburg received word from General Reynolds, pointing out the place where I was to encamp; but on approaching the town, heavy artillery firing was heard. For some little time I endeavored, by sending in different directions, to find General Reynolds, in order to report to him in person.

In the meantime I went to the top of a high building in Gettysburg, facing westward. I saw firing beyond Seminary Ridge and not far from the seminary. Toward the right, masses of cavalry were drawn up in order, to the east of the ridge and to the northeast of the town. [This was Devin's brigade of Buford's division.] A portion of the First Corps, of General Wadsworth's command, was between me and the seminary, taking position near the railroad. Another division of this corps was moving by the flank with considerable rapidity, along the ridge and in a northeasterly direction.

On hearing of the death of General Reynolds, I assumed command of the left wing, instructing General Schurz to take command of the Eleventh Corps. After an examination of the general features of the country, I came to the conclusion that the only tenable position for my limited force was the ridge to the southeast of Gettysburg, now so well known as Cemetery Ridge. The highest point at the cemetery commanded every eminence within easy range. The slopes toward the west and south [southern Seminary Ridge] were gradual, and could be completely swept by artillery. To the north, the ridge was broken by a ravine running transversely.

I at once established my headquarters near the cemetery, and on the highest point north of the Baltimore pike. Here General Schurz joined me before 12 m., when I instructed him to make the following dispositions of the Eleventh Corps. Learning from General Doubleday, commanding the First Corps, that his right was hard pressed, and receiving continued assurance that his left was safe and pushing the enemy back, I ordered the First and Third Divisions of the Eleventh Corps to seize and hold a prominent height [Oak Hill] on the right [north] of the [Mummasburg] road and on the prolongation of Seminary Ridge, each division to have a battery of artillery, the other three batteries, supported by General Steinwehr's division (Second), to be put in position near me on Cemetery Hill.

About 12.30 [p.m.] General Buford sent me word that the enemy was massing between the York and Harrisburg roads, to the north of Gettysburg, some 3 or 4 miles from the town. About this time the head of column of the Eleventh Corps entered and passed through the town, moving forward rapidly toward the position ordered.

The news of *Ewell's* advance from the direction of York was confirmed by reports from General Schurz, General Buford, and Major Charles H. Howard, my aide-de-camp, who had been sent in that direction to reconnoiter. I therefore ordered General Schurz to halt his command, to prevent his right flank being turned, but to push forward a thick line of skirmishers, to seize the point first indicated [Oak Hill], as a relief and support to the First Corps.

At 2 p.m. a report of the state of things as then existing was sent to General Meade directly. About this time I left my chief of staff to execute orders, and went to the First Corps. I found General Doubleday about a quarter of a mile beyond the seminary. His Third Division was drawn up to his front and left, facing toward the west. The artillery of this division was engaging the enemy at this time. His First Division (Wadsworth's) was located [astride] the railroad, and his Second Division (Robinson's) on Wadsworth's right. The First Corps, in this position, made a right angle with the Eleventh Corps, the vertex being near the Mummasburg road. The cavalry of General Buford was located mainly upon the flanks.

About this time (2.45 p.m.) the enemy showed himself in force in front of the Eleventh Corps. His batteries could be distinctly seen on a prominent slope [Oak Hill] between the Mummasburg and the Harrisburg roads. [*OR* 27, pt. 1, pp. 701–3]

You are on the prominent position Howard originally intended part of the Eleventh Corps to occupy. However, *Rodes's* infantry and artillery arrived here first. The Confederate artillery Howard wrote about were four batteries of *Carter's* Artillery Battalion. Two batteries, *Carter's* and *Fry's,* were positioned on top of Oak Hill, where you just came from. The other two batteries were in position on the lower part of the ridge. Captain *Richard C. M. Page's* battery with four Napoleons was deployed below you. Captain *William J. Reese's* battery with four 3-inch rifles was deployed 400 yards to the left of *Page's* guns.

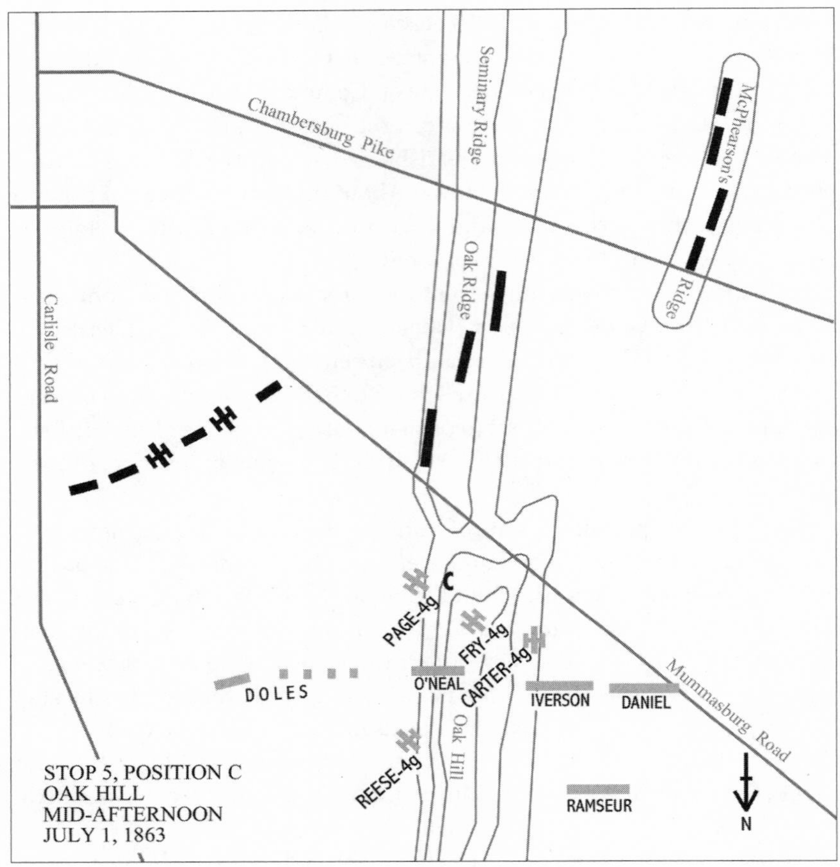

Report of Lieut. Col. *Thomas H. Carter,* CSA, Commanding *Carter's* Artillery Battalion, *Ewell's* Corps, Army of Northern Virginia

The enemy, finding their position untenable and turned by a strong force, extended their line to their right [and across the open ground], to confront us. General *Rodes,* therefore, sent for two batteries, and posted them on the left. Captains *R. C. M. Page* and *W. J. Reese,* then not engaged, were ordered to report to him. Captain *Page* opened from a point at the foot of the high ridge on the infantry advancing on Colonel *O'Neal.* The artillery of the enemy by this time had taken position in the [open ground] north of Gettysburg, and delivered a very destructive oblique fire on *Page's* battery. His loss here was heavy—2 men killed, 2 mortally wounded, 26 more or less badly wounded, and 17 horses killed and disabled; but it was borne with unflinching courage by the gallant captain and his officers and men until ordered to retire to another position.

General *Doles,* [in the open ground and] on the left of the front line of General *Rodes'* division, reported a large force massing on his front and left, near the [Carlisle] road, and asked to be supported by artillery. Leaving Captain [*Carter's*] at the first position on the high ridge, [*Fry's*], *Page's,* and *Reese's* batteries were put in position at the foot of the high ridge to prevent the enemy from turning *Rodes'* extreme left. Here these batteries rendered excellent service, driving back both infantry and artillery. Captain [*Fry's*] battery was particularly effective in its fire at this position.

General *Early* now advanced, *Doles* took it up, and *Rodes'* whole line pressed forward, forcing back the enemy at all points. My battalion followed, a few pieces unlimbering from time to time to break up the formations of the enemy as they endeavored to rally under cover of the small crests near the town. After the capture of Gettysburg, no further movement was made during the afternoon. [*OR* 27, pt. 2, p. 603]

Return to your car for the drive to Stop 6.

Drive east out of the parking lot, and follow the park road for 0.2 mile to the intersection with the Mummasburg Road. Turn left and drive on the Mummasburg Road for 0.4 mile to the first park road on your left. This is Howard Avenue. Turn left on to Howard Avenue, and drive for 0.2 mile to the monument and guns for the Thirteenth New York Independent Battery. Park, get out of your car, and stand near the monument for the Thirteenth New York Independent Battery. Look northwest toward Oak Hill and Stop 5, Position C, where you just came from.

Stop 6, Position A—Eleventh Corps Artillery in Action

Where you are standing was a wheat field in July 1863. Look northwest across the field, and you can see how commanding a position Oak Hill is. Look closely, and you can see the guns that mark the Confederate artillery positions. They are to the right of and above the farmhouse in the distance. Look to your left, toward the Mummasburg Road, and you can see the beginning of a line of monuments. These monuments mark the left flank of the Eleventh Corps. The corps's battle line, as marked by these monuments, comes toward you, passes through your location, continues to your right, crosses the Carlisle Road, and goes up on a small knoll, which is Barlow's Knoll (called Blocher's Knoll in 1863). It was not the intent of Major General Howard or Major General Carl Schurz that the line should be out in this field. The primary desired position was Oak Hill, but Confederates already occupied that. The alternate desired position was the south edge of the field near the northern edge of Gettysburg, with a strong skirmish line in the field. How they came to be out in the field will be presented at Stop 7.

You are in the center of Brigadier General Alexander Schimmelfenning's First Brigade, Third Division. The brigade's position went from the Mummasburg Road to the Carlisle Road. Colonel Wladimir Krzyzanowski's Second Brigade, Third Division, was initially deployed in a reserve position to your rear and on this side of the Carlisle Road. Brigadier General Francis Barlow's First Division was on Barlow's Knoll.

When the Union units deployed in the field, they were excellent targets for the guns of *Carter's* Artillery Battalion on Oak Hill. The only way to suppress this fire was to deploy artillery into this area for counter-battery fire.

Report of Maj. Thomas W. Osborn, USA, Commanding, Artillery Brigade, Eleventh Corps, Army of the Potomac

I moved from Emmitsburg toward Gettysburg with the artillery of the corps, consisting of five batteries, and marched in the following order: Captain Dilger in advance with the Third Division, Lieutenant Wheeler with the First Division and in the center, the three remaining batteries following closely in rear of the center division.

I herewith enumerate the batteries of the command: Battery G, Fourth U.S. Artillery, commanded by Lieut. B. Wilkeson, six [Napoleon] 12-pounders; Battery I, First Ohio Artillery, commanded by Capt. H. Dilger, six [Napoleon] 12-pounders; Battery K, First Ohio Artillery, commanded by Capt. L. Heckman, four [Napoleon] 12-pounders; Battery I, First New York Artillery, commanded by Capt. M. Wiedrich, six 3-inch [rifles], and Thirteenth New York Independent Battery, commanded by First Lieut. W. Wheeler, four 3-inch [rifles]. Total, 26 guns.

After moving 5 or 6 miles, I received notice from Major-General Howard that the First Corps was already engaged with the enemy at Gettysburg, and that I should move the artillery to the front as rapidly as possible.

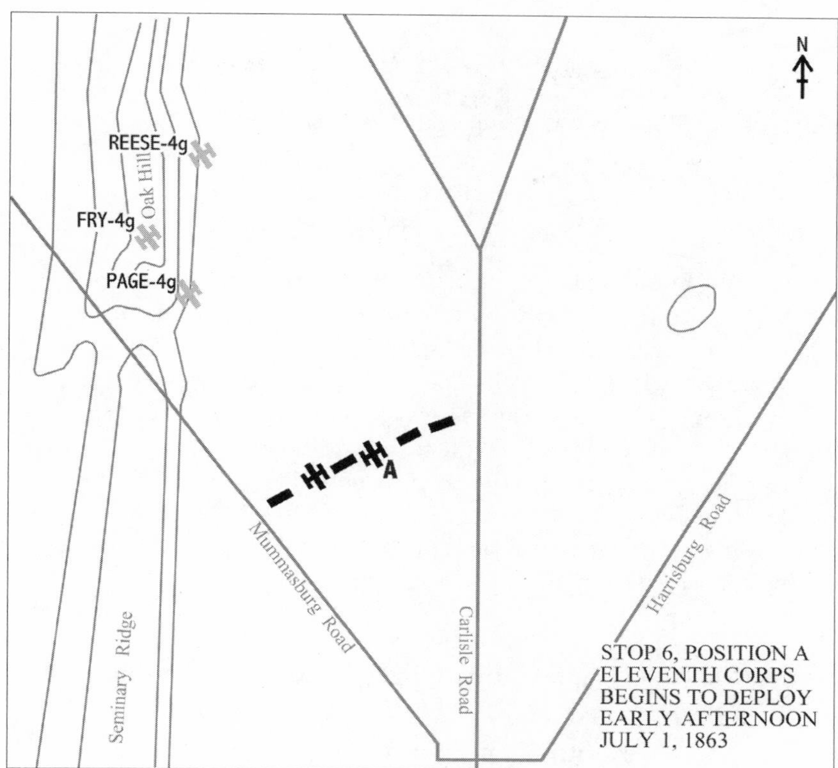

A little after 10 a.m. the first battery (Dilger's) reached the town, and was ordered by General Schurz to the front of and 300 yards beyond the town, where he took position, and at once became engaged with a rebel battery about 1,000 yards in its front [on Oak Hill]. This battery was soon supported by another, when Captain Dilger was compelled to stand the fire from both until the arrival of Wheeler's [Thirteenth New York] battery half an hour later, when I ordered Lieutenant Wheeler to report to Captain Dilger. [*OR* 27, pt. 1, p. 747]

Major Thomas W. Osborn, USA. U.S. Army Military Institute.

Face left, and walk along the park road for 100 yards to the guns and monument to Battery I, First Ohio Artillery, "Dilger's Battery." Stop, face right, and again look toward Oak Hill.

Position B—Battery I, First Ohio Artillery (Dilger's)

Coming into action in the field where you now stand was a superb battery, led by one of the best battery commanders in the Union army. The range from here to *Page's, Fry's,* and *Reese's* Batteries are approximately 1,000, 1,150, and 1,300 yards respectively. *Page's* and *Fry's* positions were just above the farmhouse in the distance. *Reese's* position was to the right of the farmhouse. Armed with six Napoleons, Dilger's battery was firing within the maximum effective range of his guns. Follow the action as Captain Dilger maneuvers his and a supporting battery to obtain maximum advantage of position and effective fire.

Report of Capt. Hubert Dilger, USA, Commanding Battery I, First Ohio Artillery, Artillery Brigade, Eleventh Corps, Army of the Potomac

The battery arrived at Gettysburg at about 10 a.m. July 1, attached to the division of Maj. Gen. C. Schurz, commanded by Brig. Gen. A. Schimmelfennig, who ordered me to take a position between the [Mummasburg] and [Carlisle] roads, wherever I might find it necessary, to which order I complied by putting one section, Lieutenant Clark Scripture commanding, on the highest point of the field. [This was behind you, about where the northern edge of the town is today.] A four-gun battery of the enemy [on Oak Hill] immediately opened fire at about 1,400 yards on this section, and compelled me very soon to bring my whole battery into action. During this heavy artillery duel, the enemy had been re-enforced to eight pieces, of which two advanced to within 800 or 1,000 yards, but I finally succeeded in silencing them, with a loss of five carriages, which they had to leave on the ground, after several efforts to bring them to the rear with new horses.

Short time afterward, a rifled battery commenced to play on me, at my request, Lieutenant Wheeler's battery [was brought] to my support, and [I had the] honor of taking charge of both batteries. I instantly advanced Lieutenant Weidman's section on our right and returned from there the

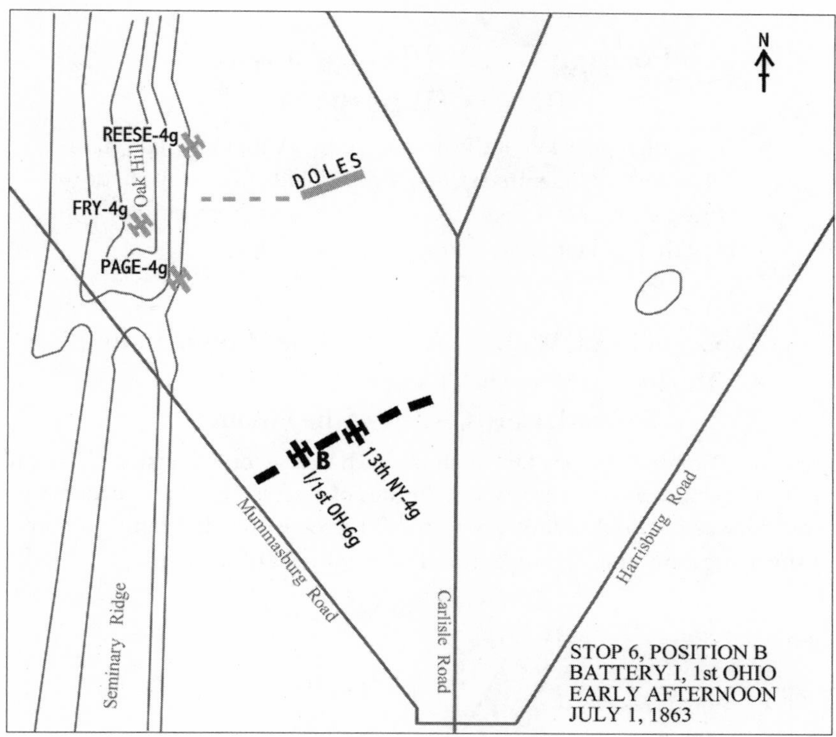

other four pieces of my battery on the left, under protection of Lieutenant Wheeler's fire. [This is where you are.]

In advancing, a ditch (5 feet wide and 4 feet deep, crossing the field in our front) had to be filled up, so as to form at least a passage for a column by pieces, which was executed under a very heavy fire. Lieutenant Wheeler followed as soon as my pieces were in position, and we remained here until the enemy's infantry commenced to mass on our right flank, supported by about four batteries, which concentrated their fire on us, one of them enfilading our line completely, causing great damage to men and horses, and disabling one piece of mine and one of Wheeler's battery. [*OR* 27, pt. 1, p. 754]

Face right and retrace your path along the park road back to the guns and monument marking the position of Lieutenant Wheeler's Thirteenth New York Independent Battery. Stand where you can look northwest and see Oak Hill.

Position C—Thirteenth New York Battery (Wheeler's)

This is the final position of the battery sent to support Dilger in his fight with the Confederate artillery on Oak Hill. Wheeler's battery was armed with four 3-inch rifles, which gave it greater range and accuracy than Dilger's Napoleons.

Report of Lieut. William Wheeler, USA, Commanding Thirteenth New York Battery, Artillery Brigade, Eleventh Corps, Army of the Potomac

On July 1, I marched from Emmitsburg with the Second Division (General Steinwehr), but, when within about 5 miles of Gettysburg, I was ordered to move forward at double-quick, which I did, proceeding at a rapid trot, and losing a large amount of forage from the roughness of the road.

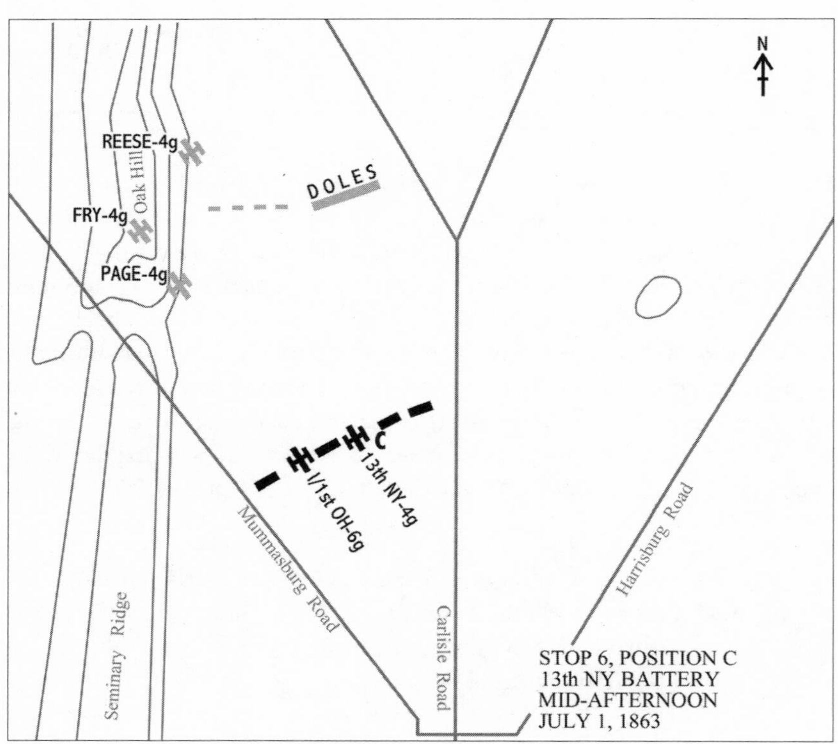

Upon arriving at Gettysburg, I took position on the right of the town, but soon received orders to move through the town to the front, and to support Captain Dilger's battery. In passing through the town, the rear body of two of my caissons broke down. One of these was subsequently recovered, but the other was too badly shattered to be repaired. I took up my position on Captain Dilger's right, and as soon as my guns had got the range of the hostile battery, they responded to it with good effect. Under their cover, Captain Dilger moved several hundred yards forward into a wheat-field. As soon as he commenced firing, I limbered up and followed, again taking position on his right. [Where you are.] A very heavy fire was opened on us here both in front and upon the right flank, but we continued to hold the position.

The enemy then massed his infantry and threw them upon the troops on our right, who fell back after some severe fighting. I changed the direction of my right section, and fired into the advancing column of the enemy with canister, but did not succeed in checking them. I did not leave this position until the enemy was almost in rear of my battery. I then moved back to a point on the road near the town, and held this until the enemy was again nearly behind me, and the infantry supports had withdrawn.

While moving across the field to this point, a shot struck the axle of one of my pieces and broke it, dismounting the piece. I slung the piece under the limber with the prolonge, and carried it for some distance until the

Oak Hill and the artillery positions of *Carter's* Battalion (Stops 5A, B, and C) as seen from the position of the 13th New York Battery (Stop 6C).

prolonge broke, when I was obliged to abandon the gun, but recovered it on the 5th, and it is now in serviceable condition. [A prolonge is a multi-purpose rope carried on the trail of a gun.] I then moved through the town, and was assigned a position on Cemetery Hill, being on the left wing of the batteries of the corps. [*OR* 27, pt. 1, pp. 752–53]

Report of Capt. Hubert Dilger, USA—continued

Our final retreat was executed in the same manner as the advance, and our infantry falling back toward the town, which could only be reached on one road, I sent all the pieces back excepting one section of each battery, commanding with them the entrance of the town as long as possible. The two rifled guns had to retire first, because I would not expose them too much at this short range, at which they commenced to become useless.

Our infantry having reached the town, I left my position, and was relieved on the [Carlisle] road by two pieces of Battery G, Fourth U.S. Artillery.

The main road was completely blockaded by artillery, infantry, and ambulances, and I took the first road to the left, marched around the town, and rejoined my command on Cemetery Hill, having lost on this day 14 men, 24 horses, and 1 piece disabled.

During the whole engagement, three of my caissons were always employed to carry ammunition, and as slowly as I directed the fire, we were twice nearly out of ammunition.

In regard to the ammunition. I must say that I was completely dissatisfied with the results observed of the fuses for 12-pounder shells and spherical case, on the explosion of which, by the most careful preparation, you cannot depend. The shell fuses, again, were remarkably less reliable than those for spherical case. The fuses for 3-inch ammunition caused a great many explosions on our right before the mouth of the guns, and it becomes very dangerous for another battery to advance in the fire of this battery, which kind of advancing of smooth-bore batteries is of very great importance on the battlefield, and should be done without danger. I would, therefore, most respectfully recommend the use of percussion shells only. [*OR* 27, pt. 1, pp. 754–55]

Both Dilger and Wheeler reported artillery fire coming from their right flank. These were the guns of Confederate Lieutenant Colonel *Hilary P. Jones's* artillery battalion in support of Major

General *Jubal Early's* infantry division. These guns were in position to the east of the Harrisburg Road and about 1,700 yards from where you are. They were firing in support of *Early's* attack against Barlow's division, which was the right of the Eleventh Corps line. The position of *Jones's* batteries and the tree cover and tree height allowed them to place enfilading fire on the right of the Eleventh Corps line and on Dilger's and Wheeler's batteries. As the fighting developed for Barlow's Knoll, Dilger and Wheeler had to face their batteries to the right to fire on *Doles's* and *Gordon's* Brigades.

Return to your car for the drive to Stop 7.

Continue to drive east on Howard Avenue for 0.5 mile. In 0.1 mile you will cross the Carlisle Road. In 0.4 mile after crossing the Carlisle Road, you will come to Barlow's Knoll. Park, get out of your car, and stand near the statue of Brigadier General Barlow.

Stop 7, Position A—The Eleventh Corps Right Flank

The small rise of ground you are on is Barlow's Knoll. It is named in honor of Brigadier General Francis C. Barlow, who commanded the First Division, Eleventh Corps that fought here. Oak Hill is west of you and can be seen from this location. Look south and you can see the northern edge of Gettysburg. On the other side of the Carlisle Road, the west side, the edge of the town is about 200 yards north of where it was in 1863. On this side of the Carlisle Road, the east side, the ground was open, with a few houses, for over one-half mile. Where the buildings mark the northern edge of the town today was the intended position for the Eleventh Corps's two divisions. However, their position was eventually out in the large field you have been moving across. How they came to be out in this exposed position is explained by the temporary corps commander, Major General Carl Schurz.

Report of Maj. Gen. Carl Schurz, USA, Temporarily Commanding Eleventh Corps, Army of the Potomac

About 10.30 o'clock I received the order to hurry forward my command as fast as possible, as the First Corps was engaged with the enemy in the neighborhood of Gettysburg. Leaving the command of the division in General

Schimmelfennig's hand, I hastened to the front, where I arrived about 11.30 o'clock, finding you [Howard] upon an eminence [Cemetery Hill] near the cemetery of Gettysburg, from which we overlooked the field of battle. You informed me that General Reynolds had just been killed; that you were in command of the whole, and that you had to turn over the Eleventh Corps to me.

You ordered me to take the Third and First Divisions of the Eleventh Corps through the town, and to endeavor to gain possession of the [northern] prolongation of the ridge [Oak Ridge] then partly held by the First Corps, while you intended to establish the Second Division and the artillery, excepting the batteries attached to the First and Third Divisions, on Cemetery Hill and the eminence east of it as a reserve.

The Third Division arrived and I ordered General Schimmelfennig, to whom I turned over the command of the Third Division, to advance briskly through the town, and to deploy on the right of the First Corps in two lines.

Shortly afterward the First Division, under General Barlow, arrived by the Emmitsburg road proper, advanced through the town, and was ordered by me to form on the right of the Third Division, its First Brigade to connect with the Third Division, while I ordered the Second Brigade to be held *en echelon* behind the right of the First Brigade east of the Mummasburg road. Each division had one battery with it. It was about 2 p.m. when the deployment of the two divisions was accomplished.

Hardly were the two divisions deployed a few hundred yards north of the town, when I received an order from you [Howard] to remain in the position I then occupied, and to push my skirmishers forward as far as possible. This was done, and our skirmishers, who became soon engaged, especially those of the Third Division, took a considerable number of prisoners.

While this was going on, two of the enemy's batteries, placed on a hillside [Oak Hill] opposite the Third Division, one above the other, opened upon us, flanking the First Corps. Captain Dilger, whose battery was attached to the Third Division, replied promptly, dismounting in a short time four of the enemy's pieces, and driving away two regiments which were on a line with the enemy's artillery at the foot of the hill.

In the meantime the firing near my extreme left seemed to increase in volume, and, leaving the point I had selected for myself and staff, on the Mummasburg road, I rode over toward the left, in order to see what was going on. The right of the First Corps seemed to be engaged in a very severe struggle. The enemy was evidently pressing upon that point. At the same time signs were apparent of an advance of the enemy upon my line, especially the right. The enemy was evidently stronger than he had been at the commencement of the battle, and the probability was that re-enforcements were still arriving. Feeling much anxiety about my right, which was liable to be turned if any of the enemy's forces were advancing by the Heidlersburg [or Harrisburg] road, I dispatched one of my aides to you, with the request to have one brigade of the Second Division placed upon the north side of the town, near the railroad depot, as an *echelon* to the First Division. My intention was to have that brigade in readiness to charge upon any force the enemy might move around my right.

After having taken the necessary observations on my extreme left, I returned to the Mummasburg road, where I discovered that General Barlow had moved forward his whole line, thus losing on his left the connection with the Third Division; moreover, the Second Brigade, of the First Division, had been taken out of its position *en echelon* behind the right of the First Brigade. I immediately gave orders to re-establish the connection by advancing the right wing of the Third Division, and hurried off aide after aide to look after the brigade of the Second Division which I had requested you to send me for the protection of my right and rear, but it had not yet arrived.

Suddenly the enemy opened upon the First Division from two batteries placed near the Harrisburg road, completely enfilading General Barlow's line. This fire, replied to by our batteries, produced but little effect upon our men. Soon afterward, however, about 3 o'clock, before the forward movement of the First Division could be arrested by my orders, the enemy appeared in our front with heavy masses of infantry, his line extending far beyond our right. [*OR* 27, pt. 1, pp. 727–28]

The knoll is the primary reason that the Eleventh Corps line was out in the open field. This piece of ground was an excellent position for 1863 artillery. It is higher than the surrounding terrain and is flat on top, with sufficient space for one or two batteries to deploy into firing positions. If Confederate artillery occupied the knoll, it would dominate any Union position to the south. To deny this position to the Confederates, Barlow moved his division forward to this vicinity. This in turn forced the division on his left to move forward in order to maintain a continuous line. Barlow attempted to refuse his right flank, but had insufficient troops to anchor his right on Gettysburg. Therefore, his right and subsequently the corps right were unprotected. As you shall see, this was not the only time during the battle that Union units were moved forward to control terrain that was a good artillery position and exposed their flank.

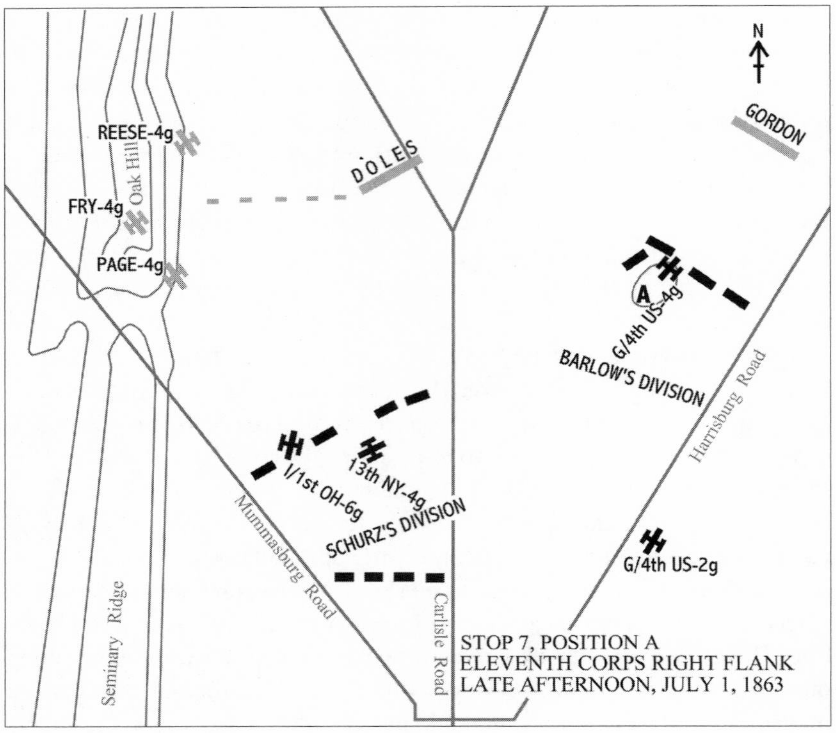

Walk to the guns representing Battery G, Fourth U.S. Artillery. They are pointed northeast. Face in that direction.

Position B—Eleventh Corps Outflanked

This is position of Battery G, Fourth U.S. Artillery. To your left rear is the Carlisle Road in front of you is Rock Creek, and to your right is the Harrisburg Road. Eight hundred yards northeast of your location is a flat ridge that was occupied by Lieutenant Colonel *Hilary P. Jones's* artillery battalion as it supported the attack of Major General *Jubal Early's* division against this position.

After you crossed the Carlisle Road, you drove along the line of monuments for Colonel Krzyzanowski's brigade. Krzyzanowski was advancing in a northeast direction to support Brigadier General Adelbert Ames's Second Brigade of Barlow's division. As Krzyzanowski advanced, Ames's line began to fall apart, then

Krzyzanowski took up a position short of Barlow's Knoll and engaged the attacking Confederates until his brigade was pushed off the position and retreated. The left regiment of Ames's brigade and Barlow's division was the 107th Ohio, two monuments to your left rear. Ames's brigade defended the position from that monument to the Seventeenth Connecticut's monument to your right rear. Barlow's other brigade, Colonel Leopold von Gilsa's First Brigade, was deployed to your right along the eastern slope of the knoll.

Report of Maj. Gen. *Jubal A. Early,* CSA, Commanding *Early's* Division, *Ewell's* Corps, Army of Northern Virginia

I encamped [on June 30] about 3 miles from Heidlersburg, and rode to see General *Ewell* at that point, and was informed by him that the object was to concentrate the corps at or near Cashtown, and received directions to move next day to that point. I was informed that *Rodes* would move by the way of Middletown [now Biglerville] and Arendtsville, but it was arranged that I should go by the way of Hunterstown and Mummasburg.

Having ascertained that the road from my camp to Hunterstown was a very rough and circuitous one, I determined next morning [July 1] to march by the way of Heidlersburg, and then from that point to the Mummasburg road. After passing Heidlersburg a short distance, I received a note from [General *Ewell*], informing me that General *Hill* was moving from Cashtown toward Gettysburg, and that General *Rodes* had turned off at Middletown, and was moving toward the same place, and directing me to move also to that point. I therefore continued to move on the road I was then on toward Gettysburg, and, on arriving in sight of that place, on the direct road from Heidlersburg, I discovered that General *Rodes'* division was engaged with the enemy to the right of me, the enemy occupying a position in front of Gettysburg, and the troops constituting his right being engaged in an effort to drive back the left of General *Rodes'* line.

I immediately ordered my troops to the front, and formed my line across the [Harrisburg] road, with *Gordon's* brigade on the right, *Hoke's* brigade (under Colonel *Avery*) on the left, *Hays'* brigade in the center, and *Smith's* brigade in the rear of *Hoke's*. *Jones'* battalion of artillery was posted in a field on the left of the [Harrisburg] road, immediately in front of *Hoke's* brigade, so as to fire on the enemy's flank, and, as soon as these dispositions could be made, a fire was opened upon the enemy's infantry and artillery by my artillery with considerable effect. [*OR* 27, pt. 2, p. 468]

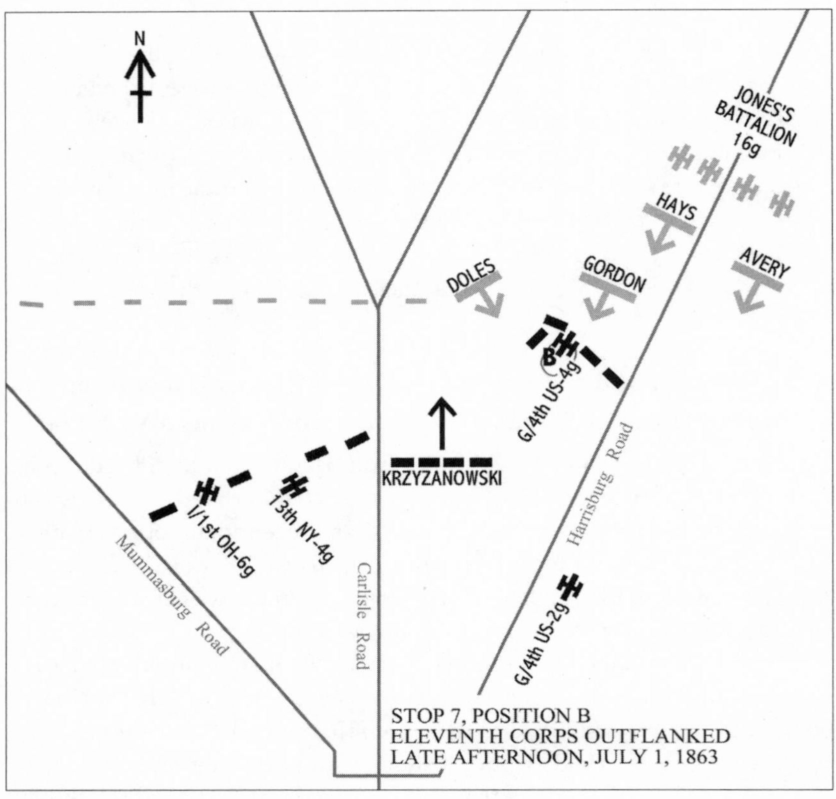

Lieutenant Colonel *Jones's* artillery battalion consisted of four batteries: Captain *James McD. Carrington's* Charlottesville (Virginia) Artillery Battery armed with four Napoleons, Captain *William A. Tanner's* Courtney (Virginia) Artillery Battery armed with four 3-inch rifles, Captain *Charles A Green's* Louisiana Guard Artillery Battery armed with two 3-inch rifles and two 10-pound Parrotts, and Captain *Asher W. Garber's* Staunton (Virginia) Artillery Battery armed with four Napoleons. Deployed into firing positions *Jones's* Battalion brought sixteen guns into the fight in an ideal location to use enfilading fire against the Eleventh Corps.

Report of Lieut. Col. *Hilary P. Jones,* CSA, Commanding *Jones's* Artillery Battalion, *Ewell's* Corps, Army of Northern Virginia

We marched back in the direction of Gettysburg, before which place we arrived on Wednesday, July 1. Here, finding the enemy heavily engaging General *Rodes* on our right, the major-general commanding ordered me to put the batteries in position, so as to open fire. Acting under his orders, I immediately placed twelve guns in position, and opened fire with considerable effect on the enemy's artillery, and upon the flank of a column of troops that were being massed upon our right. [*OR* 27, pt. 2, p. 495]

Report of Maj. Thomas W. Osborn, USA, Commanding Artillery Brigade, Eleventh Corps, Army of the Potomac

About 11 a.m. Lieutenant Wilkeson reached the field, and was ordered to report to General Barlow, commanding the First Division, which was engaged about three-fourths of a mile from the town and on the left of the York pike. The battery was assigned position by General Barlow, and when I reached the ground I found it unfortunately near the enemy's line of infantry, with which they were engaged, as well as two of his batteries, the concentrated fire of which no battery could withstand. Almost at the first fire, Lieutenant Wilkeson was mortally wounded, and carried from the field by 4 of his men. The command of the battery now devolved upon Lieutenant Bancroft. By changing position several times, the battery maintained its relative position until the division fell back to the town, when it retired to Cemetery Hill. During this engagement the battery was separated into sections or half batteries, and its struggle to maintain itself was very severe and persistent. [*OR* 27, pt. 1, p. 748]

Major Osborn mentions in his report one of the major concerns of artillerymen; that senior infantry commanders would place them in poor tactical positions. The concept of organizing artillery batteries into corps artillery brigades was to remove them from the direct control of infantry division and brigade commanders. However, once Wilkerson was ordered to report to Barlow, he came under his command.

You are standing on the initial position of Battery G in its unequal fight against *Jones's* artillery and *Early's* infantry.

Battery G, 4th U.S. Artillery in action on July 1. *Battles and Leaders of the Civil War.*

Report of Lieut. Eugene A. Bancroft, USA, Commanding Battery G, Fourth U.S. Artillery, Artillery Brigade, Eleventh Corps, Army of the Potomac

The battery, under the command of First Lieut. Bayard Wilkeson, Fourth U.S. Artillery, left camp, near Emmitsburg, Md., at 9 a.m. July 1, and marched to Gettysburg, Pa. When about 2 miles from the latter place, the order to trot was received, and, moving rapidly forward, the battery reached the town at 11 a.m.; passed directly through the village, and, turning to the right, in rear of our lines of batteries, moved about 1 mile through some fields, and immediately engaged the enemy. Leaving the left section [two Napoleons], under Second Lieut. C. F. Merkle, on the [east] side of the [Harrisburg] road, near the poor-house, the right and center sections [four Napoleons] took position on the [west] side of the road, and some distance [north] of the poor-house. [The Alms (Poor) House was located along the Harrisburg Road and south of your position. The Adams County Agricultural and Natural Resources Center is there today. It is the brick building south of you. Look past the old cemetery, and you can see it.]

At this point, Lieutenant Wilkeson was struck in the right leg by a shot from the enemy's artillery, and mortally wounded. After engaging two of the rebel batteries for about half an hour, these two sections retired a short distance, and a few minutes thereafter three of the pieces went into action on the left of their first position, to resist the advance of a line of the enemy's infantry, firing spherical case and canister, until, our infantry giving way in great disorder, the want of support compelled me to withdraw the guns. On entering the road leading into the village, I was joined by the left section, under Lieutenant Merkle, and assumed command of the whole. Halting to fill the ammunition chests of the gun limbers [from the caissons], the battery then retired slowly through Gettysburg, and took position in the cemetery, on the south side of the village, at 5 p.m., whence I fired a few shell and solid shot at the enemy, but without eliciting any reply.

The casualties during the day were as follows, viz: Lieutenant Wilkeson, mortally wounded; Private Charles F. Hofer, killed; Corporal John Monroe and Privates Ira C. Bumpus, William Clark, Taffender, and Edwin S. Libby, severely wounded; Bugler Charles A. Lockwood, Corporal Adolphus C. Hardy, Privates William Curtis and Frank E. Jordan, missing; 17 horses killed. [*OR* 27, pt. 1, p. 756]

Under Lieutenant Bancroft's command Battery G would continue fighting for the next two days. All totaled it would fire 1,380 rounds of ammunition.

Report of Maj. Gen *Jubal A. Early,* CSA—Continued

Gordon's brigade was then ordered forward to the support of *Doles'* brigade, which was on *Rodes'* left, and was being pressed by a considerable force, of the enemy, which had advanced from the direction of the town to a wooded hill [Barlow's Knoll] on the west side of Rock Creek, the stream which runs northeast of the town, and as soon as *Gordon* was fairly engaged with this force, *Hays'* and *Hoke's* [*Avery's*] brigades were ordered forward in line, and the artillery, supported by *Smith's* brigade, was ordered to follow.

After a short but hot contest, *Gordon* succeeded in routing the force opposed to him, consisting of a division of the Eleventh Corps, commanded by Brigadier-General Barlow, of the Federal Army, and drove it back with great slaughter, capturing, among a number of prisoners, General Barlow himself, who was severely wounded. *Gordon* advanced across the creek, over the hill on which Barlow had been posted, and across the fields toward the town, until he came to a low ridge, behind which the enemy had another line of battle, extending beyond his left. I directed him to halt here, and then ordered *Hays* and *Avery,* who had been halted on the east side of Rock Creek while I rode forward to where *Gordon* had been engaged, to advance toward the town, on *Gordon's* left, which they did in fine style, encountering and driving back into the town in great confusion the second line of the enemy. [*OR* 27, pt. 2, pp. 468–69]

As *Early's* Division moved forward in its attack, *Jones* began shifting guns forward to continue supporting the infantry.

Report of Lieut. Col. *Hilary P. Jones,* CSA—Continued

On the advance of General *Gordon's* brigade from our right, we directed our fire farther to the left, on the disordered masses of the enemy that were rapidly retreating before our troops. This was continued until the advance of our men rendered it dangerous to continue firing from that position. I immediately, by order of General *Early,* sent Captain *Carrington's* battery across the creek to take position in front of Gettysburg, but moving with all rapidity, as it did, before it could reach any position the enemy had been driven through the town by *Hays'* brigade. In the first position we occupied, three guns were temporarily disabled by having shots wedged in the bores, and one Napoleon permanently disabled by being struck on the face of the muzzle and bent by a solid shot from the enemy.

We had 1 man killed of Captain *Green's,* and 1 man of Captain *Garber's* battery wounded. The guns that were temporarily disabled were soon rendered fit for service again, and I was enabled to replace the Napoleon gun permanently disabled by one of the two Napoleon guns captured by General *Hays'* brigade. The disabled gun and the other captured Napoleon I had carried and turned over to the ordnance department, thereby securing them. [*OR* 27, pt. 2, p. 495]

One section of Battery G, Fourth U.S. Artillery was deployed away from the primary battery position. This section, commanded by Lieutenant Christopher Merkel, was positioned in the vicinity of the Alms House, just east of the Harrisburg Road. It was positioned there in an attempt to protect the right flank of Barlow's division. With a major portion of *Early's* Division attacking over the ground east of the Harrisburg Road, this one section had too little firepower for the task assigned.

Report of Lieut. Christopher F. Merkle, USA, Commanding Section of Battery G, Fourth U.S. Artillery, Artillery Brigade, Eleventh Corps, Army of the Potomac

I engaged one battery of the enemy for a few moments with solid shot, and then directed my attention to the rebel infantry as they were advancing in mass upon us. I used shell and spherical case shot at first, and, as the line of the enemy came closer, and I ran out of shot, shell, and case shot, I used canister; the enemy was then within canister range. At the same time, our infantry fell back rapidly, and left me almost without support. I then limbered to the rear, and retired toward the town. The enemy came rather close at the time, so I fired two double rounds of canister, with prolonge fixed, at their line at the end of the town; then limbered up and retired.

The casualties during the day were Sergeant Monroe, Privates Bumpus, Clark, and Taffender, severely wounded, and Private Curtis missing; 5 horses killed.

Ammunition expended: Solid shot 24, Case shot 24, Shells 8, Canister 14. Total 70. [*OR* 27, pt. 1, pp. 757–58]

Return to your car for the drive to Stop 8.

Drive southeast on the park road for 0.2 mile to the intersection with the Harrisburg Road. Turn right on to the Harrisburg Road, and drive for 0.3 mile to the intersection with East Broadway. Turn right on to East Broadway, and drive for one block to the intersection with Carlisle Street. Turn left on to Carlisle Street, and drive one block south to Lincoln Avenue. Turn left on to Lincoln Avenue. Park in the first available legal parking space on the right of the road. Walk back to Carlisle Street, stop, face right, and look to the north toward the large open field north of Gettysburg.

Stop 8—Attempted Delay

Report of Maj. Thomas W. Osborn, USA, Commanding Artillery Brigade, Eleventh Corps, Army of the Potomac

Captain Heckman [Battery K, First Ohio Artillery] was not ordered in until the corps had begun to fall back. He was then put into position, with a view of holding the enemy in check until the corps had time to retire through the town to the hill beyond, and though he worked his battery to the best of his ability, the enemy crowded upon it, and was within his battery before he attempted to retire. He was compelled to leave [two guns] in the hands of the enemy. I think no censure can be attached to this battery for the loss of the guns. The battery was so severely disabled otherwise that I was compelled to send it to the rear, thus losing the benefit of it during the fight of the second and third days. [*OR* 27, pt. 1, p. 748]

You are at the position occupied by the four Napoleons of Captain Lewis Heckman's Battery K, First Ohio Artillery. The area is now built up, but in 1863 it was quite open. As you face north, there is a monument to Heckman's battery on the other side of Carlisle Street. South and west of that monument were the buildings of what is today Gettysburg College. North of Lincoln Avenue there were no houses, and in front of you was the southern edge of the large field where Stops 6 and 7 are. To your right rear and on the east side of Carlisle Street, there was open ground with a scattering of houses. Heckman's battery's left was about where the monument is today. From there the battery position went east and was facing north and northeast.

Report of Capt. Lewis Heckman, USA, Commanding Battery K, First Ohio Artillery, Artillery Brigade, Eleventh Corps, Army of the Potomac

On July 1, I placed my battery in position on the [north] side of the town. The enemy was already in range when my battery went into position. I unlimbered, and commenced firing as soon as possible, as the enemy were close to me and advancing. My battery was engaged for thirty minutes. During that time I expended 113 rounds of ammunition, mostly canister.

I lost 2 men killed and 10 wounded, and 1 commissioned officer wounded severely. I lost 9 horses that died from the wounds received.

The enemy in the meantime were advancing, and had gotten very close. The order was given to limber up, but too late to save my whole battery. I fell back through the town, leaving two pieces in the hands of the enemy. [*OR* 27, pt. 1, p. 755]

Return to your car for the drive to Stop 9.

Continue driving on Lincoln Avenue to Stratton Street. Turn right on to Stratton Street, and drive south 0.1 mile to 218 Stratton Street. The address is on your right. Traffic permitting, pause briefly.

Look at the north side of the building at 218 Stratton Street. You will see embedded high up in the wall an unexploded projectile from either an Ordnance rifle or a Parrott rifle. Now look across the street at 221 Stratton Street. There you will see another rifled projectile in the south wall. A Confederate gun probably fired the projectile in the wall at 218, while the one at 221 was probably fired by a Union gun. Both projectiles must have been at their extreme range and therefore did not completely penetrate the walls.

Continue on to Stop 9, which is on Cemetery Hill.

Continue to drive south on Stratton Street for 0.2 mile to the stoplight at York Street. Proceed straight through this intersection and continue to drive south two more blocks to High Street. Turn right on to High Street, and drive west for one block to the intersection with Baltimore Street. Turn left on to Baltimore Street and drive south for 0.5 mile to Cemetery Hill. At the Y intersection go straight to follow Route 97 South, the Baltimore Pike. Find a place to park. Walk to the top of the hill, if you are not already parked there, and find the guns and monument marking the position of Battery B, Fourth U.S. Artillery. They will be close to the road and on the east side of the Baltimore Pike. Face north, the direction the guns of Battery B are pointed.

Stop 9, Position A—East Cemetery Hill

You are on Cemetery Hill. The road to your left, as you look north, is the Baltimore Pike. Going south, it is one of the main supply and communications routes, the Taneytown Road being the other, for the Army of the Potomac. To remain at Gettysburg, Meade had to have control of these roads. As the pike goes over the hill, it divides it into East and West Cemetery Hills. You are on East Cemetery Hill. To your immediate left, on the other side of the pike and the iron fence, is the Soldier's National Cemetery. The Soldier's National Cemetery was not there at the time of the battle. It was established after the battle and dedicated on November 19, 1863. At this dedication Abraham Lincoln gave his unforgettable "Gettysburg Address." At the time of the battle, the area where the Soldier's National Cemetery is located was an open field, orchards, and a cornfield.

To your left rear is the gatehouse of Evergreen Cemetery. Established in 1856, it was, and continues to be, the Gettysburg town cemetery. Evergreen Cemetery gave the high ground it was on the name Cemetery Hill, which it was called prior to the armies coming to Gettysburg. Major General George G. Meade, the Army of the Potomac's commander, came to this location when he arrived on the battlefield at 2 a.m., July 2.

Today the town of Gettysburg is closer to the top of the hill than it was in 1863. At that time the southern edge of the town was approximately one-fourth of a mile away toward the bottom of the hill. Eight hundred and fifty yards, 0.5 mile, to your right rear is a tree-covered hill. This is Culp's Hill. It was also imperative

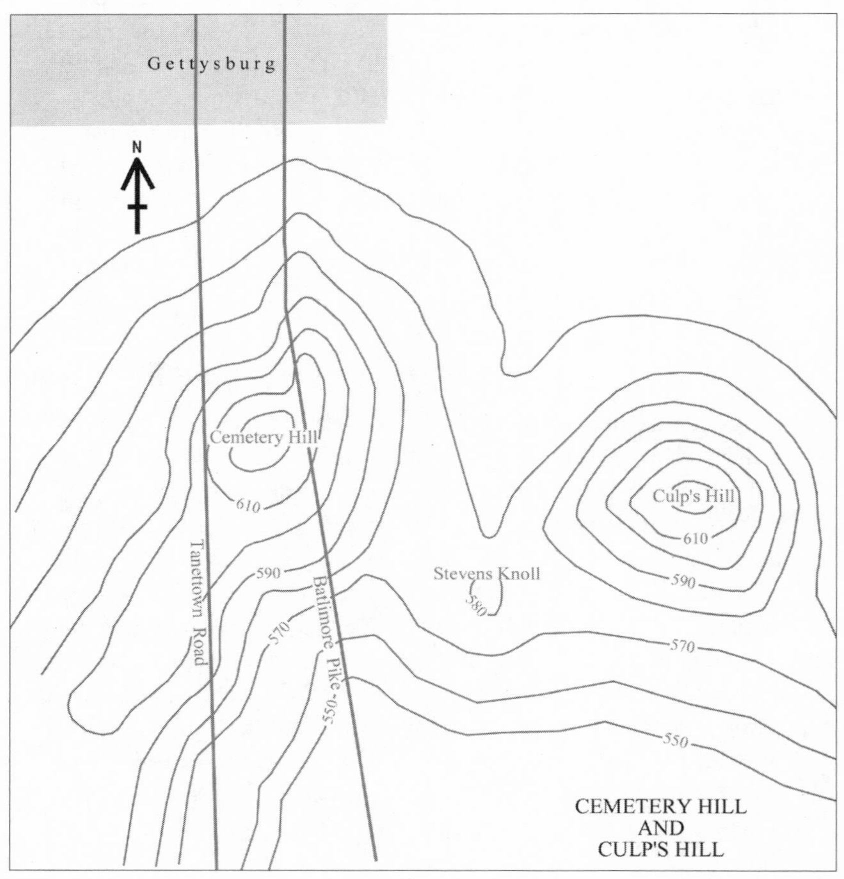

that the Union army hold Culp's Hill if it was to remain at Gettysburg. When completely deployed, the Army of the Potomac's defensive position came from Culp's Hill through where you are, continued to your left to the western edge of Cemetery Hill, then turned south along Cemetery Ridge, and went to the Round Tops.

When the Eleventh Corps marched through Gettysburg and deployed into defensive positions north of the town, Brigadier General Adolph von Steinwehr's Second Division was ordered to occupy Cemetery Hill. One of Steinwehr's brigades was eventually ordered forward to assist the other two divisions. The other brigade and Battery I, First New York Artillery, with six 3-inch rifles, remained in position on Cemetery Hill. These units provided a rallying point for retreating Union forces as they were driven back through Gettysburg.

The First and Eleventh Corps artillery retreated from positions west and north of Gettysburg to Cemetery Hill. By mutual consent, and regardless of whom they belonged to, Major Osborn took command of batteries west of the Baltimore Pike while Colonel Wainwright commanded the batteries east of the pike.

The batteries you see represented on East Cemetery Hill today were not all here on the evening of July 1. The batteries that were here included (where you are) Battery B, Fourth U.S. Artillery, (to your right) Battery B, First Pennsylvania Artillery, (to your right rear) Battery L, First New York Artillery, (to your right front) Battery I, First New York Artillery, and (halfway from your location to Culp's Hill, on the small knoll, now called Stevens's Knoll) the Fifth Maine Battery. Combined, these batteries had twenty-three guns, thirteen 3-inch rifles, and ten Napoleons. The other batteries you see represented came into position here on July 2.

Colonel Wainwright described the retreat of the First Corps Artillery through the town and deployment on to East Cemetery Hill.

Report of Col. Charles S. Wainwright, USA, Commanding Artillery Brigade, First Corps, Army of the Potomac

The batteries passed immediately through the town along with the other troops, and were placed in position again on reaching Cemetery Hill along with several of the Eleventh Corps batteries, so as to command the town

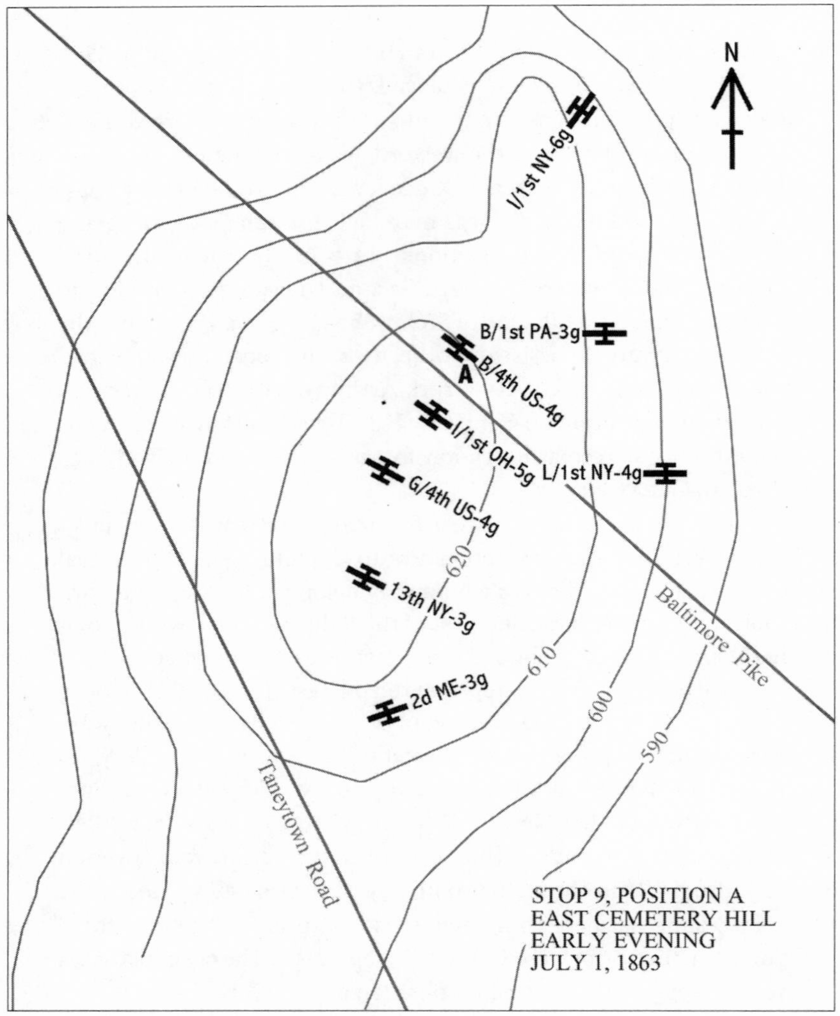

and the approach from the northwest in case the enemy should attempt to follow us through the town.

At dusk, no attack having been made, the batteries on the hill outside the cemetery gate were posted as follows, and light earthworks thrown up in front of each gun to protect the men from the fire of the enemy's sharpshooters: Four guns [Napoleons] of Battery B, Fourth U.S. Artillery, [next to] the road so as to command the approaches from the town (two guns of this battery had been disabled by loss of pointing rings) along the north front of the hill; [six 3-inch rifles] of Battery I, First New York Artillery

(Captain Wiedrich's, Eleventh Corps), on the right [of the line]; next [to Wiedrich's right was] Cooper's [Battery B, First Pennsylvania Artillery, with three 3-inch rifles], and then Reynolds's [Battery L, First New York Artillery, with four 3-inch rifles] giving thirteen 3-inch guns on this front, some of which could also be turned to bear upon the town and our old position of the morning. The Fifth Maine battery [six Napoleons] was posted to the right on a small knoll [Stevens's Knoll], from whence they could obtain an oblique fire upon the hills in front of our line as well as a flanking fire at close quarters upon any attacking columns. Captain Hall's (Second Maine) remaining three [3-inch rifles] (the others had been dismounted) were in position on the left of the cemetery [with Major Osborn] where he remained during the next day's engagement, after which he reported to General Tyler for repairs.

The loss of the batteries during the day's engagement was heavy, amounting in all to 83 officers and men and about 80 horses. A large proportion of the last were hit while passing over the short open space between Seminary Ridge and the town, the enemy having at that time a fire upon us from three sides. [*OR* 27, pt. 1, pp. 357–58]

When Meade received word that Reynolds had been killed, he sent Major General Winfield S. Hancock forward to Gettysburg to assume overall tactical control of the battlefield. Hancock arrived in the vicinity of where you are as the First and Eleventh Corps were retreating through the town. He was responsible for rallying the retreating troops and establishing the defensive position on Cemetery Hill. A statue of Hancock is to your right. Notice how his right hand is extended out palm down as if to say, "stop, stay, and rally here."

Report of Maj. Gen. Winfield S. Hancock, USA, Commanding Second Corps, Army of the Potomac

On the morning of July 1, the command marched to Taneytown, going into bivouac about 11 a.m. I then proceeded in person to General Meade's headquarters, and, on reporting to him, was informed as to his intention with reference to giving battle to the enemy, the orders for preparatory movements being then ready for issue.

A few minutes before 1 p.m., I received orders to proceed in person to the front, and assume command of the First, Third, and Eleventh Corps, in consequence of the death of Major-General Reynolds. Having been fully informed by the major-general commanding as to his intentions, I was instructed by him to give the necessary directions upon my arrival at the front for the movement of troops and trains to the rear toward the line of battle he had selected, should I deem it expedient to do so. If the ground was suitable, and circumstances made it wise, I was directed to establish the line of battle at Gettysburg.

Turning over the command of the Second Corps to Brigadier-General Gibbon, under instructions from General Meade, at 1.10 o'clock I was on the road to Gettysburg, accompanied by my personal aides, Lieutenant-Colonel Morgan, chief of staff, Second Corps, and the signal party of the corps, under command of Captain Hall.

At 3 p.m. I arrived at Gettysburg and assumed the command. At this time the First and Eleventh Corps were retiring through the town, closely pursued by the enemy. The cavalry of General Buford was occupying a firm position on the plain to the left of Gettysburg, covering the rear of the retreating corps. The Third Corps had not yet arrived from Emmitsburg. Orders were at once given to establish a line of battle on Cemetery Hill, with skirmishers occupying that part of the town immediately in our front. The position just on the southern edge of Gettysburg, overlooking the town and commanding the Emmitsburg and Taneytown roads and the Baltimore turnpike, was already partially occupied on my arrival by direction of Major-General Howard. Some difficulty was experienced in forming the troops of the Eleventh Corps, but by vigorous efforts a sufficiently formidable line was established to deter the enemy from any serious assault on the position. They pushed forward a line of battle for a short distance east of the Baltimore turnpike, but it was easily checked by the fire of our artillery. In forming the lines, I received material assistance from Major-General Howard, Brigadier-Generals Warren and Buford, and officers of General Howard's command.

As soon as the line of battle mentioned above was shown by the enemy, Wadsworth's division, First Corps, and a battery (thought to be the Fifth Maine) were placed on the eminence just across the turnpike [Stevens's Knoll and the northwest sector of Culp's Hill], and commanding completely this approach. This important position was held by the division during the remainder of the operations near Gettysburg. The rest of the First Corps, under Major-General Doubleday, was on the right and left of the Taneytown road, and connected with the left of the Eleventh Corps, which occupied that part of Cemetery Hill immediately to the right and left of the Baltimore turnpike. A division of the Twelfth Corps, under Brigadier-General Williams, arrived as these arrangements were being completed, and was established [on Culp's Hill], by order of Major-General Slocum, some distance to the right and rear of Wadsworth's division. Brigadier-General Geary's division, of the Twelfth Corps, arriving on the ground subsequently, and not being able to communicate with Major-General Slocum, I ordered the division to the high ground to the right of and near Round Top Mountain, commanding the Gettysburg and Emmitsburg road, as well as the Gettysburg and Taneytown road to our rear.

The trains of all the troops under my command were ordered to the rear, that they might not interfere with any movement of troops that might be directed by the major-general commanding [Meade].

My aide, Major Mitchell, was then sent to General Meade to inform him of the state of affairs, and to say that I would hold the position until night. Shortly after, I addressed a communication to the major-general commanding, sending it by Captain Parker, of my staff, giving in detail the information in my possession, and informing him that the position at Gettysburg was a very strong one, having for its disadvantage that it might be easily turned, and leaving to him the responsibility whether the battle should be fought at Gettysburg or at a place first selected by him.

Between 5 and 6 o'clock, my dispositions having been completed, Major-General Slocum arrived on the field, and, considering that my functions had ceased, I transferred the command to him. The head of the Third Corps appeared in sight shortly afterward, on the Emmitsburg road.

About dark I started for the headquarters of the army, still at Taneytown, 13 miles distant, and reported in person to General Meade. I then ascertained that he had already given orders for the corps in the rear to advance at once to Gettysburg, and was about proceeding there in person. [*OR* 27, pt. 1, pp. 367–69]

Lieutenant Stewart recounts Hancock's commanding presence on the battlefield and the orders he received from him.

Narrative of Lieut. James Stewart, USA, Commanding Battery B, Fourth U.S. Artillery, Artillery Brigade, First Corps, Army of the Potomac

Our corps was falling back to take position on Cemetery Hill. When I reached that point, and at the gate leading to [Evergreen Cemetery], General Hancock called to me and ask how many guns I had that were serviceable. I told him four. He then said I was to place three guns on this pike [the

Baltimore Pike] and the other at right-angles to them, and said: "I want you to remain in this position until I relieve you in person." He then called Captain Mitchell, his aide, and told him to listen to what he was going to say to me. He then said: "I am of the opinion that the enemy will mass in town and make an effort to take this position, but I want you to remain until you are relieved by me or by my written order and take orders from no one." I remained in that position from the afternoon of the 1st to the forenoon of the 4th. [Stewart, "Battery B," 189–90]

Depart from this location and follow the walking path to your right to the position of Battery I, First New York Artillery. Stand next to the right gun.

Position B—East Cemetery Hill's Fields of Fire

Report of Capt. Michael Wiedrich, USA, Commanding Battery I, First New York Artillery, Artillery Brigade, Eleventh Corps, Army of the Potomac

On arriving on the 1st instant near the cemetery at Gettysburg, I was ordered to take position on a hill on the north side of the Baltimore turnpike, and near the cemetery.

During the afternoon, we had some skirmishing with a rebel battery, which was posted near the road leading from Gettysburg to York.

When, about 5 p.m., our infantry, which had advanced through the town, was repulsed, I changed the direction of my pieces in the direction from where the enemy was advancing, and opened with shells on their columns with good effect; and after our infantry was driven out of the town, and the enemy made his appearance in our front, I received him with canister, which checked his progress, and gave our troops time to rally in rear of the battery, to advance on the enemy again, and to drive him back into town, when the fire was kept up until late in the evening. [*OR* 27, pt. 1, p. 751]

Before you leave East Cemetery Hill take a few minutes to look closely at how the artillery was positioned to cover all avenues of approach. Also notice that, with Stevens's Fifth Maine Battery on the small knoll between you and Culp's Hill, the open ground was covered by a crossfire of artillery.

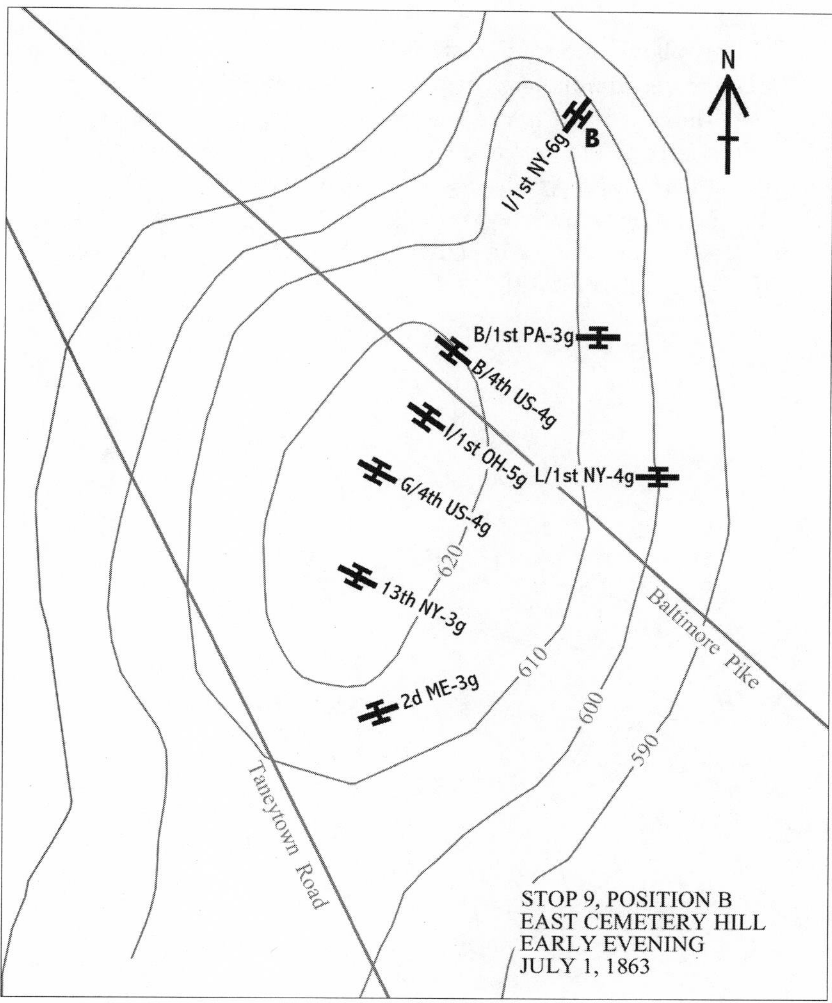

When you are ready, watch for traffic, cross the Baltimore Pike, and walk to the entrance of the Soldiers National Cemetery. This is not the same cemetery as Evergreen Cemetery.

Stop 10, Position A—Entrance Gate to National Cemetery

You are now going to walk along the rest of the Union artillery position on Cemetery Hill during the late afternoon of July 1. You will be walking in a southwesterly direction. Remember that the tree-landscaped military cemetery was not here in 1863. The area where the cemetery is today was fields and orchards. The modern built up area to the west and southwest of the hill was not there. The artillery was generally located along the higher part of the hill with the infantry lower down the slope. As you walk, you will be able to see why the long open fields of fire and observation made this a tactically key position.

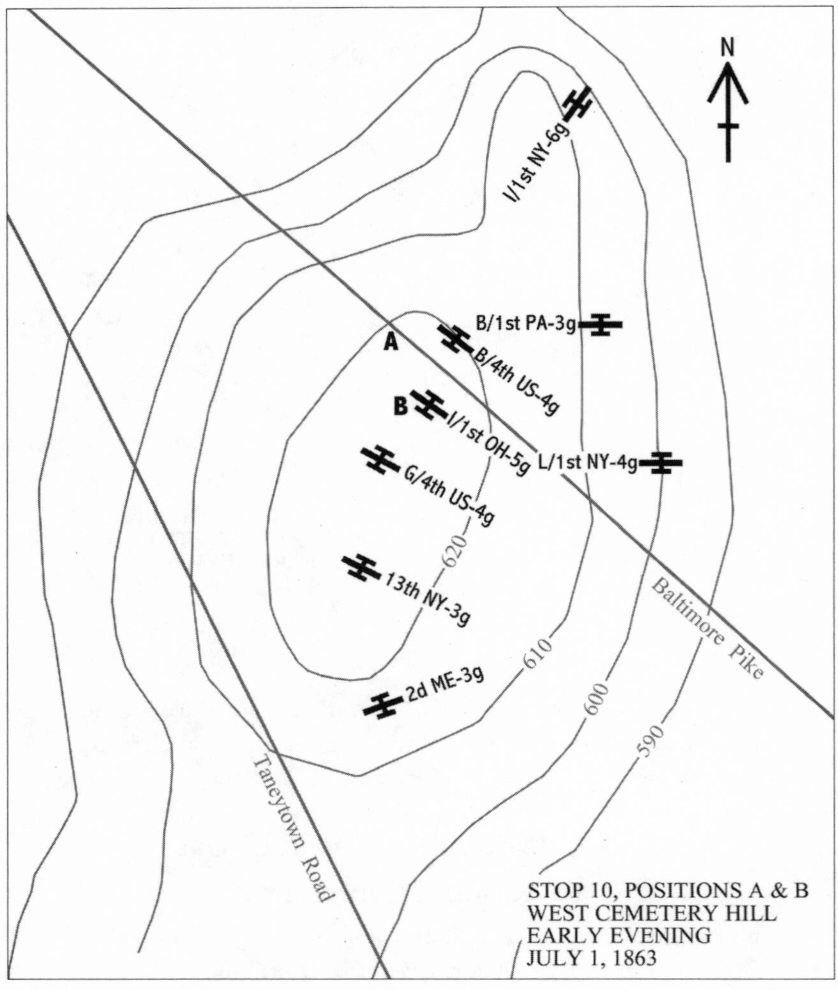

Proceed through the gate and follow the walking path. In a few yards the path will divide. Follow the left path and walk for 40 yards to the guns representing Battery I, First Ohio Artillery.

Position B—Osborn's Right Flank

On Cemetery Hill the responsibility for the artillery was divided. By mutual consent Major Osborn, the Eleventh Corps's Artillery Brigade Commander, commanded all artillery on the left side of the Baltimore Pike while the First Corps's Artillery Brigade commander, Colonel Wainwright, assumed command of all batteries to the right of the pike. You are at the position of Captain Dilger's Battery I, First Ohio Artillery. The last time you saw this battery was at Stop 6 in the open field north of Gettysburg. Late in the afternoon Dilger retreated the five surviving Napoleons of his battery through the town to this position, where he was the right flank of Osborn's artillery line.

Continue to walk along the path for 150 yards to the position of Battery G, Fourth U.S. Artillery.

Position C—Osborn's Artillery Line.

Major Osborn initially had five batteries in his artillery brigade. One of them, Battery I, First New York, was deployed with Colonel Wainwright on East Cemetery Hill. Captain Heckman's Battery K, First Ohio, was so badly damaged on the northern edge of Gettysburg, Stop 8, that it may have stopped here for a short time but went to the rear for repairs. You have just walked from Battery I, First Ohio Artillery. Where you are now was the location of Battery G, Fourth U.S. Artillery, after it retreated from Barlow's Knoll, Stop 7. Battery G, now commanded by Lieutenant Eugene Bancroft, arrived at this location with four Napoleons, Lieutenant Merkle's section having been temporarily positioned in another location. To Battery G's left were the three surviving 3-inch rifles of Wheeler's Thirteenth New York Battery. To Wheeler's left were the three remaining 3-inch rifles of Captain Hall's Second Maine Battery, who you last saw between the Chambersburg Pike and the railroad cut, Stop 1. These batteries gave Osborn fifteen guns to defend this position. Infantry were deployed on the lower slope of the hill.

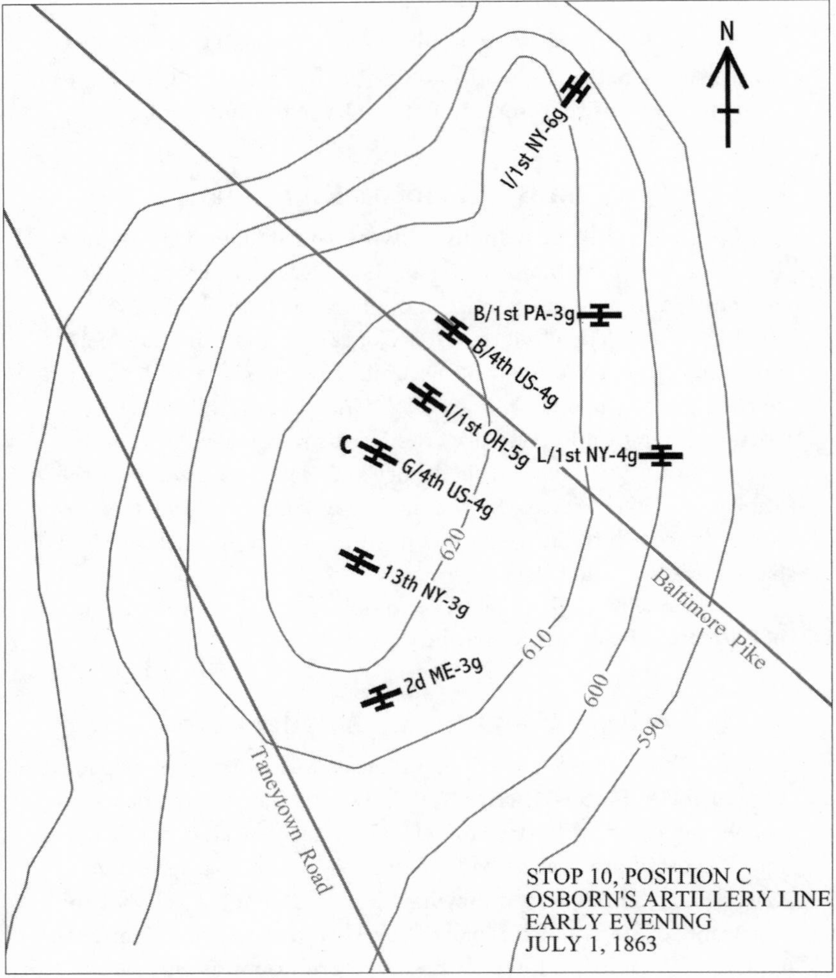

Continue to walk along the path. Look to your right, northwest, and you will see the steeple that marks the seminary. Continue walking, and you will pass a large white monument, the Soldiers National Monument. From here you can see Oak Hill. Look for the large Eternal Peace Light Memorial.

You should by now begin to appreciate the importance of this hill. It controlled the three major roads (Baltimore Pike, Taneytown Road, and Emmitsburg Road) to Baltimore and Washington, provided the northern anchor for the Union line, and with its short- and long-range fields of fire and observation was an excellent defensive position.

Continue walking past the large white monument for another 75 yards, then stop and face west, to your right.

Position D—Osborn's Left Flank

The road directly in front of you on the other side of the stonewall is the Taneytown Road. At a greater distance you can see the Emmitsburg Road. If you look just south of west, you can see the

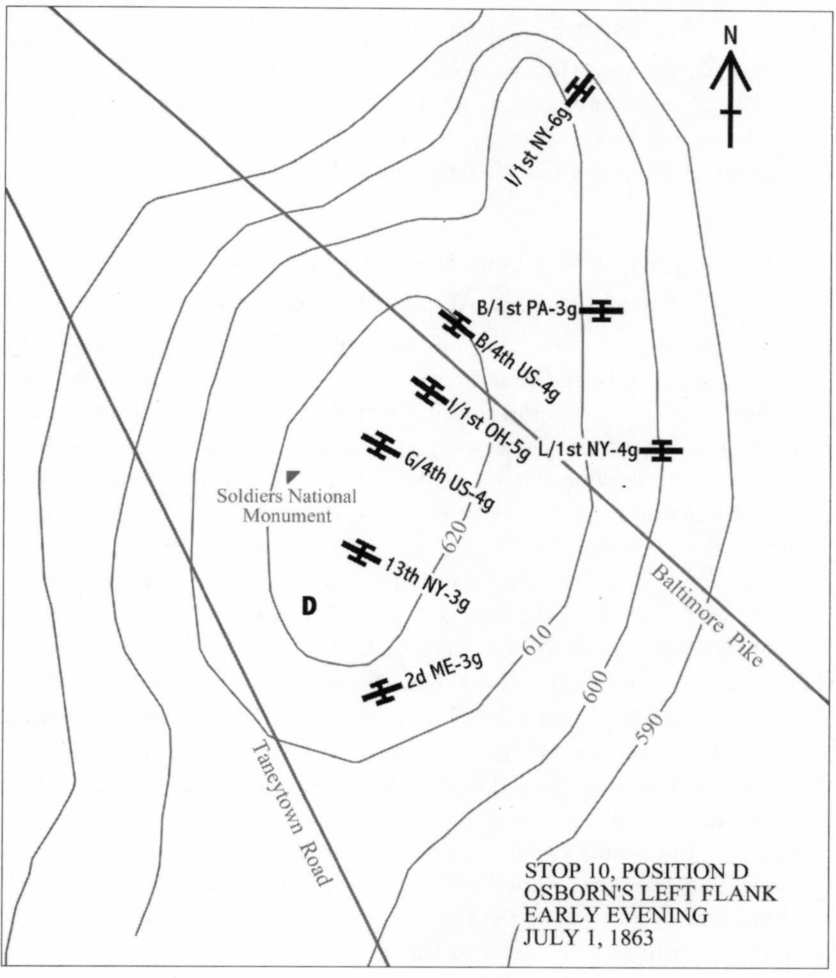

STOP 10, POSITION D
OSBORN'S LEFT FLANK
EARLY EVENING
JULY 1, 1863

large white Virginia Monument on Seminary Ridge. This monument is approximately in the center of the Confederate July 2 and 3 positions on Seminary Ridge. As you walked along the path, you saw monuments and guns to other batteries. This is artillery that reinforced Osborn on July 2 and 3. After they arrived, Osborn had over 40 guns on West Cemetery Hill. Before you depart this location, you may wish to look around and study the artillery positioning and the fields of interlocking fire.

Retrace your steps on the path back to the Soldiers National Monument.

Position E—Hunt Reinforces Osborn

Brigadier General Henry J. Hunt was the chief of artillery for the Army of the Potomac. As such he exercised supervision over all of Meade's artillery. During the early hours of July 2 he began to deploy artillery to strengthen Cemetery Hill and Culp's Hill

Report of Brig. Gen. Henry J. Hunt, USA, Chief of Artillery, Army of the Potomac

On the night of July 1, the commanding general [Meade] left Taneytown, and reached Gettysburg about 2 a.m. of the 2d. Soon after his arrival, he directed me to see to the position of the artillery, and make such arrangements respecting it as were necessary. I examined the positions at Cemetery Hill, so far as the darkness would permit, and then accompanied the general and Major-General Howard in an inspection of the west front of the field, occupied by the Second and Third Corps. Cemetery Hill commanded the positions which could be occupied by the enemy to the north and northwest. Toward the south the line occupied the crest of a gentle elevation [Cemetery Ridge], which, concealing everything immediately behind it from the observation of the enemy, commanded the ground to the west, which sloped down gradually for a few hundred yards, and then rising, formed another crest [Seminary Ridge], varying from half to three-quarters of a mile distant. The summit of this crest was wooded, and toward the south bent eastwardly and crossed the Emmitsburg road, forming a very favorable position for the enemy's artillery, and affording concealment to his movements in that direction. About half or three-quarters of a mile south of the cemetery our own crest and the ground in front of it were broken by groves of trees, and still farther on by rough and rocky ground. At a distance of about 2 miles from Cemetery Hill, a high, rocky, and broken peak formed the natural termination of our lines. The broken character of the ground in front of the southern half of our line was unfavorable to the use of artillery. From the cemetery, as a center, the right of our line extended toward the east, and lay on the north [side] of the Baltimore pike. The ground is hilly, heavily wooded, and intersected with ravines and small water-courses, very unfavorable to the use of artillery. The First and Eleventh Corps were stationed on and near Cemetery Hill. The Second Corps (Hancock's) stretched along the crest on the left [south] of the Cemetery Hill, with the Third Corps (Sickles') on its left. To the right of the cemetery lay a portion of the First Corps (Newton's), and beyond it the Twelfth (Slocum's) [on Culp's Hill].

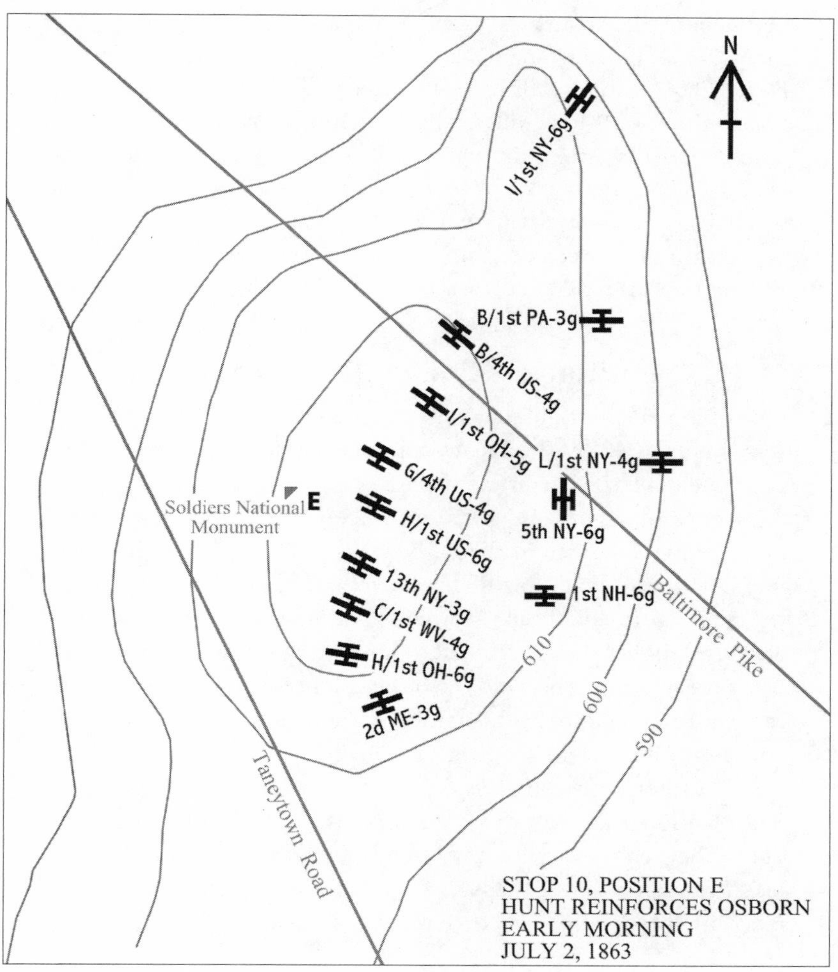

STOP 10, POSITION E
HUNT REINFORCES OSBORN
EARLY MORNING
JULY 2, 1863

The batteries at the cemetery, under command of Colonel Wainwright, remained as they were, and Major Osborn, chief of artillery of the Eleventh Corps, was directed to take command on the south [west] of the road. I re-enforced him with five batteries (Eakin's, H, First United States, six 12-pounder [Napoleons]; Taft's, Fifth New York, six 20-pounder [Parrotts]; Hill's, C, First West Virginia, four 10-pounder [Parrotts]; Huntington's, H, First Ohio, six 3-inch [rifles], and Edgell's, First New Hampshire, six 3-inch [rifles]) from the Artillery Reserve. [*OR* 27, pt. 1, pp. 232–33]

When Hunt reinforced Osborn with five batteries, he brought an additional twenty-eight guns to this position. These reinforcements and Osborn's fifteen guns gave him command of forty-three pieces of artillery on West Cemetery Hill. This was increased to forty-five when Lieutenant Merkle's section rejoined Battery G, Fourth U.S. Artillery. They were fifteen (then seventeen) Napoleons, nineteen 3-inch rifles, four 10-pound Parrotts and six 20-pound Parrotts. This mixture provided Osborn the capability to engage area targets, such as infantry formations, or point targets when firing at enemy artillery in a counter battery role.

Continue to retrace your steps, and walk to the guns and marker for Battery G, Fourth U.S. Artillery.

Position F—End of the First Day

One of the much discussed controversies of the Gettysburg battle was the decision by the Lieutenant General *Richard Ewell* not to continue his attack, after his successes north of the town, and try to capture all or part of Cemetery Hill. *Robert E. Lee* had given him a discretionary order to do so, but had left the implementation decision up to *Ewell.* The full details of this decision are not within the purview of this book. However, you may wonder if such an attack might have been successful. Located lower down on the hill was a fresh infantry brigade and other infantry brigades. Although reduced in strength by casualties, these brigades were rallying and assuming defensive positions on or near the hill. In addition to Osborn's fifteen guns on this side of the pike, Wainwright had positioned twenty-three guns on the other side. This provided the defenders with thirty-eight guns among nine batteries. Although many of them had been in a sustained action, upon reaching this position, any battery, on both sides of the road, needing ammunition was resupplied from Osborn's ammunition train, as Wainwright's had not arrived. The artillery and infantry made this a formidable position that became stronger as late afternoon turned to evening.

With the successful withdrawal of what remained of the First and Eleventh Corps infantry and their two artillery brigades to positions on and near Cemetery Hill and *Ewell's* decision not to continue his attack, the first days fighting came to a close.

July 1 had been the first test of the Army of the Potomac new artillery organization. In past battles artillery assigned to divisions,

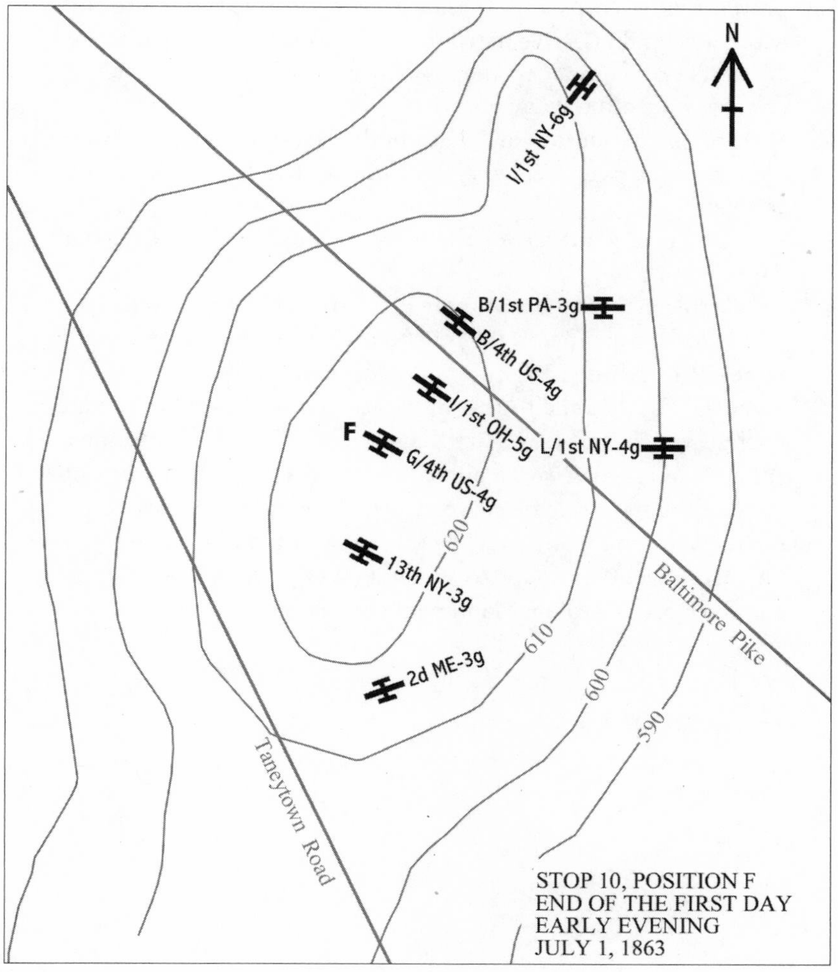

and even brigades, had arrived and gone into battle in a piecemeal fashion. This method of committing the batteries reduced their effect on the battle and in many cases placed artillery in tactically disadvantageous positions. Except for the few batteries that had been temporarily attached to the leading division of each corps, the batteries of the corps arrived together with their command and control structure intact. This allowed Wainwright and Osborn to deploy the batteries as they thought best and to use their artillery to maximum advantage.

This was also the first large battle for the Army of Northern Virginia's new artillery organization. Again the fighting on July 1 proved that at corps and division level the artillery organization was viable and effective. Arriving by battalions under control of an artillery commander, the Confederate batteries were able to employ concentrated and effective fire.

This ends your tour and study of the first day's artillery action. You will return to Cemetery Hill during the July 2 and July 3 actions.

Return to your car for the drive to Stop 11 and the second day's action.

Drive north on the Baltimore Pike, which turns into Baltimore Street, for approximately 0.5 mile to the intersection with Middle Street, Pennsylvania Highway 116. Turn left on to Middle Street, and drive for 0.7 mile to the intersection with West Confederate Avenue, which is on Seminary Ridge. Turn left onto West Confederate Avenue, and drive 0.8 mile to the North Carolina Monument. Park on the right side of the road, get out of your car, walk across the road and to a position a few yards in front of the North Carolina Monument, and face to the east. West Confederate Avenue and the North Carolina Monument are behind you.

Chapter 3

THURSDAY, JULY 2, 1863

Stop 11—Lee's Decision

You are once again on Seminary Ridge. The ridge was part of the Confederate position on July 2–4. Oak Hill, Stop 5, is 2.3 miles to your left, north. The Lutheran Seminary is one mile to your left. To your right, south, Seminary Ridge continues for another 1.9 miles to its intersection with the Emmitsburg Road.

In the early morning hours of July 2, the Confederate position began to take form and was shaped roughly like an upside-down L. The short part of the L was generally along or south of Middle Street through the town and then east across the fields south of the Hanover Road. This part of the line was occupied by Lieutenant General *Richard S. Ewell's* corps and faced south. The long part of the L was occupied by Lieutenant General *Ambrose P. Hill's* corps and then extended south by Lieutenant General *James Longstreet's* corps when it came into position late in the afternoon. Both of these corps faced generally east. Where you are was the general vicinity of the left and right flanks of two of *A. P. Hill's* divisions. Major General *Dorsey Pender's* division was to your left and Major General *Richard H. Anderson's* division was to your right. *Pender's* Division had been in action on July 1 and moved into positions on Seminary Ridge late that afternoon. *Heth's* Division was deployed in a reserve position a short distance behind *Pender's. Anderson's* Division had not see action on July 1. During the morning hours of July 2, it moved forward to positions on your right. When his division's deployment was completed, *Anderson's* line went about 0.7 mile to your right. Beyond that there were no Confederate forces on the south part of Seminary Ridge until late afternoon.

Hill's Corps had five battalions of artillery totaling 84 guns, 41 rifles, and 43 smooth bores. Four of these battalions were deployed on a frontage of 1,400 yards (0.8 mile). You are standing in the

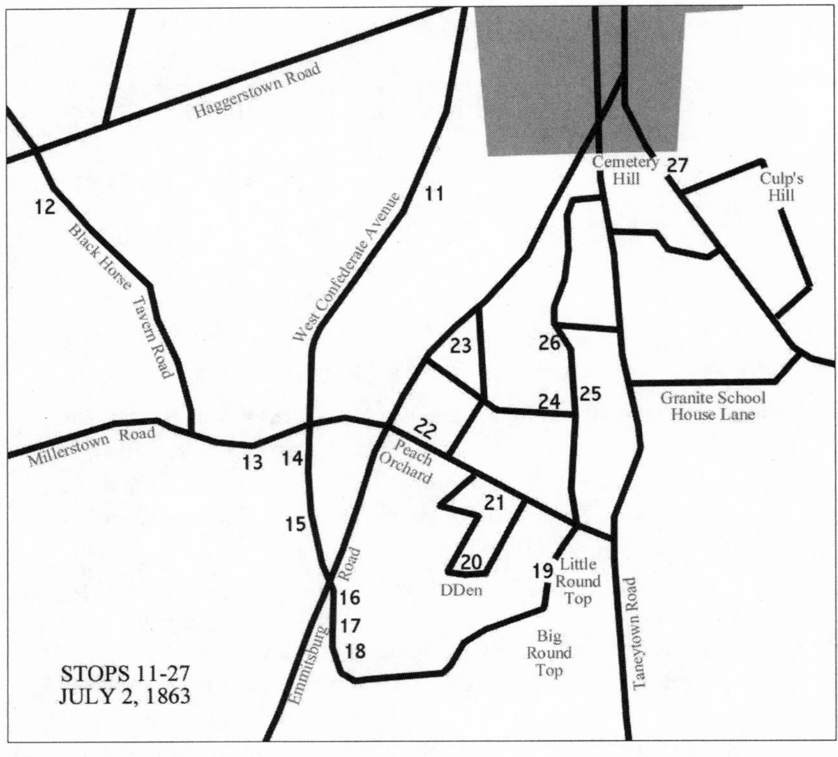

center of the position occupied by two batteries of Major *John Lane's* Sumter Artillery Battalion. Two hundred yards to *Lane's* left was the right of Major *William Pegram's* artillery battalion. *Pegram's* Battalion occupied a 300-yard front. To the left of *Pegram's* Battalion and deployed on a 350-yard front was Lieutenant Colonel *John Garnett's* artillery battalion. After a 100-yard open interval, Major *David McIntosh's* artillery battalion occupied the next 350 yards of the position. To the left of *Hill's* artillery and across the Fairfield Road were two batteries of Captain *Willis Dance's* artillery battalion from *Ewell's* Corps. The fifth artillery battalion of *Hill's* Corps was Major *William Poague's* battalion, which was kept in reserve during the second day's fighting. To the rear of and among the artillery were the infantry of *Pender's* Division.

The range from all of the batteries to your left, or north, to the Union positions on West Cemetery Hill was approximately 1,400 to 1,600 yards. The range to the right center of the Union line, marked by the "Copse of Trees" and "The Angle" on Cemetery Ridge, was approximately 1,200 to 2,000 yards. Union targets on Cemetery Hill and Cemetery Ridge were within the maximum effective range of *Hill's* rifled artillery. Some of these targets were at the maximum effective range of the Napoleons and were beyond the effective range of the smooth-bore howitzers. However, the smooth-bore guns could provide defensive fire if the position on this part of Seminary Ridge was attacked by Meade's infantry.

Report of Gen. *Robert E. Lee,* CSA, Commanding Army of Northern Virginia

It had not been intended to deliver a general battle so far from our base unless attacked, but coming unexpectedly upon the whole Federal Army, to withdraw through the mountains with our extensive trains would have been difficult and dangerous. At the same time we were unable to await an attack, as the country was unfavorable for collecting supplies in the presence of the enemy, who could restrain our foraging parties by holding the mountain passes with local and other troops. A battle had, therefore, become in a measure unavoidable, and the success already gained gave hope of a favorable issue.

The enemy occupied a strong position, with his right upon two commanding elevations adjacent to each other, one southeast [Culp's Hill] and the other, known as Cemetery Hill, immediately south of the town, which lay at its base. His line extended thence upon the high ground along the Emmitsburg road, with a steep ridge [Cemetery Ridge] in rear, which was also occupied. This ridge was difficult of ascent, particularly the two hills above mentioned as forming its northern extremity, and a third [Little Round Top] at the other end, on which the enemy's left rested. Numerous stone and rail fences along the slope served to afford protection to his troops and impede our advance. In his front, the ground was undulating and generally open for about three-quarters of a mile. [*OR* 27, pt. 2, p. 318]

Look east, and you will see the terrain generally as *Lee* saw it on the morning of July 2. The Union position was shaped like an upside down J or fishhook. The tip or barb of the fishhook was on Culp's Hill, which you cannot see from this location. Culp's Hill is on the other side of Cemetery Hill, the large hill to your left front with trees on it. On the morning of July 2, the Union line went from Culp's Hill to and around Cemetery Hill. It then came into your view on the western part of Cemetery Hill. From Cemetery Hill the line went south, to your right, along Cemetery Ridge, which is the long, low ridge in front of you. The line went past the "Copse of Trees" and continued south past today's U.S. Regulars Monument (the tall monument that looks like the Washington Monument in Washington, D.C.), then past today's large monument with the dome on top. This is the Pennsylvania Monument, the largest monument on the battlefield, and it will be used from time to time as a landmark to locate positions. From there the line continued on south to the two pieces of high ground to your right front. The largest of these, which look like a bowl turned upside-down, is Big Round Top. To its left the smaller hill is Little Round Top. Big Round Top is the highest piece of ground on the battlefield, but because of its dense foliage, which restricts fields of fire and observation, it has minimal tactical value. Little Round Top with open fields of observation and fire to the west was the most important terrain feature on the Union south flank. Going from north to south, your left to right, across the open ground between Seminary Ridge and Cemetery Ridge is the Emmitsburg Road. That road and the ridge you are on intersect 1.9 miles to your right.

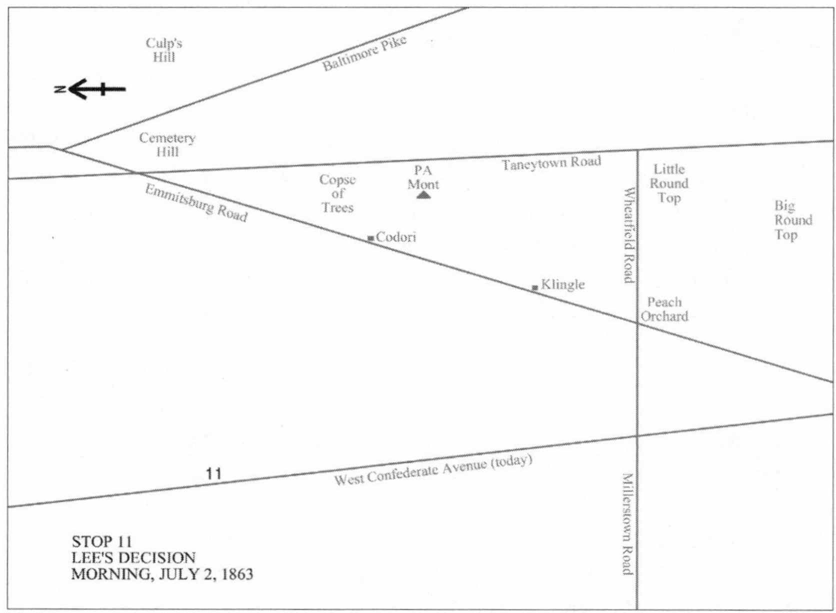

Report of Gen. *Robert E. Lee,* CSA—continued

General *Ewell's* corps constituted our left, *Johnson's* division being opposite the height adjoining Cemetery Hill [Culp's Hill], *Early's* in the center, in front of the north face of the latter, and *Rodes* upon his right. *Hill's* corps faced the west side of Cemetery Hill, and extended nearly parallel to the Emmitsburg road, making an angle with *Ewell's* [Corps], *Pender's* division formed his left, *Anderson's* his right, *Heth's,* under Brigadier-General *Pettigrew,* being in reserve. His artillery, under Colonel *R. L. Walker,* was posted in eligible positions along his line.

It was determined to make the principal attack upon the enemy's left, and endeavor to gain a position from which it was thought that our artillery could be brought to bear with effect. *Longstreet* was directed to place the divisions of *McLaws* and *Hood* on the right of *Hill,* partially enveloping the enemy's left, which he was to drive in.

General *Hill* was ordered to threaten the enemy's center, to prevent reenforcements being drawn to either wing, and co-operate with his right division [*Anderson's*] in *Longstreet's* attack.

General *Ewell* was instructed to make a simultaneous demonstration upon the enemy's right, to be converted into a real attack should opportunity offer. [*OR* 27, pt. 2, pp. 318–19]

Lee planned not only to capture ground favorable for artillery, but also to outflank and envelop the left of Meade's defensive line, to attack it, drive it in, or collapse it, and then sweep the defenders up along the axis of the Emmitsburg Road. *Lee's* final objective was the linchpin of Meade's defenses, Cemetery Hill, and his routes of supply and communication.

If *Lee's* plan had worked and you were standing here in the mid-afternoon hours on July 2, 1863, you would have seen *Longstreet's* two divisions attacking along the Emmitsburg Road, moving from your right to left. However, before *Lee's* plan could be successful he had to overcome or solve four problems. Three of them he knew about in the morning; one he would not know of until late afternoon.

The first problem was the Union position. It was shaped like an upside-down J, or a fishhook. Meade with the advantage of interior lines could move reinforcements rapidly to either of his flanks across the inside of the arc. Union troops would have to move only a maximum of two and a half miles to reach either flank. On the other hand with exterior lines, *Lee's* units would have to move almost six miles to reinforce from one flank to the another. To prevent Meade from using his advantage of interior lines and reinforcing his south flank with units from Culp's or Cemetery Hills, *Lee* ordered *Ewell* to conduct a demonstration and possible attack against those positions. This action was to begin simultaneously with *Longstreet's* attack.

The second problem was the terrain itself. As you look east across the fields, you can see that the Union defenses occupied a long ridge, with excellent fields of fire and observation, which was higher than the Confederate position. Meade's position was also anchored on both flanks by dominant high ground. There was no location on the Confederate position where they could see beyond the Union front line. On the other hand, from the Union position, especially the high hills, Meade's soldiers could not only see behind the Confederate position but also deep into the Confederate rear area. This gave the defenders the capability of observing large Confederate forces moving into position and thereby warning of an attack. Because of the defender's advantages in observation and reinforcement, *Lee* had to move *Longstreet's* force to the south without it being seen. *Lee's* instructions were for *Longstreet* to keep his force out of sight behind Seminary Ridge while moving south to attack positions.

The higher ground occupied by the Union defenders provided them an advantage for their artillery. Any Confederate artillery firing from positions on this part of Seminary Ridge could observe the strike of their rounds only if they were on target or short. The strike of any rounds going over the targets was unobservable. This severely limited their ability to adjust fire on targets. However, Union artillery from many of their positions could observe the strike of their rounds to determine if they were short, on target, or long. This gave them the advantage of being able to adjust their fire onto targets accurately.

Time was the other problem facing *Lee,* and time did not favor him. Civil War armies normally did not conduct night attacks. It was difficult enough to control long battle lines in the smoke of gunfire and in woods; it was impossible in the dark. *Lee* issued his order to *Longstreet* sometime around 10:00 a.m., and *Longstreet* began the march south about noon. The distance from where the lead brigade of the column started marching to its designated attack position was 3.3 miles. Average speed of a marching column was 2.25 to 2.5 miles per hour. At that speed, if all went well, *Lee* could reasonably expect the lead elements to move into position for attack around 1:30 p.m. *Longstreet's* column was composed of two divisions, four battalions of artillery, and a combat supply train of perhaps 150 wagons. This formation had a road space of just under eight miles and at a normal march speed required from three to three and a half hours to pass a given point. With units deploying simultaneously, this time could be cut down to about one and one-half to two hours. Therefore, by the time the infantry and artillery were deployed for attack, it would be, at best, about 3:00 or 3:30 p.m. Sunset was 7:41 p.m., and by 8:13 it was too dark to conduct an attack. If the attack began at 3:30, there would almost be five hours of daylight to complete it.

There was one other problem confronting *Lee,* but at the time he developed his plan and issued orders he was not aware of it. On June 25, while still in northern Virginia, Major General *J. E. B. Stuart* took a part of the Confederate cavalry on a ride around the Union army. *Stuart* expected to be gone for only a short time. However, as events unfolded, the Army of the Potomac moved north and was between *Stuart* and the Army of Northern Virginia, and he was forced to march farther and farther north in an attempt to return to *Lee. Stuart* did not return to the Confederate army until late afternoon, July 2. Because of *Stuart's* absence and poor use of the remaining cavalry, *Lee* was operating without cavalry, his eyes and ears, to provide him information on Union dispositions and terrain. *Lee* developed a plan without good intelligence.

Directly in front at a distance of 1,200 yards (0.7 mile) is the Emmitsburg Road. An additional 260 yards beyond the Emmitsburg Road is the "Copse of Trees" that played a predominant role on July 3. The high ground to the left of the trees is Cemetery Hill. Beyond that, but not observable, is Culp's Hill. Meade's defensive line began on Culp's Hill and came west to Cemetery Hill. At that location, which could be seen from here, the line of deployed Union troops turned south and went along Cemetery Ridge. It went past the "Copse of Trees," then to your right past the U.S. Regulars Monument, and on toward the Pennsylvania Monument. In that vicinity *Lee* would have lost view of this line of troops. However, he could see along the Emmitsburg Road—from about where the red barn marks the Codori farm—a line of troops that went south to where you see a small white building. This white building marks the location of the Klingle House, which is the red brick building next to it. Because the ground dropped away and out of view, the line of troops appeared to end at the Klingle House.

To the left and farther on from the white building, you can see Little Round Top and Big Round Top. Captain *Samuel R. Johnston* of *Lee's* staff had led a small group on a reconnaissance to the south. He reported to *Lee* that there were no Union troops in the vicinity of Big Round Top or Little Round Top. However, this information was incorrect.

Based upon *Johnston's* report and what he could observe, *Lee* believed the southern portion of the Union line was "upon the high ground along the Emmitsburg road, with a steep ridge in rear, which was also occupied." [OR 27, pt. 2, p. 318]

Lee thought the Union left, or south, flank was in the vicinity of the Emmitsburg Road and south of the Klingle House. This situation, if actual, would have presented *Lee* with an unprotected flank that he could envelop and attack. In reality, Meade's position extended almost a mile farther south. With faulty information *Lee* drew a faulty conclusion and developed a flawed plan. When he

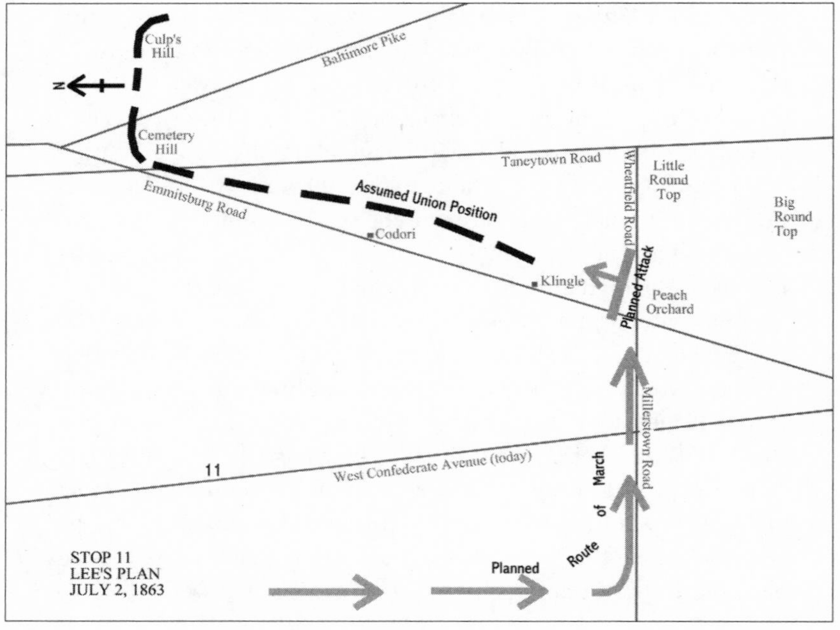

sent *Longstreet's* force south, he did not have them go far enough south before turning east. Instead of moving to the flank of the Union defenses, *Longstreet's* divisions ran directly into them.

Return to your car for the drive to Stop 12.

If you do not wish to go to Stop 12 and follow *Longstreet's* infantry and artillery as it approached their attack positions, at the intersection of the Millerstown Road and West Confederate Avenue (1.2 miles), continue on straight for 0.1 mile. Turn left into the parking area at the base of the steel tower. Park, get out of your car, walk pass the tower, and through the thin tree line. Stand 20 yards in front of the tower with the thin tree line behind you so that you have a view of the open fields and the Peach Orchard. Page forward to Stop 14.

If you wish to go to Stop 12 and follow *Longstreet's* march use these instructions:

Drive south on West Confederate Avenue for 1.2 miles to the intersection with the Millerstown Road. At the intersection of West Confederate Avenue and Millerstown Road, turn right and drive west for 0.5 mile to the intersection with Black Horse Tavern Road. Turn right on to Black Horse Tavern Road, and drive north 1.3 miles to a raised piece of ground. Be careful of traffic in both directions. Do a U-turn and park alongside the road so that you are looking back to where you just came from. Be sure to park so that you can be seen by traffic coming from both directions.

Stop 12—*Longstreet* Orders the Countermarch

Late morning on July 2 *Longstreet* had two of his three divisions and four of his five artillery battalions in position behind Seminary and Herr Ridges. Colonel *Henry C. Cabell's* artillery battalion was supporting *McLaws's* Division and marched with them. Major *Mathias W. Henry's* artillery was supporting *Hood's* Division and accompanied them on the march. *Pickett's* Division and Major *James Dearing's* supporting artillery battalion did not arrive near the battlefield in time to participate in the second day's action. Colonel *E. Porter Alexander's* and Major *Benjamin F. Eshleman's* battalions of the corps artillery reserve were ordered to march independently to positions where they could support the infantry attack.

Black Horse Tavern Road intersects with the Hagerstown Road 0.5 mile behind you. At the northeast section of this intersection is

Black Horse Tavern. Black Horse Tavern Road continues on from there in a north and northwest direction. Major General *Lafayette McLaws's* and Major General *John B. Hood's* divisions began their march toward the Union left on Black Horse Tavern Road from the other side of the intersection. With *McLaws* leading, they marched in this direction. Riding a little ahead of his division, *McLaws* stopped the march when he came up on this piece of ground. *Longstreet* then came forward to find out why the column was halted. Look directly ahead, and at a distance of 3,900 yards (2.2 miles) you will see Big Round Top. To the left of Big Round Top is Little Round Top. Today you cannot see it because of the height of the trees along Seminary Ridge. However, in 1863 Little Round Top was visible from this location. Conversely this location could be seen from there. *Longstreet* and *McLaws* saw the flags of the Union signal station on Little Round Top and knew if they continued on this route they would be seen and their movement reported. Meade's receipt of this information would remove the element of surprise from *Lee's* plan.

Narrative of Maj. Gen. *Lafayette McLaws,* CSA, Commanding *McLaws's* Division, *Longstreet's* Corps, Army of Northern Virginia

Suddenly, as we rose a hill [where you are] on the road we were taking, the [Little] Round Top was plainly visible, with the flags of the [Union] signal men in rapid motion. I sent back and halted my division and rode with Major *Johnson* rapidly around the neighborhood to see if there was a road by which we could go into position without being seen. Not finding any I rejoined my command and met General *Longstreet* there, who ask, "What is the matter?" I replied, "Ride with me and I will show you that we can't go on this route according to instructions without being seen by the enemy." We rode to the top of the hill and he at once said, "Why this won't do. Is there no way to avoid it?" I told him of my reconnaissance in the morning, and he said: "How can we get there?" I said: "Only by going back—by countermarching." He said: "Then alright," and the movement [countermarch] commenced. [Lafayette McLaws, "Gettysburg," *Southern Historical Society Papers* 7, no. 2 (1879): 69. Hereafter cited as McLaws, "Gettysburg," followed by page numbers.]

This conversation and *Longstreet's* decision placed the countermarch into motion. *McLaws's* and *Hood's* Divisions turned around, retraced part of their routes, and crossed over a ridge into a low area where Willoughby Run flows south. Their new route of march was to your left and allowed them to continue moving south without being observed.

Colonel *E. Porter Alexander* had also passed this way with his artillery battalion. When he arrived at this location, rather than turn around, he went off to your right, moved around the higher ground, and regained the road farther on.

Narrative of Col. *E. Porter Alexander,* CSA, Commanding *Alexander's* Artillery Battalion, *Longstreet's* Corps, Army of Northern Virginia

[Lieutenant General] *Longstreet* pointed out the enemy's position and said that we would attack his left flank. He told me to take command of all of [his corps's] artillery on the field for the attack, and suggested I go at once, first, and get an idea of the ground, and then go and bring my own battalion up. But he told me to leave the Washington Artillery [*Eshleman's* Battalion] in bivouac where they were. And he specially cautioned me to keep all movements carefully out of view of a signal station whose flags we could see wig-wagging on Little Round Top. In ten minutes after I reported, I had my orders, and was off to examine all the roads leading to the right and front, and to get an understanding of the enemy's position and how where we could best get at it. I rode fast—having a courier or two with me, and I don't think it took me much over an hour to get a very fair idea of the ground and the roads and to find *Cabell's* and *Henry's* battalions, and give them what instructions were needed.

I do not remember looking at my watch this whole day, and all of my ideas of the hours are guesses, but it seems to me that before 11 a.m. [probably closer to noon or 1:00 p.m.] I had gotten my battalion down in the valley of Willoughby Run, in a few hundred yards of the school house, where I had to wait on the infantry and *Cabell's* and *Henry's* battalions before going further. I had come there by a short and direct road, which at one point passed over a high bare place [where you are now] where it was in full view of the Federal signal station [on Little Round Top]. But I avoided that part of the road by turning out to the [right], and going through fields and hollows, and getting back on the road again a quarter mile or so beyond. Then I recall riding back for something, and finding the head of one of our infantry divisions standing halted [where you are] in sight of the signal station. It had been put on that road to march, but told, as I had been, to keep out of view.

Of course I told the officers at the head of the column of the route my artillery had followed—which was easily seen—but there was no one with authority to vary the orders they were under, and they momentarily expected new ones for which they had sent and which were very explicit when they came after the long delay. [Gary W. Gallagher, ed., *Fighting for the Confederacy: The Personal Recollections of Edward Porter Alexander,* Chapel Hill: University of North Carolina Press, 1989), 235–37]

You will now follow beside and then on the route of *McLaws's* Division after it completed the countermarch and moved onto lower ground. This will take you back to the intersection of the Millerstown Road and West Confederate Avenue.

Drive south on Black Horse Tavern Road for 1.3 miles to the intersection with the Millerstown Road. After you have driven 0.9 mile, you will cross Willoughby Run. *McLaws's* Division rejoined the road in this vicinity.

At the intersection of Black Horse Tavern Road and Millerstown Road, turn left and drive east for 0.1 mile, pull off to the side of the road, and stop.

Stop 13—Marching toward a Surprise

You are in the vicinity of where Colonel *Alexander* positioned his artillery battalion to await the arrival of the infantry and *Cabell's* and *Henry's* Battalions. The schoolhouse he referred to was the Pitzer School House, which was located to your left rear.

Along this part of the route, *McLaws* and *Longstreet* had a conversation as to how *McLaws's* Division would deploy. To *Longstreet's* question, "How are you going in?" *McLaws* replied, "That will be determined when I can see what is in my front." *Longstreet* then said, "There is nothing to your front; you will be entirely on the flank of the enemy." *McLaws* then told *Longstreet,* "Then I will continue on my march in column of companies, and after arriving on the flank, as far a necessary will face to the left and march on the enemy." Satisfied with this answer *Longstreet* rode away and *McLaws's* Division, lead by Brigadier General *Joseph B. Kershaw's* brigade continued along the road. [McLaws, "Gettysburg," 69–70]

This conversation between *McLaws* and *Longstreet* shows that, as they approached Seminary Ridge, they were not aware that they had not flanked the Union position.

The tall tower you see in front of you is on West Confederate Avenue. It is in the vicinity of your next stop. Continue driving for 0.4 mile to the intersection of Millerstown Road with West Confederate Avenue. Turn right on to West Confederate Avenue, and drive for 0.1 mile, then turn left into the parking area at the base of the steel tower. Park, get out of your car, walk pass the tower, and through the thin tree line. Stand 20 yards in front of the tower with the thin tree line behind you so that you have a view of the open fields and the Peach Orchard.

Stop 14, Position A—The Plan Collapses

As you look east across the fields, the terrain appears much as it did in 1863. Going from your left to right, north to south, is the Emmitsburg Road. Directly in front of you on the other side of the Emmitsburg Road is the Peach Orchard. In the northern part of the orchard was the Wentz home, of which only a foundation remains today. To your left the modern house is an add-on to the small stone Warfield House that was there in 1863. Further to your left along the road, you can see the houses and barns of the Sherfy, Klingle, and Codori farms. They look much today as they did at the time of the battle. *Lee* thought Meade's left, or south, flank was in the vicinity or slightly south of the Klingle home. To your right front you can see Little Round Top and Big Round Top. Between them and you, but hidden by the trees in the distance, is the Devil's Den. On the other side of the trees to the right of and beyond the Peach Orchard is the Wheatfield.

According to *Lee's* plan, *Longstreet's* force was to march along the Millerstown Road, cross over the ridge, follow the road to your left, cross the Emmitsburg Road, where it would turn left, and attack the Union left flank. It was not to be.

Narrative of Maj. Gen. *Lafayette McLaws,* CSA—continued

My head of column soon reached the edge of the woods, and the enemy at once open on it with numerous artillery, and one rapid glance showed them to be in force much greater than I had, and extending considerably beyond

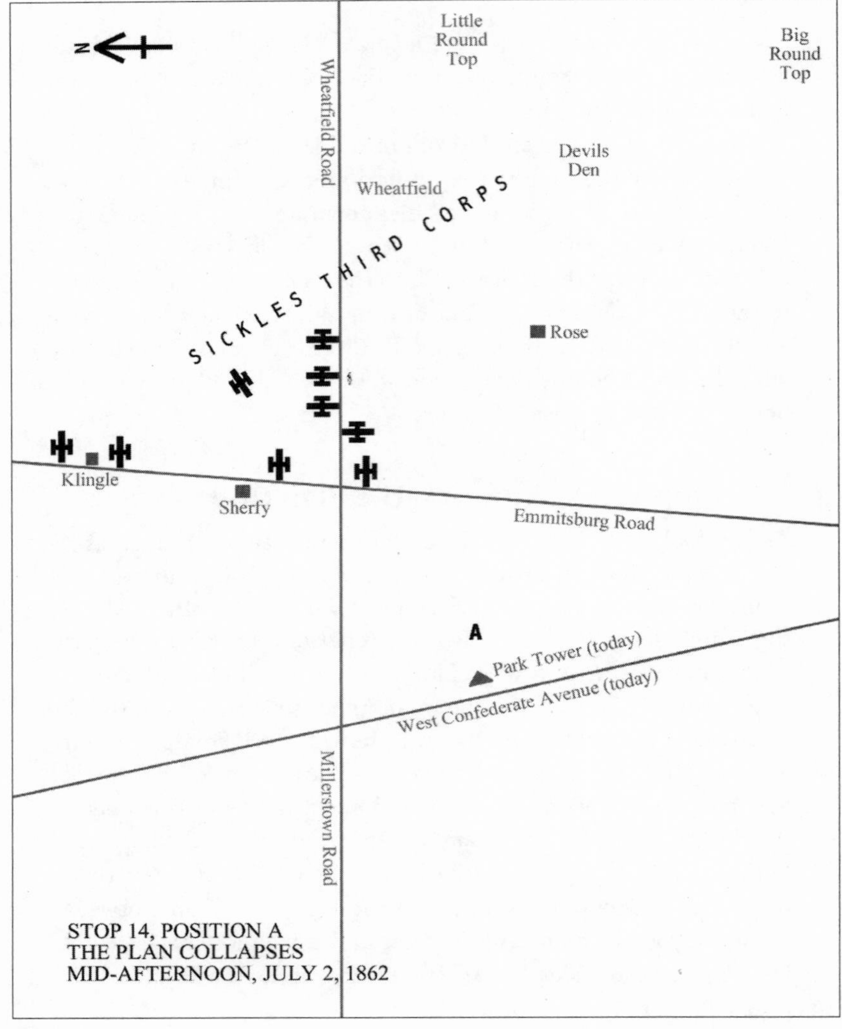

my right. My command therefore, instead of marching on as directed, by head of column, deployed at once. *Kershaw* immediately turned the head of his column [brigade] and marched by flank to the right, and put his men under cover of a small stonewall. *Barksdale,* following came into line on the left of *Kershaw,* his men sheltered by trees and part of a stonewall and under a general declivity. I hurried back to quicken the march of those in rear, and sent orders for my artillery to move to my right and open fire, so as to draw the fire of the opposite artillery from my infantry.

While this was going on I rode forward, and getting off my horse, went to some trees and took a good look at the situation, and the view presented astonished me, as the enemy was massed in my front, and extended to my right and left as far as I could see. [McLaws, "Gettysburg," 70]

McLaws's two other brigades, *Wofford's* and *Semmes's,* deployed in a supporting line behind *Barksdale* and *Kershaw.* Colonel *Henry Cabell's* artillery battalion went into position to your right.

Face left and walk north for 40 yards, stop, then face right so that you are again looking to the east and at the Peach Orchard.

Position B—A New Plan

When *McLaws* and *Longstreet* arrived in this vicinity, they were completely surprised by what they saw.

In the early afternoon hours of July 2, Major General Daniel E. Sickles's Third Corps, composed of two infantry divisions and a five-battery artillery brigade, formed the left of the Union line. Their initial position went from the southern part of Cemetery Ridge, across low ground, and up onto the northern slope of Little Round Top. Before *Longstreet's* divisions completed their march and approached Seminary Ridge, Sickles moved his corps forward to a new position. Why he did this will be discussed later.

From Seminary Ridge the Confederates saw a Union infantry line that went from the south edge of the Peach Orchard north, to your left, along the Emmitsburg Road for 1,400 yards. Deployed with the infantry were four batteries of artillery, two from the Third Corps and two from the Artillery Reserve, with twenty-four Napoleons. Supporting this position and protecting its south flank were an additional five batteries with twenty-eight guns. These batteries were in position on the other, east, side of the Peach Orchard and could not be seen from this location.

Faced with this new situation, *Longstreet* decided to deploy *McLaws's* Division where you are and march *Hood's* Division to the south in an attempt at still striking Meade's left flank. As the Confederate infantry moved into position, *Alexander's, Cabell's* and *Henry's* artillery battalions deployed and opened fire on the Union defenders.

Turn around and walk west toward West Confederate Avenue. Walk to the marker and guns representing *Jordan's* Bedford

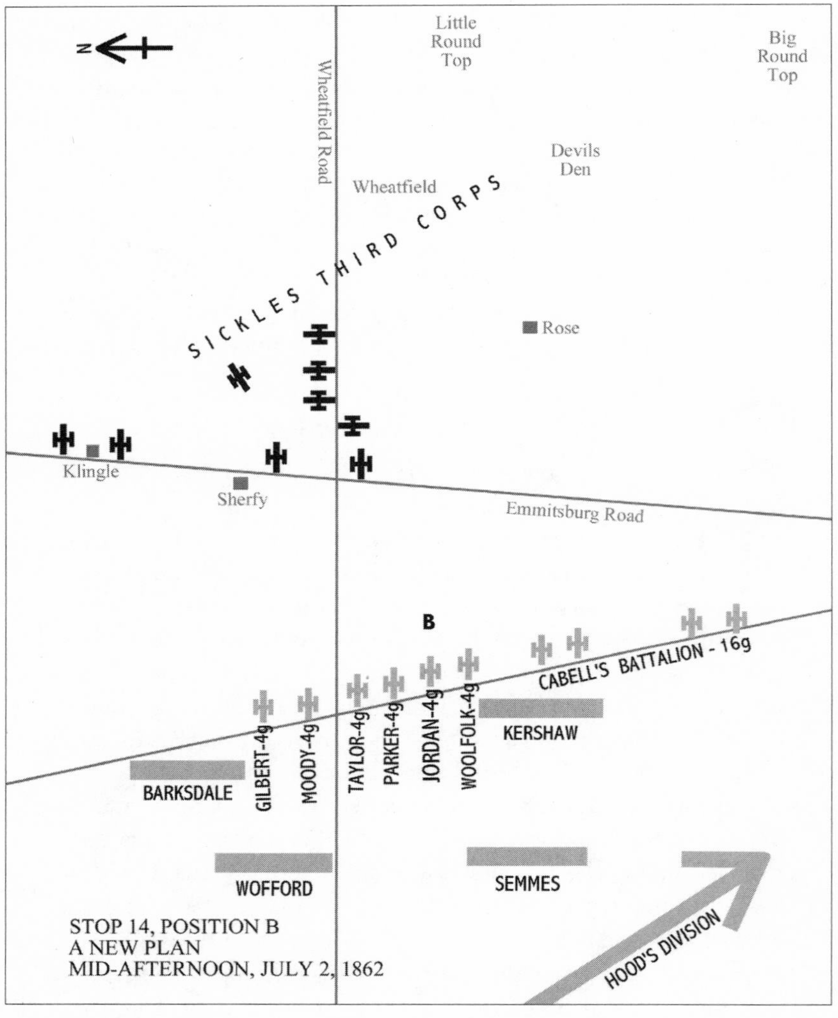

(Virginia) Artillery Battery. Stop at that position, turn around, and look back toward the Peach Orchard.

Position C—*Alexander's* Battalion in Action

When the fighting commenced in this vicinity, Colonel *Alexander* brought his battalion forward and deployed at this location. You are standing in the right center of *Alexander's* Battalion. Where you are was the position Captain *Tyler C. Jordan's* Bedford (Virginia)

Artillery Battery with four 3-inch rifles. To *Jordan's* right were the two Napoleons and two 20-pound Parrotts of Captain *Pichegru Woolfolk's* Ashland (Virginia) Artillery Battery. To *Jordan's* left was Captain *William W. Parker's* Virginia Battery with three 3-inch rifles and one 10-pound Parrott. To *Parker's* left were the four Napoleons of Captain *Osmond B. Taylor's* Virginia Battery. Farther left across the Millerstown Road were Captain *George V. Moody's* Madison (Louisiana) Artillery Battery with four 24-pound howitzers and then the four 12-pound howitzers of Lieutenant *S. Capers Gilbert's* (*Rhett's*) Brooks (South Carolina) Artillery Battery. The range from these twenty-four guns to the Union position at the Peach Orchard and along the Emmitsburg Road, depending on the location of the battery, was from 500 to 700 yards. This was well with in the maximum effective range of all of *Alexander's* guns.

Report of Col. *E. Porter Alexander,* CSA, Commanding *Alexander's* Artillery Battalion, *Longstreet's* Corps, Army of Northern Virginia

About 4 p.m. I placed four batteries (those of Captains *Moody, Parker, Taylor,* and *Rhett,* the latter commanded by Lieutenant *Gilbert,* and the whole commanded by Maj. *Frank Huger,* I having been ordered to control also the other battalions of artillery on the field) in action against a heavy artillery and infantry force of the enemy, about 500 yards distant, in a peach orchard on the Emmitsburg pike.

Colonel *E. Porter Alexander,* CSA. National Archives.

After a spirited engagement of a half hour, assisted by *Cabell's* battalion from a short distance on our right, the enemy's guns were silenced, and the position was immediately carried by the infantry, and the enemy fell back to his position on the mountain [Little Round Top], where our infantry gallantly pursued him.

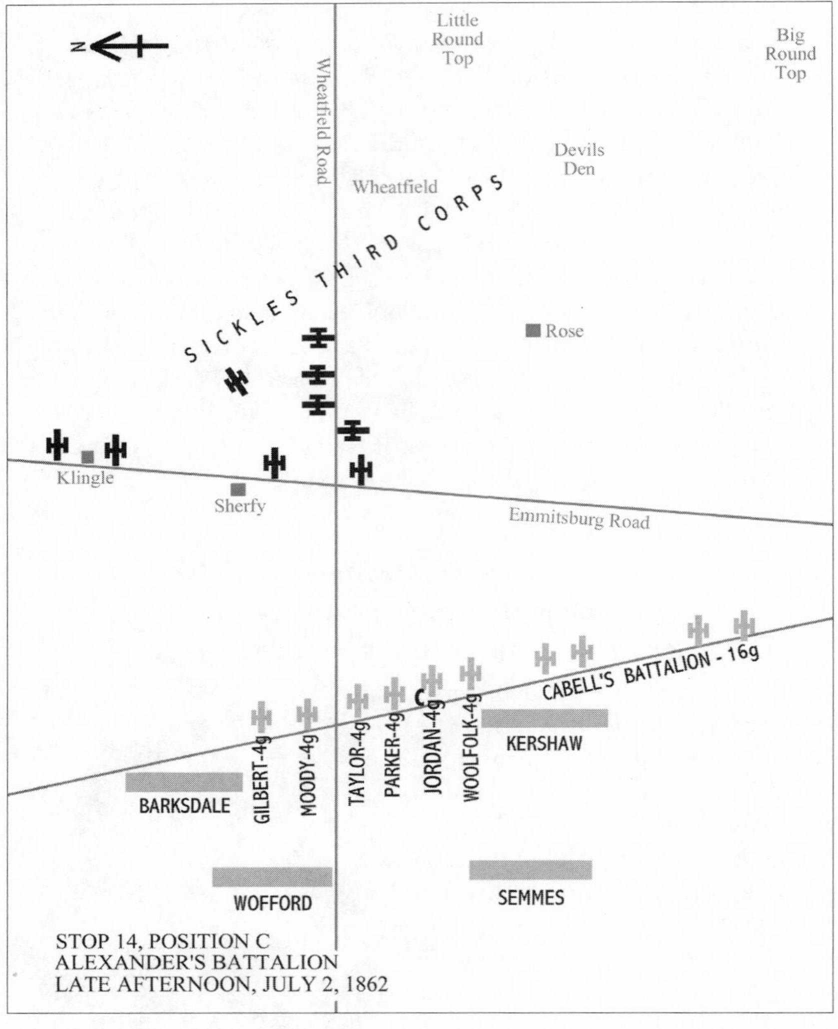

Just before the enemy ceased his fire, annoyed by his obstinacy, I had ordered up my two remaining batteries, *Jordan's* and *Woolfolk.* These, arriving on the ground just as the infantry charge was made, joined in it, under the immediate command of Maj. *James Dearing,* who had volunteered his services to me. Major *Huger* also followed with the four batteries under his control as soon as the teams could be disencumbered of killed and wounded animals (for his loss had been serious), and occupied the enemy's original position, in time to seriously annoy their retreat to the mountain, and to assist the infantry in causing them to abandon several guns at its foot. From this new position a spirited duel now ensued with their new line, which our infantry attacked in vain, and was kept up till dark, shortly before which our infantry fell back, and the enemy, who attempted to pursue, were checked and driven back by our fire. [*OR* 27, pt. 2, pp. 429–30]

Face left; walk north along the park road for 60 yards to the guns and marker for *Taylor's* Battery, stop, and face right.

Position D—*Taylor's* Battery

Captain *Taylor,* whose battery was initially deployed where you are, gives an account of the action from the battery perspective.

Report of Capt. *Osmond B. Taylor,* CSA, Commanding Virginia Battery (Bath Artillery), *Alexander's* Artillery Battalion, *Longstreet's* Corps, Army of Northern Virginia

About 4 p.m. I was ordered into position within 500 yards of the enemy's batteries, and to dislodge them, if possible, from a commanding position which they held. I opened upon the batteries with my four Napoleons, firing canister and spherical case until our infantry, who were present, began their charge. I then ceased firing, limbered to the front, and advanced some 800 or 1,000 yards, and took another position, which I held till after dark, though several attempts were made by the enemy, both with infantry and artillery, to drive me from it.

I lost at the first position one of my best gunners (Corpl. *William P. Ray*). He was killed while in the act of sighting his gun. He never spoke after receiving the shot, walked a few steps from his piece, and fell dead. I had also while in this, my first position, the following men wounded: *Vincent F. Burford,* badly bruised on shoulder; *Silas C. Gentry,* cut on the wrist; *Joseph Moody,* cut in the face and bruised on the back; *Byrd McCormick,* shot through the calf of the leg by a bullet from a spherical case; *Edward J. Sheppard,* wounded badly in heel, and several others slightly wounded. I had killed in the lane while going to my second position another excellent gunner (*Corpl. Joseph T. V. Lantz*). He had both legs broken above the knees; lived but a little while. His only words were, "You can do me no good; I am killed; follow your piece." While in my second position, I had two men wounded: *Hill Carter Eubank,* shot through the leg. *Eubank* was a very promising youth, about eighteen years of age; left the Military Institute at Lexington, Va., to join the army; was brave and attentive to his duties. The other (*Claiborne Y.*

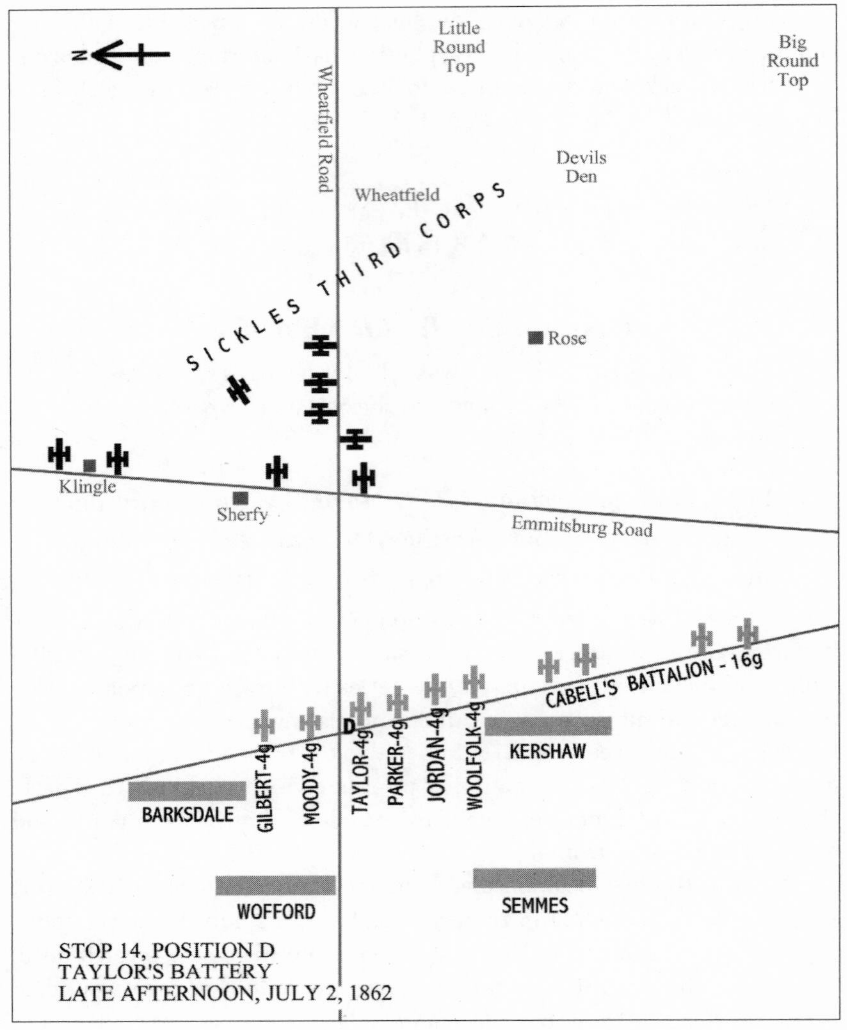

Atkinson) struck on the leg by a piece of shell; seriously wounded. [*OR* 27, pt. 2, p. 432]

Return to your car for the drive to Stop 15.

Drive south on West Confederate Avenue for 0.3 mile to the marker for *Fraser's* Pulaski (Georgia) Artillery Battery; it is on your left. Park on the right side of the road, leave your car, cross the road, and stand in front of the marker.

Stop 15—*Cabell's* Battalion In Action

To your right front is Big Round Top. To its left is Little Round Top. The stone building in front of you is the Rose Farm House. To your left front, you can see the Peach Orchard and the red Sherfy Barn.

Colonel *Henry C. Cabell's* artillery battalion was assigned to support *McLaws's* Division. Its four batteries marched with that division to the southern flank and was the first of *Longstreet's* artillery in action.

You are in the position of the right flank battery. This was *Captain John C. Fraser's* Pulaski (Georgia) Artillery Battery armed with two 3-inch rifles and two 10-pound Parrotts. To *Fraser's* left was Captain *Edward S. McCarthy's* First Richmond Howitzers with two 3-inch rifles and two Napoleons. Farther to your left after an open interval of 350 yards were *Cabell's* other two batteries, Captain *Basil C. Manly's* Battery A, First North Carolina Artillery, with two 10-pound Parrotts and two 12-pound Howitzers, and Captain *Henry H. Carlton's* Troup (Georgia) Artillery Battery, armed with two 10-pound Parrotts and two 12-pound howitzers.

The range to the Peach Orchard from this location is 900 yards. The range from *Cabell's* left two batteries to the Peach Orchard is 700 yards. To the right of the Peach Orchard, along Wheatfield Road, were four batteries from Meade's artillery reserve. The range from where you are to that position is 1,000 yards. To your right at a distance of 1,700 yards, you can see Little Round Top. There was a Union battery there during the fighting.

Report of Col. *Henry C. Cabell,* CSA, Commanding *Cabell's* Artillery Battalion, *Longstreet's* Corps, Army of Northern Virginia

On July 2, moved up with the division. When we commenced to ascend the road leading to the crest of the hill [Seminary Ridge], where the battle was subsequently fought my battalion moved to the head of the column. Near the crest of the hill, I turned to the right, and placed the battalion in position on the edge of the wood, the right resting near the road leading from Gettysburg to Emmitsburg. One horse was wounded while crossing the field, although this movement was made beyond the view of the enemy. On our right, and slightly in front, the enemy occupied a rocky mountain with several batteries, and directly in front, about 600 or 700 yards distant, were a large number of batteries, occupying a peach orchard. Receiving orders,

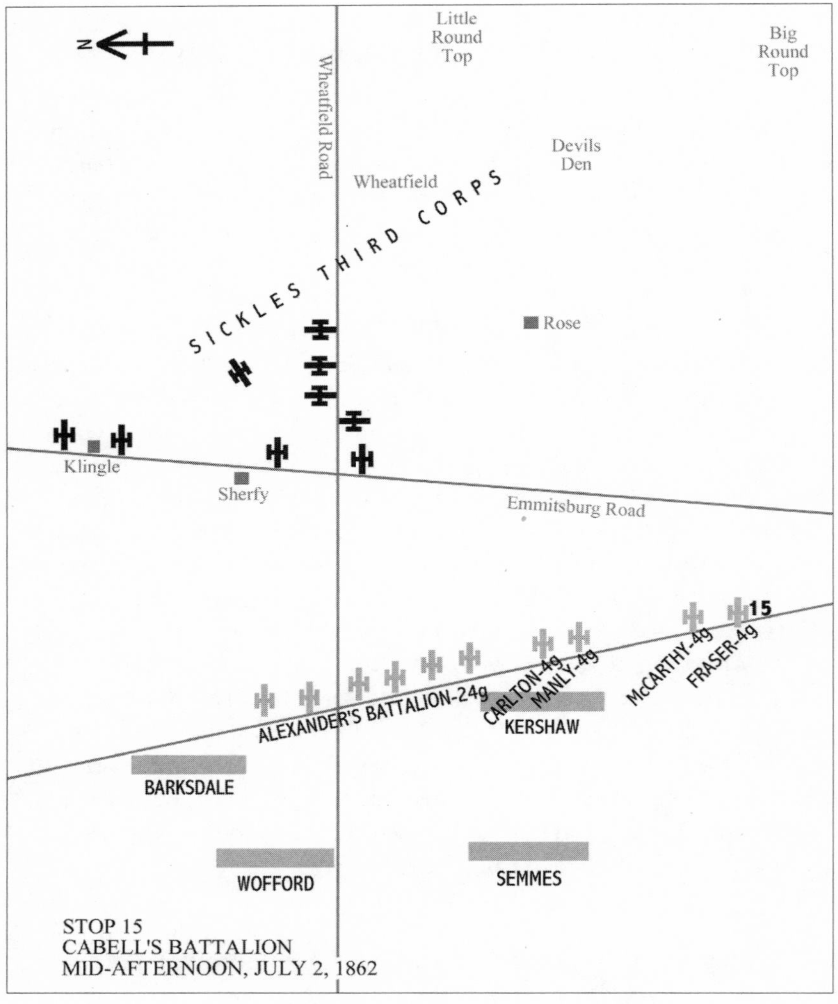

we opened a most effective fire upon these batteries. Exposed ourselves to a flanking fire from the enemy's mountain batteries, our position gave us a similar advantage in firing upon a large part of his line, which was drawn up nearly parallel with the Emmitsburg road. The battalion, being first to open fire, received for a short time a concentrated fire from the enemy's batteries. The fire from our lines and from the enemy became incessant, rendering it necessary for us sometimes to pause and allow the smoke to clear away, in order to enable the gunners to take aim. During the same time, two guns were ordered to play upon the batteries on the stony mountain.

The loss of my battalion was very heavy during this cannonading, Captain *Fraser,* who had always in previous engagements, as in this, set an example of the highest courage, coolness, and gallantry, fell, dangerously wounded by the bursting of a shell. The same shell killed 2 sergeants and 1 man.

Lieutenant *R. H. Couper,* of the same battery, was wounded during the same engagement.

The batteries in the peach orchard were driven off, and our fire was suspended to allow the infantry to advance. The guns on the right continued to fire on the enemy's batteries on the mountain as soon as the infantry had charged. [*OR* 27, pt. 2, p. 375]

You are at the position of *Cabell's* right flank battery. The battery commander, Captain *Fraser,* was wounded during the action and Lieutenant *William Furlong* took command and continued to fight the battery.

Report of Lieut. ***William J. Furlong,*** CSA, Commanding ***Fraser's*** Pulaski (Georgia) Artillery Battery ***Cabell's*** Artillery Battalion, ***Longstreet's*** Corps, Army of Northern Virginia

On the 2d, the battery was placed in position on the right of the battalion, behind a loose rock fence. The battery was in position a short time before the order was given to commence firing. At the command, the battery opened fire from four guns (two 10-pounder Parrotts and two 3-inch rifles) on some light batteries of the enemy which had taken a position on our left. The firing at first was rapid, but soon became slow and cautious, the gunners firing slow, evidently making each shot tell with effect on the enemy's batteries.

In the meantime, the enemy replied with spirit, their fire being incessant, severe, and well directed. After being engaged about an hour, Capt. *J. C. Fraser,* commanding, fell, dangerously wounded. I then took command of the battery, using but two guns; our loss being so great, both in cannoneers and drivers, I could muster but two detachments. Immediately after I took command, the enemy's fire began to slacken, and finally stopped altogether, with the exception of one piece, which was in position a little to the left of my right piece, and was annoying us considerably. I opened fire on it with one piece, and, after firing half a dozen rounds, silenced it for a short time; but it soon began to play on us again.

In the meantime, the order was given to cease firing, after which I took no further notice of it.

On calling the roll, the following officers and men were found to be either killed or wounded:

Officers and men.	Killed	Wounded	Total
Officers		2	2
Non-commissioned officers	2		2
Enlisted men	1	10	11
Total	3	12	15

I had one caisson disabled and rendered unfit for service, the pole and splinter-bar being shot away. I had 15 horses killed and disabled. [*OR* 27, pt. 2, p. 382]

Return to your car for the drive to Stop 16.

Continue driving for 0.2 mile on West Confederate Avenue to the intersection with the Emmitsburg Road. Cross the Emmitsburg Road and drive for 120 yards to the Texas State Monument. It is a red granite monolithic shaped monument on the right side of the road. Park on the side of the road, get out of your car, and walk left to the other side of the road to the marker and artillery. Where you cross the Emmitsburg Road, West Confederate Avenue becomes South Confederate Avenue. The Texas Monument and the park road are now behind you. Look toward the northeast and east, where the guns are pointed.

Stop 16—Attack on the Union Left

With your back to the park road as you look east, Big Round Top is 1,400 yards (0.8 mile) in front of you. Little Round Top is slightly to the left of Big Round Top and 1,600 yards (0.9 mile) from your location. Between you and Little Round Top at a distance of 1,100 yards (0.6 mile) is the Devil's Den. The Devil's Den was the left flank of Meade's defense; no one was on Little Round Top, yet. The Peach Orchard and the Wheatfield Road are 1,400 yards (0.8 mile) to your left. The stone Rose Farm House is between you and the Peach Orchard and the Wheatfield Road.

Major General *John B. Hood* deployed his division at this location late on Thursday afternoon. *Hood's* Division was following *McLaws's* as they turned off the Black Horse Tavern Road onto Millerstown Road. When *McLaws's* Division made contact with Sickles's position at the Peach Orchard, *Hood* moved to the right of the intended route and marched south to this location. Brigadier General *Jerome B. Robertson's* brigade deployed where you are. The Arkansas State Monument on the other side of the Emmitsburg Road marks its left flank. Brigadier General *Evander M. Law's* brigade deployed to the right of *Robertson's.* Brigadier General *George T. Anderson* deployed his brigade in a supporting position behind *Robertson's* and Brigadier General *Henry L. Benning* deployed behind *Law's.*

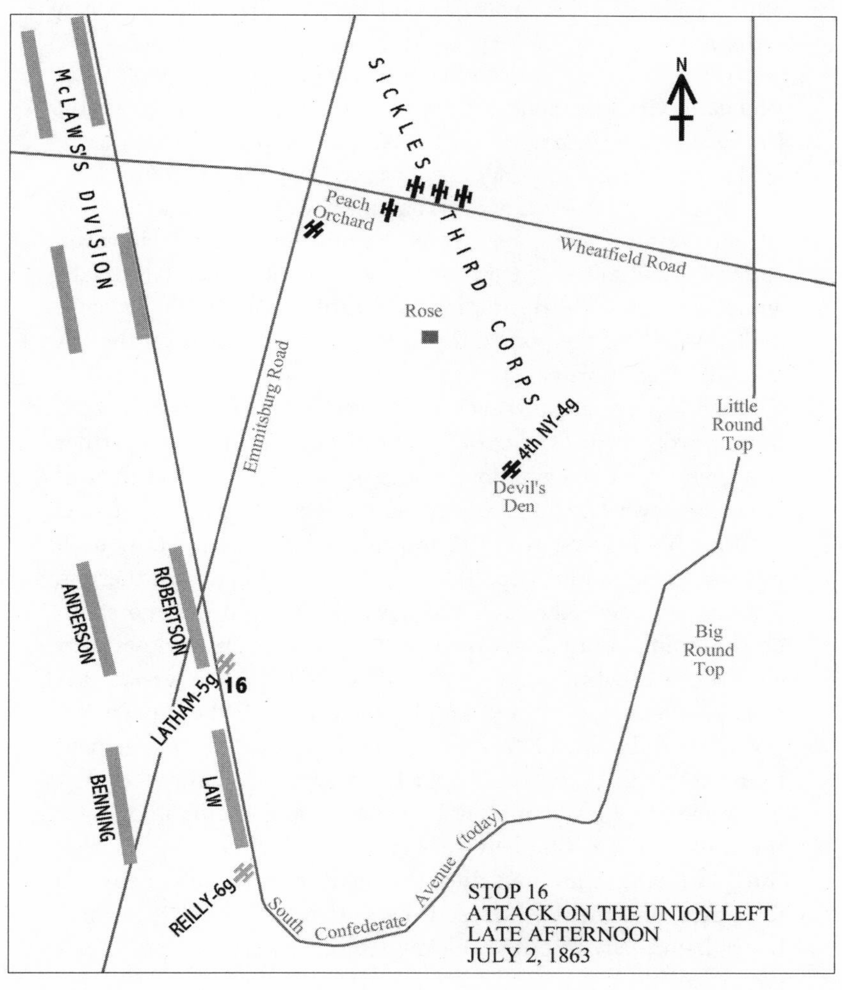

STOP 16
ATTACK ON THE UNION LEFT
LATE AFTERNOON
JULY 2, 1863

Major *Mathias W. Henry's* four-battery battalion provided artillery support for *Hood's* Division. Because of the limited space available, *Henry* deployed only two of his batteries to support *Hood's* attack. Captain *Alexander C. Latham's* Branch (North Carolina) Artillery Battery, with one 6-pound gun, one 12-pound howitzer, and three Napoleons, was deployed where you are. The most likely targets for this battery were the Union batteries at the Peach Orchard and along Wheatfield Road. The distance to these targets precluded using the howitzer; however, it could have been used to fire at the Union battery at Devil's Den. Although we do not know for sure, it was probably held back in a protected position. *Henry's* other deployed battery was Captain *James Reilly's* Rowan (North Carolina) Artillery Battery. *Reilly's* Battery was positioned 700 yards to your right. *Henry's* other two batteries, Captain *William K. Bachman's* German (South Carolina) Artillery Battery and Captain *Hugh R. Garden's* Palmetto (South Carolina) Artillery Battery, were held in reserve and did not participate in the fighting on July 2.

By the time the infantry and artillery were in position, it was late in the afternoon, some time around four o'clock. However, *Longstreet* had followed through on *Lee's* intent. When faced with an unexpected tactical situation in the area of the Peach Orchard, he had modified the plan and placed part of his corps on the left flank of Meade's army.

While preparing to attack, *Hood* received information that led him to propose to *Longstreet* that *Hood* move his division farther east then attack. Such a move would place *Hood* in the vicinity of the Taneytown Road, 2,300 yards (1.3 miles) directly east of your location. This would give him the capability of outflanking both Big and Little Round Top. The question was how to get there in a timely manner? The fastest way would have been to go south on the Emmitsburg Road for 0.7 mile where there is a road that goes southeast. In 0.5 mile this road intersects with a road that goes northeast for 1.2 miles and intersects with the Taneytown Road. Total distance is 2.4 miles. The time for the lead element to move this distance would have been about one hour after they began marching. Add another hour or one and one-half hours for the trail units to complete the march and then at least another thirty minutes to an hour until the division was totally deployed for attack, and there is a lapse time of two and one-half to three hours before *Hood* could attack. At best, his attack would have been started around 6:30 or 7:00 p.m. Sunset on July 2, 1863, was at 7:41 p.m. and it was dark in another thirty minutes.

In addition, *Hood's* Division was no longer out of sight of the Union defenders. Major *Henry's* two batteries were actively engaging Union targets. Brigadier General Gouverneur K. Warren, on Little Round Top, had already sent out request for troops to come to that location. In another hour or two the entire defensive situation on Meade's left would have been different.

Longstreet turned down *Hood's* repeated request, several times, and ordered him to attack from where he was. The meeting between *Hood* and *Longstreet* was about where you are. Shortly after the attack began, *Hood* was wounded, just in front of you, by a fragment of an artillery shell.

Return to your car for the drive to Stop 17.

Continue driving forward on South Confederate Avenue for 0.2 mile to the Alabama State Monument. It is on your right. Pull off to the side of the road, park, get out of your car, and face left. You should be looking at Big Round Top.

Stop 17—*Law* Goes for the Artillery

Big Round Top is 1,400 yards (0.8 mile) in front of you. Little Round Top is just to the left of Big Round Top and 1,600 yards (0.9 mile) from your location. The Devil's Den, and the Union left flank, is 1,100 yards (0.6 mile) to your left front. Five hundred yards from Little Round Top was one of Meade's supply and communication routes, the Taneytown Road. Any attack going forward from here will pass over and around Big Round Top then arrive south and southeast of Little Round Top. From there the right of an attack could flank or bypass the Union defenses.

You are in the center of *Law's* Brigade after it deployed for attack. The Fifteenth Alabama was where you are. To your right were the Forty-fourth and then Forty-eighth Alabama. To your left were the Forty-seventh and then the Fourth Alabama. Four hundred yards behind you, Brigadier General *Henry L. Benning* deployed his four Georgia regiment to support *Law's* attack.

As *Law's* regiments attacked across the open ground in front of you, they began to receive fire from Captain James E. Smith's Fourth New York Battery, located on the ground just above Devil's Den. In response to this fire, *Law* ordered his two right regiments,

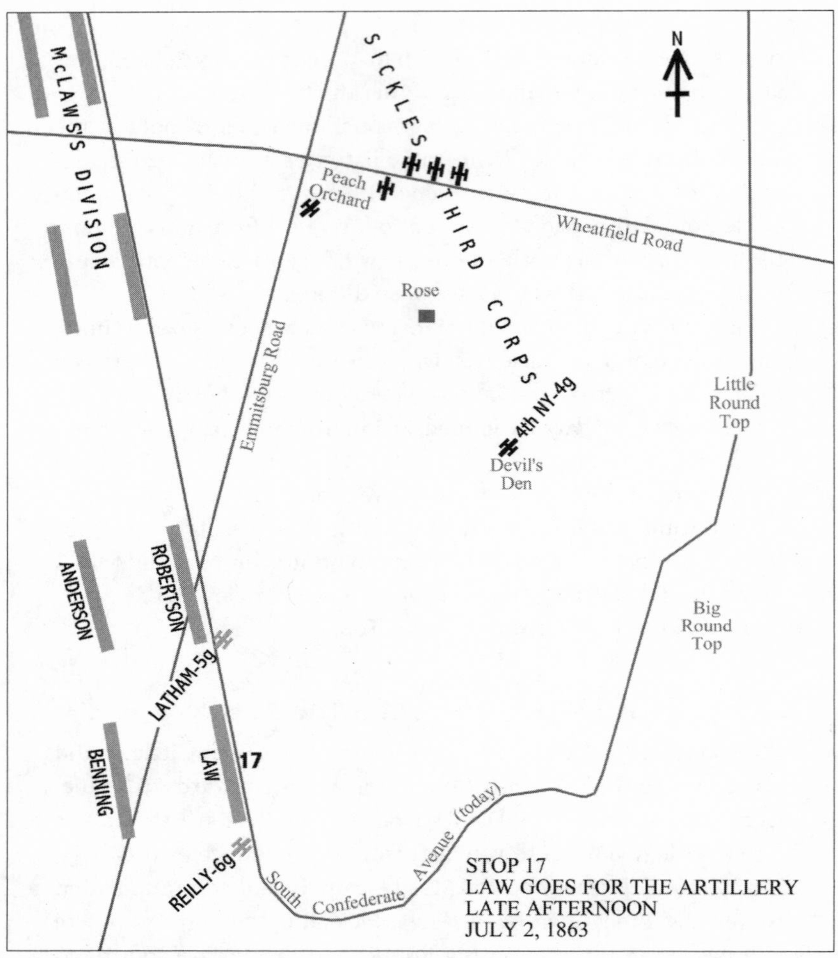

the Forty-fourth and Forty-eight, out of line and had them cross behind the three regiment to their left in order to attack Smith's battery.

When *Benning's* Brigade, following behind *Law's,* came forward, it moved through the trees that are behind you. As *Benning* came out of the trees, he saw the Forty-fourth and Forty-eight Alabama as they departed from the line of attack and moved toward Devil's Den. Not seeing *Law's* other three regiment as they went on toward the Round Tops, *Benning* shifted his direction of movement to the left and followed the Forty-fourth and Forty-eighth Alabama. This shift carried *Benning* into the fight for the Devil's

Den. Had he continued moving straight behind *Law's* other three regiments, he would have been in position to support the flanking attack against the defenses on Little Round Top or to isolate the position completely by moving east a short distance.

Return to your car for the drive to Stop 18.

Continue to drive on South Confederate Avenue for 150 yards. Stop, park on the side of the road, get out of your car, and walk to the marker for *Reilly's* Rowan (North Carolina) Artillery Battery. Face toward Big and Little Round Tops.

Stop 18—The Confederate Right

Late in the afternoon of July 2, this was the location of Captain *James Reilly's* Rowan (North Carolina) Artillery Battery. This was the right battery of the two batteries Major *Henry* deployed to support *Hood's* attack. *Reilly's* Battery was armed with two 3-inch rifles, two 10-pound Parrotts, and two Napoleons. Not only was this battery the right of *Hood's* Division, it was also the right flank unit of the Army of Northern Virginia.

This was a good position for a battery as it is a small plateau with sufficient space to deploy guns. Being elevated, it provided long-range observation and fire and allowed artillery to fire over the heads of attacking infantry.

As you look northward, you can see at a range of 1,400 yards the Devil's Den and the left flank of Sickle's Corps. The Devil's Den is just above the treetops. Smith's Fourth New York Battery was in that vicinity. All targets at that location were well within the range of *Reilly's* guns. To the right, as you view it, of the Devil's Den and at a range of 1,800 yards is Little Round Top. Targets on Little Round Top were close to the maximum effective range of *Reilly's* 3-inch rifles and 10-pound Parrotts. They were beyond the effective range of the Napoleons.

In front of you are the open fields that *Law's* and *Robertson's* Brigades crossed as they began their attack. While crossing these fields, *Law* began to receive the fire from Smith's guns that caused him to shift his right regiments to the left.

Return to your car for the drive to Stop 19.

Drive on South Confederate Avenue for 1 mile to a road intersection. You drove past Big Round Top and are now at the south base of Little Round Top. Continue driving north for 0.1 mile to

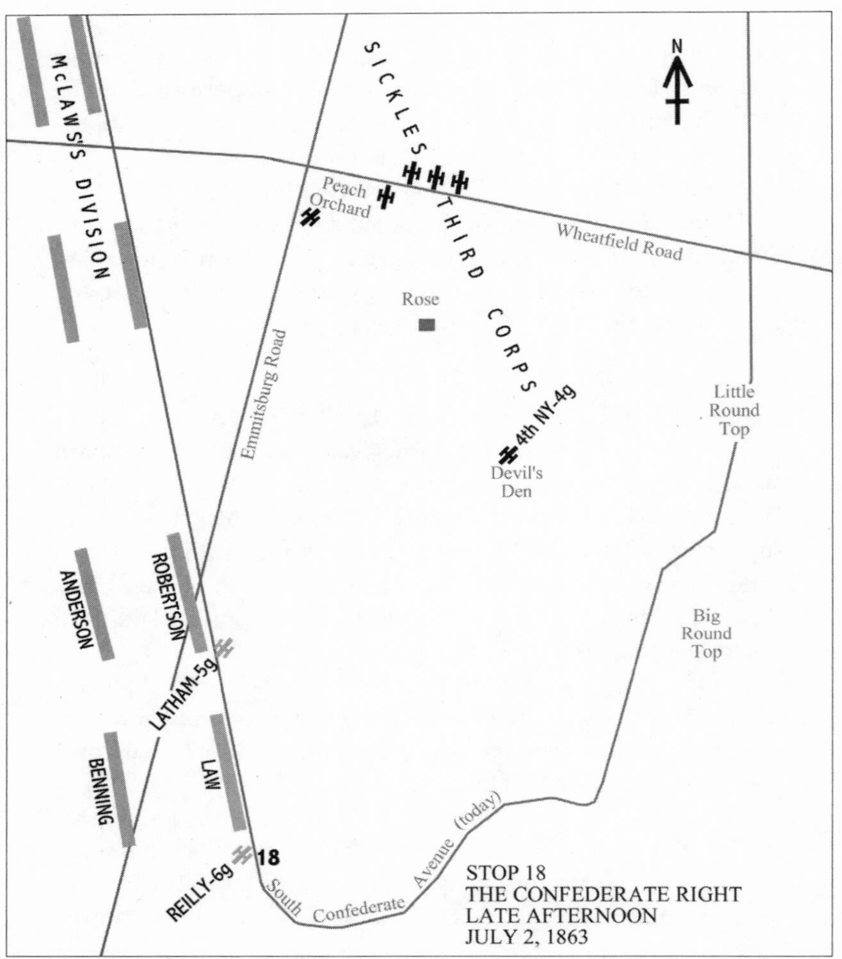

the crest of Little Round Top. Park, get out of your car, follow one of the walking trails, and walk to the highest point on Little Round Top. Stand in front of the guns and marker for Battery D, Fifth U.S. Artillery, and look toward the west.

Stop 19, Position A—Battery D, Fifth U.S. Artillery (Hazlett's)

This is where the signal station that *Longstreet* and *McLaws's* could see from the Black Horse Tavern Road was located. The low ground directly in front of you is Plum Run Valley. The small ridge on the other side of the valley is Houck's Ridge. Sickle's left flank units, also the left flank of the Army of the Potomac, were located on Houck's Ridge. At the left end of the ridge, where the large boulders are, is Devil's Den. This was the position of Smith's Fourth New York Battery. Look beyond Devil's Den, and, at a distance of 1,600 yards, you can see the intersection of Emmitsburg Road and West/South Confederate Avenue, where there is an opening in the tree line. *Hood's* Division was located on both sides of this intersection. Farther to the right of the intersection was *Cabell's* Artillery Battalion. From the location of *Cabell's* Battalion, look right along

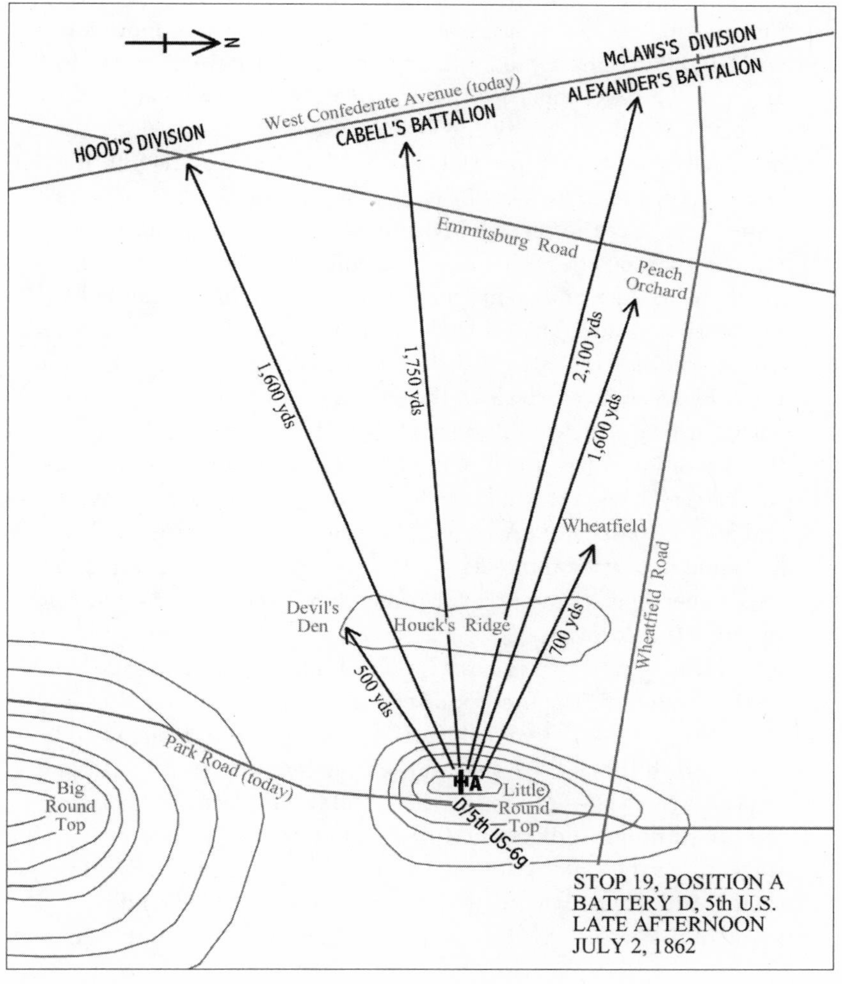

the far tree line that marks West Confederate Avenue until you see the tall steel tower. *Alexander's* Artillery Battalion extended from right of the tower to the other side of the intersection of West Confederate Avenue and Millerstown Road. This intersection is near the house to the right of the tower. *McLaws's* infantry brigades were deployed on either side of this intersection. Look slightly to the right and slightly closer toward you, and at 1,600 yards you can see the small plateau that the Emmitsburg Road goes over and the Peach Orchard. Between you and the Peach Orchard is the Wheatfield. It is 700 yards from you. You can see a corner of the field to your right front.

Initially only the troops operating the signal station were on this position. As *Law's* and *Robertson's* Brigades began to move forward in their attack, Union infantry from the Fifth Corps began to arrive on Little Round Top. The first to arrive was Colonel Strong Vincent's Third Brigade of the First Division. Vincent's four regiments were positioned to your left on the south side of the hill. The next infantry to arrive was Brigadier General Stephen H. Weed's Third Brigade of the Second Division. Weed's four regiments went into position on the west side of the hill. Their line was forward of where you are and went from your left to right. As the fighting continued, additional brigades from the Sixth Corps and Fifth Corps occupied this area and the ground across the road to your right. Between the arrivals of the two infantry brigades, Lieutenant Charles E. Hazlett's Battery D, Fifth U.S. Artillery went into firing position where you are. Armed with six 10-pound Parrotts, this battery had the capability of hitting targets as far away as West and South Confederate Avenues. The guns could not be depressed low enough to fire on targets at the base of Little Round Top and were dependent on infantry for protection from any enemy force reaching that location.

Hazlett's battery is the one Colonel *Cabell* mentioned as being on the mountain. The first rounds from Hazlett's guns were probably fired at *Cabell's* two right batteries (Stop 15). Hazlett would have then shifted his fire against the Confederate infantry attacking through the low ground to the left of Devil's Den. The battery then fired upon Confederate infantry at Devil's Den and on the ridge across the valley after they captured those positions. During the fighting Lieutenant Hazlett was mortally wounded, and command of the battery went to Lieutenant Benjamin F. Rittenhouse.

The next day, July 3, Battery D brought enfilading fire into the ranks of *Pickett's* Division as it attacked the Union center. If you look to your right front at a distance of 2,500 yards (1.4 miles), you can see the center of the open ground crossed by the Confederate third day attack. Continue to turn your head to the right, and you can see the location of the Union defenses as they went from Little Round Top to Cemetery Hill.

Retrace your path back to the park road where you parked. When you reach the road, turn left and walk north on or beside the road for 80 yards. You will be walking downhill. In 80 yards turn left off the road, and walk 10 yards to the 121st New York monument. At this monument, angle slightly left, and walk 40 yards to the guns and monument for Battery L, First Ohio Artillery. The monument has stone cannonballs on top of it. Stand in front of the monument so that you are again looking west at Plum Run Valley and beyond.

Position B—Battery L, First Ohio Artillery (Gibbs's)

Four hundred yards directly in front of you is Houck's Ridge, the western edge of Plum Run Valley. Beyond it through the trees is the Wheatfield. West of the Wheatfield at a distance of 1,500 yards from your location is the Peach Orchard. The road to your right that goes west is the Wheatfield Road. It continues past the Wheatfield to the Peach Orchard, where it intersects with the Emmitsburg Road and changes names to the Millerstown Road. Seven hundred yards west of the Emmitsburg Road–Wheatfield/Millerstown Road intersection was the initial firing positions for *Alexander's* Artillery Battalion.

Across the valley in front of you, the Wheatfield was the area of many attacks and counterattacks by both sides. Initially Colonel Regis De Trobriand's Third Brigade of Major General David B. Birney's First Division, Third Corps, defended the area and was attacked by Brigadier General *George T. Anderson's* brigade of *Hood's* Division. This resulted in the two brigades of Brigadier General James Barnes's First Division, Fifth Corps reinforcing the Wheatfield position. Next *Anderson's* Brigade with part of Brigadier General *Joseph B. Kershaw's* brigade again attacked and drove the Union defenders across the Wheatfield. The Confederate success was nullified with the counterattack of Brigadier General John C. Caldwell's four-brigade First Division, Second Corps, that pushed Confederate out of the field.

Simultaneously with Caldwell's attack, Brigadier General *Paul Semmes's* Brigade of *McLaws's* Division reinforced *Anderson* and *Kershaw.* After Caldwell crossed over the Wheatfield two brigades of U.S. Regulars, Colonel Hannibal Day's and Colonel Sidney Burbank's brigades, occupy the ground in front of you on Houck's Ridge.

A fourth Confederate brigade, Brigadier General *William T. Wofford's,* advancing astride the Wheatfield Road joined the fight

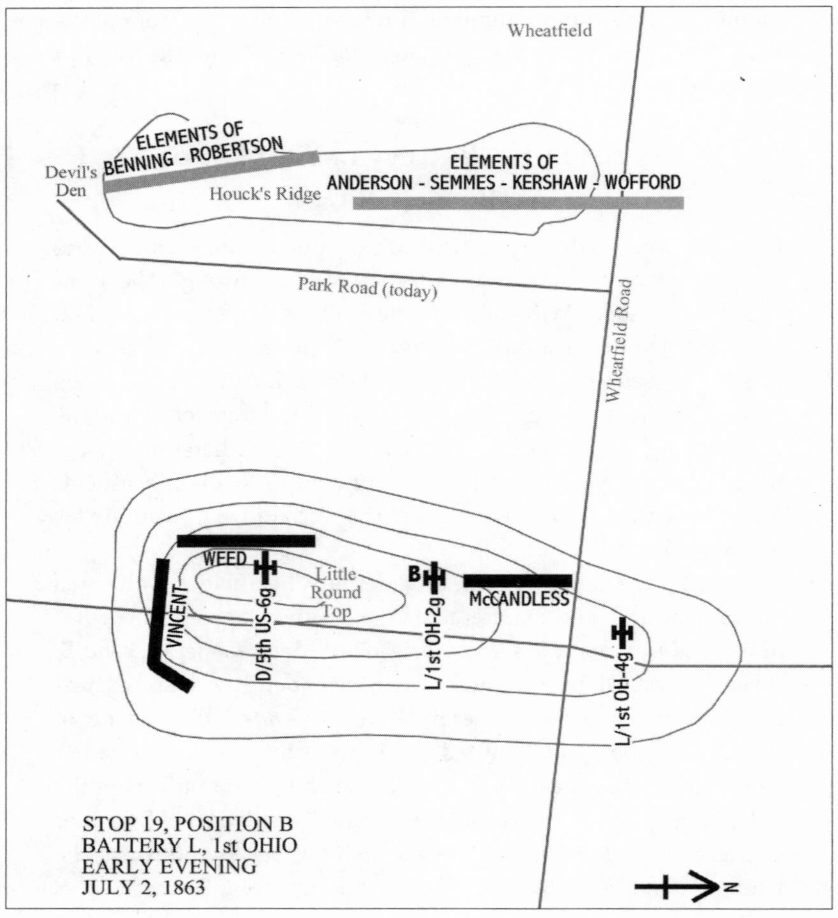

and *Anderson, Kershaw,* and *Semmes* attacked again. This attack drove the Union forces out of the Wheatfield. The two brigades of U.S. Regulars were pushed off Houck's Ridge and retreated back across the valley, toward where you are.

When the Confederates arrived on Houck's Ridge, they began to attack in this direction and commenced crossing the valley below you. In addition *Wofford's* Brigade was approaching astride the Wheatfield Road. To receive this attack, there were five Pennsylvania Reserve Regiments from the Third Division, Fifth Corps, under command of Colonel William McCandless and the Ninety-eighth Pennsylvania from the Third Brigade, Third Division, Sixth Corps.

Captain Frank C. Gibbs's Battery L, First Ohio Artillery, was deployed at this location and to your right. Two of Gibbs's Napoleons were positioned where you are. The other four were positioned on the other side of the road to your right. When firing canister, the large-bore Napoleons of this battery made it ideal for defense. The six Napoleons of Lieutenant Aaron F. Walcott's Third Massachusetts Battery was deployed 350 yards to your right front. Their position was to the right of the intersection of the park road in the valley and Wheatfield Road. Having no infantry support as the Confederate attack approached, Walcott's men fell back.

Report of Capt. Frank C. Gibbs, USA, Commanding Battery L, First Ohio Artillery, Artillery Brigade, Fifth Corps, Army of the Potomac

About the middle of the afternoon an orderly came rapidly up, asking our battery to come to the assistance of the Fifth Corps. I started on the trot, and reported to General Sykes, who ordered the battery to cover the valley. The rocky nature of the ground compelled us to unhitch our horses and place our guns in position by hand; the left section, in charge of Lieut. H. F. Guthrie, on the left of a road leading from the valley, and on the right slope of Little Round Top; the center and right sections, in charge of Lieuts. James Gildea and William Walworth, on the right of said road. We had hardly placed our guns in position when the Fifth Corps was forced back by a terrific charge of *Longstreet's* corps, and came rushing through us, but began rallying on us as soon as they understood matters. Our front was hardly clear when the irregular, yelling line of the enemy put in his appearance, and we received him with double charges of canister, which were used so effectively as to compel him to retire. So rapidly were the guns worked that they became too hot to lay the hand on. But for the position of the battery, and the gallantry with which it was handled by the men, I have no doubt the enemy would have accomplished his purpose of breaking our lines at this point, and possibly changed the fortunes of the day. [*OR* 27, pt. 1, p. 662]

The Confederate attack stopped, the Pennsylvania Regiments counterattack across the valley and captured the section of the low ridge in front of you.

Return to your car for the drive to Stop 20.

Depart Little Round Top by driving north on the park road. At 0.2 mile from the top of Little Round Top, you will come to a road intersection. This is the eastern portion of Wheatfield Road. At the intersection turn left, and drive west on Wheatfield Road for 0.2 mile to the first road on your left. This is Crawford Avenue. As you drive on Crawford Avenue, Little Round Top will be to your left. From the road you can see the positions of Gibbs's battery, Stop 19—Position B, and Hazlett's battery, Stop 19—Position A. Turn left on to Crawford Avenue, and drive south in Plum Run Valley for 0.3 mile to a parking area, turn into the parking area, park, and get out of your car. Cross the road, follow the walking trail up through the boulders for 100 yards to the guns and monument of the Fourth Battery, New York Artillery, and face the directions in which the guns are pointed, which are west and southwest.

Stop 20—Artillery at the Devil's Den

The guns represent part of Captain James E. Smith's Fourth New York Battery. There is some controversy as to actually where this part of Smith's battery was positioned. Opinion is divided as to whether the guns were placed just forward of where you are or approximately 60 yards to your right. Smith's battery was armed with six 10-pound Parrotts. Because of space constraints, Smith could deploy only four of his six guns in this vicinity. The other two guns were positioned 150 yards to your right rear in Plum Run Valley. They were sited so as to fire south and cover the ground between Big Round Top and Devil's Den.

The large boulders that you walked through and to your left are the Devil's Den. When Major General Daniel E. Sickles moved forward to occupy the ground in the vicinity of the Peach Orchard, this position became the extreme left flank of his corps and the Army of the Potomac.

The intersection of the Emmitsburg Road and West/South Confederate Avenue is 1,100 yards directly in front of you. In the vicinity of this intersection, Major General *John B. Hood* deployed his division. To the left of the intersection was one battery, *Latham's* Branch (North Carolina) Artillery Battery, of Major *Mathias W. Henry's* artillery battalion. *Henry's* other deployed battery, *Reilly's* Rowan (North Carolina) Artillery Battery, was farther to your left, or east. As you view it, to the right of the Emmitsburg Road and West Confederate Avenue intersection was Colonel *Henry C. Cabell's* artillery battalion. The Peach Orchard and the Wheatfield Road artillery positions are 1,100 yards, through the trees, to your right front. The ground to your right is Houck's Ridge, which goes north and forms the western side of Plum Run Valley. Little Round Top is 500 yards behind you.

To Smith's right was Brigadier General J. Hobart Ward's Second Brigade of Major General David B. Birney's First Division. Ward's defensive line went north, to your right, for 350 yards to the Wheatfield. At the Wheatfield, Birney's division's position continued northwest with Colonel Regis De Trobriand's brigade, along the edge of the field. Then there was a gap in the line, and Brigadier General Charles K. Graham's brigade occupied the Peach Orchard and an area along the Emmitsburg Road. To Graham's right was Sickles's other division, commanded by Brigadier General Andrew A. Humphreys.

Smith and his gunners could observe and fire on *Latham's* and *Reilly's* Batteries and *Robertson's* and *Law's* Brigades of *Hood's* Division as they went into position and began their attack late in the afternoon. Various regiments from *Law's, Benning's,* and *Robertson's* Brigades (all from *Hood's* Division) assaulted the Devil's Den–Houck's Ridge position from the front and to your left and right. It was the effective fire from Smith's guns that caused *Law* to move his right regiments over to his left to attack this position. This maneuver placed two of *Law's* regiments in the middle of *Robertson's* battle line and broke its continuity. It caused *Benning* to follow the wrong segment of the attacking front line. He assaulted this position rather than follow the remainder of *Law's* Brigade and provide additional combat power to the attack against the defenders on Little Round Top.

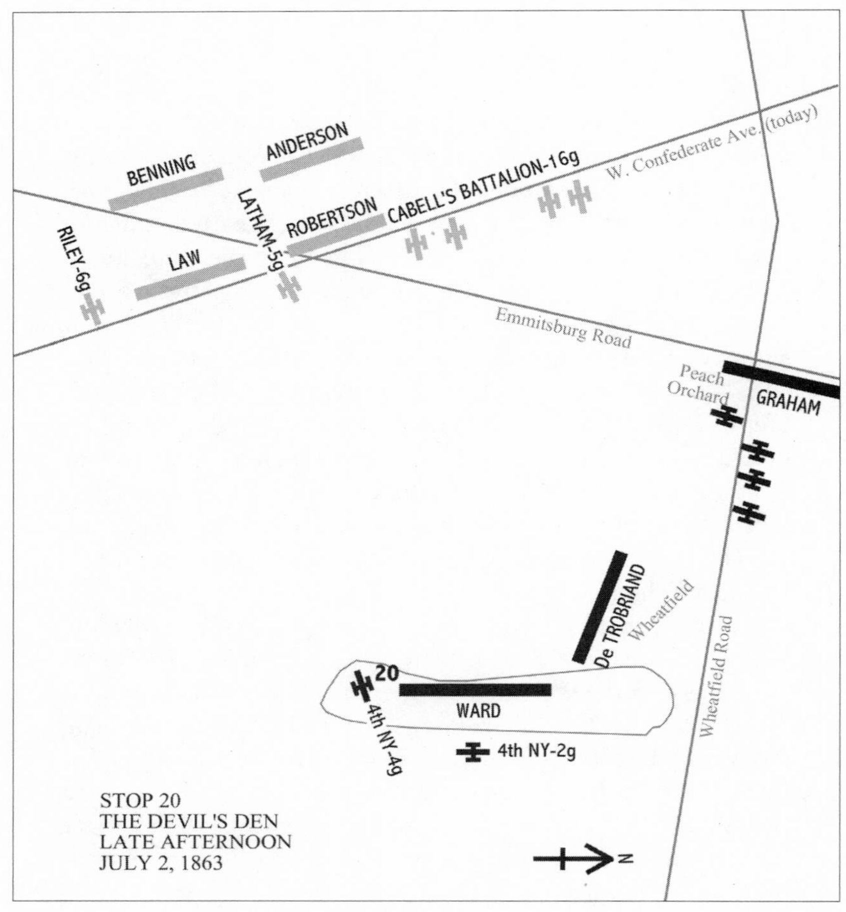

Report of Capt. James E. Smith, USA, Commanding Fourth New York Battery, Artillery Brigade, Third Corps, Army of the Potomac

In compliance with instructions received from you [Hunt], I placed two sections of my battery on a hill (near the Devil's [Den]) on the left of General Birney's line, leaving one section, together with caissons and horses, 150 yards in the rear. The Fourth Maine Regiment was detailed as support, forming line in rear under cover of a hill. On my left, extending half way to the Emmitsburg road, was a thick wood, in which I requested Lieutenant Leigh, aide-de-camp to General Ward, to place supports. He informed me that a brigade had already been placed there, but this must have been a mistake.

The enemy opened fire on my right and front from several guns, directing a portion of their fire upon my position. I was ordered by one of General Ward's aides to return their fire, which order I complied with. Twenty minutes later I discovered the enemy was endeavoring to get a section of light 12-pounder guns in position on my left and front, in order to enfilade this part of our line, but I succeeded in driving them off before they had an opportunity to open fire. Soon after, a battery [probably *Latham's* Battery] marched from the woods near the Emmitsburg road, and went in battery in the field in front, about 1,400 yards distant. A spirited duel immediately began between this battery and my own, lasting nearly twenty minutes, when *Hood's* division, *Longstreet's* corps (rebel), charged upon us.

At this time I requested the officer in command of the Fourth Maine Regiment to place his regiment in the woods on my left, telling him I could take care of my front, but my request was not complied with. I used case shot upon the advancing column until it entered the woods, when I fired shell until they emerged from the woods on my left flank, in line of battle 300 yards distant; then I used canister with little effect, owing to numerous large rocks, which afforded excellent protection to their sharpshooters. I saw it would be impossible for me to hold my position without assistance, and therefore called upon my supports, who gallantly advanced up the hill and engaged the enemy. Fighting became so close that I ordered my men to cease firing, as many of the Fourth Maine had already advanced in front of the guns. I then went to the rear, and opened [fire with] that section of guns [150 yards to your right rear], firing obliquely through the gully, doing good execution.

At this time the Sixth New Jersey Volunteers, Lieutenant-Colonel Gilkyson commanding, and Fortieth New York Regiment, Colonel Egan commanding, came to our support. These regiments marched down the gully, fighting like tigers, exposed to a terrific fire of musketry, and, when within 100 yards of the rebel line, the Fourth Maine, which still held the hill, were forced to retreat. Very soon afterward the Fortieth New York and Sixth New Jersey Regiments were compelled to follow. I then ordered my remaining guns to the rear.

When I left three guns on the hill (one having been sent to the rear disabled), I was under the impression we would be able to hold that position, but, if forced to retreat, I expected my supports would save the guns, which, however, they failed to do. I could have run my guns to the rear, but expecting to use them at any moment, and the position difficult of access, I thought best to leave them for awhile. Again, I feared if I removed them the infantry might mistake the movement for a retreat. In my opinion, had supports been placed in the woods, as I wished, the hill could not have been taken.

I regret to report the loss of 2 brave men, viz, Corpl. John A. Thompson and Private Isaiah Smith, and the wounding of 10 privates, many severely. Eleven horses were killed and disabled. Three 10-pounder Parrott guns and gun carriages were lost.

Total amount of ammunition expended, 240 rounds. [*OR* 27, pt. 1, pp. 588–89]

Return to your car for the drive to Stop 21.

Continue to drive on the park road for 0.5 mile to the Wheatfield. After you depart the parking area, you will drive up on top of Devil's Den and go past Smith's Fourth New York Battery, Stop 20. In another 0.2 mile, you will come to the Wheatfield. Continue on for another 0.1 mile to the parking area on the right of the road. Park here, and get out of your car. You can remain at this position, or you can walk 125 yards into the Wheatfield to the position of Captain George B. Winslow's Battery D, First New York Artillery. In either case face toward the west, the direction you car is pointed.

Stop 21—Battery D, First New York Artillery (Winslow's)

You are in the Wheatfield. Today it looks much as it did in 1863. There are trees on all four sides of the field, with only three small openings that allow a view from the field. Two of these openings are to your front and right front, and one is to your right rear. From the woods around the field, it is possible to observe into the field, but from the field it is difficult to look outward. The Wheatfield Road, which was the only road in the field that was here in 1863, is to your right along the northern edge of the field. The ground in front of you is rocky and 25 feet higher in elevation than the Wheatfield. Some reports refer to this as "the stony hill." Whoever occupied this piece of ground controlled the Wheatfield.

As you drove along the park road from Smith's battery (Stop 20) to the Wheatfield, you traveled along the defensive line of the Third Corps left flank brigade, Brigadier General Hobart Ward's Second Brigade of Major General David B. Birney's First Division. Birney's Third Brigade, commanded by Colonel Regis De Trobriand, was deployed to your left and left front, along the south side and southwest corner of the Wheatfield. Birney's First Brigade, commanded by Brigadier General Charles K. Graham, was deployed 700 yards in front of you (west) at the Peach Orchard. On the stony hill and facing west were Colonel William S. Tilton's and Colonel Jacob B. Sweitzer's brigades of the Fifth Corps's First Division.

Captain Winslow was ordered to deploy his battery's six Napoleons into this field. It occupied a position in the center of the field and faced generally southwest. The limited fields of observation and fire from inside the field make this a poor position for artillery. The advantage of the cannon's longer range is negated, and any engagement is well within the range of the infantry's rifled muskets.

Report of Capt. George B. Winslow, USA, Commanding Battery D, First New York Artillery, Artillery Brigade, Third Corps, Army of the Potomac

The position assigned my battery was near the left of the line, in a small wheat field near the base of [Little Round Top].

A battery of the enemy posted nearly in my front opened between 3 and 4 p.m. upon our lines. I could only see the smoke of their guns as it rose above the tree tops, but, by command of General Hunt, fired a few rounds of solid shot in that direction, probably with no effect, as it was evidently beyond the range of my guns. Soon after, the two lines of infantry became hotly engaged, but I was unable from my obscure position to observe the movements of the troops, and was compelled to estimate distances and regulate my fire by the reports of our own and the enemy's musketry.

By direction of Major-General Birney, I opened with solid shot, giving but sufficient elevation to clear our own troops in front, and firing in the direction of the heaviest musketry, lessening the range as our troops fell back and the enemy advanced. Our line of skirmishers fell back on their supports at the edge of the woods, little, if any, more than 400 yards from the front of my guns. This line was a weak one and soon fell back, but by using shell and case shot at about one degree elevation, and from 1 to 1½ second fuse, I kept the enemy from advancing from the cover of the woods. Having been just directed by General Birney, through an aide, to closely watch the movements and look for a route upon which I might withdraw in case it became necessary, I rode through the woods on my left, perhaps 200 yards in width, and found our line there formed perpendicular to my own, instead of parallel, as I had supposed, facing from me and closely pressed by the enemy. This line soon fell back irregularly, but slowly, passing in front of and masking my guns. A portion of Smith's battery, on my left, also withdrew by my rear.

The enemy's advance being within 25 yards of my left, and covered by woods and rocks, I ordered my left section limbered, with a view of moving it a short distance to the left and rear. Before this was accomplished, the enemy had advanced under cover of the woods upon my right, and was cutting down my men and horses. Having no supports in rear, and being exposed to a heavy fire of musketry in front and upon both flanks, I deemed it necessary to withdraw in order to save my guns, which was done by piece in succession from the left, continuing to fire until the right and last piece was limbered. Several horses were killed and disabled before moving 25 yards. In one instance it became necessary to use the limber of a caisson to secure the piece. By impressing 2 passing horses of Captain Smith's, not in use, the former was secured. Meeting Major-General Sickles and Captain Randolph immediately after leaving the field, I was ordered by them to move my battery to the rear, and refit as far as possible.

Captain George B. Winslow, USA. U.S. Army Military History Institute.

The casualties were 10 men wounded and 8 missing. Ten horses were killed and disabled. [*OR* 27, pt. 1, pp. 587–88]

Return to your car for the drive to Stop 22.

Continue driving west on the park road. This will bring you up on "the stony hill" where the road turns to the right, or north, and then makes a T intersection with the Wheatfield Road. At this intersection turn left and drive on the Wheatfield Road for 0.2 mile to a parking area on the left of the road. Park in this area, get out of your car, and walk west beside the road, the direction you were driving, for 90 yards to the highest point of ground where you can look west across the Emmitsburg Road. Stand off the road. Turn around and face to the east, back toward where your car is parked, so that you can look down Wheatfield Road. You are standing in the Peach Orchard.

Stop 22, Position A—The Peach Orchard

Look left and right, and you will see that you are standing on a small slightly elevated plateau. The plateau is 450 yards wide north to south, or your left to right. Its depth ranges from 350 yards to 140 yards, from east to west. It has width and depth and is flat, which made it an ideal position for Civil War artillery. As you look east down the Wheatfield Road, you can see how the ground drops away. There is a 40-foot difference in elevation between this plateau and where the center of Sickles's line initially was.

When Sickles's Corps deployed into position, it was initially located on the left of the Second Corps. From there his corps position went south along Cemetery Ridge into the low ground, 1,400 yards (0.8 mile) in front of you and then up on Little Round Top. Probably remembering his experience at Chancellorsville when Confederate infantry and artillery occupied the key terrain at Hazel Grove, Sickles decided to move forward to this location to deny it to *Lee's* infantry and artillery. Although it placed his corps in an unsupported position, it presented *Longstreet* and *McLaws* with a totally unexpected tactical situation.

Turn around, and walk west beside the Wheatfield Road for 50 yards. Just before you reach the Emmitsburg Road, turn left off the road and walk 25 yards to the monument to Battery G, First New York Artillery. Stand to the left of the monument and face west so that you are looking across the Emmitsburg Road and can see the tall metal observation tower.

Position B—Battery G, First New York Artillery (Ames's)

In 1863 the Peach Orchard was on the east side of the Emmitsburg Road and on both sides of the Wheatfield Road. The remains of the Wentz House are just on the other side of the Wheatfield Road. The Sherfy House is 350 yards to your right on the other side of the Emmitsburg Road. On this side of the road and 700 yards to your right is the Klingle House. The Rose House is the stone building 600 yards to your left. The tree line 500 yards in front of you marks the southern end of Seminary Ridge, which is also called Warfield Ridge at that location.

At 4:00 p.m. on July 2 this was part of Major General Daniel E. Sickles's Third Corps position. You are standing in the right center of Major General David B. Birney's First Division of the Third Corps. Brigadier General Charles K. Graham's First Brigade was deployed where you are and to your right for approximately 400 yards. Birney's other two brigades, De Trobriand's and Ward's, were deployed in the Wheatfield and along Houck's Ridge, with the left flank at the Devil's Den. To Graham's right was Brigadier General Andrew A. Humphreys's Second Division. Humphreys had two brigades deployed along the Emmitsburg Road. To Graham's immediate right was Colonel William R. Brewster's Second Brigade. To Brewster's right was Brigadier General Joseph B. Carr's First Brigade. Colonel George C. Burling's Third Brigade was in reserve. In this position Sickles's right flank was exposed and 900 yards forward of the Second Corps left flank. Sickle's left flank in Devil's Den was exposed and Little Round Top was undefended.

The Third Corps Artillery Brigade consisted of five batteries with thirty guns, eighteen Napoleons, and twelve 10-pound Parrotts. The Fourth New York was deployed at the Devil's Den (Stop 20), and Battery D, First New York, was deployed in the Wheatfield (Stop 21). The other three batteries were deployed in the vicinity of the Peach Orchard and along the Emmitsburg Road. They were reinforced with six batteries from the Artillery Reserve. Two of these batteries were deployed along the Emmitsburg Road. Four reserve batteries were positioned along the Wheatfield Road to fill in the gap between Graham's and De Trobriand's brigades.

At your location was the Artillery Reserve's Fourth Volunteer Brigade's Battery G, First New York Artillery, with six Napoleons. These guns were positioned to fire both west and south. One hundred yards to your right was Third Corps Artillery Brigade's Battery E, First Rhode Island Artillery, with six Napoleons. To that batteries right and 650 yards from your location was another Third Corps battery, Battery K, Fourth U.S. Artillery, with six Napoleons. Nine hundred yards to your right was the Artillery Reserve's First Regular Brigade's Battery F and K (Combined), Third U.S. Artillery, with six Napoleons. These four batteries deployed on a 900-yard front a total of twenty-four Napoleons to support the infantry along the Emmitsburg Road.

Five hundred yards directly in front of you is the Warfield House. It is near where West Confederate Avenue and Millerstown Road intersect. To your left front at a distance of 600 yards you can see the steel observation tower. The area between the tower and the Warfield House is Stop 14's Positions A, B, C, and D (*Alexander's* Battalion).

As his lead units marched into view and began receiving fire from this location, Major General *Lafayette McLaws* deployed the four brigades of his division. *Kershaw's* Brigade deployed in the vicinity of the steel observation tower, with *Semmes's* Brigade in a supporting line behind. To *Kershaw's* left, your right as you view it, and just beyond the Warfield House was *Barksdale's* Brigade with *Wofford's* Brigade in a supporting line behind. To *Kershaw's* left, your right, and in front of *Barksdale* was Colonel *E. Porter Alexander's* artillery battalion. On Kershaw's right, 850 yards to your left front, was Colonel *Henry C. Cabell's* artillery battalion. *Cabell* deployed sixteen guns, and *Alexander* deployed twenty-four guns. Look to your direct left. On this side of the Emmitsburg Road at a distance of 1,400 yards was the position of Captain *Alexander C. Latham's* Branch (North Carolina) Artillery Battery of one 6-pound gun, one 12-pound howitzer, and three Napoleons. On both sides of and behind this battery were the four deployed brigades of *Hood's* Division. All of this Confederate artillery could place fire on this location and was also in range of the Union batteries at the Peach Orchard and along Wheatfield Road.

In the tree line 850 yards to your right front on Seminary (Warfield) Ridge was the southernmost brigade of Major General *Richard H. Anderson's* division of *Hill's* Corps. *Wilcox's* Brigade was *Anderson's* southernmost (right) brigade. To that brigade's left and reaching north for over 1,400 yards, almost to where the North Carolina Monument is today (Stop 11), were *Perry's, Wright's, Posey's,* and *Mahone's* Brigades. Once *Longstreet's* began his attack *Anderson's* Division was to join in with a supporting attack.

As the Confederate artillery went into position, it and the Union guns engaged in an artillery duel. *McLaws* began his attack when *Kershaw's* Brigade went forward. The left wing of *Kershaw's* Brigade struck the southern front of the Peach Orchard but was repulsed. The remainder of the brigade passed by to the south and went toward the Rose House and "the stony hill." Shortly after *Kershaw* moved forward, *Barksdale's* Brigade commenced its attack.

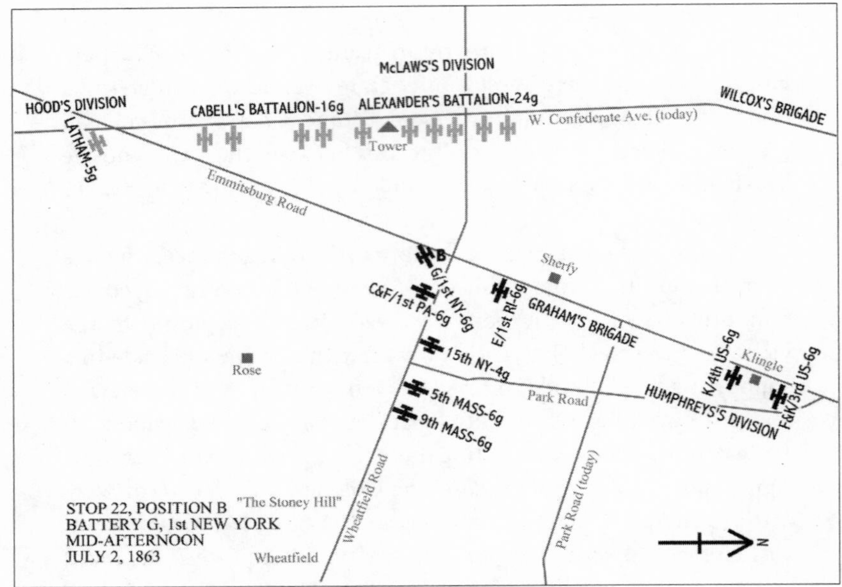

Barksdale's regiments attacked directly toward the Union positions in the Peach Orchard and along the Emmitsburg Road to the north.

Report of Capt Nelson Ames, USA, Commanding Battery G, First New York Artillery, Fourth Volunteer Artillery Brigade, Artillery Reserve, Army of the Potomac

I was ordered to move forward and shelter the battery behind the piece of woods on the Emmitsburg road, near the stone barn. I remained there until 3 p.m., when Captain Randolph, chief of artillery Third Army Corps, ordered me to move forward about 800 yards, take position in a thick peach orchard, and engage the enemy's batteries at a distance of 850 yards. I immediately moved forward, and, while crossing a cleared field, the enemy opened fire from one of their batteries. They got an excellent range of my battery, nearly all of their shot striking in my battery, but fortunately they did no other damage than killing 2 horses.

Before gaining the position assigned me, I was obliged to halt in plain sight of the enemy, to clear away two fences, which the supporting infantry had failed to throw down as they had been ordered to do. As soon as I could come into battery, I opened upon the battery in my front with spherical case and shell, and, after firing about thirty minutes, the enemy's fire greatly slackened, and in a few moments more it nearly ceased; but before I had time to congratulate myself or men upon our success with this battery, a four-gun battery of light 12-pounders opened upon my right from a grove 500 yards distant, and at the same time a new battery opened on my front. I immediately ordered Lieutenant McClellan, commanding the right section, to turn his two pieces upon the flank battery, while Lieutenants Hazelton and Goff kept up their fire upon the battery in front, and for a short time I had as sharp an artillery fight as I ever witnessed. I was soon pleased to see one piece of the flank battery dismounted, and the cannoneers of another either killed or wounded, when the other two pieces were taken from the field. I then turned my whole attention upon the batteries in front, but was obliged to fire very slowly, as my ammunition was getting exhausted, having but a few rounds of spherical case left, with a small supply of solid shot and canister.

About this time the rebel infantry advanced in line of battle across the wheat-field to my left and front. [Not The Wheatfield behind you where Stop 21 is.] Lieutenant Hazelton opened upon them with spherical case—he having collected all there was in the battery—with great success as long as that kind of ammunition lasted. He then ceased firing, and ordered his cannoneers to shelter themselves until the enemy advanced within canister range, when he purposed to drive them back with the unwelcome messenger—canister—Lieutenants McClellan and Goff meanwhile keeping up a steady, slow fire with solid shot upon the batteries in front.

My loss during the two and a half hours' fighting was 7 men wounded, 1 mortally and 2 seriously; also a loss of 11 horses killed. [*OR* 27, pt 1, pp. 900–901]

Their ammunition expended, Ames's battery withdrew from the Peach Orchard to resupply. However, their fighting at Gettysburg was not done.

Retrace your steps to the Wheatfield Road. Continue across the road, and walk north, past the Wentz House foundation, for 80 yards to the monument to Battery E, First Rhode Island Artillery. Position yourself next to the monument and guns, and face left so that you are looking west across the Emmitsburg Road.

Position C—Battery E, First Rhode Island Artillery

This was the position of Lieutenant John K. Bucklyn's Battery E, First Rhode Island Artillery. The battery was armed with six

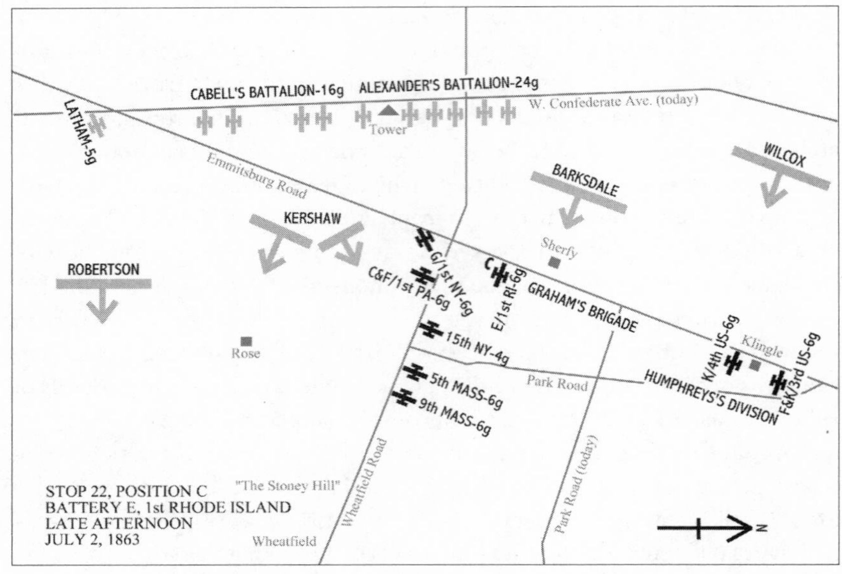

Napoleons. Four of the guns were deployed were you are. Two guns were farther to the right and on the other side of the Emmitsburg Road. Deploying under fire, the battery engaged the artillery of *Alexander's* Battalion directly to its front. When *Barksdale's* Brigade (to *Kershaw's* left, your right) attacked directly toward the Peach Orchard and this position, Bucklyn's gunners shifted their fire to the infantry. During this action Lieutenant Bucklyn was wounded, and Lieutenant Benjamin Freeborn assumed command of the battery.

Report of Lieut. Benjamin Freeborn, USA, Commanding Battery E, First Rhode Island Artillery, Artillery Brigade, Third Corps, Army of the Potomac

We moved up and took a position near the Emmitsburg road, under a heavy artillery fire from the enemy. Commenced firing immediately, and succeeded in siléncing several of the enemy's guns, but they soon opened from different points, and, owing to the peculiar formation of the line, we were at times exposed to a heavy cross-fire. The right section was detached from the rest of the battery and operated on the road near a small house. We were somewhat annoyed by sharpshooters, who were in a barn in front of the section, but dislodged them by a shell or two.

Lieutenant Benjamin Freeborn, USA. U.S. Army Military History Institute.

The enemy appeared to have massed their infantry on the left of the battery, and the fighting was severe there, so that our supports were either sent to that point or some other, as for twenty minutes before we left the battery was without any support, and nothing in front but a few sharpshooters. Some of them reported to me that the enemy was advancing in line in the ravine in front, probably with a view of charging on the battery. Nearly at the same time the artillery and infantry on our left fell back. It was deemed best to withdraw the battery, which was done, the enemy appearing within a few yards of us and delivering a heavy musketry fire, from which we suffered severely. We abandoned one caisson for want of horses, but regained it when our forces reoccupied the ground.

Lieutenant Bucklyn being wounded in coming off the field, the command devolved upon me, and the battery was ordered to the rear, and, being badly cut up, did not participate in any of the subsequent fighting.

The casualties were as follows: 2 officers wounded, 3 enlisted men killed, and 24 wounded; 17 horses killed and 23 disabled and abandoned. [*OR* 27, pt. 1, pp. 589–90]

Five hundred and fifty yards to your right and just this side of the Klingle house were the six Napoleons of Battery K, Fourth U.S. Artillery. Another 250 yards to that battery's right was Battery F/K, Third U.S. Artillery, with another six Napoleons. Both batteries were interspaced with the infantry regiments of Brigadier General Joseph B. Carr's First Brigade of the Third Corps's Second Division. Attacking that position were regiments from *Wilcox's* and *Perry's* Brigades. You will go to Battery K, Fourth U.S. Artillery position later on.

Face left, and walk south back to the Wheatfield Road. Be careful of traffic, turn left, and walk east beside the road for 150 yards to the Fifteenth New York Battery monument. Stand across the road from the monument and face south, your right as you walked beside the Wheatfield Road.

Position D—The Right of McGilvery's First Artillery Line

When Birney's division went into position, there was a gap between Graham's brigade to your right and De Trobriand's brigade in the Wheatfield to your left. To fill this gap, the four batteries of Lieutenant Colonel Freeman McGilvery's First Volunteer Brigade of the Artillery Reserve were deployed, facing south, along the Wheatfield Road. You are standing in the right part of McGilvery's artillery position.

Captain Patrick Hart's Fifteenth New York Battery with four Napoleons was at this location. To Hart's right were the six 3-inch rifles of Batteries C and F (Combined), Pennsylvania Artillery. To Hart's left was Captain Charles A. Phillips's Fifth Massachusetts Battery with the Tenth New York Battery attached for a combined total of six 3-inch rifles. The six Napoleons of Captain John Bigelow's Ninth Massachusetts Battery was to the left of Phillips. The Third Corps's Second New Jersey Battery with six 10-pound Parrotts was also in this vicinity.

In front of you at a range of 1,400 yards, where there is a small rise of ground with woods, was *Latham's* Branch (North Carolina) Artillery Battery of *Henry's* Battalion, *Hood's* Division (Stop 16). Latham had one 6-pound gun, one 12-pound howitzer, and three Napoleons. To your right front at a range of 1,000 yards were the right two batteries of *Cabell's* Battalion, *McLaws's* Division (Stop 15): *Fraser's* Pulaski (Georgia) Artillery Battery with two 3-inch rifles and two 10-pound Parrotts and *McCarthy's* Battery (First Richmond Howitzers) with two 3-inch rifles and two Napoleons. The other two batteries of *Cabell's* Battalion and the six batteries of *Alexander's* Battalion were in position to your right. The higher terrain to your right prevented *Alexander's* gunners from seeing the batteries here, except for Batteries C and F, Pennsylvania Artillery. However, any rounds from *Alexander's* guns that went over their intended targets in the Peach Orchard probably landed among McGilvery's guns.

As the brigades of *McLaws's* and *Hood's* Divisions moved into position for attack, their artillery fired upon the Union position at

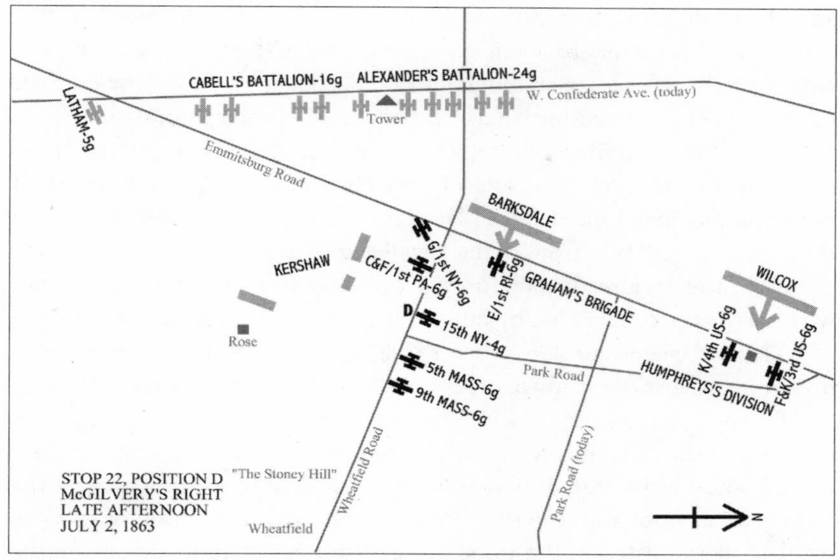

the Peach Orchard and along the Emmitsburg Road. The Union artillery at those locations and here began returning fire on the artillery and infantry.

Lieutenant Colonel McGilvery gave an excellent over view of his brigade as it went into action here.

Report of Lieut. Col. Freeman McGilvery, USA, Commanding First Volunteer Artillery Brigade, Artillery Reserve, Army of the Potomac

My brigade—Battery C and F, consolidated Pennsylvania artillery, Captain Thompson; Ninth and Fifth Massachusetts Batteries, Captains Bigelow and Phillips; Fifteenth New York Independent Battery, Captain Hart—being in park at a central position near our line of battle, at about 3.30 p.m. on July 2, I received an order to report to General Sickles with one light 12-pounder and one rifled battery.

The Fifth Massachusetts Battery, Captain Phillips, and Ninth Massachusetts Battery, Captain Bigelow, were marched immediately to a position occupied by General Sickles, near a belt of oak woods, considerably in front of the prolongation of the natural line of defenses of our army, on the left center, in which General Sickles' command was then engaged with the enemy. By General Sickles' order, I made an examination of the grounds, and placed the two Massachusetts batteries in a position [to your left] that commanded most of the open country between the woods held by our troops on the left center and high ground occupied by the enemy on their right. A New Jersey battery [Second New Jersey Battery] immediately on the right of the two Massachusetts batteries was receiving the most of the fire of two or more rebel batteries. Hart's Fifteenth New York Independent Battery reporting at that time, I placed it in position in a peach orchard on the right and a little in front of the New Jersey battery.

The batteries already mentioned presented a front nearly at right angles with the position occupied by our troops, facing toward our left, the fire of which I concentrated on single rebel batteries, and five or more were driven in succession from their positions. Captain Thompson's battery (C and F, consolidated Pennsylvania artillery), of my brigade, took position on the right of the Fifteenth New York Battery, two sections of which battery fronted and fired in the direction of those heretofore mentioned, and the right section fronted to the right, and opened fire on a section or more of rebel artillery posted in the woods, at canister range, immediately on the right of the batteries under my command, the enfilade fire of which was inflicting serious damage through the whole line of my command.

At about 5 o'clock a heavy column of rebel infantry [elements of *Robertson's* and *Anderson's* Brigades of *Hood's* Division] made its appearance in a grain-field about 850 yards in front, moving at quick time toward the woods on our left, where the infantry fighting was then going on. A well-directed fire from all the batteries was brought to bear upon them, which destroyed the order of their march and drove many back into the woods on their right, though the main portion of the column succeeded in reaching the point for which they started, and sheltered themselves from the artillery fire.

Lieutenant Colonel Freeman McGilvery, USA. U.S. Army Military History Institute.

In a few minutes another and larger column [*Kershaw's* Brigade of *McLaws's* Division] appeared at about 750 yards, presenting a slight left flank to our position. I immediately trained the entire line of our guns upon them, and opened with various kinds of ammunition. The column continued to move on at double-quick until its head reached a barn and [the Rose] farm-house immediately in front of my left battery, about 450 yards distant, when it came to a halt. I gave them canister and solid shot with such good effect that I am sure that several hundred were put *hors de combat* in a short space of time. The column was broken—part fled in the direction from whence it came; part pushed on into the woods on our left; the remainder endeavored to shelter themselves in masses around the house and barn.

After the battle, I visited the position where this column in its confusion massed up around the house and barn heretofore mentioned, and found 120 odd dead, belonging to three South Carolina regiments. This mortality was no doubt from the effect of the artillery fire. The asperities of the ground in front of my batteries were such as to enable the enemy's sharpshooters in large numbers to cover themselves within very short range. [*OR* 27, pt. 1, pp. 881–82]

The four Napoleons of Hart's Fifteenth New York Battery were able to engage the Confederate artillery south and southwest of this location. These guns were the ideal weapons to fire upon the infantry attacks that crossed their front or came at their position.

Report of Capt. Patrick Hart, USA, Commanding Fifteenth New York Battery, First Volunteer Artillery Brigade, Artillery Reserve, Army of the Potomac

On the 2d [of July] I was ordered by [Lieutenant Colonel] McGilvery to go to the front with him, to take a position in the line of battle. I proceeded to the left and center, when we met General Sickles, with whom [McGilvery] consulted. I halted my battery, and received orders to go with [McGilvery] to reconnoiter the enemy. [He], General Tyler's aide, and I proceeded to the front, when [he] pointed out the position I was to occupy. According to [Lieutenant Colonel] McGilvery's orders, I formed my battery into line, and was proceeding to take position when I met General Hunt, chief of artillery, who ordered me to take a position on the left of the peach orchard. I immediately obeyed the general's orders, and came into battery as directed. I then directed the fire of my battery on one of the enemy's batteries, which was doing heavy execution on our line of battle. This battery was to my right and front, and distant about 900 yards. I used solid shot and shell with such effect that the enemy was compelled to withdraw their battery. They then brought a battery still farther to my right. They poured a tremendous crossfire into me, killing 3 of my men and wounding 5, also killing 13 horses.

At this time my attention was drawn to a heavy column of infantry advancing on our line. I directed my fire with shrapnel on this column to good effect. I then changed to canister, repulsing the attack made on my battery. At this time the batteries on my right were abandoned, with the exception of Captain Ames', which retired in good order to the rear.

After the first repulse of the enemy, they reformed and advanced on me a second time, and were repulsed. At this very moment I saw a very heavy column of the enemy advancing on the left of the [Rose] barn and through a wheat-field, distant about 400 yards. I directed the fire of the left piece of my battery with canister upon this column, which did excellent execution, the enemy breaking in confusion. At this time the enemy were advancing in heavy force on me. I fired my last round of canister at this column before I retired. Previous to this I had sent to the rear for two of my caissons. There came word to me that they were not where I left them. I sent another messenger to bring them up. When they were convenient to me, they were again ordered to the rear. The only projectiles I had left were a few solid shot. I then limbered to the rear, and retired. [*OR* 27, pt. 1, p. 887]

Face to your left, and continue walking east along side the Wheatfield Road. Walk for 250 yards to the monument to the Ninth Massachusetts Battery. Stand across the road from the battery monument so than you are again looking south and southwest toward the stone Rose Farm House.

Position E—The Left of McGilvery's Artillery Line

You are standing in the left part of the artillery position occupied by Lieutenant Colonel McGilvery's artillery brigade. Captain John Bigelow's Ninth Massachusetts Battery was at this location. To Bigelow's right was Captain Charles A. Phillips's Fifth Massachusetts Battery.

Report of Lieut. Col. Freeman McGilvery, USA—Continued

At about a quarter to 6 o'clock the enemy's infantry gained possession of the woods immediately on the left of my line of batteries, and our infantry fell back both on our right and left, when great disorder ensued on both flanks of the line of batteries. At this period of the action, all of the batteries were exposed to a warm infantry fire from both flanks and front, whereupon I ordered them to retire 250 yards and renew their fire. The New Jersey bat-

The 9th Massachusetts Battery going into position. U.S. Army Military History Institute.

tery mentioned, being out of ammunition, retired to the rear. The Fifteenth New York Battery also retired from the field. Captains Bigelow and Phillips, who were under my observation about all the time, evinced great coolness and skill in retiring their batteries. Captain Phillips, Lieutenant Scott, and 4 men hauled one of his pieces off by hand, every horse in the limbers having been shot down, at which work Lieutenant Scott received a serious wound in the face, and it is a mystery to me that they were not all hit by the enemy's fire, as they were surrounded and fired upon from almost every direction. Captain Bigelow retired by prolonge, firing canister, which, with Captains Phillips and Thompson firing on his right in their new position, effectually checked the enemy in his advance for a short time. Captain Thompson, having all his horses belonging to one of the limbers of one of his pieces killed while retiring, was compelled to leave the piece, which fell into the hands of the enemy. [*OR* 27. pt. 1, p. 882]

Fighting from this location, the six Napoleons of Bigelow's Ninth Massachusetts Battery were positioned to inflict maximum damage on the attacking Confederate infantry in front of them. Captain Bigelow was wounded later in the fighting and did not write a report. However, in 1910 he published an account of his battery's fighting on July 2.

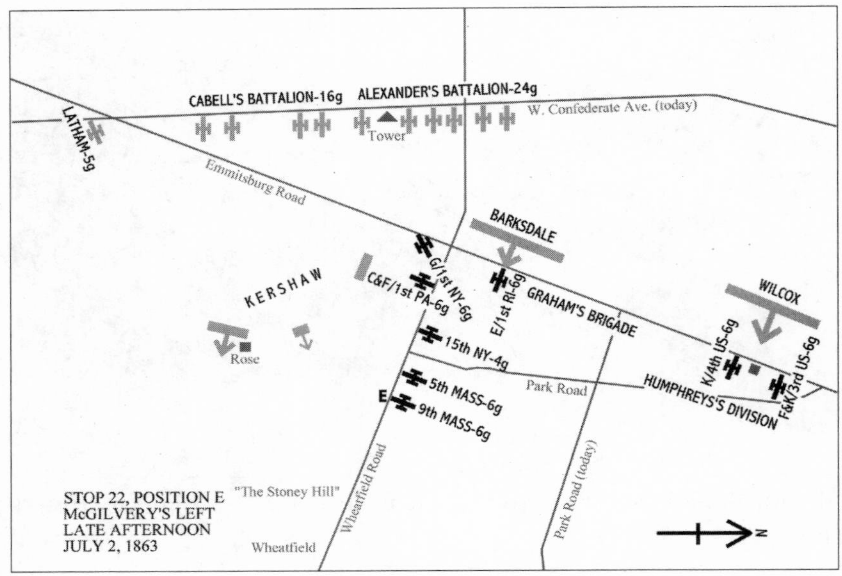

Narrative of Capt. John Bigelow, USA, Commanding Ninth Massachusetts Battery, First Volunteer Artillery Brigade, Artillery Reserve, Army of the Potomac

We dropped our guns in battery about 200 yards back [east] of the Peach Orchard angle, under a heavy fire from sharpshooters and two Confederate batteries. One man was killed and several wounded before we could fire a single gun, but, the wind being light, we soon covered ourselves in a cloud of powder smoke, for our six [Napoleons] were rapidly served, as we engaged the enemy's batteries 1,400 yards away down the Emmetsburg Road, whose attention we were receiving. Our position was in the open and exposed. Besides the sharpshooting, the air seemed alive with the bullets from the Peach Orchard struggle, just on our right. . . . It seemed but a short time, after we opened fire, before two of the enemy's limber chests were blown up and their fire silenced.

With the batteries disposed of, we immediately turned an effective fire on a large body of Confederate infantry whom we saw forming around the Rose building, 600 yards in our front. As a swell of ground interfered with the new range of the left section, it was quickly moved around to the right flank of the battery where the view was unobstructed. Our case shot and shell broke beautifully. One struck beneath the horse of the officer, who had apparently ridden out to give the order to advance—and brought down both horse and rider.

Captain John Bigelow, USA. U.S. Army Military History Institute.

Hardly had the enemy around the Rose buildings disappeared, before a battle line started across an open field in our front for a skirt of woods on our left, some 400 yards away. [This was part of *Kershaw's* Brigade advancing to "the stony hill."] The battery immediately enfiladed them with a rapid fire of canister, which tore through their ranks and sprinkled the field with their dead and wounded, until they disappeared in the woods on our left. . . .

[Lieutenant] Colonel McGilvery rode up at this time, told me "all of Sickles' men had withdrawn; limber up and get out." I replied that, "if I attempted to do so, the sharpshooters, on my left front, would shoot us all down. I must retire by prolonge and firing in order to keep them off." He assented and rode away.

Glancing towards the Peach Orchard on my right, I saw that the Confederates had come through and were forming a line 200 yards distant, extending back, parallel with the Emmitsburg Road and I must therefore move almost parallel with and in front of their line, in order to reach the exit of the stone wall at the Trostle's house 400 yards away. [The Confederate infantry were elements of *Barksdale's* Brigade. The red barn across the field behind you is the Trostle Barn. The house is next to it.] Bullets were coming into our midst from many directions and a Confederate battery added to our difficulties. Still, prolonges were fixed and we withdrew—the left section keeping *Kershaw's* skirmishers back with canister, and the other two sections bowling solid shot towards *Barksdale's* men. We moved slowly, the recoil of the guns retiring them, while the prolonges enabled us to keep the alignment; but the loss in men and horses was severe. [John Bigelow, *The Peach Orchard, Gettysburg, July 2, 1863* (Minneapolis: Kimball-Storer Co. 1910), 52–56. Hereafter cited as Bigelow, *The Peach Orchard*.]

The prolonge is a rope that was fixed on the trail of the gun. When a gun was retired by prolonge, one end of the rope was attached to the trail of the gun and the other end to the limber. When the gun was fired, it rolled back, and at the same time the horses pulled the limber to keep the gun pointed in the desired direction. The gun was then reloaded and fired. This kept the crew from having to hook and unhook the gun from the limber whenever they wanted to fire. This process was repeated until the desired location was reached or the enemy attacked ceased. Retiring by prolonge was normally used only when a battery was under close attack by enemy infantry and there were no friendly infantry available to cover the withdrawing battery.

Using this technique, the Ninth Massachusetts Battery fell back across the open ground behind you to the vicinity of the Trostle's house and barn. You will visit that location after the next stop.

The Ninth Massachusetts Battery was one of the last batteries to depart the defensive position at the Peach Orchard. Shortly after the Union infantry and artillery had retreated from this vicinity, Colonel *E. Porter Alexander* ordered his artillery forward to occupy the plateau at the Peach Orchard. From there he was able to continue providing fire support to the east and to the northeast.

Return to your car for the drive to Stop 23.

As you walk back to your car, take time to look south across the open terrain and study the fields of fire McGilvery's artillery had.

Do a U-turn from the parking area, and drive east for 50 yards to the first park road on your left. This is Sickles Avenue. Turn left on Sickles Avenue and drive 0.2 mile across the open field to the intersection with another park road. This is United States Avenue. Drive straight through the intersection, and continue driving for another 0.2 mile to the intersection with the Emmitsburg Road. At the intersection with the Emmitsburg Road be extremely careful, make a hard left turn, and drive for 0.2 mile to the monument for Battery K, Fourth U.S. Artillery. It is just past the Klingle House and on your left. Pull into the small stop area on the left side of the road and park. Be careful of traffic, get out of your car, stand beside the monument, and look west across the Emmitsburg Road.

Stop 23—Battery K, Fourth U.S. Artillery (Seeley's)

The Klingle House is to your immediate right. On the other side of the house was the position of Batteries F and K (Consolidated), Third U.S. Artillery. The red Sherfy Barn is to your left. At that location were two guns of Battery E, First Rhode Island Artillery. The remainder of the battery, four guns, was positioned just past the barn but on this side of the road. You are at the position of the six Napoleons of Battery K, Fourth U.S. Artillery.

Battery K, Fourth U.S. Artillery, was positioned in the left sector of Brigadier General Joseph B. Carr's First Brigade of Brigadier General Andrew A. Humphreys's Second Division of the Third Corps. Regiments from Brigadier General *Cadmus Wilcox's* brigade of Major General *Richard H. Anderson's* division attacked this position. *Wilcox's* Brigade was initially deployed in the trees 880 yards in front of you, where West Confederate Avenue is today.

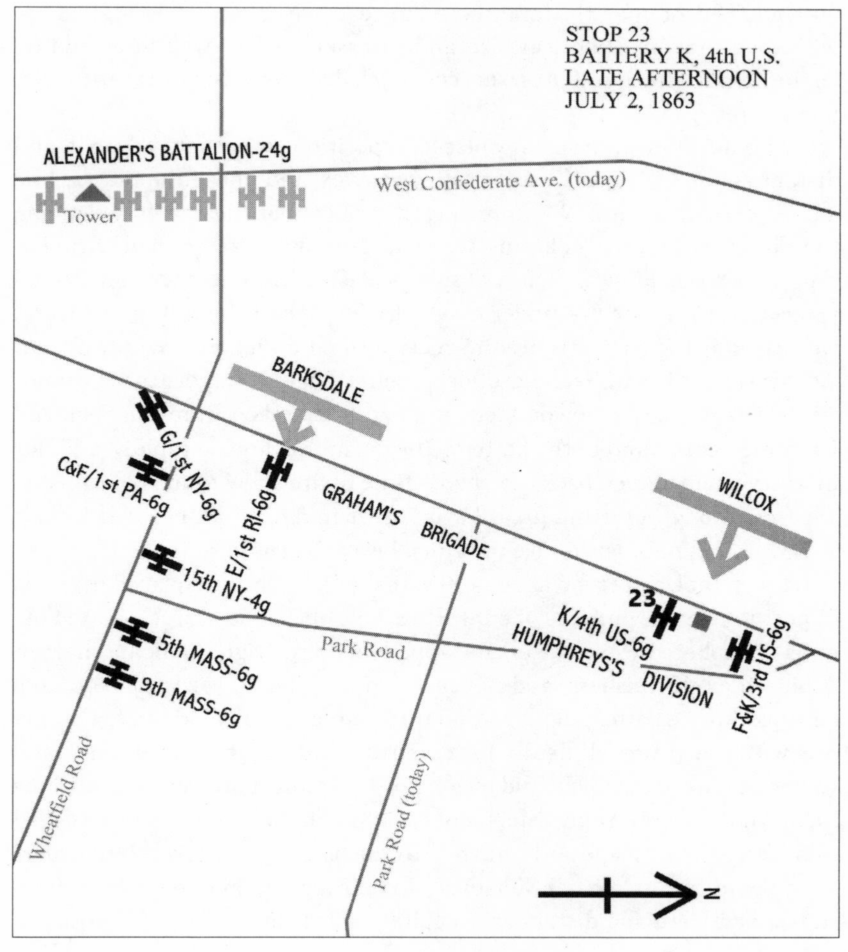

Anderson's Division was on the left of *Longstreet's* Corps and was ordered to attack with *Longstreet's* divisions.

Report of Lieut. Robert James, USA, Commanding Battery K, Fourth U.S. Artillery, Artillery Brigade, Third Corps, Army of the Potomac

About 3 p.m. on the afternoon of the 2d instant, the battery, under command of First Lieut. F. W. Seeley, Fourth U.S. Artillery, was ordered to a position on the crest of a small hill near the left center of our line, and immediately in front of the Second Division, Third Corps. The enemy had a battery posted in our front, and distant about 800 yards, and were firing with good effect upon the infantry in our rear. We immediately opened fire with solid shot and spherical case, and, after a rapid and well-directed fire, lasting about fifteen minutes, succeeded in silencing this battery and causing it to retire.

About 5.30 p.m. the enemy placed in position to our left and front, and distant about 1,000 yards, some four batteries, and opened upon our line a most destructive fire. We immediately replied, but the enemy advancing their infantry in heavy columns, we turned our attention to them, firing as rapidly as possible shot, shell, and spherical case. The enemy having gained protection from our fire under cover of the slope of the hill in our front, we ceased firing, and prepared to receive them on its crest with canister. At this time it is with feelings of deep regret I have to report that Lieutenant Seeley was severely wounded, and had to be taken from the field, and I assumed command of the battery. The enemy advancing rapidly, and our infantry having fallen back, I had only time to fire a few rounds of canister, which, although creating great havoc in their ranks, did not check their advance, and, in order to save my guns, I was obliged to retire.

I then took a position about 400 yards to the right, and placed my guns in position for the purpose of enfilading their line. I had scarcely gotten my guns unlimbered when the enemy appeared on my right flank and in rear, deployed as skirmishers, and not more than some 30 yards distant, and, getting into the battery along with our own infantry, I could not fire, and it was with the utmost difficulty I succeeded in moving by the left flank and retiring to the rear, which I did in good order, losing, however, several of my men, who were taken prisoners, but most of whom fortunately succeeded in making their escape and returned to the battery. I then received orders from [Lieutenant Colonel] McGilvery to take a position in an open field to the rear and left, and distant about 1,200 yards from our original position.

Not having a sufficient number of men to man my six guns, I sent a section of the battery to the rear, and went into this position with only four guns. [*OR* 27, pt. 1, pp. 590–91]

Return to your car for the drive to Stop 24.

Be extremely careful, pull on to the road, and continue driving south for 0.1 mile to the first park road on your left. Make a left turn on to this road, United States Avenue, and drive 0.2 mile to the parking area near the Trostle Barn. Park in the area on the right of the road, get out of your car, stand off the road, and look to the south, which was to your right as you were driving.

Stop 24—Bigelow Buys Time

The Ninth Massachusetts Battery retreated toward this corner of the field where there was an opening in the stonewall that they could pass through. However, when they arrived here, Lieutenant Colonel McGilvery had other plans for Bigelow's battery. We pick up the action with McGilvery's report as his batteries fell back from their positions along the Wheatfield Road.

Report of Lieut. Col. Freeman McGilvery, USA, Commanding First Volunteer Artillery Brigade, Artillery Reserve, Army of the Potomac

At about a quarter to 6 o'clock the enemy's infantry gained possession of the woods immediately on the left of my line of batteries [along the Wheatfield Road], and our infantry fell back both on our right and left, when great disorder ensued on both flanks of the line of batteries. At this period of the action, all of the batteries were exposed to a warm infantry fire from both flanks and front, whereupon I ordered them to retire 250 yards and renew their fire. The New Jersey battery [Second New Jersey Battery] mentioned, being out of ammunition, retired to the rear. The Fifteenth New York Battery also retired from the field. Captains Bigelow [Ninth Massachusetts Battery] and Phillips [Fifth Massachusetts Battery], who were under my observation about all the time, evinced great coolness and skill in retiring their batteries. Captain Phillips, Lieutenant Scott, and 4 men hauled one of his pieces off by hand, every horse in the limbers having been shot down, at which work Lieutenant Scott received a serious wound in the face, and it is a mystery to me that they were not all hit by the enemy's fire, as they were surrounded and fired upon from almost every direction. Captain Bigelow retired by prolonge, firing canister, which, with Captains Phillips and Thompson [Batteries C and F, Pennsylvania Artillery] firing on his right in their new position, effectually checked the enemy in his advance for a short time. Captain Thompson, having all his horses belonging to one of the limbers of one of his pieces killed while retiring, was compelled to leave the piece, which fell into the hands of the enemy.

The crisis of the engagement had now arrived. I gave Captain Bigelow orders to hold his position [where you are now] as long as possible at all hazards, in order to give me time to form a new line of artillery, and justice demands that I should state Captain Bigelow did hold his position and execute his firing with a deliberation and destructive effect upon the enemy in a manner such as only a brave and skillful officer could, until—one officer killed and the others wounded, and more than half his men either killed or wounded, and his horses all shot down at the limbers—he was forced to leave four guns and retire. Two guns under command of Lieutenant Milton were taken safely to the rear. [*OR* 27, pt. 1, p. 882]

Captain Bigelow's narrative provides a detail description of his battery's fight in this corner of the field.

Narrative of Capt. John Bigelow, USA, Commanding Ninth Massachusetts Battery, First Volunteer Artillery Brigade, Artillery Reserve, Army of the Potomac

When we reached the angle of the stone wall at Trostle's house, a swell of ground, 50 yards on our right front, covered us from *Barksdale's* approaching line and we began to limber up, hoping to get out and back to our lines before they closed in on us; but McGilvery, again rode up, told me that back of me for nearly 1,500 yards, between [Little] Round Top and the left of the Second Corps, the lines were open; there were no reserves, and said, I must hold my position at all hazards until he could find some infantry or could collect and place some batteries in position to cover the gap. The position, in which we were halted, was an impossible one for artillery. We were far in advance of our lines, without supports of any kind. . . . Further, we were shut in by the angle of a stone wall, along one line of which, the left, *Kershaw's* sharpshooter were following us; while on its other line, in front and on our right, *Barksdale's* Brigade was advancing; nearly half our men and horses were lying killed and wounded at our first position [along the Wheatfield Road], or on the field between that and where we then were.

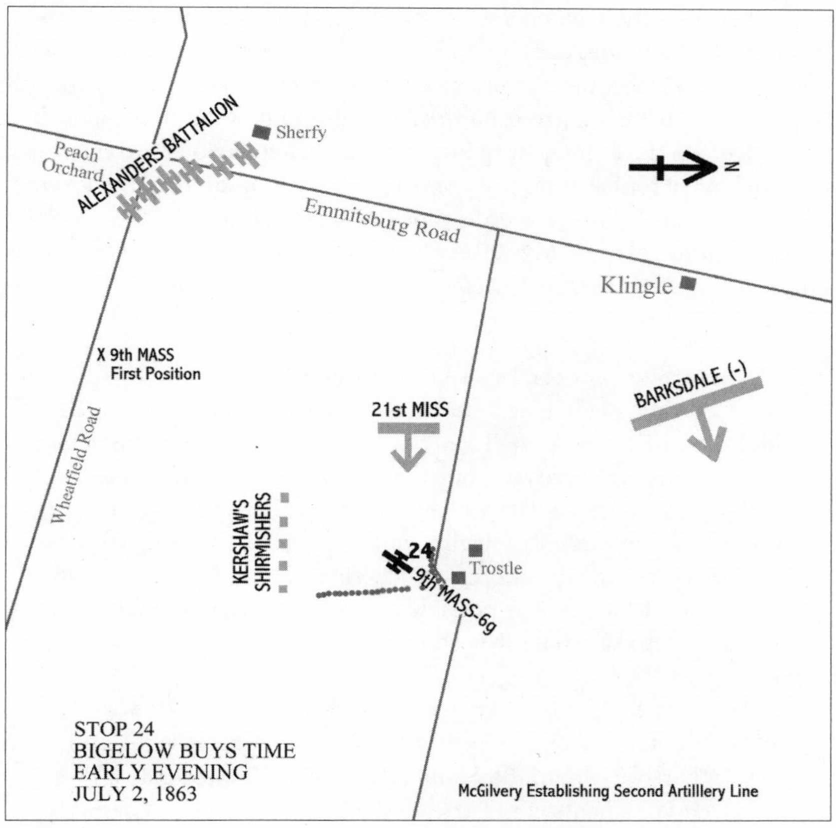

. . . However, the orders were given to unlimber, take the ammunition from the chest, place it near the guns for rapid firing and load the guns to the muzzle. They were hardly executed before the enemy appeared breast high above the swell of ground 50 yards in front, already referred to, and firing on both sides began. Notwithstanding repeated efforts, I don't think any of *Barksdale's* men came in on the front of the battery, weak as we were; but his lines extended far beyond our right flank, and the Twenty-first Mississippi swung without opposition and came in from that direction, pouring in a heavy fire all the while. Just before they closed in, the left section, Lieutenant Milton, could not be used, owing to some stone boulders, and was ordered to the rear. One piece went through the gateway of the stone wall, was upset, righted amid a shower of bullets and, Lieutenant Milton assisting, was dragged to the rear, the other piece was driven directly over the stone wall. . . . [At this point in the fighting Bigelow was wounded, but remained in command until he ordered the rest of the battery to fall back.]

I then saw the Confederates swarming in on our right flank, some standing on the limber chest and firing at the gunners, who were still serving their pieces; the horses were all down; overhead the air was alive with missiles from batteries [from *Alexander's* Battalion], which the enemy had now placed on the Emmetsburg Road, and glancing anxiously to the rear, I saw the longed for batteries just coming into position on the high ground, 500 yards away. I then gave orders for the small remnant of the four-gun detachment to fall back. My battery had delayed the enemy thirty precious minutes. [Bigelow, *The Peach Orchard,* 56–57]

Return to your car for the drive to Stop 25.

Continue driving east on United States Avenue for 0.2 mile. Pull off to the side of the road. Stay in your car, but look to your left. Seventy-five yards to your left, in the field, you will see two markers. They are for Battery I, Fifth U.S. Artillery, and the Thirty-ninth New York Infantry Regiment, the "Garibaldi Guards."

There is some question as to whether Battery I's marker is in the correct location. It is possible that the battery may have been slightly south of where it is shown, which would place it just to your right.

Battery I, Fifth U.S. Artillery, with four 3-inch rifles was the left flank of a line of artillery established by McGilvery to fill in where there was no infantry and hold back the Confederate attack until reinforcements could arrive. The Twenty-first Mississippi of *Barksdale's* Brigade having over run Bigelow's Ninth Massachusetts Battery continued on and attacked Lieutenant Watson's Battery I, Fifth U.S. Artillery. Lieutenant Watson was wounded during the fighting, and Lieutenant Charles MacConnell took command of the battery. There is no complete report from MacConnell, but fragments of his report are in the Fifth Corps's Artillery Brigade Commander's report and give a brief description of what happened here.

Report of Capt. Augustus P. Martin, USA, Commanding Artillery Brigade, Fifth Corps, Army of the Potomac

Second Lieutenant MacConnell, upon whom the command of the battery devolved when Lieutenant Watson was wounded, says:

> The battery was without support of any kind. The enemy appeared shortly—say twenty minutes—after taking position, nearly in front, at a distance of about 350 yards, and the battery immediately opened on them with shell. As they approached nearer, the battery poured in canister, some twenty rounds, until men and horses were shot down or disabled to such an extent that the battery was abandoned.

It was, however, soon recaptured by the bravery and determination of Second Lieut. Samuel Peeples, Fifth U.S. Artillery, who, having procured the services of the Garibaldi Guards, took a musket and led the charge himself, driving the enemy from the guns, and retaking everything that was lost, and conveyed it safely to the rear. [*OR* 27, pt. 1, p. 660]

The counterattack by the Thirty-ninth New York was part of a general counterattack made by Union reinforcements that came to this area. However, it was not made until later in the fighting. First the artillery had more fighting to do on it's own.

Continue driving east on United States Avenue for 0.2 mile to the T intersection with another park road. This road is a north-south road that goes along Cemetery Ridge. To your right it is called Sedgwick Avenue. To your left it is called Hancock Avenue. Turn left on to Hancock Avenue, and drive north for 75 yards to the statue of Father William Corby, which is on the right side of the road. Park along the right half of the road in the area provided, get out of your car, and walk to the other side of the road to the guns representing the Sixth Maine Battery. Position yourself beside the guns and look west, the direction the guns are pointed.

Stop 25—McGilvery's Second Artillery Line

You are on the southern part of Cemetery Ridge. In this area McGilvery established an artillery position to delay the Confederate attack until infantry reinforcements could arrive. Late in the afternoon, this area was critical for the success of Meade's defense.

Four hundred yards through the woods behind you is the Taneytown Road. This road and the Baltimore Pike were Meade's two major supply and communications routes. A penetration of the Union defenses at this point and the capture of Taneytown

Road would pose a serious threat to Meade's supply lines and his army's rear area. It would also breach the continuity of the defensive position and pose a threat to the separated parts of the army south and north of this location.

Earlier in the day, Brigadier General John C. Caldwell's four-brigade First Division, Second Corps, had occupied the ground where you are and to your right. In late afternoon it was sent southwest into the Wheatfield to reinforce the Third Corps. This left an opening in the defensive position that extended from where you are to past the large Pennsylvania Monument you see 600 yards to your right. Prior to McGilvery reaching this location, there were only a few infantry regiments and two artillery batteries defending this large gap in the line. Reinforcements had been called for and were on the way, but time was needed for them to arrive.

Lee's plan called for Major General *Richard H. Anderson's* division of *Hill's* Corps to support *Longstreet* by an attack on his left. *Anderson's* Division was initially positioned from 1,950 yards (1.1 miles) to your front along today's West Confederate Avenue to just north of the Virginia Monument, 2,100 yards (1.2 miles) to your right front. The far tree line generally marks *Anderson's* position.

Longstreet's left brigade, *Barksdale's,* and *Anderson's* two right brigades— *Wilcox's* and *Perry's (Lang's)*—attacked the Third Corps position along the Emmitsburg Road. They drove the defenders back then continued their attacks toward this position and the area immediately to your right.

You will notice a large amount of guns representing batteries from where you are to the Pennsylvania Monument. Many of these batteries were not here late in the afternoon of July 2, but were present the next day, July 3. You will look at this position again as part of the third day at Gettysburg later on.

The terrain in front of you today looks much like it did in 1863. It was open and provided for good fields of observation and fire. The ground gently fell away from this location for 400 to 500 yards to Plum Run, where there was low growth and bushes. From Plum Run the ground gently ascended 700 yards to the Emmitsburg Road. The park road, Hancock Avenue, was not here in 1863.

Although the guns and battery markers are along Hancock Avenue, on July 2 the actual positions were about 50 to 75 yards forward of these markers. At that location McGilvery established his second artillery line with all or parts of five batteries. From left

View to the west of the 6th Maine Battery (Stop 25) on McGilvery's Second Line on July 2. Trostle barn in the left, Sherfy barn in the left center, and Klingle house in the right of the photo.

to right they were: Battery I, Fifth U.S. Artillery, Fifth Corps Artillery Brigade with four 3-inch rifles; Lieutenant Edwin B. Dow's Sixth Maine Battery, Fourth Volunteer Artillery Brigade with four Napoleons; Captain Charles A. Phillips's Fifth Massachusetts Battery with three 3-inch rifles; Captain James Thompson's Batteries C and F (Consolidated) Pennsylvania Artillery with two 3-inch rifles (both from the First Volunteer Artillery Brigade); and Captain James M. Rorty's Battery B, First New York Artillery, Second Corps Artillery Brigade, with four 10-pound Parrotts. These five batteries, or parts thereof, gave McGilvery seventeen guns.

Report of Lieut. Col. Freeman McGilvery, USA, Commanding First Volunteer Artillery Brigade, Artillery Reserve, Army of the Potomac

I formed a new line of artillery about 400 yards to the rear, close under the woods, and covering the opening which led into the Gettysburg and Taneytown road, of the following batteries and parts of batteries: Battery I, Fifth Regular, and a volunteer battery which I have never been able to learn the name of; three guns of the Fifth Massachusetts and two of Captain Thompson's Pennsylvania battery, and commenced firing on the enemy's

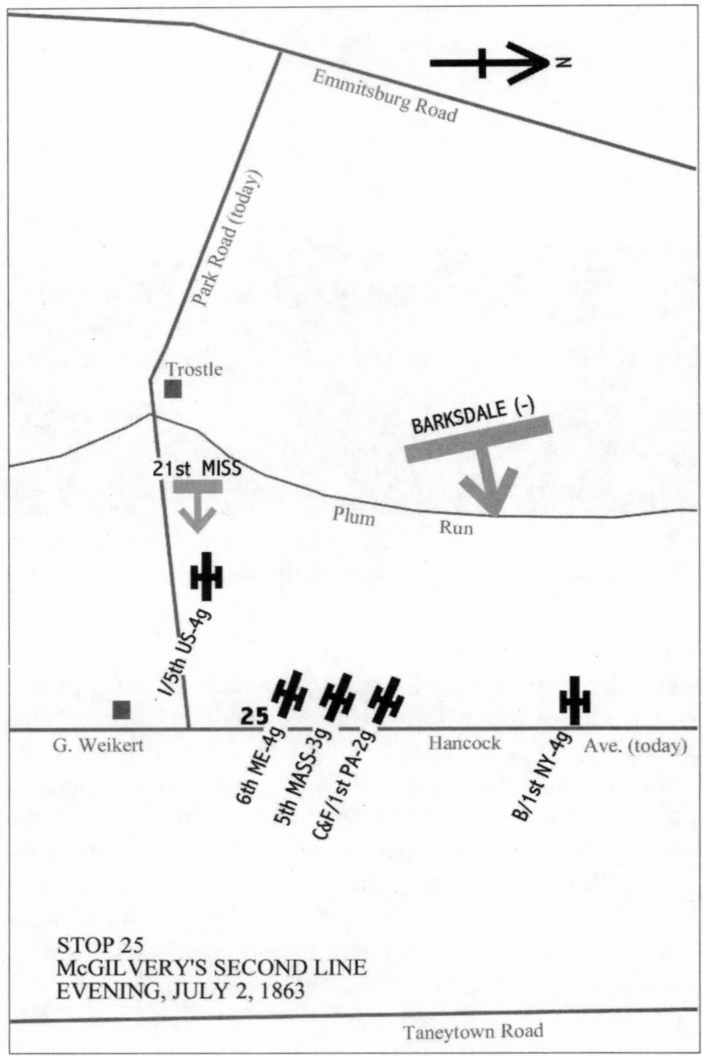

line of infantry and artillery, which had formed in the open field only about 700 or 800 yards in our front. A brook [Plum Run], running through low bushes parallel to our front, midway between ours and the enemy's lines, was occupied by, rebel sharpshooters. As soon as the Sixth Maine Battery reported, which was just before sundown, I ordered canister to be used on the low bushes in front, which compelled them to retire. About this time [Rorty's] New York battery reported, and changed position on the right of the Sixth Maine.

At this time the enemy's artillery fire was very heavy and rapid. The unknown volunteer battery, heretofore mentioned, left the field; the guns of Battery I, Fifth Regulars, were abandoned; Captain Thompson's guns, being out of ammunition, were sent to the rear: [Rorty's] First New York Battery B remained only a few minutes, and left [moving farther to the right] while I was directing the fire of the Sixth Maine and a section of the Fifth Massachusetts, Captain Phillips. Lieutenant Dow, with the Sixth Maine and one section of the Fifth Massachusetts, Captain Phillips, remained in position, and kept up a well-directed fire upon the enemy's lines until they had ceased firing, which was about 8 o'clock. I then placed Captain Seeley's regular battery [Battery K, Fourth U.S. Artillery], Lieutenant James [commanding], in position near Lieutenant Dow's battery, with instructions to watch the enemy closely and fire upon any advancing column, or reply to any artillery that might be opened upon us. Here ended the engagement of July 2.

At 8 p.m. a detail was made from the Sixth Maine and Seeley's battery to go to the front and haul off the guns of Battery I, [Fifth] Regulars. I instructed Lieutenant Dow to procure an infantry detail, and haul off the four guns of the Ninth Massachusetts, all of which was accomplished. The guns of the two batteries, numbering eight, were brought safely to the rear, and arrangements immediately made to secure their safe transportation in the event of any contingency that might necessitate a retreat or other movement. [*OR* 27, pt. 1, pp. 882–83]

Lieutenant Dow's report provides an excellent account of the artillery action at this location and the recovery operations on the night of July 2.

Report of Lieut. Edwin B. Dow, USA, Commanding Sixth Maine Battery, Fourth Volunteer Artillery Brigade, Artillery Reserve, Army of the Potomac

I received orders from General Tyler, through Lieutenant Blucher, to report to General Sickles' (Third) corps, on the left center, about 6 p.m. [July] 2d. I immediately marched my command to the front, meeting an ambulance with General Sickles in it, badly wounded.

I had not gone far when [Lieutenant Colonel] McGilvery ordered me into position in rear of the first line, remarking that he had charge of the artillery of the Third Corps. On going into position, my battery was under a heavy fire from two batteries of the enemy, situated some 1,000 yards in my front. I replied to them with solid shot and shell until the enemy's line of skirmishers and sharpshooters came out of the woods to the left front of my position and poured a continual stream of bullets at us. I soon discovered a battle line of the enemy coming through the wood about 600 yards distant, evidently with design to drive through and take possession of the road to Taneytown, directly in my rear. I immediately opened upon them with spherical case and canister, and, assisted by a section of Captain Phillips' (Fifth Massachusetts) battery, drove them back into the woods. Their artillery, to which we paid no attention, had gotten our exact range, and gave us a warm greeting.

We continued to shell the woods after their infantry retired, and upon visiting the spot the same night, about 9 o'clock, found many rebels dead and wounded. It was evidently their intention, after capturing the Ninth Massachusetts Battery and [Battery] I, Fifth Regulars, to have charged right through our lines to the Taneytown road, isolating our left wing and dividing our army: but owing to the prompt and skillful action of [Lieutenant Colonel] Freeman McGilvery, in forming this second line as soon as he found the first line lost, their plan was foiled, for they no doubt thought the woods in our rear were filled with infantry in support of the batteries, when the fact is we had no support at all. At this crisis, my orders from [Lieutenant Colonel] McGilvery were to hold my position at all hazards until he could re-enforce the position and relieve me. It was about 7 o'clock when the enemy retired, and I was in action altogether about one hour and a half.

At 7.30 p.m. I was relieved by [Lieutenant Colonel] McGilvery, who placed Seeley's battery, under command of Lieutenant James, in my position, and I retired into the edge of the woods. Lieutenant Rogers, of this battery, in reconnoitering found the enemy had retired from the field in haste, and had not taken the captured guns with them, nor even spiked them. He immediately reported the fact to me, and as many men as I could spare were sent under his charge to bring them off the field. With the aid of the Garibaldi Guard [Thirty-ninth New York Infantry], he brought off, under a fire from the enemy's sharpshooters, four 3-inch rifled guns and two limbers belonging to Company I, Fifth Regulars, which we immediately limbered on our caissons and ran to the rear.

I was then ordered to go to the front and see if any other public property was on the field, which order I obeyed, and discovered four light 12-pounder guns and a limber of the Ninth Massachusetts Battery. The remnant of the One hundred and fiftieth New York Regiment, although tired and weary, took hold of the guns and ran them up to Lieutenant James' position, where I turned them over to Lieutenant James, not having force sufficient to bring them off the field. Lieutenant James brought the guns off, and, I understood, turned them over to the Ninth Massachusetts Battery.

By order of [Lieutenant Colonel] McGilvery, I reported to Generals Tyler and Hunt what we had done. General Hunt ordered me to go to the rear near the reserve train with the guns. I did so, and next morning had the satisfaction of returning the guns of [Battery] I, Fifth Regulars, to their commanding officer.

I am happy to state that in this action, although under the most severe artillery and sharpshooters' fire, I had only 8 men wounded, not one killed. Ammunition expended, 244 rounds. [*OR* 27, pt. 1, pp. 897–98]

On July 3 the Sixth Maine Battery returned to this location and again was in action.

As the artillery fired into the attacking Confederates infantry, reinforcements arrived. It was Colonel George Willard's four-regiment Third Brigade from the Third Division of Hancock's Second Corps. Initially deployed on the right of the Second Corps line, it had been sent to this location. Arriving in time, it counterattacked and drove the Confederate attackers back.

Before you depart this location, walk to your right for 50 yards to the guns and monument to the Second Connecticut Artillery. These weapons are James rifles. The Second Connecticut Battery had four of them. Made of bronze, these rifles had a maximum effective range of 1,700 yards at five degrees of elevation when firing a 14-pound solid shot. Because of the softer bronze metal construction, the wear-out of the bore was faster than other rifled cannon. This weapon was more common in the western theater armies, and only four were with the Army of the Potomac. This battery was not here on July 2, but you will see it in action on July 3.

Return to your car for the drive to Stop 26.

Continue driving north on Hancock Avenue for 0.3 mile to the Pennsylvania Monument. It is the large monument directly in front of you. Follow the road where it veers to the left, if possible, and park. If necessary, you can park where the road goes straight ahead or even before where the road veers left. Get out of your car, and walk down the road so that the Pennsylvania Monument is on your right. Walk to the intersection where a park road comes in from your right. This is Pleasonton Avenue. In 1863 it was the Hummelbaugh Lane, and it intersects with Taneytown Road 500 yards to your right. At the intersection walk off to the left side of the road, stop and face left, west.

Stop 26, Position A—*Wilcox* and *Lang* Are Repulsed

Eight hundred yards to your left are the George Weikert House and the intersection of United States Avenue with Hancock Avenue. This is in the vicinity of Stop 25 and the left part of McGilvery's second artillery line. Directly west of you at a distance of 700 yards, you can see the Emmitsburg Road as it goes generally from southwest to northeast. Nine hundred and seventy yards to your left front is the Klingle House. To your right front, 500 yards distant, is the red Codori Barn. Five hundred yards to your right is the Copse of Trees of July 3 fame. Three hundred yards in front of you is Plum Run.

When Caldwell's Division moved south to reinforce the Third Corps, the ground 700 yards to your left and 200 yards to your right was virtually empty of defensive units. Three hundred yards to your right was the Nineteenth Maine Infantry Regiment. To your left was the First Minnesota Infantry Regiment. Both of these regiments were from Brigadier General John Gibbon's Second Division, Second Corps, and had been redeployed to this vicinity from a position farther north on the ridge. One hundred yards forward of your location was Lieutenant Evan Thomas's six Napoleons of Battery C, Fourth U.S. Artillery, First Regular Brigade of the Artillery Reserve. Approximately 350 yards to your left was Lieutenant Albert S. Shelton/Captain James M. Rorty's Battery B, First New York Artillery, from the Second Corps Artillery Brigade, with four 10-pound Parrotts.

Look west to the Emmitsburg Road. Seven hundred yards in front of you, along the Emmitsburg Road, and to the right of the Klingle House was the initial position of Batteries F and K (Consolidated) Third U.S. Artillery. To the left of the Klingle House was the initial position of Battery K, Fourth U.S. Artillery. These batteries were supporting part of Brigadier General Andrew A. Humphrey's Second Division of the Third Corps's defensive line that went northeast along the Emmitsburg Road from the Peach Orchard. Look to your right along the Emmitsburg Road to the red Codori Barn. On line with your position and the red Codori Barn at a distance of 350 yards was the initial location of Lieutenant Gulian V. Weir's Battery C, Fifth U.S. Artillery, with six Napoleons. To Weir's right rear and 400 yards from your location was Lieutenant T. Frederick Brown's Battery B, First Rhode Island Artillery, with six Napoleons. Farther to your right and on the other side of the Copse of Trees were two more Second Corps artillery batteries.

The intersection of the Millerstown Road and today's West Confederate Avenue is 1.1 miles southwest of where you are now, in the vicinity of where you see the tall steel observation tower above the trees. This is also Stop 14. This was the general location of *Longstreet's* left flank. To *Longstreet's* left, north, *Anderson* had deployed the five brigades of his division along Seminary Ridge. You can see the tree line that runs along Seminary Ridge, which is from south to north (your left to right) 1,900, 1,800, and 1,500 yards from your present position. *Anderson's* right flank, south, brigade was *Wilcox's* Brigade. To *Wilcox's* left, north, was *Perry's* (*Lang's*) Brigade. *Perry's* Brigade was 1,600 yards directly west of you in the trees on Seminary Ridge. *Wright's* Brigade was to *Perry's* Brigade's left. *Wright* was to your right front in the vicinity of where the Virginia Monument, with a statue of *Robert E. Lee* on top, is located today. To *Wright's* left were *Posey's* Brigade and then *Mahone's* Brigade. On *Anderson's* right was artillery from *E. Porter Alexander's* Battalion and, from his own divisional artillery, one battery from *Lane's* Battalion. The remainder of *Lane's* batteries and artillery from *Hill's* Corps reserve battalions were interspersed with *Anderson's* left, north, flank brigades and farther north.

General *Lee's* plan was for *Longstreet's* Corps to flank the Union left and attack up the Emmitsburg Road. When *Longstreet's* attack commenced, Major General *Richard H. Anderson's* division was also to attack the Union defenses along Cemetery Ridge. *Longstreet* had to modify his attack when he found the Union forces were not in the positions *Lee* thought when he had developed his plan. Once *Longstreet's* attack began, *Anderson* ordered his brigades forward.

Report of Major General *Richard H. Anderson,* CSA, Commanding *Anderson's* Division, *Hill's* Corps, Army of Northern Virginia

. . . the line of battle was formed, with the brigades in the following order: *Wilcox's, Perry's* (commanded by Col. *David Lang*), *Wright's, Posey's,* and *Mahone's.* The enemy's line was plainly in view, about 1,200 yards in our front, extending along an opposite ridge somewhat more elevated than that which we occupied, the intervening ground being slightly undulating, enclosed by rail and plank fences, and under cultivation. Our skirmishers soon became engaged with those of the enemy, and kept up an irregular fire upon one another. Shortly after the line had been formed, I received notice that Lieutenant-General *Longstreet* would occupy the ground on the right; that his line would be in a direction nearly at right angles with mine; that he would assault the extreme left of the enemy and drive him toward Gettysburg, and I was at the same time ordered to put the troops of my division into action by brigades as soon as those of General *Longstreet's* corps had progressed so far in their assault as to be connected with my right flank.

About 2 o'clock in the afternoon, the engagement between the artillery of the enemy and that of [*Longstreet's*] Corps commenced, and was soon followed by furious and sustained musketry; but it was not until 5.30 o'clock in the evening that *McLaws'* division (by which the movement of my division was to be regulated) had advanced so far as to call for the movement of my troops. The advance of *McLaws'* division was immediately followed by the brigades of mine, in the manner directed. [*OR* 27, pt. 2, p. 614]

As the Confederate attack developed along the Emmitsburg Road, Brown's (B, First Rhode Island) and Weir's (C, Fifth U.S.) batteries moved forward to support the defenders. When the infan-

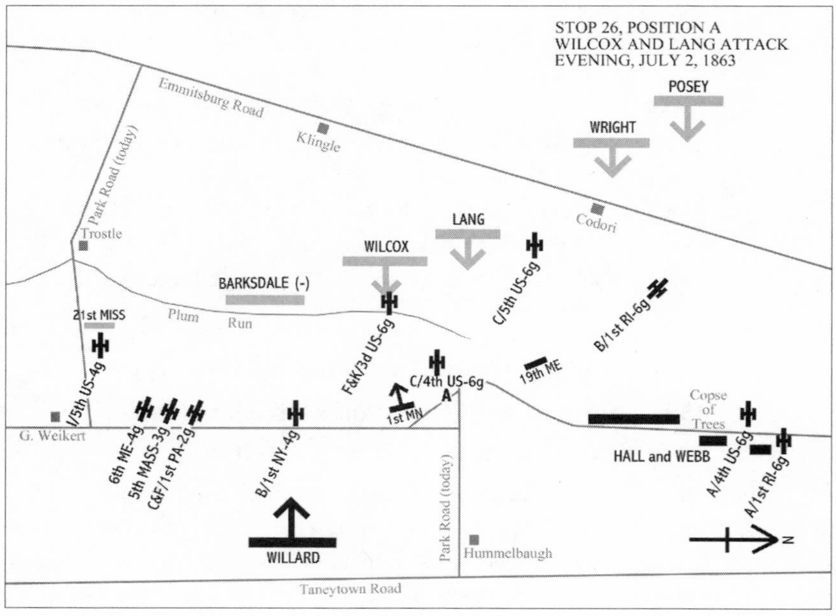

try defenses began to falter, Turnbull's Battery F and K, Third U.S. Artillery, fell back from the Emmitsburg Road. Just as Bigelow's battery did, the guns were retired by prolonge. The battery deployed to a second firing position just west of Plum Run. As Weir turned his six Napoleons more to the southwest and fired to cover Turnbull's retreat, the Nineteenth Maine Infantry Regiment moved forward to Weir's left.

Report of Lieut. Gulian V. Weir, USA, Commanding Battery C, Fifth U.S. Artillery, First Regular Artillery Brigade, Artillery Reserve, Army of the Potomac

About 4 o'clock was ordered by Major-General Hancock to take up a position about 500 yards to the front, with orders to watch my front, as our troops were falling back on the left at the time. I was ordered by General Gibbon to open fire to the left with solid shot at 4 degrees elevation. In a short time the enemy showed themselves in front, and, in their advance toward the battery, met with no opposition whatever from our infantry, who were posted on my right and front. I opened with solid shot and spherical case, and as they continued to advance, I opened with canister. Soon it was reported to me that we were out of canister. The enemy being within a few rods [1 rod = 5½ yards] of us, I immediately limbered up, and was about to retire when a regiment of infantry [Nineteenth Maine] took position on my left and rear, and opened fire. I immediately came into battery again, hoping that our infantry would drive the enemy back, as their force seemed to be small and much scattered. The enemy were too close. I endeavored to get my guns off the field; succeeded in getting off but three, as some of the drivers and horses were disabled while in the act of limbering up.

My horse was shot at this time, and, as I was rising from the ground I was struck with a spent ball, and everything seemed to be very much confused. I hastened off with the remaining guns. After the enemy had been driven back by the infantry, the other guns were brought off. [*OR* 27, pt. 1, p. 880]

Wright's Brigade overran Weir's position and captured three of his guns. The reminder of Weir's battery retreated back to a position to your right rear.

In the meantime Turnbull's Battery, F & K, Third U.S. Artillery, and the Nineteenth Maine were engaged with regiments from *Wilcox's* and *Perry's* Brigades. Although Turnbull's cannoneers fought hand to hand with the attacking Confederates, they were overwhelmed and four of his guns captured. When the survivors of Turnbull's battery with the two remaining Napoleons reached Thomas's battery [C, Fourth U.S.], directly in front of you, his six Napoleons opened fire on the Confederate infantry around the abandoned guns. Turnbull's guns were recaptured later by an infantry counterattack.

Colonel *David Lang* commanding *Perry's* Brigade wrote an account of the effectiveness of this artillery fire after his attack crossed the Emmitsburg Road.

Report of Col. *David Lang,* CSA, Commanding *Perry's* Brigade, *Anderson's* Division, *Hill's* Corps, Army of Northern Virginia

At 6 p.m., General *Wilcox* having begun to advance, I moved forward, being met at the crest of the first hill with a murderous fire of grape, canister, and musketry. Moving forward at the double-quick, the enemy fell back beyond their artillery, where they were attempting to rally when we reached the crest of the second hill. Seeing this, the men opened a galling fire upon them, thickly strewing the ground with their killed and wounded. This threw them into confusion, when we charged them, with a yell, and they broke and fled in confusion into the woods and breastworks beyond, leaving four or five pieces of cannon in my front, carrying off, however, most of the horses and limbers. Following them rapidly, I arrived behind a small eminence at the foot of [Cemetery Ridge], where, the brigade having become much scattered, I halted for the purpose of reforming, and allowing the men to catch breath before the final assault upon the [ridge].

While engaged in reforming here, an aide from the right informed me that a heavy force had advanced upon General *Wilcox's* brigade, and was forcing it back. At the same time a heavy fire of musketry was poured upon my brigade from the [thin] woods [along Plum Run] 50 yards immediately in front, which was gallantly met and handsomely replied to by my men. A few moments later, another messenger from my right informed me that General *Wilcox* had fallen back, and the enemy was then some distance in rear of my right flank. Going to the right, I discovered that the enemy had passed me more than 100 yards, and were attempting to surround me. I immediately ordered my men back to the [Emmitsburg] road, some 300 yards to the rear. Arriving here, I found there was no cover under which to rally, and continued to fall back, rallying and reforming upon the line from which we started.

In this charge, the brigade lost about 300 men killed, wounded, and missing. [*OR* 27, pt. 2, pp. 631–32]

Walk north, to your right, on Hancock Avenue for 250 yards to the guns and monument for Battery B, First New York Artillery. The monument is just before the tall U.S. Regulars Monument, which looks like the Washington Monument. When you reach Battery B's monument, face left, and again look toward the west.

Position B—*Wright* Reaches Cemetery Ridge

Lieutenant Albert S. Shelton had commenced the fight as Battery B's commander. The battery had initially deployed approximately 700 yards to your left with Caldwell's division. When Caldwell was sent to reinforce the Third Corps, Shelton kept his battery in position and then later moved farther south and joined the artillery at McGilvery's second artillery line. Hancock ordered Captain James M. Rorty to find Battery B, take command, and bring it to this location. Rorty rode south along the ridge, found Shelton and the battery, took command, and pulled the guns off McGilvery's

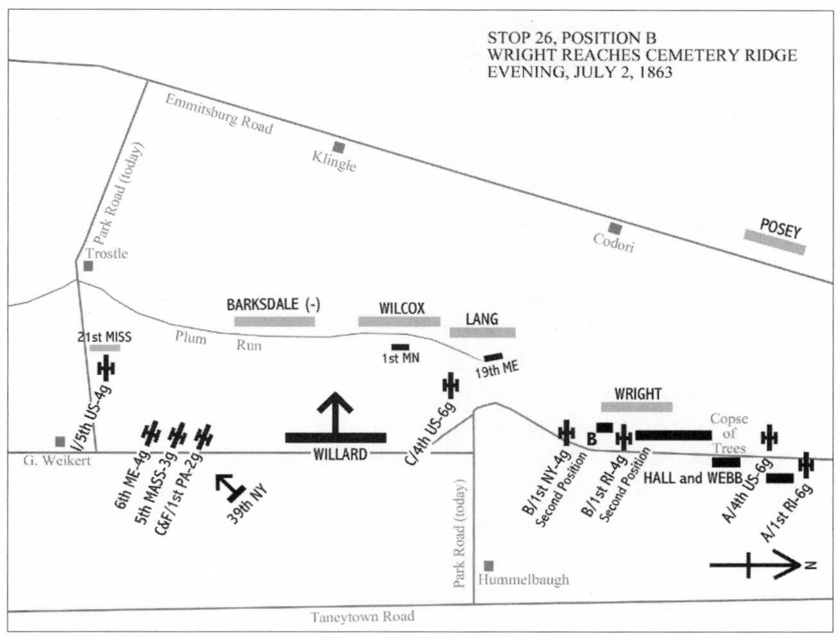

artillery line. The battery was brought north along the east side of the ridge to protect it from direct fire from the west, and its 10-pound Parrotts went into a firing position at this location. From here Battery B fired into *Wright's* infantrymen around Weir's three captured guns.

Lieutenant T. Frederick Brown's Battery B, First Rhode Island Artillery, with six Napoleons was 400 yards to your right front and 150 yards in front of the trees to your right. Initially the battery was in position along that portion of Cemetery Ridge about where you are now. As the action developed during the late afternoon, it was deployed forward of the main defensive positions on the ridge.

Sergeant John H. Rhodes in his *History of Battery B* recorded the position and actions of the battery.

Narrative of Sergeant John H. Rhodes, USA, Battery B, First Rhode Island Artillery, Artillery Brigade, Second Corps, Army of the Potomac

The guns of Battery B, at four o'clock, were advanced to the right and front, a few hundred rods, to a ridge in front of the main battle line at General Gibbon's [position] known as the Godori [Codori] field.

General Gibbon's line ran nearly parallel with the Emmitsburg road; we were on a slight ridge in [Codori] field between his line [on Cemetery Ridge] and the road at an angle of about 45°. The battery's left was nearest the road with the right extending back to within one hundred yards of the main line, at the stone wall, facing nearly northwest. The Fifteenth Massachusetts and the Eighty-second New York regiments lay along the road beside the fences [just to the right of the Codori Barn].

A large force of the enemy was seen coming out of the woods [on Seminary Ridge] on our left flank, moving to the road in the direction of the gap [between the Second and Third Corps]. At first we mistook them for our own men, supposing that the Third Corps was falling back to its old position [on Cemetery Ridge]; but when we commenced to receive their fire and heard that well known "rebel yell" as they charged for our battery, we were no longer in doubt. This force of the enemy proved to be General *Wright's* brigade. Lieutenant Brown ordered the battery to change front left oblique and then to begin firing four-second [fuse] spherical case shell.

By the change of fronts, only the left and center sections (four guns) of the battery could be brought to bear effectually on the advancing enemy, while the right section shelled the woods [on Seminary Ridge]. By their exposed position the battery received the concentrated fire of the enemy, which was advancing so rapidly that our fuses were cut at three, two, and one second, and then canister at point blank range, and, finally double charges [of canister] were used. Then came the order to "Limber to the rear."

During this time the enemy were advancing and firing by volleys. Their objective point seemed to be the capture of the battery, but, as we were well supported by the Sixty-ninth and One Hundred and sixth Pennsylvania boys, we succeeded in retiring with four pieces leaving two on the field, the horses having been killed.

In retiring the battery came under a heavy enfilading fire from the wing of the flanking foe, which had overlapped us, and many of our men and horses were wounded before we could retire behind our line of support, for only one piece at a time could go through the narrow gap in the stone wall which afforded a breastwork for our infantry.

The pieces, which reached the rear of our battle line, got in battery at once and opened fire upon the advancing foe. When the rebels were finally driven back across the Emmitsburg road, we with drew our two pieces from the field to the position occupied by the battery

Owing to the loss of men and horses the fifth and sixth pieces were sent to the rear, where the reserve artillery was parked, while the serviceable horses and men were put into the other four [guns] making them complete. [John H. Rhodes, *The History of Battery B, First Regiment Rhode Island Light Artillery in the War to Preserve the Union, 1861–1865.* (Providence, RI: Snow and Farnham Printers, 1894), 200–203]

Lieutenant Brown was wounded in this action, and command of the battery went to Lieutenant Walter S. Perrin.

This battery was hit hard by *Wright's* attack. Two of Brown's Napoleons were temporarily captured, but the remainder fell back and went into a firing position in this vicinity. From this vicinity Brown's and Rorty's guns fired upon *Wright's* advancing infantry. At the same time Lieutenant Alonzo H. Cushing's Battery A, Fourth U.S. Artillery, located on the other side of the "Copse of Trees," opened fire on *Wright's* infantry near Brown's two captured guns, with their six 3-inch rifles.

Report of Brig. Gen. *Ambrose R. Wright*, CSA, Commanding *Wright's* Brigade, *Anderson's* Division, *Hill's* Corps, Army of Northern Virginia

About noon, I was informed by Major-General *Anderson* that an attack upon the enemy's lines would soon be made by the whole division, commencing on our right by *Wilcox's* brigade, and that each brigade of the division would begin the attack as soon as the brigade on its immediate right commenced the movement. I was instructed to move simultaneously with *Perry's* brigade, which was on my right, and informed that *Posey's* brigade, on my left, would move forward upon my advance.

This being the order of battle, I awaited the signal for the general advance, which was given at about 5 p.m. by the advance of *Wilcox's* and *Perry's* brigades, on my right. I immediately ordered forward my brigade, and attacked the enemy in his strong position on a range of hills running south from the town of Gettysburg. In this advance, I was compelled to pass for more than a mile across an open plain, intersected by numerous post and rail fences, and swept by the enemy's artillery, which was posted along the Emmitsburg road and upon the crest of the heights a little south of Cemetery Hill.

My men moved steadily forward until reaching within musket range of the Emmitsburg [road], when we encountered a strong body of infantry posted under cover of a fence near to and parallel with the road. Just in rear of this line of infantry were the advanced batteries of the enemy, posted along the Emmitsburg [road], with a field of fire raking the whole valley below.

I immediately charged upon the enemy's line, and drove him in great confusion upon his second line, which was formed behind a stone fence, some 100 or more yards in rear of the Emmitsburg [road].

At this point we captured several pieces of artillery, which the enemy in his haste and confusion was unable to take off the field. Having gained the Emmitsburg [road], we again charged upon the enemy, heavily posted behind a stone fence which ran along the abrupt slope of the heights some 150 yards in rear of the [road].

Here the enemy made considerable resistance to our farther progress, but was finally forced to retire by the impetuous charge of my command.

We were now within less than 100 yards of the crest of the heights [where you are], which were lined with artillery, supported by a strong body of infantry, under protection of a stone fence. My men, by a well-directed fire, soon drove the cannoneers from their guns, and, leaping over the fence, charged up to the top of the crest, and drove the enemy's infantry [to] a rocky gorge on the eastern slope of the heights, and some 80 or 100 yards in rear of the enemy's batteries.

Unfortunately, just as we had carried the enemy's last and strongest position, it was discovered that the brigade on our right had actually given way, and was rapidly falling back to the rear, while on our left we were entirely unprotected, the brigade ordered to our support having failed to advance.

It was now evident, with my ranks so seriously thinned as they had been by this terrible charge, I should not be able to hold my position unless speedily and strongly re-enforced. My advanced position and the unprotected condition of my flanks invited an attack which the enemy were speedy to discover, and immediately passed a strong body of infantry in a southeasterly direction, and, emerging on the western slope of the ridge, came upon my right and rear at a point equidistant from the Emmitsburg [road] and the stone fence, while a large brigade advanced on my left.

We were now in a critical condition. The enemy's converging line was rapidly closing upon our rear; a few moments more, and we would be completely surrounded; still, no support could be seen coming to our assistance, and with painful hearts we abandoned our captured guns, faced about, and prepared to cut our way through the closing lines in our rear. This was effected in tolerable order, but with immense loss. The enemy rushed to his abandoned guns as soon as we began to retire, and poured a severe fire of grape and canister into our thinned ranks as we retired.

In this charge, my loss was very severe, amounting to 688 in killed, wounded, and missing, including many valuable officers. [*OR* 27, pt. 2, pp. 622–24]

With the repulse of *Wright's* Brigade and *Perry's* and *Wilcox's* Brigades to his right, your left, the fighting along this portion of Cemetery Ridge came to a halt for the day. The artillery had played a significant role in defending this portion of Meade's defensive position. However, their work at Gettysburg was not done.

Return to your car for the drive to Stop 27.

Drive forward to the intersection of Hancock Avenue with Pleasonton Avenue, turn right, and drive east for 0.3 mile to the intersection with the Taneytown Road. Turn right on the Taneytown Road, and drive south for 0.2 mile to Granite School House Lane. Be very observant to your left, as this road is easy to miss. Turn left on Granite School House Lane, drive east for 0.2 mile, then pull off to the side of the road, and pause for a few minutes.

The large open area to your right was the assembly area of the Army of the Potomac's artillery reserve. From this location batteries were dispatched to various part of the battlefield, as you have seen at the last four stops and will see in future stops. Batteries or their ammunition caissons also returned to this location to resupply with ammunition. Many of the batteries retreating back from the Peach Orchard and the Emmitsburg Road defensive positions came to this location to repair battle damage. After resupply and repair, they were again sent back into action.

Continue to drive on Granite School House Lane for 0.4 mile to the intersection with Blacksmith Shop Road. Follow Blacksmith Shop Road to the left for 0.1 mile to its intersection with the Baltimore Pike. Turn left, and drive northwest on the Baltimore Pike for 1.1 miles to the top of Cemetery Hill. Park in a legal space, get out of your car, cross the road, and follow the path to the monument to Batteries F and G (Combined), First Pennsylvania Artillery.

Stop 27, Position A—East Cemetery Hill

You are standing on East Cemetery Hill. You were here before, at the end of the fighting on July 1 (Stop 9). West Cemetery Hill is located on the other side of the Baltimore Pike. Located there is Evergreen Cemetery, a civilian cemetery that was there at the time of the battle, and the military cemetery, established after the battle. The large brick structure just across the road is the gatehouse for Evergreen Cemetery.

The First and Eleventh Corps artillery batteries retreated to Cemetery Hill late in the afternoon of July 1. Regardless of which corps the batteries belonged to, the commander of the Eleventh Corps artillery, Major Thomas W. Osborn, assumed command of all of the artillery on the hill west of the Baltimore Pike, and Colonel Charles S. Wainwright, commander of the First Corps artillery, commanded all batteries east of the pike. On July 1, as it became dark, there were on Cemetery Hill four batteries with a total of seventeen guns, thirteen 3-inch rifles, and four Napoleons, all east of the pike, and four batteries with fifteen guns, six 3-inch rifles, and nine Napoleons to the west of the pike.

Deployed along northeast base of East Cemetery Hill were the remains of the eight infantry regiments of Brigadier General Francis C. Barlow's First Division, Eleventh Corps, now commanded by Brigadier General Adelbert Ames as Barlow was wounded on July 1. The remainder of the Eleventh Corps infantry occupied defensive positions at the west and northwest base of West Cemetery Hill.

East face of Cemetery Hill. Union artillery was positioned high on the hill, while infantry was at the base, where the road is today.

With the Baltimore Pike behind you, look to the east. Eight hundred and fifty yards in front of you is wooded Culp's Hill. The right flank of the Army of the Potomac was on this hill. Regiments from the First Corps occupied the northern side, and two divisions of the Twelfth Corps occupied the northeastern and eastern side. Between you and Culp's Hill is a small knoll. It is slightly to the right of a line from your location and the top of Culp's Hill, and it is 550 yards from you. You may be able to see a monument with a man on horseback. This is Stevens's Knoll. It was named after the commander of the battery, with six Napoleons, there on July 2 and 3. Look to the left of Culp's Hill, and you can see the open fields that stretch from the base of East Cemetery Hill to the Hanover Road. In the distance, to the left of these fields, you can see part of Gettysburg. Look on a line halfway between Gettysburg and Culp's Hill. At a distance of 1,600 yards from your location, you can see a small hill with a shallow ridge running north from it. The ridge crosses the Hanover Road. The hill is Benner's Hill. On the afternoon of July 2, it and the small ridge were a Confederate artillery position.

At noon on Thursday, July 2, there were four batteries in position on East Cemetery Hill. All of them had participated in the previous days fighting. Only one battery was at full strength. To your left was Captain Michael Wiedrich's Battery I, First New York Artillery, with it full complement of six 3-inch rifles. To your immediate right was Captain James H. Cooper's Battery B, First Pennsylvania Artillery, with three of its surviving 3-inch rifles. To Cooper's right was Captain Gilbert A. Reynolds's Battery L, First New York Artillery, with four of its surviving 3-inch rifles. Reynolds had been wounded the day before, and Lieutenant George Breck now

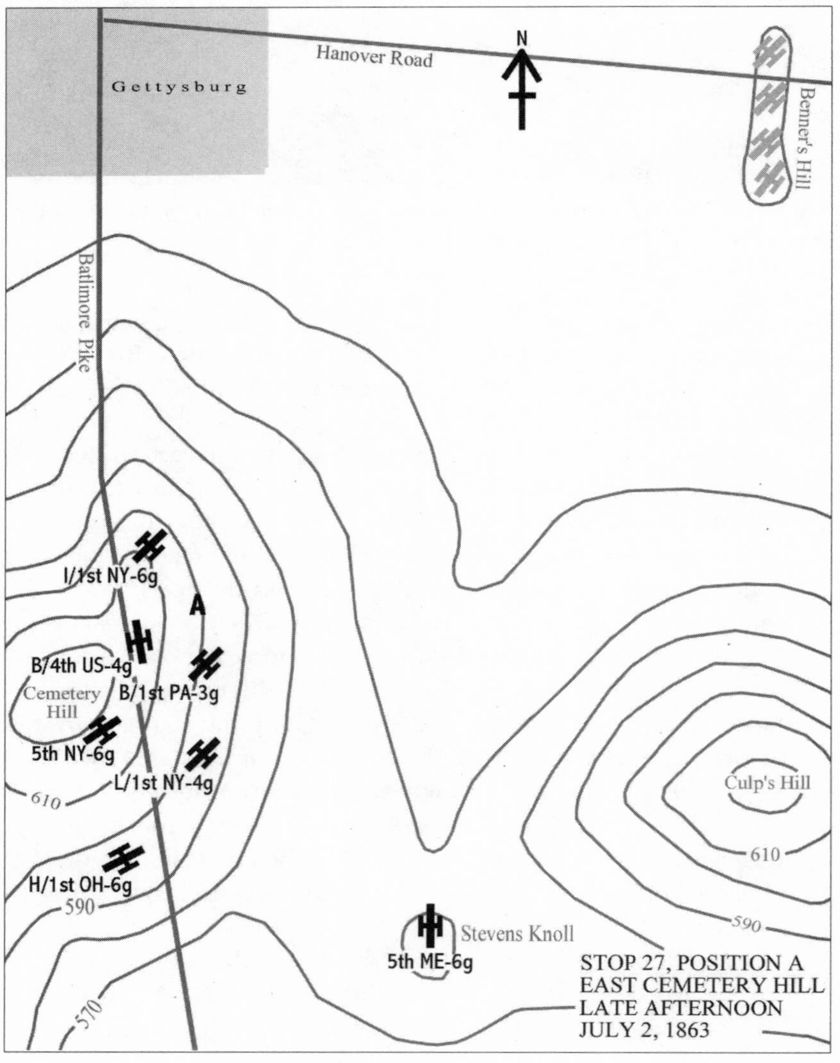

commanded the battery. Behind you, astride the Baltimore Pike and facing north, were the four remaining Napoleons of Lieutenant James Stuart's Battery B, Fourth U.S. Artillery. Where you are was the position late that afternoon of Captain R. Bruce Ricketts's Batteries F and G (Consolidated), First Pennsylvania Artillery of the Third Volunteer Artillery Brigade, Artillery Reserve. Ricketts's six 3-inch rifles replaced Cooper's battery's after it was withdrawn around 7:00 p.m. Behind you on the other side of the pike and partially in Evergreen Cemetery were the six 20-pound Parrotts of Captain Elijah D. Taft's Fifth New York Battery, Second Volunteer Artillery Brigade, Artillery Reserve. These powerful guns had a field of fire to the northeast, but they could also be turned to fire to the north if necessary. Behind but to Taft's right were the six 3-inch rifles of Lieutenant George W. Norton's Battery H, First Ohio Artillery, Third Volunteer Artillery Brigade, of the Artillery Reserve. Norton's guns also had a field of fire to the northeast. The six Napoleons of Captain Greenleaf T. Stevens's Fifth Maine Battery were positioned on Stevens's Knoll. Stevens was wounded on the morning of July 2, and the battery was commanded by Lieutenant Edward N. Whittier. The Fifth Maine Battery's guns were position to fire across the front of the East Cemetery Hill defenses and thus provide an artillery crossfire on the open ground.

While *Longstreet's* Corps was attacking the Union south flank, *Lee's* two other corps had significant missions to carry out. One of those missions would bring about an artillery duel and then infantry attacks in this vicinity.

Report of Gen. *Robert E. Lee,* CSA, Commanding Army of Northern Virginia

General *Ewell's* corps constituted our left, *Johnson's* division being opposite the height [Culp's Hill] adjoining Cemetery Hill, *Early's* in the center, in front of the north face of the latter, and *Rodes* upon his right. *Hill's* corps [along Seminary Ridge] faced the west side of Cemetery Hill, and extended nearly parallel to the Emmitsburg road, making an angle with *Ewell's, Pender's* division formed his left, *Anderson's* his right, *Heth's,* under Brigadier-General *Pettigrew,* being in reserve. His artillery, under Colonel *R. L. Walker,* was posted in eligible positions along his line.

It was determined to make the principal attack upon the enemy's left, and endeavor to gain a position from which it was thought that our artillery could be brought to bear with effect. *Longstreet* was directed to place the divisions of *McLaws* and *Hood* on the right of *Hill,* partially enveloping the enemy's left, which he was to drive in.

General *Hill* was ordered to threaten the enemy's center, to prevent re-enforcements being drawn to either wing, and co-operate with his right division [*Anderson's*] in *Longstreet's* attack.

General *Ewell* was instructed to make a simultaneous demonstration upon the enemy's right, to be converted into a real attack should opportunity offer. [*OR* 27, pt. 2, pp. 318–19]

In tactical operations, attacks are categorized as main and supporting attacks. The main attack is the one the commander designs to capture the enemy's position or to achieve his overall objective. Usually it has the majority of troops assigned to it and has priority of supporting artillery fire. The reserve, if there is one, is normally placed so as to support or exploit the success of the main attack. Supporting attacks are designed to assist the main attack by causing the enemy to disperse his forces and fight in several locations, hold enemy forces in position, cause a premature or incorrect commitment of enemy reserves, and confuse the enemy as to which is the main attack.

Using modern military terminology, *Longstreet* was to make the main attack while *Hill* and *Ewell* were to conduct supporting attacks. *Hill's* and *Ewell's* attacks were to hold the Union defenders on the northern part of Cemetery Ridge, Cemetery Hill, and Culp's Hill in position to keep them from reinforcing the center or south sectors of Meade's defensive position. In addition, *Hill* and *Ewell* might create confusion as to which attack was the main attack and cause Meade to commitment reserve units to the wrong area.

In carrying out his mission, *Ewell* ordered Major General *Edward Johnson* to prepare his infantry to attack Culp's Hill, to deploy his divisional artillery battalion to Benner's Hill, and to open fire on the Union positions where you are located. Late in the afternoon these orders brought about an intense artillery verses artillery duel.

Johnson's divisional artillery was Lieutenant Colonel *R. Snowden Andrews's* battalion. *Andrews* was wounded on June 13 in the fight for Winchester, Virginia, and Major *Joseph W. Latimer* temporarily commanded the battalion. *Andrews's* Battalion was composed of four batteries with a total of sixteen guns. The guns were six Napoleons, five 10-pound Parrotts, three 3-inch rifles, and two 20-pound Parrotts. These weapons occupied a frontage of 450 yards from Benner's Hill north along the ridge to just on the other side of the Hanover Road. The four 20-pound Parrotts of Captain *Archibald Graham's* Rockbridge Artillery from *Dance's* Battalion of the corps reserve artillery reinforced them.

Facing this array of Confederate artillery were the seventeen guns, thirteen 3-inch rifles, and four Napoleons, all on East Cemetery Hill, and the six Napoleons on Stevens Knoll; all these were under the command of Colonel Wainwright. Supporting Wainwright's artillery from the other side of the pike were the twelve guns, six 20-pound Parrotts and six 3-inch rifles, of Taft's and Norton's batteries. If necessary, Major Osborne could shift some of his other batteries to fire on Benner's Hill. As the fighting developed, although the terrain was not good for artillery, five guns from the Twelfth Corps Artillery Brigade were positioned on Culp's Hill. They were three 10-pound Parrotts from Battery E, Pennsylvania Artillery, and two Napoleons from Battery K, Fifth U.S. Artillery. After the artillery fighting was over, they withdrew to a reserve position.

Forty Union guns, with additional guns readily available if needed, faced the twenty Confederate guns on the Benner's Hill position. In addition to being outgunned, the Confederate artillery position was a poor location. It was open with no cover or concealment and was forty to fifty feet lower than the Union positions. In addition the batteries on East Cemetery Hill and Stevens Knoll had occupied their positions for almost twenty-four hours, and the crews had constructed earthen embankments, called a lunette, in front of and to the sides their guns.

Report of Major General *Edward Johnson*, CSA, Commanding *Johnson's* Division, *Ewell's* Corps, Army of Northern Virginia

Early next morning, skirmishers from *Walker's* and *Jones'* brigades were advanced for the purpose of feeling the enemy, and desultory firing was maintained with their skirmishers until 4 p.m., at which hour I ordered Major *Latimer* to open fire with all of his pieces from the only eligible hill within range, *Jones'* brigade being properly disposed as a support. The hill [Benner's] was directly in front of the wooded mountain [Culp's Hill] and a little to the left of the Cemetery Hill; consequently exposed to the concentrated fire from both, and also to an enfilade fire from a battery near the Baltimore road. The unequal contest was maintained for two hours with considerable damage to the enemy, as will appear from the accompanying report of Lieutenant-Colonel *Andrews.* Major *Latimer* having reported to me that the exhausted condition of his horses and men, together with the terrible fire of the enemy's artillery, rendered his position untenable, he was ordered to cease firing and withdraw all of his pieces excepting four, which were left in position to cover the advance of my infantry. [*OR* 27, pt. 2, p. 504]

Colonel Wainwright gives an overall view of his artillery at this location.

Report of Col. Charles S. Wainwright, USA, Commanding, Artillery Brigade, First Corps, Army of the Potomac

During the morning several moving columns of the enemy were shelled at intervals, but no engagements occurred until about 4 p.m., when they planted a battery of four 20-pounders and six 10-pounder Parrotts in a wheat-field on our immediate front, at about 1,300 yards, and opened the most accurate fire I have ever yet seen from their artillery. We replied with our thirteen 3-inch guns with good effect. It was an hour and a half, however, before we were able to compel them to withdraw, and then they hauled off their two right pieces by hand. Twenty-eight dead horses were found on the knoll occupied by this battery. A portion of the guns again took position farther to the right, but were soon silenced, as we could bring an additional number of pieces to bear on them there. Soon after, Captain Cooper's battery, which had suffered considerably, was relieved by Captain Ricketts' battery of six 3-inch guns. [*OR* 27, pt. 1, p. 358]

Face to your right, and walk 25 yards to the guns and monument for Battery B, First Pennsylvania Artillery. When you reach that location, stop and face to your left, back to the northeast, as the guns are pointed.

Position B—Battery B, First Pennsylvania Artillery (Cooper's)

Late in the afternoon the three 3-inch rifles of Captain James H. Cooper's Battery B, First Pennsylvania artillery was at this loca-

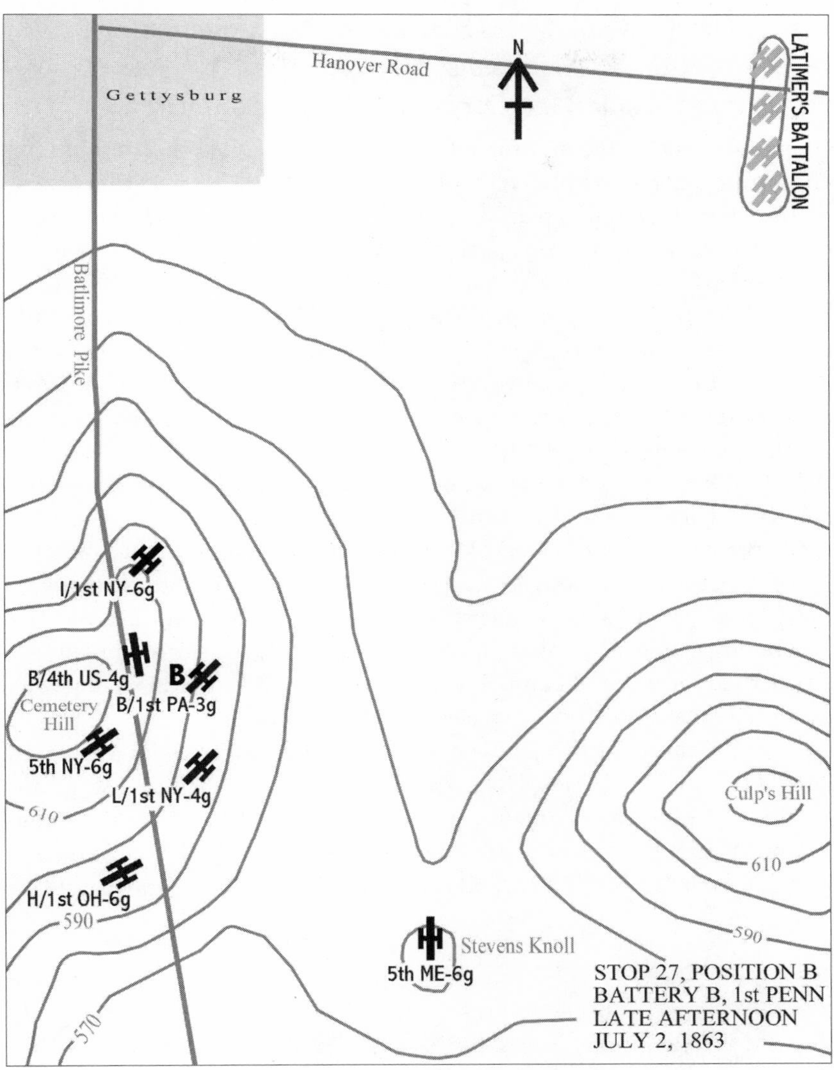

tion. If you look the direction the guns are pointed, you can see the line of sight they had to *Latimer's* guns. All of *Latimer's* position was with in effective range of Cooper's guns.

Report of Capt. James H. Cooper, USA, Commanding Battery B, First Pennsylvania Artillery, Artillery Brigade, First Corps, Army of the Potomac

At about sunset in the evening [of July 1], having refilled the ammunition chests, the battery was placed in position, by order of Colonel Wainwright, on the crest of the hill in rear of Gettysburg, and fronting to the northeast. The battery remained in this position without firing until 9.30 a.m., July 2, when occasional shots were fired at small bodies of the enemy's infantry and cavalry which were maneuvering in the skirts of timber from 1 mile to 1¼ miles distant until 4 p.m., when the enemy brought a number of 10 and 20 pounder Parrott guns into position in the open field about 1,400 and 2,000 yards distant, and opened a vigorous fire upon the position. To this fire the battery replied, and, with the assistance of a battery on its left [Wiedrich's Battery I, First New York Artillery], Reynolds' [Battery L, First New York Artillery] and Stevens' [Fifth Maine Battery] batteries on the right, the enemy's guns were silenced in about two and a half hours firing. The battery fired occasional shots into the position of these batteries until about 7 p.m., when it was relieved by Captain Ricketts' battery, and ordered by Colonel Wainwright to report to General Tyler, commanding Artillery Reserve, to refit and fill ammunition chests, one gun having been dismounted late in this day's engagement.

The casualties of this day's engagement were: Private J. H. McCleary, killed; Private P. G. Hoagland, killed; Private Jesse Temple, wounded severely; Private J. C. Cornelius, wounded slightly; Private D. W. Taylor, wounded slightly; Corpl. Joseph Reed, wounded slightly: 1 horse killed, 2 horses disabled. About 500 rounds of ammunition were expended. [*OR* 27, pt.1, p. 365]

Cooper had one gun disabled on July 1. With the disabling of a second gun on July 2, his battery was down to 50 percent in firepower. Wainwright ordered the battery to the Artillery Reserve park, beside Granite School House Lane, to refit and resupply. On July 3 Cooper's battery reinforced the artillery on Cemetery Ridge.

Again face right, and walk for 50 yards to the guns representing Battery L, First New York Artillery. When you reach that location, stop, and face left so you are looking back to the northeast.

Position C—Battery L, First New York Artillery (Breck's)

You are now standing at the position of Battery L, First New York Artillery. This is the battery mentioned by Cooper as being on his right. Captain Gilbert A. Reynolds was wounded on July 1, and Lieutenant George Breck commanded the battery's remaining four 3-inch rifles during this and subsequent actions.

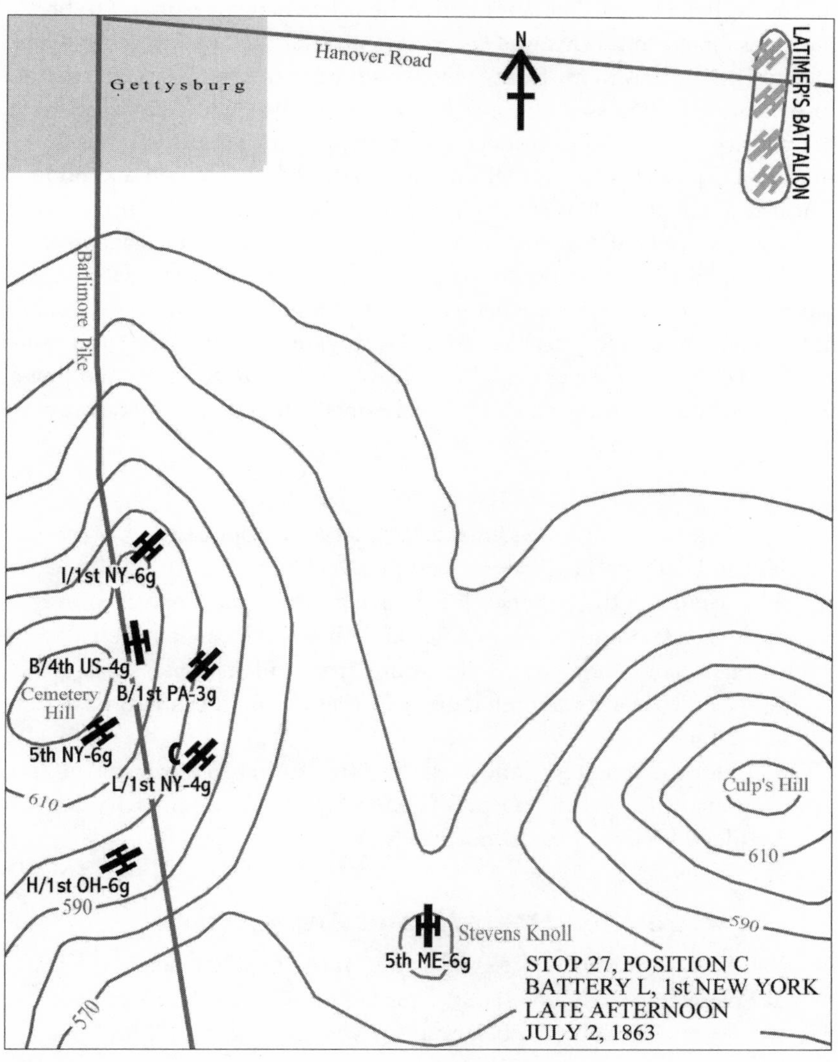

Report of Lieut. George Breck, USA, Commanding Battery L, First New York Artillery, Artillery Brigade, First Corps, Army of the Potomac

I took position with the remaining pieces of the battery to the front and right of the cemetery gate, which position, by order of Colonel Wainwright, I caused to be intrenched, and held during the two following days of the battle. In the position last assumed, my command was the third battery to the right of the right angle formed by our line of artillery near the town. With the exception of picket firing, a general quiet was maintained along the lines on the 2d instant, until about 4 p.m., when the enemy attempted to break our lines on the left. [This was *Longstreet's* attack.] At the same time, a line of batteries directly in my front opened a simultaneous and very severe fire, to which we replied steadily, and before dusk succeeded in silencing most of their fire. This action continued about [two] hours, almost without intermission. The battery to the right of our front, and situated on a knoll in a wheat-field about 1,800 yards distant, upon which I principally directed my fire, was silenced and forced to retire in the early part of the engagement.

In this action the axle of one of my guns was broken, disabling the piece, in consequence of which it was sent to the Artillery Reserve, by order of Colonel Wainwright, to be repaired. During the cannonade, an ammunition chest of one of my caisson limbers was struck by a shell, exploding a few rounds of ammunition, which it contained, and completely destroying it. [*OR* 27, pt. 1, p. 363]

As a result of the concentrated artillery fire from East Cemetery Hill and Culp's Hill, *Andrews's* Battalion had ten men killed, thirty-four wounded, thirty horses killed, one gun damaged, one caisson exploded, and one caisson damaged. While withdrawing the battalion, Major *Latimer* received a wound from which he later died.

You will have the opportunity to visit the Benner's Hill position later.

Retrace you steps, and walk back north for 75 yards to the monument for Batteries F and G (Combined), First Pennsylvania Artillery. Face back to the northeast.

Position D—*Hays* and *Avery* Attack

You have now returned to the center of the artillery position on East Cemetery Hill. The six 3-inch rifles of Captain Ricketts's Batteries F and G (Combined), First Pennsylvania Artillery, Third Volunteer Artillery Brigade, Artillery Reserve, were at this location. Ricketts's battery was positioned here to relieve Cooper's Battery B, First Pennsylvania Artillery, which was sent to the rear to refit and resupply. Although Wainwright had two guns disabled and the two remaining guns of Cooper's battery withdrawn, with the arrival of Ricketts's six guns, he had increased his strength by two more guns than he had earlier. Ricketts arrived in time to participate in

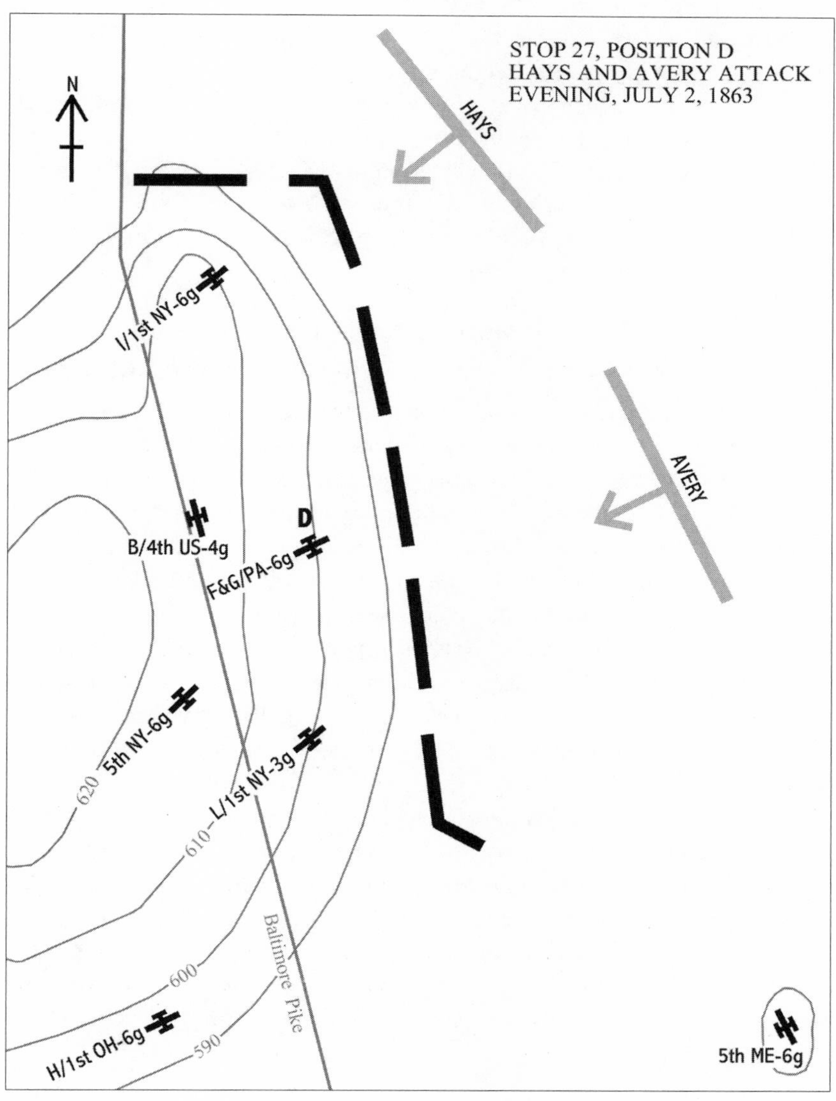

the last part of the artillery duel, which was shortly followed by an infantry assault.

Located directly below you at the base of the hill were the remains of six regiments of the First Division, Eleventh Corps. Two other regiments were positioned at a right angle to them and covered that part of the hill to your left.

Ewell not only employed an artillery battalion against the Union right; he followed up with two infantry assaults. Major General *Edward Johnson's* division was sent against Culp's Hill. This attack was too late to prevent Meade from shifting troops from there to reinforce the south center sector of his defenses. Although stripped of a majority of the forces on Culp's Hill, the remaining defenders were successful in limiting *Johnson's* success. *Ewell's* other attack was made against this location by two brigades from Major General *Jubal A. Early's* division. These two brigades came across the open ground in front of you and up against this position.

Report of Maj. Gen. *Jubal A. Early,* CSA, Commanding *Early's* Division, *Ewell's* Corps, Army of Northern Virginia

The fire from the artillery having opened on the right and left at 4 o'clock, and continued for some time, I was ordered by General *Ewell* to advance upon Cemetery Hill with my two brigades that were in position as soon as General *Johnson's* division, which was on my left, should become engaged at the wooded hill [Culp's Hill] on the left, which it was about to attack, information being given me that the advance would be general, and made also by *Rodes'* division and *Hill's* divisions on my right.

Accordingly, as soon as *Johnson* became warmly engaged, which was a little before dusk, I ordered *Hays* and *Avery* to advance and carry the works on the heights in front. These troops advanced in gallant style to the attack, passing over the ridge in front of them under a heavy artillery fire, and then crossing a hollow between that and Cemetery Hill, and moving up this hill in the face of at least two lines of infantry posted behind stone and plank fences; but these they drove back, and, passing over all obstacles, they reached the crest of the hill, and entered the enemy's breastworks crowning it, getting possession of one or two batteries. But no attack was made on the immediate right, as was expected, and not meeting with support from that quarter, these brigades could not hold the position they had attained, because a very heavy force of the enemy was turned against them from that part of the line which the divisions on the right were to have attacked, and these two brigades had, therefore, to fall back. [*OR* 27, pt. 2, p. 470]

Again Colonel Wainwright provides an overview of the fighting here.

Report of Col. Charles S. Wainwright, USA—continued

About dusk they again opened from a knoll on our left and front, distant 1,800 yards, which fire was followed by a strong attack upon our position. As their column filed out of the town they came under the fire of the Fifth Maine Battery [on Stevens Knoll] at about 800 yards. Wheeling into line, they swung around, their right resting on the town, and pushed up the hill, which is quite steep at this corner. As their line became fully unmasked, all the guns which could be brought to bear were opened on them, at first with shrapnel and afterward with canister, making a total of fifteen guns in their front and six on their left flank. Their center and left never mounted the hill at all, but their right worked its way up under cover of the houses, and pushed completely through Wiedrich's battery into Ricketts'. The cannoneers of both these batteries stood well to their guns, driving the enemy off with fence-rails and stones and capturing a few prisoners. [*OR* 27, pt. 1, p. 358]

Wiedrich's six 3-inch rifles, Ricketts's six 3-inch rifles, and Breck's three 3-inch rifles at this position and Whittier's six Napoleons on Stevens Knoll fired into the attacking Confederate infantry. Stewart's, Taft's, and Norton's batteries, because of the steep drop in the hill's elevation, were unable to fire at the attackers as they closed with the defenders. However, if the Confederate infantry had been able to hold their gains on East Cemetery Hill, they would have been confronted by these guns when Wiedrich's, Ricketts's, and Breck's gunners had fallen back across the Baltimore Pike.

Face left, and walk for 40 yards to the monument to Battery I, First New York Artillery. Stop at the monument, and face right.

Position E—The Artillery Is Overrun

You are at the position of Captains Michael Wiedrich's Battery I, First New York Artillery. The battery's six 3-inch rifles were the left of Wainwright's artillery line. Earlier in the day they had participated

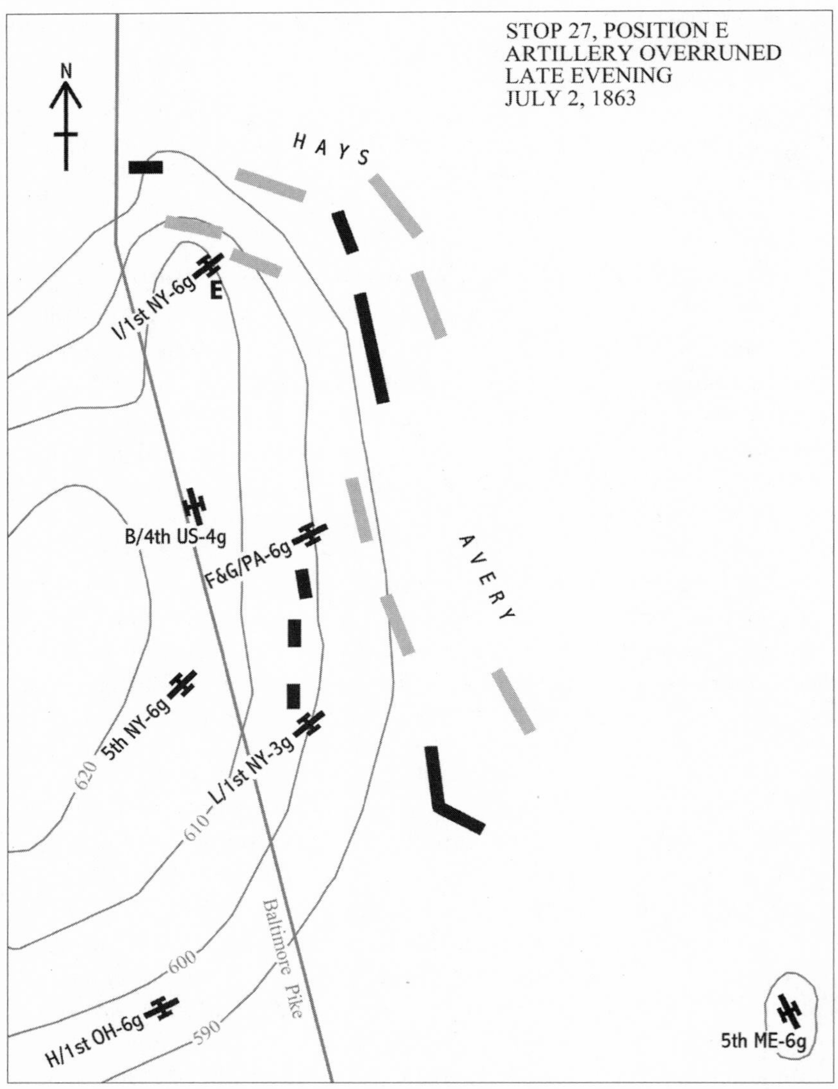

in the duel with *Latimer's* artillery. Now, in the early evening, they were the objective of the right of the Confederate infantry attack.

To their left were deployed two infantry regiments, which faced north, and below them was the left of the infantry line that ran along the base of the hill. Brigadier General *Harry T. Hays's* brigade attacked this portion of the hill.

Report of Brig. Gen. *Harry T. Hays,* CSA, Commanding *Hays's* Brigade, *Early's* Division, *Ewell's* Corps, Army of Northern Virginia

A little before 8 p.m. I was ordered to advance with my own and *Hoke's* [*Avery's*] brigade on my left, which had been placed for the time under my command. I immediately moved forward, and had gone but a short distance when my whole line became exposed to a most terrific fire from the enemy's batteries from the entire range of hills in front, and to the right and left; still, both brigades advanced steadily up and over the first hill, and into a bottom at the foot of Cemetery Hill.

Here we came upon a considerable body of the enemy, and a brisk musketry fire ensued; at the same time his artillery, of which we were now within canister range, opened upon us, but owing to the darkness of the evening, now verging into night, and the deep obscurity afforded by the smoke of the firing, our exact locality could not be discovered by the enemy's gunners, and we thus escaped what in the full light of day could have been nothing else than horrible slaughter.

Taking advantage of this, we continued to move forward until we reached the second line, behind a stonewall at the foot of a fortified hill. We passed such of the enemy who had not fled, and who were still clinging for shelter to the wall, to the rear, as prisoners. Still advancing, we came upon an abatis of fallen timber and the third line, disposed in rifle-pits. This line we broke, and, as before, found many of the enemy who had not fled hiding in the pits for protection. These I ordered to the rear as prisoners, and continued my progress to the crest of the hill.

Arriving at the summit, by a simultaneous rush from my whole line, I captured several pieces of artillery and a number of prisoners. At that time every piece of artillery which had been firing upon us was silenced. [*OR* 27, pt. 2, p. 480]

The right part of *Hays's* Brigade had struck Wiedrich's battery. In hand-to-hand fighting, it drove many of the cannoneers from their guns.

Report of Captain Michael Wiedrich, USA, Commanding Battery I, First New York Artillery, Artillery Brigade, Eleventh Corps, Army of the Potomac

About 8 p.m. the enemy charged on the battery with a brigade of infantry, which succeeded in turning our infantry, and got into the intrenchments of my battery. After they were repulsed by our forces, I opened on them again with canister with good effect. [*OR* 27, pt. 1, p. 752]

Face right, and walk 25 yards back to the cannon barrel pointed up and set in stone.

Position F—*Hays* and *Avery* Are Stopped

Overrunning the infantry supporting Wiedrich's battery and then the battery itself caused a penetration of the defensive position. *Hays's* infantry continued moving forward and struck the left of Ricketts's battery.

Report of Capt. R. Bruce Ricketts, USA, Commanding Batteries F and G (Combined), First Pennsylvania Artillery, Third Volunteer Artillery Brigade, Artillery Reserve, Army of the Potomac

At about 8 p.m. a heavy column of the enemy charged on my battery, and succeeded in capturing and spiking my left piece. The cannoneers fought them hand to hand with handspikes, rammers, and pistols, and succeeded in checking them for a moment, when a part of the Second Army Corps charged in and drove them back. During the charge I expended every round of canister in the battery, and then fired case shot without the fuses. [*OR* 27, pt. 1, p. 894]

Hays's penetration reached this far, was halted, and was repulsed with assistance of infantry reinforcements from the Second Corps.

Report of Brig. Gen. *Harry T. Hays,* CSA—Continued

A quiet of several minutes now ensued. Their heavy masses of infantry were heard and perfectly discerned through the increasing darkness, advancing in the direction of my position. Approaching within 100 yards, a line was discovered before us, from the whole length of which a simultaneous fire was delivered. I reserved my fire, from the uncertainty of this being a force of the enemy or of our men, as I had been cautioned to expect friends both in front, to the right, and to the left, Lieutenant-General *Longstreet,* Major-General *Rodes,* and Major-General *Johnson,* respectively, having been assigned to these relative positions; but after the delivery of a second and

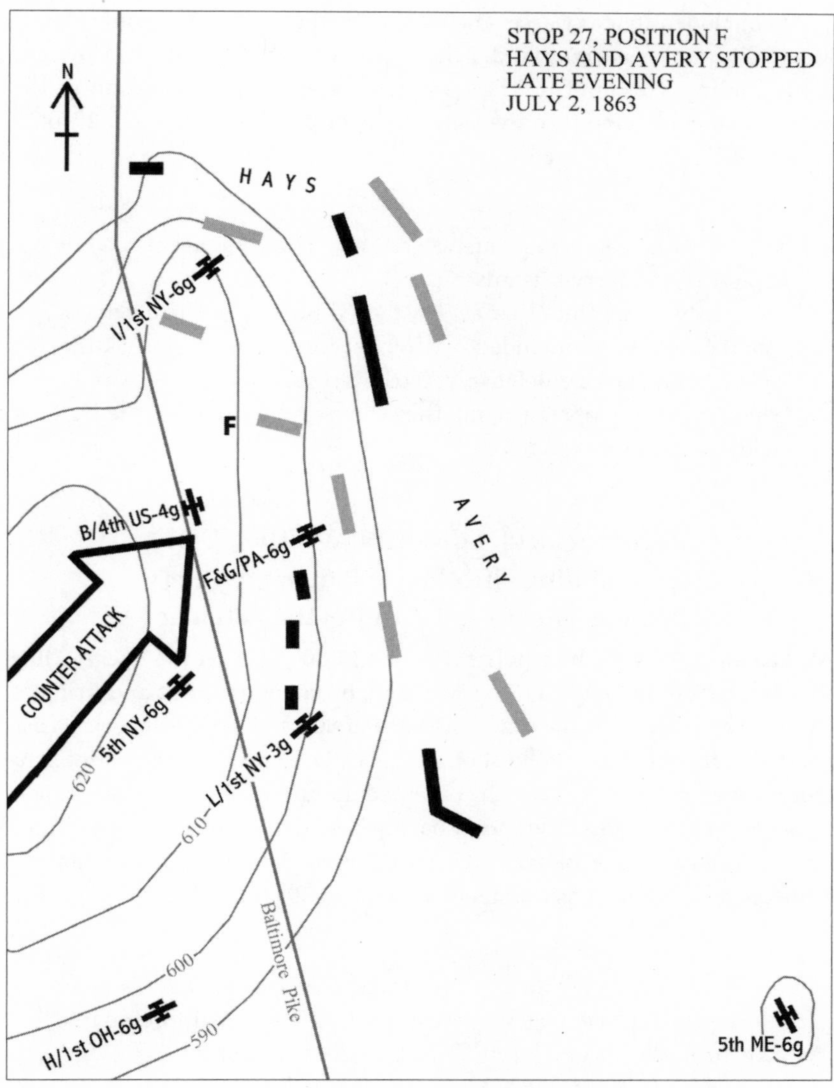

third volley, the flashing of the musketry disclosed the still-advancing line to be one of the enemy.

I then gave the order to fire; the enemy was checked for a time, but discovering another line moving up in rear of this one, and still another force in rear of that, and being beyond the reach of support, I gave the order to retire to the stone wall at the foot of the hill, which was quietly and orderly effected. From this position I subsequently fell back to a fence some 75 yards distant from the wall, and awaited the further movements of the enemy.

I concluded that any assistance would be too late, and my only course was to withdraw my command. I therefore moved my brigade by the right flank, leading it around the hill, so as to escape the observation of the enemy, and conducted it to the right of my original position. [*OR* 27, pt. 2 pp. 480–81]

Hays's losses during this attack were twenty-one killed, 119 wounded, and forty-one missing.

At the same time that *Hays* attacked the left of the defenses, *Hoke's* Brigade, commanded by Colonel *Isaac E. Avery,* struck the right portion of the defenses. As the brigade conducted a right wheel across the open ground, they came under fire from the Napoleons on Stevens's Knoll.

Report of Lieut. Edward N. Whittier, USA, Commanding Fifth Maine Battery, Artillery Brigade, First Corps, Army of the Potomac

At dusk opened with the whole battery at 1,200 yards on the enemy's line advancing from the edge of the town, and, by changing front and firing to the left, enfiladed their lines, at a distance of 800 yards, with spherical case and shell, and later with solid shot and canister, expending the entire contents of the limber chests, which contained upward of 46 rounds of canister repacked from caissons. The enemy having been driven back and the ammunition exhausted, the battery was withdrawn, the caissons and limbers refilled, and the same position reoccupied at 10.30 p.m. [*OR* 27, pt. 1, p. 361]

Avery was killed during the attack; his brigade attack stalled and was then driven back by a counterattack by a reinforcing brigade from the Second Corps. This brought the fight for East Cemetery Hill to an end.

Once again Cemetery Hill had become the focus of *Lee's* tactical operations. Had his overall attack plan been successful, *Longstreet's* divisions supported by *Hill's* Corps would have attacked northeast along the Emmitsburg Road, collapsed the Union defensive position, and gained the northern part of Cemetery Ridge and maybe West Cemetery Hill. As we know, *Longstreet's* part of the plan was flawed from its conception, and a flanking attack up the Emmitsburg Road did not occur.

Eastern face of East Cemetery Hill as seen from the position of the 5th Maine Battery on Steven's Knoll. Attacking Confederates were subjected to enfilading fire from this position.

To support *Longstreet's* attack, *Ewell* had been given the mission of conducting a demonstration against East Cemetery Hill and Culp's Hill and at his discretion making an actual attack against the Union positions at those two locations. *Ewell* began his demonstration with five batteries, twenty guns, under command of Major *Latimer* deployed on Benner's Hill and firing on East Cemetery Hill. Against this artillery Colonel Wainwright initially had five batteries, with twenty-three guns, was reinforced with a sixth battery of six guns, was supported by two additional batteries, with twelve guns, immediately behind him, and if necessary could call on the support of the Eleventh Corps artillery on West Cemetery Hill. In addition there were five guns from the Twelfth Corps artillery on Culp's Hill that participated in the fight. Outgunned and on an inferior position, the Confederate artillery was eventually forced to withdraw.

After the artillery duel, *Ewell* committed his infantry to an attack on Culp's Hill and East Cemetery Hill. Two Confederate infantry brigades attacked the Union infantry and artillery on East Cemetery Hill. Elements of the attacking infantry were able to penetrate the defenses and overrun some of the artillery and infantry. The other defenders and a reinforcing infantry brigade halted this penetration. This attack was the closest *Lee's* forces came to capturing Cemetery Hill. Although the attack was defeated, for a brief time the supporting attacks had the potential of accomplishing the mission of the main attack.

Return to your car for the drive to Benner's Hill or to Stop 28 on Seminary Ridge.

If you wish to visit the Confederate position on Benner's Hill, turn to appendix VI and follow the instructions. If not, follow the instructions in the next paragraph, which take you back to Seminary Ridge for the third day's action.

Depart East Cemetery Hill by drive northwest on the Baltimore Pike into Gettysburg. In 0.2 mile from the top of Cemetery Hill, the road will make a half turn to the right and become Baltimore Street. Continue north to the intersection with Middle Street. Make a left turn on Middle Street, and drive west for 0.6 mile to the intersection with West Confederate Avenue, which is on Seminary Ridge. Once you leave Gettysburg, Middle Street becomes the Hagerstown Road. You will see the Lutheran Seminary on your right front as you approach Seminary Ridge. At the intersection with West Confederate Avenue, turn left and drive for 1.1 miles to the Virginia State Monument. Park in the area provided or along the side of the road, leave your car, and walk east for 250 yards on the walking path that goes past the monument and on to a rise of ground. As you walk east on the path, there will be a woods to your right. When you reach the rise of ground, stand so that you are facing east.

Chapter 4

FRIDAY, JULY 3, 1863

Stop 28, Position A—*Lee* Continues to Attack

As darkness fell on the night of July 2, *Lee* must have felt that victory was almost within his grasp. He could look back on the events of the day and attribute the failure of his army to have won the battle to a lack of coordinated action by all of his corps.

Lee was faced with the three tactical options available to any commander. He could attack, defend, or move away from the enemy. *Lee* did not believe he could remain static in a defensive position. He was concerned about supplying his army while east of South Mountain, he worried that a Union force might occupy a position between him and the mountain passes, and he realized that Meade could probably outwait him if he went on the defense. To move away from Meade, in other words, to retreat, would be to give up one of the major objectives of the campaign. *Lee* had brought the Army of Northern Virginia north in order to defeat the Army of the Potomac on northern soil. To move away now would be to give that up. Therefore, as *Lee* saw it, he was left with only one option: attack. The only question that remained was where?

Report of Gen. *Robert E. Lee,* CSA, Commanding Army of Northern Virginia

The result of [July 2] operations induced the belief that, with proper concert of action, and with the increased support that the positions gained on the right would enable the artillery to render the assaulting columns, we should ultimately succeed, and it was accordingly determined to continue the attack. The general plan was unchanged. *Longstreet,* re-enforced by *Pickett's* three brigades, which arrived near the battlefield during the afternoon of the 2d, was ordered to attack the next morning, and General *Ewell* was directed to assail the enemy's right [on Culp's Hill] at the same time.

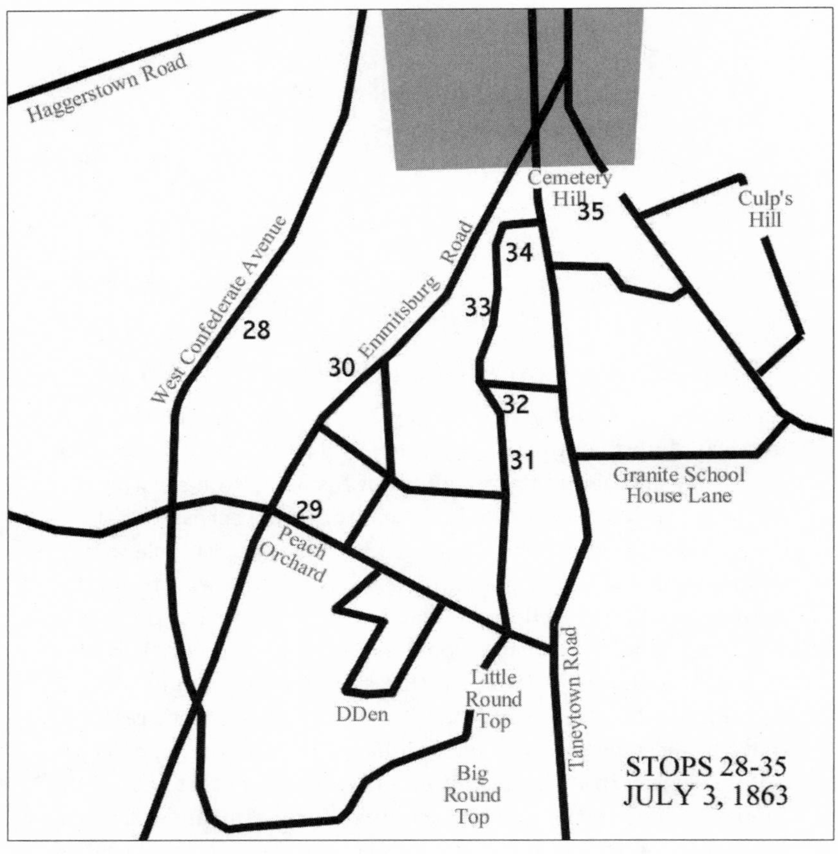

The latter, during the night, re-enforced General *Johnson* with two brigades from *Rodes'* and one from *Early's* division. [*OR* 27, pt. 2, p. 320]

Early on the morning of July 3, *Lee* rode to the southern part of his line, near the Peach Orchard, to confer with *Longstreet.* During this meeting *Longstreet* informed *Lee* that *McLaws's* and *Hood's* Divisions had taken so many casualties on the previous day that they did not have the strength to attack. Not only could they not attack, if counterattacked, he was not sure of being able to hold the ground they had gained. *Longstreet* also pointed out that if he continued his attack toward the northeast, he would be leaving a large Union force behind him that might come down off the Round Tops and attack him in the rear. *Lee* conceded to *Longstreet's* points and canceled his initial plan. However, by then *Johnson's* reinforced division of *Ewell's* Corps was already decisively committed to a battle for Culp's Hill. By the time *Lee* had formulated his second plan for July 3, *Johnson's* force was fought out and could not be included in any immediate future attack.

With his initial plan falling apart, *Lee's* options as to where to attack were severely limited. He had already planned for and canceled an attack on the left part of the Union line because of the condition of *Longstreet's* force. *Johnson's* attack on the right of the Union line had been conducted and repulsed. Had *Lee* been able to cancel this attack, it might have been an option for the main attack if properly reinforced. At the least, it could serve to support his main attack. However, none of these options were available to him, and time constraints prevented major redeployment of divisions along the Confederate position unless *Lee* was prepared to attack very late in the afternoon. These parameters limited *Lee's* option to an attack in the center. His tactical objective was to break the Union center, as represented by the "Copse of Trees."

Report of Gen. *Robert E. Lee,* CSA—Continued

General *Longstreet's* dispositions were not completed as early as was expected, but before notice could be sent to General *Ewell,* General *Johnson* had already become engaged, and it was too late to recall him.

A force occupying the high, rocky hills on the enemy's extreme left, from which his troops could be attacked in reverse as they advanced, delayed General *Longstreet.* His operations had been embarrassed the day previous by the same cause, and he now deemed it necessary to defend his flank and rear with the divisions of *Hood* and *McLaws.* He was, therefore, re-enforced by *Heth's* division and two brigades of *Pender's,* to the command of which Major-General *Trimble* was assigned. General *Hill* was directed to hold his line with the rest of his command, afford General *Longstreet* further assistance, if required, and avail himself of any success that might be gained. [*OR* 27, pt. 2, p. 320]

As he moved to various locations, *Lee* made his decision to attack in the center. Initially he was at the Peach Orchard when *Longstreet* informed him he could not carry out the original plan. From there he came back toward your present location along a route that allowed him to study Meade's defenses. He probably issued the attack order to *Longstreet* on the ground to your right and observed the attack from this vicinity.

Eleven hundred yards directly in front of you is the "Copse of Trees" and "The Angle" on Cemetery Ridge. To the left of these two features, where the ground rises to form Cemetery Hill, is Ziegler's Grove. These were the terrain objectives of the attack on July 3. Slightly to the right along the Emmitsburg Road and 900 yards from where you are is the red Codori Barn. Look to your right, and you will see the Spangler House 650 yards from your location. Beyond the Spangler House is the Sherfy House. Beyond the Sherfy House and just across the Emmitsburg Road is the Peach Orchard. The Peach Orchard is 1,400 yards (0.8 mile) from your location.

Beginning at the Peach Orchard and coming in your direction was the artillery of *Longstreet's* Corps. *Longstreet* had sixty-five guns deployed from the Peach Orchard northward for 1,350 yards to almost where you are now. The low ground and woods to your right and right rear was where *Pickett's* Division formed for the attack.

Sixty-eight guns from *Hill's* Corps were deployed left of your position, along West Confederate Avenue. To your left also was where Brigadier General *J. Johnston Pettigrew,* temporarily commanding *Heth's* Division, and Major General *Isaac R. Trimble,* temporarily commanding *Pender's* Division, formed their infantry for the attack.

Report of Gen. *Robert E. Lee,* CSA—Continued

A careful examination was made of the ground secured by *Longstreet,* and his batteries placed in positions, which, it was believed, would enable them to silence those of the enemy. *Hill's* artillery and part of *Ewell's* was ordered to open simultaneously, and the assaulting column to advance under cover of the combined fire of the three. The batteries were directed to be pushed forward as the infantry progressed, protect their flanks, and support their attacks closely. [*OR* 27, pt. 2, p. 320]

Lee's chief of artillery, Brigadier General *William N. Pendleton,* provided an overview of the Confederate artillery deployment on July 3.

Report of Brig. Gen. *William N. Pendleton,* CSA, Chief of Artillery, Army of Northern Virginia

Brigadier General *William N. Pendleton,* CSA. Jennings C. Wise, *The Long Arm of Lee* (1915).

By direction of the commanding general, the artillery along our entire line was to be prepared for opening, as early as possible on the morning of the 3d, a concentrated and destructive fire, consequent upon which a general advance was to be made. The right, especially, was, if practicable, to sweep the enemy from his stronghold on that flank. Visiting the lines at a very early hour toward securing readiness for this great attempt, I found much (by Colonel *Alexander's* energy) already accomplished on the right. *Henry's* battalion held about its original position on the flank. [Part of *Cabell's* battalion was] in front of the peach orchard. *Alexander's* was next then came the Washington Artillery Battalion, under Major *Eshleman,* and *Dearing's* battalion on his left, these two having arrived since dusk of the day before; and beyond *Dearing,* [part of] *Cabell's* battalion had been arranged, making nearly sixty-five guns for that wing, all well advanced in a sweeping curve of about [three-fourths] mile. In the posting of these there appeared little room for improvement, so judiciously had they been adjusted. To Colonel *Alexander,* placed here in charge by General *Longstreet,* the wishes of the commanding general were repeated. The battalion and battery commanders were also cautioned how to fire so as to waste as little ammunition as possible. To [*Hill's*] Corps artillery attention was also given. Major *Poague's* battalion had been advanced to the line of the right wing, and was not far from its left. His guns also were well posted. Proper directions were also given to him and his officers. The other battalions of this corps [*Pegram's, Lane's, McIntosh's,* and], a portion of *Garnett's,* under Major *Charles Richardson,* being in reserve, held their positions of the day before, as did those of [*Ewell's*] Corps, each group having specific instructions from its chief. Care was also given to the convenient posting of ordnance trains, especially for the right, as most distant from the main depot, and due notice given of their position. [*OR* 27, pt. 2, pp. 351–52]

The right of the *Hill's* Corps artillery position began to your left rear on this side of West Confederate Avenue. From there it went north, generally along the trace of West Confederate Avenue to the Hagerstown Road. It began with the four batteries (sixteen guns) of *Pogue's* Battalion and continued north in the order of two batteries (eleven guns) of *Lane's* Battalion, five batteries (twenty guns) of *Pegram's* Battalion, the nine rifled guns of *Garnett's* Battalion, two and one half batteries (ten guns) of *Dance's* Battalion from *Ewell's* Corps, and then three batteries (twelve guns) of *McIntosh's* Battalion. Farther north on Oak Hill were the two Whitworth rifles from *McIntosh's* Battalion. All total counting *Dance's* guns and the two Whitworths, eighty guns were in position.

The target area for *Hill's* guns was Meade's defensive position from the "Copse of Trees" to Ziegler's Grove. All of this target area was with in effective range of the majority of *Hill's* artillery.

In addition, thirty-four more guns from the *Ewell's* Corps were in position to support the attack. On Seminary Ridge north of the Hagerstown Road, there were three batteries (ten guns) from *Carter's* Battalion and one and one-half batteries (six guns) from *Dance's* Battalion. East of Gettysburg, along the north-running ridge from Benner's Hill, were positioned three batteries (twelve guns) from *Nelson's* Battalion, two guns from *Andrews's* Battalion, and the four remaining guns from *Dance's* Battalion.

Ewell's artillery was in the often-sought and highly prized position to place cross fire and enfilading fire on the Union artillery on Cemetery Hill. In addition the infantry and artillery on Cemetery Ridge north of the "Copse of Trees" were vulnerable to enfilading fire from some of *Ewell's* artillery. However, as you will see later, this advantage was not used to the maximum.

Eight hundred yards to your left front and midway between the Emmitsburg Road and today's West Confederate Avenue was the Bliss farmhouse and barn. These two buildings and the surrounding terrain offered a tactical advantage to whichever side held them. From there each opponent was offered an excellent observation post into the other's central positions from which they could report movements and give early warning of an attack. The relative low ground in proximity to these buildings also offered protected locations to assemble an attacking force closer to the other's defenses. Major General *Isaac R. Trimble,* who commanded *Pender's* Division during the attack, commented afterward that, if

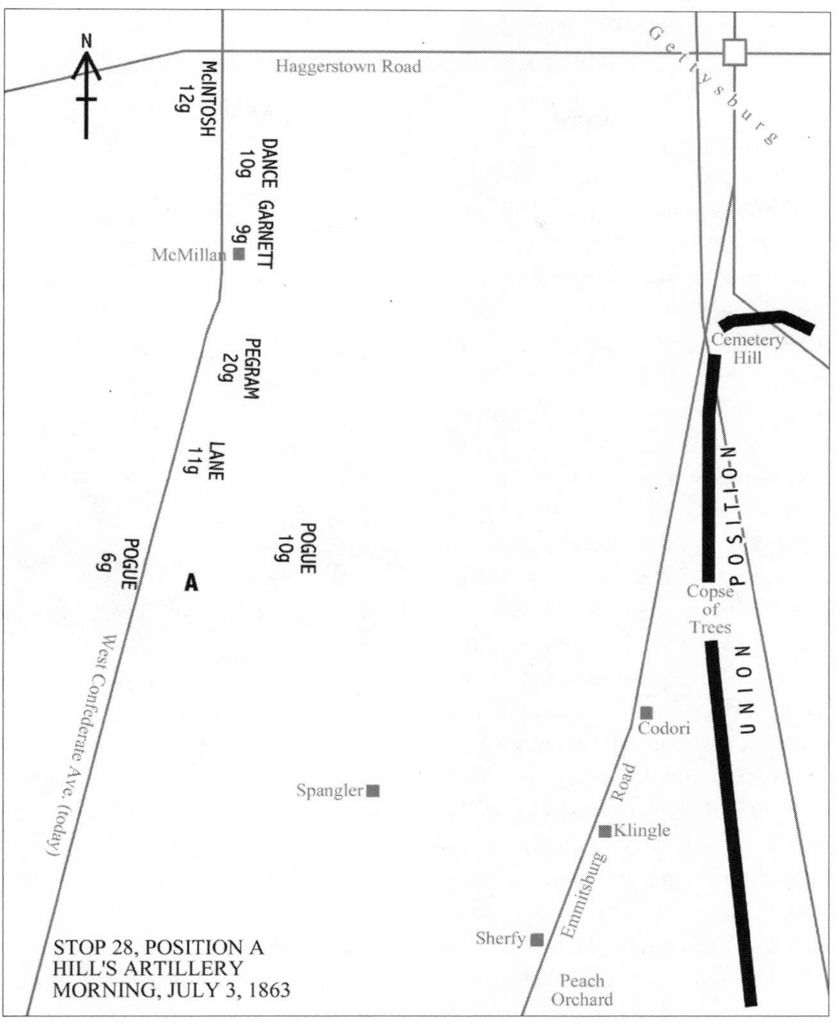

his troops had been moved forward to that area during darkness and attacked at first light, they would have had much less open area to cross and would have had more combat power as they approached the Union defenses.

On the morning of July 3, there were actions and counteractions by both sides to control the Bliss house and barn. Batteries from each side supported these actions. The buildings changed hands several times, but when the Union infantry fell back from the position in late morning, both the house and barn were burned.

Report of Maj. *William T. Poague*, CSA, Commanding *Poague's* Artillery Battalion, *Hill's* Corps, Army of Northern Virginia

Late in the evening of the 2d [July] I reported to Major-General *Anderson* for duty, and at last succeeded in getting ten of my guns into position. The balance (six howitzers) were kept a short distance in rear, as no place could be found from which they could be used with advantage. Of the ten guns in position, three rifles and two Napoleons were posted on the left of *Anderson's* division, and not far from *Pegram's* battalion, and on the right of these and in front of *Anderson's* left, at the distance of 400 yards, five Napoleons were placed. These positions, separated by a body of timber, were about 1,400 yards from the enemy's batteries, strongly posted on an eminence. Immediately on my right were the batteries of [*Longstreet's*] Corps. My battalion being necessarily separated, that part of it next to *Pegram's* position, consisting of three of *Wyatt's* and two of *Graham's* guns, was placed in charge of Captain [*James W.*] *Wyatt,* while Captain [*George*] *Ward* was directed to superintend the guns of his own and of *Brooke's* battery.

Major *William T. Poague,* CSA. Jennings C. Wise, *The Long Arm of Lee* (1915).

About 7 o'clock on the morning of the 3d, while I myself was at the position occupied by Captain *Ward,* the guns under Captain *Wyatt* opened on the enemy's position. In a few minutes, the fire of several of their batteries was concentrated on these five guns, and seeing that the contest was a very unequal one, and not knowing the origin of the order for opening, I directed the firing to cease. In this affair, Captain *Wyatt* lost 8 of his best horses. A caisson of the enemy was exploded.

In the general engagement that occurred about the middle of the day, the battalion participated. Upon the repulse of our troops, anticipating an advance of the enemy, I ordered up the howitzers. The enemy, however, failed to follow up his advantage, and I got no service out of those useless guns. [*OR* 27, pt. 2, pp. 673–74]

Find an opening in the fence to your right, and walk southeast for 30 yards. Stop at the last gun on the right, and face left toward Cemetery Ridge, the direction the guns are pointed.

Position B—*Longstreet's* Artillery

Look to your right. On a line between the Spangler House and the Sherfy House, which is farther on, you can see the plateau of

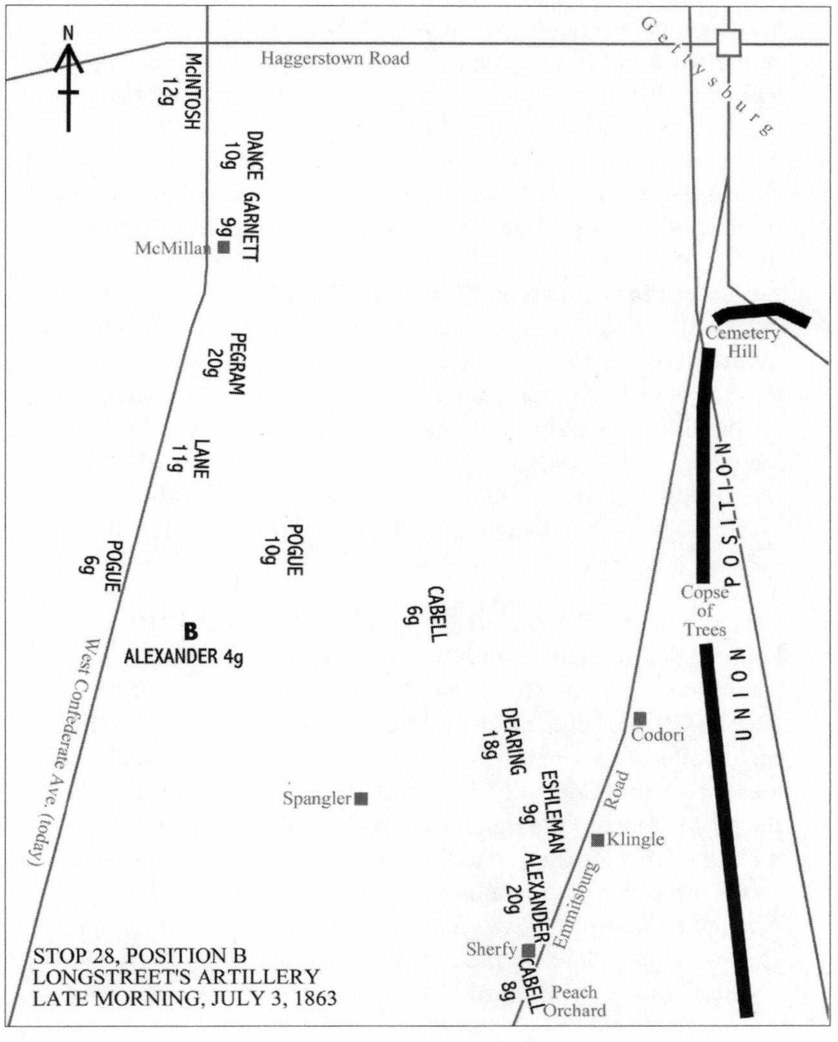

ground where the Peach Orchard is located. The Peach Orchard is 1,370 yards from your location.

Placed from your right to the Peach Orchard were sixty-five of the eighty-seven available guns of *Longstreet's* Corps artillery. The line of guns went along the open ridges to your front and right to the Emmitsburg Road, then south along the road, and across it to the plateau where the Peach Orchard is. From your present location *Longstreet's* artillery was deployed as follows: directly in front of you was one and one-half batteries (six guns) of *Cabell's* Battalion; one battery (four guns) of *Alexander's* Battalion was where you are; the four batteries (eighteen guns) of *Dearing's* Battalion were to your right front; and to *Dearing's* right in order were three batteries (nine guns) of *Eshleman's* battalion, five batteries (twenty guns) of *Alexander's* Battalion, and the other two and one-half batteries (eight guns) of *Cabell's* Battalion. South of the Peach Orchard was *Henry's* Battalion. All total *Lee* had 179 guns that could potentially support his infantry attack by direct fire on the objective or divert the fire of the defending artillery.

Return to your car for the drive to Stop 29.

Continue to drive south on West Confederate Avenue for 0.9 mile to the intersection with the Millerstown Road. At the intersection turn left, and drive east for 0.4 mile to the small parking area for the Peach Orchard. In doing this, you will cross the Emmitsburg Road. Park, leave your car, and walk back west 90 yards beside the road to its highest point. Stand beside the Sixty-eighth Pennsylvania Monument, and look northeast toward Cemetery Hill.

Stop 29—The Right of the Artillery Line

Find the tall monument with the dome on top that is 1,500 yards from your location. This is the Pennsylvania State Monument. Now look to the left of the Pennsylvania State Monument, and find the U.S. Regulars Monument (it looks like the Washington Monument), then the "Copse of Trees" a little farther to the left. This and the position just to the right of the Pennsylvania Monument were the target area for the Confederate artillery located here and just on the other side of the Emmitsburg Road.

Eight guns from *Cabell's* Battalion were in this vicinity. *Cabell's* guns were positioned on the northern edge of the Peach Orchard and near the red Sherfy Barn. They were oriented so as to be able to fire on Cemetery Ridge and Little Round Top, which is 1,600 yards to your right

Across the road and north of the Sherfy Barn was the right of *Alexander's* Battalion. *Alexander's* gun line went north along the west side of Emmitsburg Road for 400 yards to the vicinity of the Klingle House.

Narrative of Col. *E. Porter Alexander,* CSA, Temporarily Commanding Corps Artillery, *Longstreet's* Corps, Army of Northern Virginia

A clump of trees in the enemy's line was pointed out to me as the proposed point of our attack, which I was incorrectly told was the cemetery of the town, and about 9 a.m. I began to revise our artillery line and post it for the cannonade. Of *Longstreet's* [Corps artillery, 65 guns] were posted in an irregular line about 1,300 yards long, beginning in the Peach Orchard and ending near the northeast corner of the Spangler wood.

A few hundred yards to the left and rear of my line began the artillery of *Hill's* [Corps] under Col. *Walker.* It extended on Seminary Ridge as far as the Hagerstown road, and two Whitworth rifles located nearly a mile farther north on the same ridge. [E. Porter Alexander, *Military Memoirs of a Confederate* (New York: Charles Scribner's Sons, 1907), 418–19. Hereafter cited as Alexander, *Military Memoirs,* followed by page numbers.]

Return to your car for the drive to Stop 30.

Continue to drive east on Wheatfield Road for 50 yards to the first park road on your left. This is Sickles Avenue. Turn left on Sickles Avenue, and drive 0.2 mile across the open field to the intersection with another park road. This is United States Avenue. Drive straight through the intersection, and continue driving for another 0.2 mile to the intersection with the Emmitsburg Road. DO NOT drive on to Emmitsburg Road, but park in the small gravel parking area on your right by the statue of Brigadier General Andrew A. Humphreys. To your left across the road is a sign: "The Site of the Rogers House 1863." Get out of your car, be extremely careful of traffic, cross the road, walk through the opening in the fence, turn left, and walk southwest for 200 yards on the trail that parallels the Emmitsburg Road. After walking 200 yards stop and face left.

Stop 30, Position A—*Eshleman's* Battalion

Find the U.S. Regulars Monument (it looks like the Washington Monument) on Cemetery Ridge. It is 1,100 yards from your location. Now look to the right of the U.S. Regulars Monument, and find a tall column monument with a statue on top. This is the Vermont Monument. A statue of Brigadier General George Stannard is on top. It is 900 yards from your location. These two monuments mark the center of the target area for *Eshleman's* guns, which extended out to the left and right of these two monuments to the "Copse of Trees" and the Pennsylvania Monument.

You are at the position of the right most battery of *Eshleman's* Battalion, also called the Washington (Louisiana) Battalion. The battery at this location was Captain *Merritt B. Miller's* Third Company armed with three Napoleons. *Miller* was tasked with firing the two signal guns that commenced the artillery preparatory fire against the Union defenders. To *Miller's* left were Captain *Joseph Norcom's* Fourth Company, temporarily commanded by *Lieutenant H. A. Battles,* with two Napoleons and one 12-pound howitzer, and then Captain *John Richardson's* Second Company with two Napoleons and one 12-pound howitzer. These three batteries, with

View from the right of *Eshleman's* Battalion's position (Stop 30A) to Cemetery Ridge.

nine guns, occupied the ground from where you are to the Roger's House.

To *Eshleman's* right was *Alexander's* Battalion, deployed from left to right: Captain *Osmond B. Taylor's* Virginia Battery, four Napoleons; Lieutenant *S. Capers Gilbert's* Brooks (South Carolina) Artillery Battery, four 12-pound howitzers; Captain *William W. Parker's* Virginia Battery, three 3-inch rifles and one 10-pound Parrott; Captain *George V. Moody's* Madison (Louisiana) Artillery Battery, four 24-pound howitzers; and Captain *Tyler C. Jordan's*

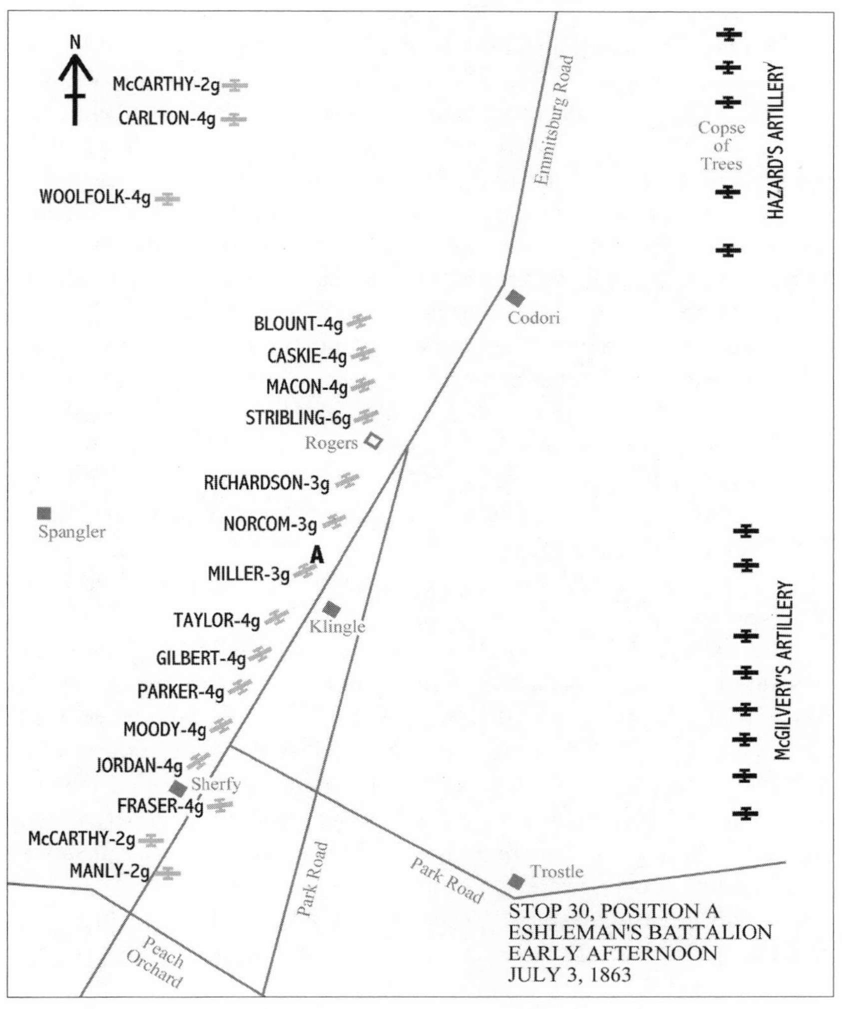

Bedford (Virginia) Artillery Battery, four 3-inch rifles. These batteries were deployed from just to your right for 400 yards to the vicinity of the red Sherfy Barn.

Report of Major *Benjamin F. Eshleman,* CSA, Commanding Washington (Louisiana) Artillery Battalion, *Longstreet's* Corps, Army of Northern Virginia

Between 1 and 2 p.m. [I was] ordered to give the signal for opening along the entire line. Two guns in quick succession were fired from Captain *Miller's* battery, and were immediately followed by all the battalions along the line opening simultaneously upon the enemy behind his works. The enemy answered vigorously, and a most terrific artillery duel ensued. Notwithstanding a most galling fire from the enemy's artillery from behind his works, and an enfilade fire from the mountain [Little Round Top] on my right, my men stood bravely to their work.

About [sixty] minutes after the signal guns had been fired, our infantry moved forward over the plateau in our front. It having been understood by a previous arrangement that the artillery should advance with the infantry, I immediately directed Captain *Miller* to advance his and *Norcom's* batteries. Captain *Miller* having suffered severely from the loss of men and horses, could move forward only three pieces of his own battery and one of *Norcom's* section. He took position 400 or 500 yards to the front, and opened with deadly effect upon the enemy. With the exception of these [four] guns, no others advanced.

Captain *Taylor* [Virginia Battery, *Alexander's* Battalion, with four Napoleons], on my right, and Major *Dearing,* on my left, at this juncture ran out of ammunition and withdrew, leaving my battalion alone to bear the brunt of this portion of the field.

The advanced position of *Miller* and *Norcom's* [Batteries] made them, as soon as the batteries on their flanks had ceased firing, the center of a concentrated fire from several of the enemy's batteries. [This was probably Battery I, First Michigan, Fifteenth New York Battery, and others along McGilvery's position.] Our artillery fire seemed to have slackened upon the whole line, and our infantry, unable to hold the works they had so gallantly taken, were falling back, and being pressed by the enemy, who had advanced from behind his breastworks.

At this juncture, General *Longstreet* ordered that all the artillery that could be spared from the right should be sent to the position just evacuated by Major *Dearing* [on the left of *Eshleman's* Battalion]. Finding my advanced guns were suffering severely, I determined to change their position to that indicated by General *Longstreet.*

This change, however, could not be made, I regret to say, under such a galling fire, without the loss of several of my gallant men, who fell, killed and wounded; among whom was Lieutenant *Brown,* commanding the First Company piece, severely wounded in the abdomen by a Minie ball. Lieutenant *Battles* [*Norcom's* Battery] had both of his pieces disabled—one struck on the face and so badly indurated as to prevent loading, and the other by having the axle broken. Captain *Miller's* loss in horses was so great that he could maneuver but one piece. Three pieces of the [*Miller's*] Third Company and the section of [*Norcom's*] Fourth Company were, therefore, sent to the rear. A [earlier] captured rifle (Captain *Richardson's*), after having fired away all its ammunition, was struck on the axle by a solid shot and disabled, and was also withdrawn.

My casualties were: Wounded, 3 officers. Killed, 3; wounded, 23, and missing, 16, non-commissioned officers and privates; 37 horses killed and disabled; 3 guns disabled; 1 limber blown up. [*OR* 27, pt. 2, pp. 434–36]

Retrace your path back to the site of the Rogers House. When you reach the Rogers House marker, stop, face right, and look across the Emmitsburg Road.

Position B—*Dearing's* Battalion

Again find the U.S. Regulars Monument on Cemetery Ridge and the "Copse of Trees" to its left. The monument is 900 yards and the "Copse of Trees" is 975 yards from your location. This was the center of the target area for the guns that were here and to your left. Union batteries left and right of this center were engaged when they reveled their location by firing.

You are standing in the right of Major *James Dearing's* artillery battalion's position. Captain *Robert M. Stribling's* Fauquier (Virginia) Artillery Battery with four Napoleons and two 20-pound Parrotts was deployed here. To *Stribling's* left was Captain *Miles C. Macon's* Richmond Fayette Artillery Battery with two Napoleons and two 10-pound Parrotts, then Captain *William H. Caskie's* Hampden (Virginia) Artillery Battery with two Napoleons, one 3-inch rifle, and one 10-pound Parrott, and then Captain *Joseph G. Blount's* Virginia Battery of four Napoleons. To *Blount's* left rear was Captain

View from the right of *Dearing's* Battalion's position (Stop 30B) to Cemetery Ridge.

Pichegru Woolfolk's Ashland (Virginia) Battery from *Alexander's* Battalion with two Napoleons and two 20-pound Parrotts. Directly to *Blount's (Dearing's)* left were six guns from *Cabell's* Battalion. They included two 12-pound howitzers and two 10-pound Parrotts from Captain *Henry Carlton's* Troup (Georgia) Artillery Battery and two Napoleons from Captain *Edward S. McCarthy's* First Richmond Howitzers. This was the left flank of *Longstreet's* Corps artillery. The right flank comprised the remaining guns of *Cabell's* Battalion in the vicinity of the Peach Orchard. Farther south of the Peach Orchard was *Henry's* Battalion, which was positioned to protect *Longstreet's* and the army's right flank. *Henry's* guns did not participate in the preparatory artillery bombardment, but five of them were later redeployed so as to support the infantry attack. To the left of *Woolfolk's* battery and behind *Carlton's* and *McCarthy's* batteries was the right of *Hill's* Corps artillery. *Hill's* artillery extended north to the Hagerstown Road.

Having looked at the artillery deployment, look now at the deployment of the Confederate infantry in their preattack positions.

Turn around, and walk west for 20 yards, then stop.

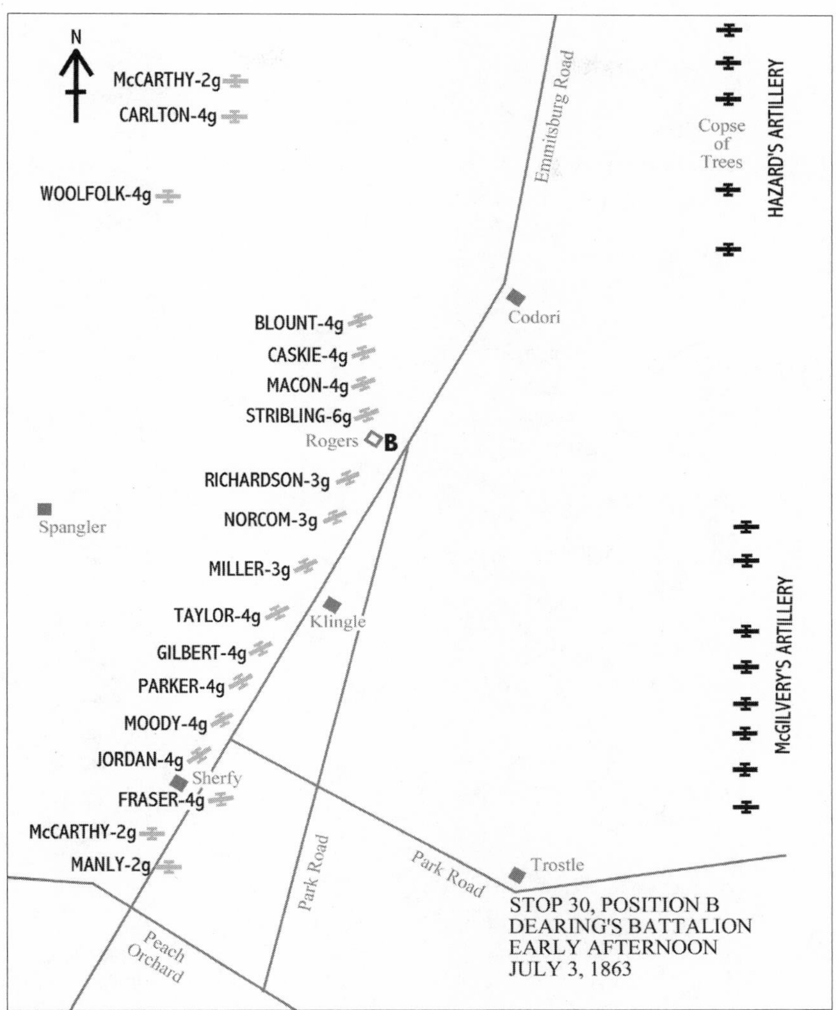

Position C—The Attacking Infantry

Six Hundred yards directly in front of you is the Spangler Woods. Look slightly left, and at a distance of 450 yards, you will see the Spangler House. This side of the house and on either side of the dirt road going from the house to the Emmitsburg Road was the first line of *Pickets* Division. From your viewpoint, *Kemper's* Brigade was to the left, and *Garnett's* Brigade was to the right. Deployed behind *Garnett* along the edge of Spangler Woods was *Pickett's* second

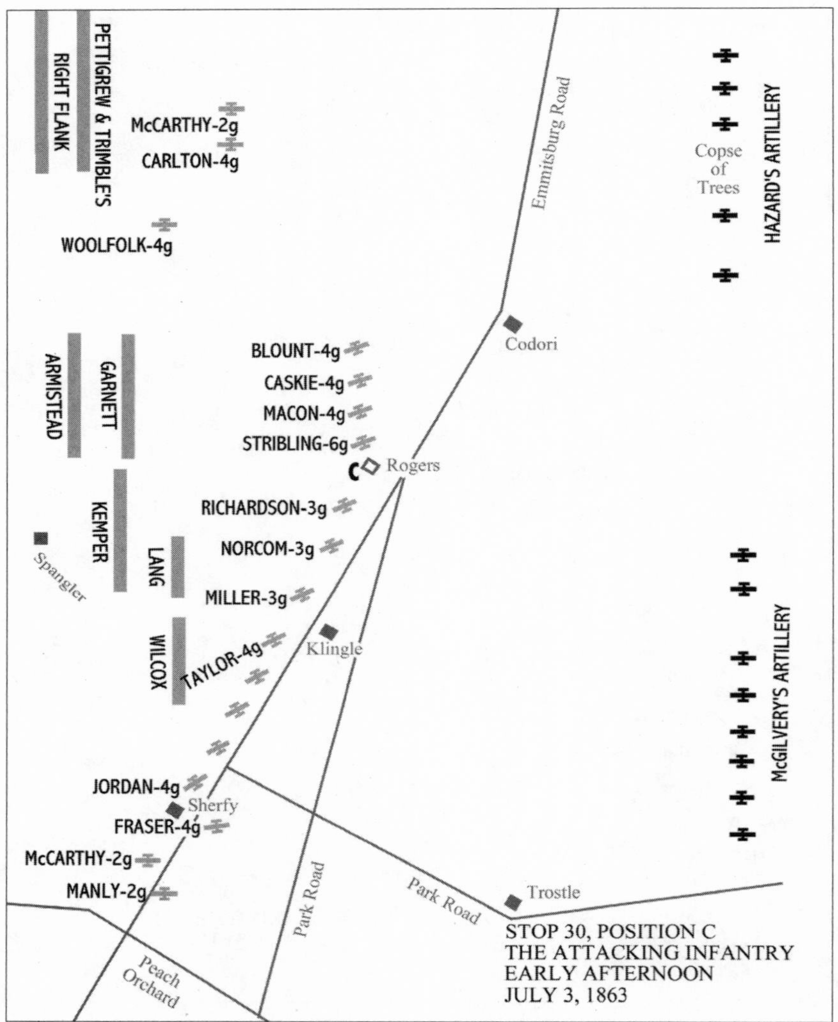

line, *Armistead's* Brigade. These three brigades were in a defilade position and could not be observed from Cemetery Ridge. However, any Union artillery fire from Cemetery Ridge that went over *Eshleman's* and *Dearing's* guns hit among *Pickett's* waiting troops. To *Pickett's* right front, the left as you view it, were *Lang's* and *Wilcox's* Brigades from *Anderson's* Division. You can see, to your right front at a distance of 800 yards, the northeast corner of Spangler Woods, the same one *Alexander* mentioned. Just around this corner but out of sight is the Virginia Monument. To the right of the Spangler Woods, the line of trees going north marks the location of today's West Confederate Avenue and the line of *Hill's* Corps artillery. Continue to look northward along this tree line, and you will see the North Carolina Monument 1,200 yards from your location. Six brigades of infantry from *Hill* Corps were deployed to attack with *Pickett's* Division. In the first line were four brigades from *Heth's* Division, commanded by Brigadier General *J. Johnston Pettigrew. Pettigrew's* right two brigades were deployed on either side of and behind where the North Carolina Monument is today. The other two brigades were positioned farther to the north. Behind *Pettigrew's* two right brigades were two brigades from *Pender's* Division, commanded by Major General *Isaac Trimble.* All six brigades were behind the line of artillery and on the west side of today's West Confederate Avenue.

Turn around and reverse your route back to the vicinity of the Rogers House sign. Stop and look toward the "Copse of Trees" on Cemetery Ridge.

Position D—The Artillery Bombardment

The nine brigades of infantry that were deployed behind you and to your left rear were to advance so that the center of the attack struck the Union defenses on Cemetery Ridge in the vicinity of the "Copse of Trees" and to the left. To accomplish this, the brigades of *Hill* Corps would attack straight ahead from their positions. *Pickett's* brigades, however, would have to keep echeloning to their left so as to bring their left flank in close proximity to *Hill's* right before they struck the Union defenses.

Prior to the infantry assault all of the artillery whose positions you have seen fired a preassault bombardment. When the infantry was in position and ready, *Alexander* was ordered to open fire. This order was communicated to the batteries by firing two guns in *Miller's* Battery. At this signal all of the artillery opened fire. When the artillery had done its maximum damage, *Alexander* was to inform *Pickett* so the infantry attack could begin.

Alexander provides an overview of the action.

Narrative of Col. *E. Porter Alexander,* CSA, Temporarily Commanding Corps Artillery, *Longstreet's Corps,* Army of Northern Virginia

It was just after 1 p.m. by my watch when the signal guns were fired and the cannonade opened. The enemy replied rather slowly at first, though soon with increasing rapidity. Having determined that *Pickett* should charge, I felt impatient to launch him as soon as I could see that our fire was accomplishing anything. I guessed that a half-hour would elapse between my sending him the order and his column reaching close quarters. I dare not presume on using more ammunition than one hour's firing would consume, for we were far from supplies and had already fought for two days.

At the end of 20 minutes no favorable development had occurred. More guns had been added to the federal line than at the beginning, and its whole length, about two miles, was blazing like a volcano. It seemed madness to order a column in the middle of a hot July day to undertake an advance of three-fourths of a mile over open ground against the center of that line.

But something had to be done. I wrote the following note and dispatched it to *Pickett* at 1:25:

> "General: If you are to advance at all, you must come at once or we will not be able to support you as we ought. But the enemy's fire has not slackened materially and there are still 18 guns firing from the cemetery." [*Alexander* was incorrectly told that the "Copse of Trees" was where the cemetery was.]

I had hardly sent this note when there was a decided falling off in the enemy's fire, and as I watched I saw other guns limbered up and withdrawn. We frequently withdrew from fighting Federal guns in order to save our ammunition for their infantry. The enemy had never heretofore practiced such economy. After waiting a few minutes and seeing that no fresh guns replaced those withdrawn, I felt sure the enemy was feeling the punishment, and at 1:40 I sent a note to *Pickett* as follows:

> "For God's sake come quick. The 18 guns have gone. Come quick or my ammunition will not let me support you properly."

The suspense was brief and was ended by *Garnett* riding in front of his brigade. He saluted and I mounted and rode with him while his brigade swept through our guns. I then rode down the line of guns, asking what each gun had left. Many had canister only. These and all having but a few

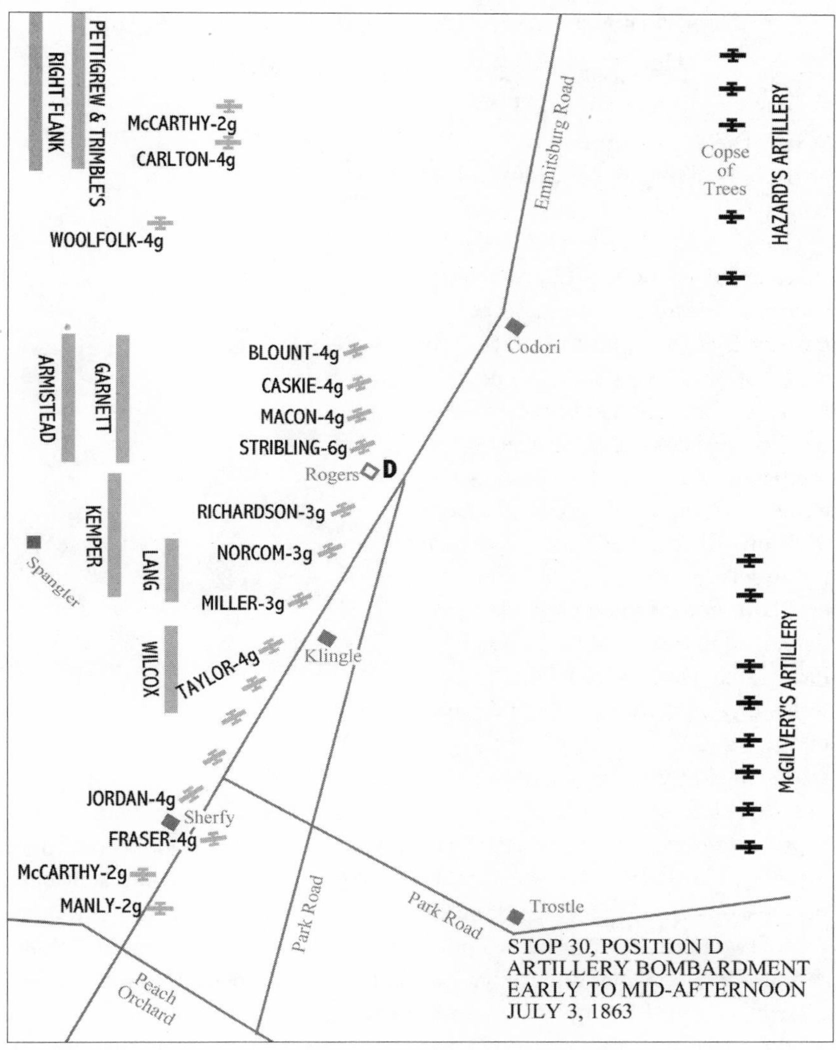

shells were ordered to stand fast. Those with a moderate amount of suitable ammunition were ordered to limber up and advance [to support the infantry]. [Alexander, *Military Memoirs,* 422–24]

Dearing provided a view of the action from the battalion level.

Report of Maj. *James Dearing,* CSA, Commanding *Dearing's* Artillery Battalion, *Longstreet's* Corps, Army of Northern Virginia

Major *James Dearing,* CSA. U.S. Army Military History Institute.

When the signal guns were fired, I at once brought my battalion in battery to the front, and commenced firing slowly and deliberately. To insure more accuracy and to guard against the waste of ammunition, I fired by battery. The firing on the part of my battalion was very good, and most of the shell and shrapnel burst well. My fire was directed at the batteries immediately in my front, and which occupied the heights charged by *Pickett's* division. Three caissons were seen by myself to blow up, and I saw several batteries of the enemy leave the field. At one time, just before General *Pickett's* division advanced, the batteries of the enemy in our front had nearly all ceased firing; only a few scattering batteries here and there could be seen to fire.

About this time my ammunition became completely exhausted, excepting a few rounds in my rifled guns, which were used upon a column of infantry, which advanced on General *Pickett's* right flank. I had sent back my caissons an hour and a half before for a fresh supply, but they could not get it. Two of my batteries and a part of Captain *Moody's* battery, of Colonel *Alexander's* battalion, under command of Captain *Moody,* remained under a very heavy fire for upward of an hour without being able to fire a single shot. My own batteries remained on the field after every round of ammunition was exhausted and until I could receive some fresh batteries, which Colonel *Alexander* sent to me.

Captain *Moody's* four 24-pounder howitzers, two of Captain *Norcom's* [*Battles's*] guns, and one of Captain *Miller's,* and Captain *Taylor's* battery were sent to me. I put them in position, and succeeded in driving back the column of infantry, which was at that time advancing. After the enemy was driven back at this point, nothing but desultory picket firing could be heard on that part of the line for the rest of the day.

In this engagement, Captain *Stribling's* battery had 3 men wounded and 10 horses killed and left on the field. Captain *Macon* had 3 men killed, 3 wounded, and 8 horses killed and left on the field; Captain *Caskie,* 3 men wounded and 7 horses killed and left on the field; Captain *Blount* had 5 men killed and wounded, and 12 horses killed. [*OR* 27, pt. 2, pp. 388–89]

Alexander continues with his description as the attack passed by where you are and crossed the Emmitsburg Road.

Narrative of Col. *E. Porter Alexander,* CSA—Continued

During the cannonade the reserve ordnance train had been moved from the position first occupied, and caissons sent to it had not returned. Only about one gun in four could be ordered forward from the center, but from the right Maj. *Haskell* [from *Henry's* battalion] took five [guns], and Maj. *Eshleman,* of the Washington artillery, sent four somewhat to *Haskell's* left.

Returning to the center I joined the few guns advancing from the batteries there, whence we opened upon troops advancing to attack the right of *Pickett's* division. [This was the Brigadier General George J. Stannard's brigade located in the vicinity of the tall column monument with the statue on top.] The charging [infantry] brigades were now close in front of the Federal lines and the musketry was heavy.

As we watched, we saw them close in upon the enemy in the smoke and dust, and we ceased firing and waited the result. It was soon manifest in a gradual diminution of the fire and in a stream of fugitives coming to the rear pursued by some fire but not as much, it seemed to me, as might have been expected.

After perhaps 20 minutes, during which the firing had about ceased, to my surprise there came forward from the rear *Wilcox's* fine Alabama brigade. It had been sent to reinforce *Pickett,* but was not in the column. Now when it was all over, the single brigade was moving forward alone. They were about 1,200 strong and on their left were about 250, the remnant of *Perry's* [*Lang's*] Florida brigade. It was at once both absurd and tragic.

They advanced several hundred yards beyond our guns, under a sharp fire. Then they halted and opened fire from some undergrowth and brushwood along a small ravine. [This is Plum Run, 500 yards to your right front.] Federal infantry soon moved out to attack their left, when [*Lang*] fell back past our guns; *Wilcox* moved by his right flank and regained out lines at the Peach Orchard.

While *Wilcox's* brigade was making its charge General *Lee* rode up and joined me. . . . When all the fugitives had passed and there was no sign of a [Union] counter-stroke, *Lee* rode off. I continued to hold my line of guns with few changes until after dark. . . . I quietly withdrew guns, one at a time, sending them to be refitted, and by 10 [p.m.] our whole line had been retired to the position from which the attack began [along today's West Confederate Avenue] on the 2d. [Alexander, *Military Memoirs,* 424–26]

The Confederate artillery had not been as effective as it was thought. After the war *Alexander* had time to reflect on the third day at Gettysburg and wrote a sharp analysis of the use of *Lee's* artillery and the selection of the terrain objective for the attack.

Narrative of Col. *E. Porter Alexander,* CSA –Continued

The great criticism which I have to make on the artillery operations of the [3d] day is upon the inaction of the artillery of *Ewell's* Corps. Our position on the exterior line placed us under many and serious disadvantages. But it gave us one single advantage. It enabled us to enfilade any of the enemy's positions, near the center of their line, with our artillery fire. Now, a battery established where it can enfilade others need not trouble itself about aim. It has only to fire in the right direction and the shot finds something to hurt wherever it falls. No troops, infantry or artillery, can long submit to an enfilade fire. But, both the infantry and artillery lines which we were to attack could have been enfiladed from somewhere in our lines near Gettysburg. This is where the use of a chief of artillery for the army comes in. [For the Army of Northern Virginia this was the tactically ineffective Brigadier General *William N. Pendleton.*] He visits and views the entire field and should recognize and know how to utilize his opportunities. The chief of each corps only sees his own ground. I never had an idea of the possibility of this being done at the time, for I had but the vaguest notion of where *Ewell's* Corps was. And *Ewell's* chief [of artillery] doubtless had as vague ideas of my situation. Only one of *Ewell's* five fine battalions participated in the bombardment at all. It only fired a few dozen shots. But, every shot was smashing up something, and, had it been increased and kept up, it is hard to say what might have resulted.

I think that all, who will study the field, will agree that the point selected for *Pickett's* attack was very badly chosen—almost as badly chosen as it was possible to be.

The point we attacked [was] upon the long shank of the fishhook [on Cemetery Ridge] of the enemy's position, and our advance was exposed to the fire of the whole length of that shank, some two miles. Not only that, that shank is not perfectly straight, but it bends forward at [Little] Round Top end, so that rifled guns there could and did enfilade the assaulting lines. Now add that the advance must be over 1,400 yards of open ground, none of it sheltered from fire, and very little from view.

I think any military [officer] would, instead, select for the attack the bend of the fishhook [on Cemetery Hill]. There, at least, the assaulting lines cannot be enfiladed. The assaulting column will only be exposed to the fire of the front less than half, even if over one-fourth, of the firing front upon the shank. [Gary W. Gallagher, *Fighting for the Confederacy,* p. 252]

You will now drive to the Union side of the field and look at the artillery action from their point of view.

Return to your car for the drive to Stop 31.

Be extremely careful, and make a hard left turn on to the Emmitsburg Road. Drive southeast for 0.3 mile to the park road on the left. Turn left on to this road, United States Avenue, and drive east for 0.7 mile to the intersection with Hancock and Sedgewick Avenue. Turn left on to Hancock Avenue, and drive for 0.1 mile. Park on the right side of the road, get out of your car, and stand facing west.

Stop 31, Position A—Artillery Positions

The fighting on July 3 presents an excellent example of the effectiveness of the Army of the Potomac's new centralized artillery organization and command and control structure. On the third day the Army of the Potomac's artillery was deployed for defense in seven tactical areas. Fifteen hundred yards to your left is Little Round Top. One battery and the section of another, eight guns all total, from the Fifth Corps artillery were positioned there. These guns had the capability of firing at *Longstreet's* Corps artillery and the attacking infantry. Where you are was Lieutenant Colonel Freeman McGilvery's artillery position. McGilvery's position went 260 yards to your left and 350 yards to your right, near the Pennsylvania Monument. At noon it consisted of eight batteries, totaling thirty-nine guns. Beginning on the other side of the Pennsylvania Monument and going north for 325 yards was a space occupied only by infantry. North of this area was the Second Corps artillery position under the command of Captain John Hazard. Five batteries for a total of twenty-six guns initially occupied a 650-yard-long position. Just prior to and during the attack seven batteries, for a total of thirty-seven guns (twenty-five 3-inch rifles, six 10-pound

Parrotts, and six Napoleons), reinforced McGilvery's and Hazard's positions. One of the reinforcing batteries went into position in the center of McGilvery's line. The remainder deployed with McGilvery's right flank batteries and in the open space between McGilvery and Hazard. As the Confederate infantry attack developed, one of these batteries was shifted farther north to strengthen Hazard's position.

To Hazard's right flank was the Eleventh Corps artillery position on West Cemetery Hill. Major Thomas W. Osborn commanded seven batteries and a section of one battery for a total of thirty-nine guns deployed on a 500-yard-long position. Most of Osborn's guns, without changing position, could fire into the positions of *Hill's* Corps artillery on Cemetery Ridge. The guns on the left of Osborn's position, without redeploying, could fire into the attacking Confederate infantry. Just across the Baltimore Pike on East Cemetery Hill, Colonel Charles S. Wainwright had four batteries with seventeen guns. If necessary any or all of these guns could be called upon to reinforce Osborn.

In addition there were batteries in two other locations that could be used to reinforce the artillery on Cemetery Ridge. The four batteries, twenty guns, of the Twelfth Corps artillery were positioned south of Cemetery Hill, along the Baltimore Pike. Depending on the fighting around Culp's Hill, these batteries could reinforce the Cemetery Ridge defenses or counter a Confederate penetration of the center. The park of the Artillery Reserve was positioned east of where you are. At that location were located reserve batteries, some of which had already been sent forward to reinforce, and batteries that were refitting and resupplying. These batteries were also available to reinforce the defenses or to counter a Confederate penetration of the center.

On the morning of July 3, Brigadier General Henry J. Hunt, the Army of the Potomac's chief of artillery, had been in the vicinity of Culp's Hill checking the condition of the artillery that had been supporting the infantry against the final Confederate attack on the right of Meade's position. Hunt's concept for the use of the artillery to obtain maximum advantage is contained in an article he wrote after the war.

Narrative of Brig. Gen. Henry J. Hunt, USA, Chief of Artillery, Army of the Potomac

Between 10 and 11 a.m., everything looking favorable at Culp's Hill, I crossed over to Cemetery Ridge, to see what might be going on at other points. Here a magnificent display greeted my eyes. Our whole front for two miles was covered by [enemy] batteries already in line or going into position. They stretched—apparently in one unbroken mass—from opposite the town to the Peach Orchard, which bounded the view to the left, the ridges of which were planted thick with cannon. Never before had such a sight been witnessed on this continent, and rarely, if ever, abroad. What did it mean? It might possibly be to hold that line while the infantry was sent to aid *Ewell* [the attack on Culp's Hill], or to guard against a counter-stroke from us, but it most probably meant an assault on our center, to be preceded by a cannonade in order to crush our batteries and shake our infantry; at least to cause us to exhaust our ammunition in reply, so that the assaulting troops might pass in good condition over the half mile of open ground which was beyond our effective musketry fire. . . . From the great extent of the ground occupied by the enemy's batteries, it was evident that all the artillery on our west front, whether of the army corps or the reserve, must be concentrated as a unit, under the chief of artillery, in the defense. . . . It was of the first importance to subject the enemy's infantry, from the first moment of their advance, to such a cross-fire of our artillery as would break their formations, check their impulse, and drive them back, or at least bring them to our lines in such condition as to make them an easy prey. . . . Beginning on the right, I instructed the chiefs of artillery and battery commanders to withhold their fire for fifteen or twenty minutes after the cannonade commenced, then to concentrate their fire with all possible accuracy on those batteries which were most destructive to us—but slowly, so that when the enemy's ammunition was exhausted, we should have sufficient left to meet the assault. I had just given these orders to the last battery on Little Round Top, when the signal-gun was fired, and the enemy opened with all his guns. [Henry J. Hunt, "The Third Day at Gettysburg," in *Battles and Leader of the Civil War,* vol. 3, 371–72]

Cross the road, stand next to the marker for Battery H, Third Pennsylvania Heavy Artillery, and look west.

Position B—McGilvery's Artillery Position

You are in the center of McGilvery's artillery position. The two 3-inch rifles of Captain William D. Rank's Battery H, Third Pennsylvania Heavy Artillery from the Cavalry's First Brigade, Horse Artillery were here. Captain John W. Sterling's Second Connecticut Battery with four James rifles and two 12-pound howitzers from the Second Volunteer Artillery Brigade was to Rank's left. Next to the left was Lieutenant Edwin B. Dow's Sixth Maine Battery with four Napoleons. Captain Nelson Ames's Battery G, First New York Artillery, with six Napoleons was to Dow's left and was the position's left flank. The last two batteries were from the Fourth Volunteer Artillery Brigade. During the attack Captain James H. Cooper's Battery B, First Pennsylvania Artillery, from the First Corps Artillery Brigade with four 3-inch rifles reinforced McGilvery and went into position to your left between Rank's and Sterling's batteries.

Captain Patrick Hart's Fifteenth New York Battery from McGilvery's First Volunteer Artillery Brigade with four Napoleons was to Rank's right. To Hart's right was Captain Charles A. Phillips's Fifth Massachusetts Battery with six 3-inch rifles and to his right Captain James Thompson's Batteries C and F (Combined), Pennsylvania Artillery, with five 3-inch rifles. All three of these batteries were from McGilvery's First Volunteer Artillery Brigade. To their right, forming the right flank of the position was Lieutenant Evan Thomas's Battery C, Fourth U.S. Artillery with six Napoleons from the First Regular Artillery Brigade.

The eight batteries initially deployed on this position consisted of twenty Napoleons, thirteen 3-inch rifles, four James rifles, and two 12-pound howitzers for a total of thirty-nine guns. They came from five different artillery brigades and were all under the temporary command of Lieutenant Colonel McGilvery. The deployment of the artillery to this location is another example of the effectiveness of the Army of the Potomac's new artillery organization and its command and control structure.

Deployed with and behind the artillery was the surviving infantry of Brigadier General John C. Caldwell's First Division, Second Corps, which had seen heavy fighting on July 2 and was at a reduced strength.

Plum Run is 350 yards in front of you. It goes across the entire front of McGilvery's position. The Klingle House is 1,050 yards

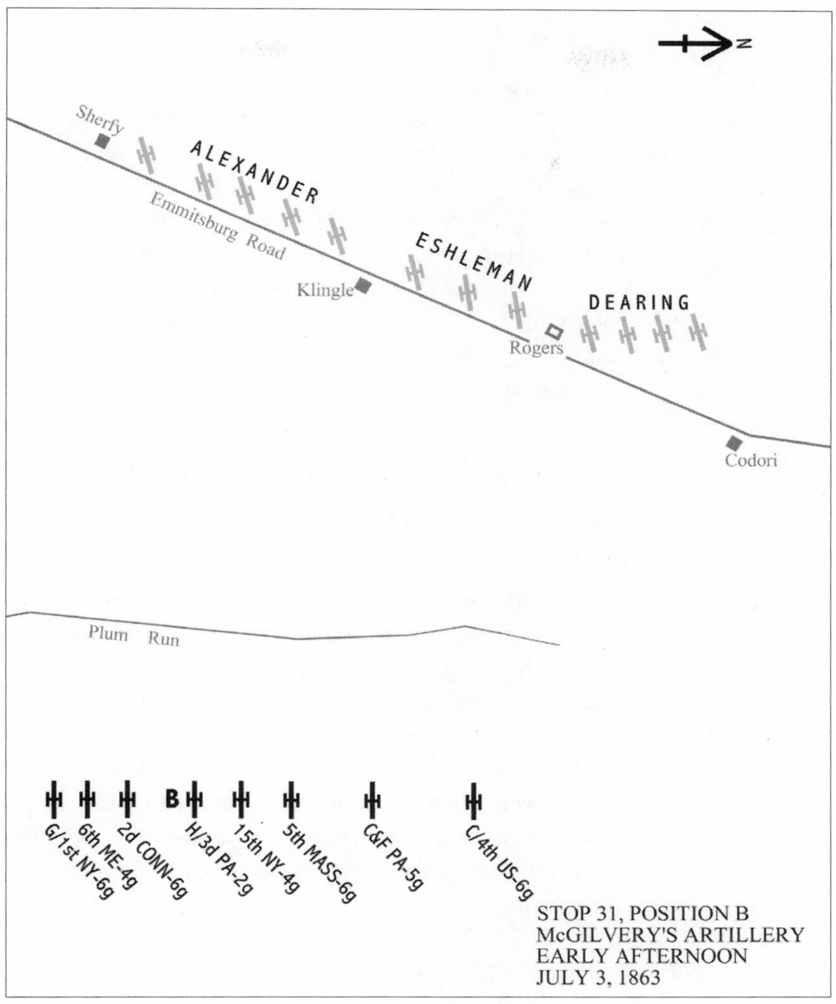

directly in front of you. To the left of the Klingle House and 1,400 yards from your location are the Sherfy House and Barn. To the right of the Klingle House and 900 yards from you are the Codori House and Barn. Along the line from the Sherfy Barn to the Codori Barn you can see the low ridges where *Alexander's, Eshleman's,* and *Dearing's* artillery battalions were deployed. As you view it, *Alexander's* Battalion was between the Sherfy Barn and the Klingle House, *Eshleman's* Battalion was to the right of the Klingle House, and *Dearing's* Battalion was to the right of *Eshleman's.* The center of *Pickett's* Division was on a line that went from your location, through the Klingle House and on to the west for another 500 yards. *Pickett's* infantry was in the low ground behind the Confederate artillery and could not be seen from where you are. However, any artillery rounds fire from McGilvery's guns that went over the Confederate artillery landed among *Pickett's* troops.

Look just to the right of and beyond the Codori Barn, and you will see the North Carolina Monument 1,900 yards to your right front. This monument marks the approximate location of *Hill's* Corps artillery's right, or south, flank. *Hill's* artillery extended north from that location. Behind the artillery near the North Carolina Monument were *Pettigrew's* and *Trimble's* waiting infantry.

Report of Lieut. Col. Freeman McGilvery, USA, Commanding First Volunteer Artillery Brigade, Artillery Reserve, Army of the Potomac

During the night [of July 2d] I ascertained the whereabouts of all my batteries, and early on the morning of July 3 brought them into line on the low ground on our left center, fronting the woods and elevated position occupied by the enemy along the Gettysburg and Emmitsburg road, a point at which it was plain to be seen they were massing artillery in great force.

In front of [my] guns I had a slight earthwork thrown up, which proved sufficient to resist all the projectiles which struck it, and the commanders of batteries were repeatedly ordered that, in the event of the enemy opening a cannonading upon our lines, to cover their men as much as possible, and not return the fire until ordered.

At about 12.30 o'clock the enemy opened a terrific fire upon our lines with at least one hundred and forty guns. This fire was very rapid and inaccurate, most of the projectiles passing from 20 to 100 feet over our lines. About one-half hour after the commencement, some general commanding the infantry line ordered three of the batteries to return the fire. After the discharge of a few rounds, I ordered the fire to cease and the men to be covered. After the enemy had fired about one hour and a half, and expended at least 10,000 rounds of ammunition, with but comparatively little damage to our immediate line, a slow, well-directed fire from all the guns under my command was concentrated upon single batteries of the enemy of those best in view, and several badly broken up and successively driven from their position to the rear. [*OR* 27, pt. 1, pp. 883–84]

Face right, and walk north to the monument and guns for the Fifteenth New York Battery. Stand beside the guns, and look west.

Position C—Fifteenth New York Battery

Captain Hart wrote an account describing the fighting by the four Napoleons of his battery at this position.

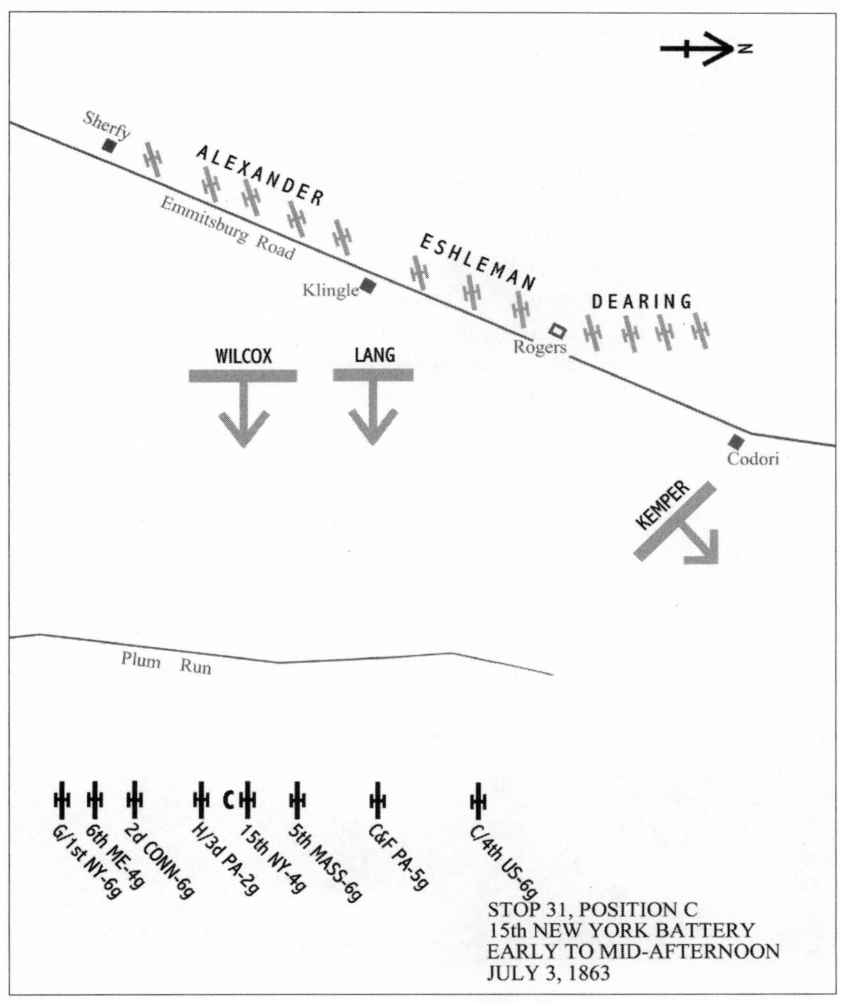

Report of Capt. Patrick Hart, USA, Commanding Fifteenth New York Battery, First Volunteer Artillery Brigade, Artillery Reserve, Army of the Potomac

Early on the morning of the 3d, I received orders by Lieut. Col. McGilvery's orderly to proceed to the front, which order I immediately obeyed. When I reached the front, not being able to find Lieut. Col. McGilvery, I reported to Captain Thompson [Batteries C & F, Pennsylvania Artillery]. He told me to come into position anywhere on his left, so as to leave room for Captain Phillips [Fifth Massachusetts Battery]. I took position accordingly. A short time after, General Hunt, passing along the line, told me to hold my position and not to return the enemy's fire unless I saw his infantry advancing; then to open fire to the best advantage. This order was afterward repeated to me by Lieut. Col. McGilvery, which I obeyed, until ordered by General Hancock to open on the enemy's batteries. I obeyed this order, but after firing a few rounds Lieut. Col. McGilvery ordered me to cease firing. After the enemy opened with all of his batteries, I was ordered by Lieut. Col. McGilvery to return their fire, which I did.

While firing at the enemy's batteries I used solid shot and shell, but when his infantry commenced to advance, I fired shell and shrapnel until the right of his first column came within about 500 yards of me, when I opened with canister, which took good effect. His second line [*Lang's* and *Wilcox's* Brigades] appeared to be coming direct for my battery. I turned all

Area west of the 15th New York Battery (Stop 31C) in the center of McGilvery's July 3 artillery position. Codori barn is in right of photo.

my guns on this line, every piece loaded with two canisters. I continued this dreadful fire on this line until there was not a man of them to be seen.

At this time the enemy opened a battery on his right, in front of a barn, his projectiles killing many of my horses. I directed my fire on this battery and on his caissons, which were partly covered by the barn. I candidly believe it was I who caused his caissons to explode and set the barn on fire. Immediately afterward he brought a section to bear on me. I brought all the guns of my battery to bear on this section. The first gun that I fired exploded one of his limbers. Corporal Hammond with the next shot dismounted, I believe, one of his guns. Sergt. William Sheehy, I believe, followed with equal success. There was not a gun fired or a man to be seen at this section afterward, until, late in the evening, they sent down horses and took away one limber. [*OR* 27, pt. 1, p. 888]

Face right and walk north along side the park road for 25 yards to the marker and guns for the Fifth Massachusetts Battery, stop, face left, and again look west.

Position D—The Fifth Massachusetts Battery

You are at the position of Captain Charles A. Phillips's battery. Armed with six 3-inch rifles, this battery was more accurate at longer ranges that those with Napoleons.

Area west of McGilvery's artillery position on July 3 as seen from the position of the 5th Massachusetts Battery (Stop 31D). The Klingle farm buildings are in the left of the photo.

Directly in front of you at a distance of 1,050 yards is the Klingle House. Brigadier General *Cadmus Wilcox's* brigade and Colonel *David Lang's* brigade of *Anderson's* Division were in position behind the artillery on the low ridge across the Emmitsburg Road from the Klingle House. They were to attack, when ordered, to protect *Pickett's* right flank. However, the order for them to advance came after *Kemper's* Brigade had passed well beyond the Emmitsburg Road. Following their orders, these two brigades moved for-

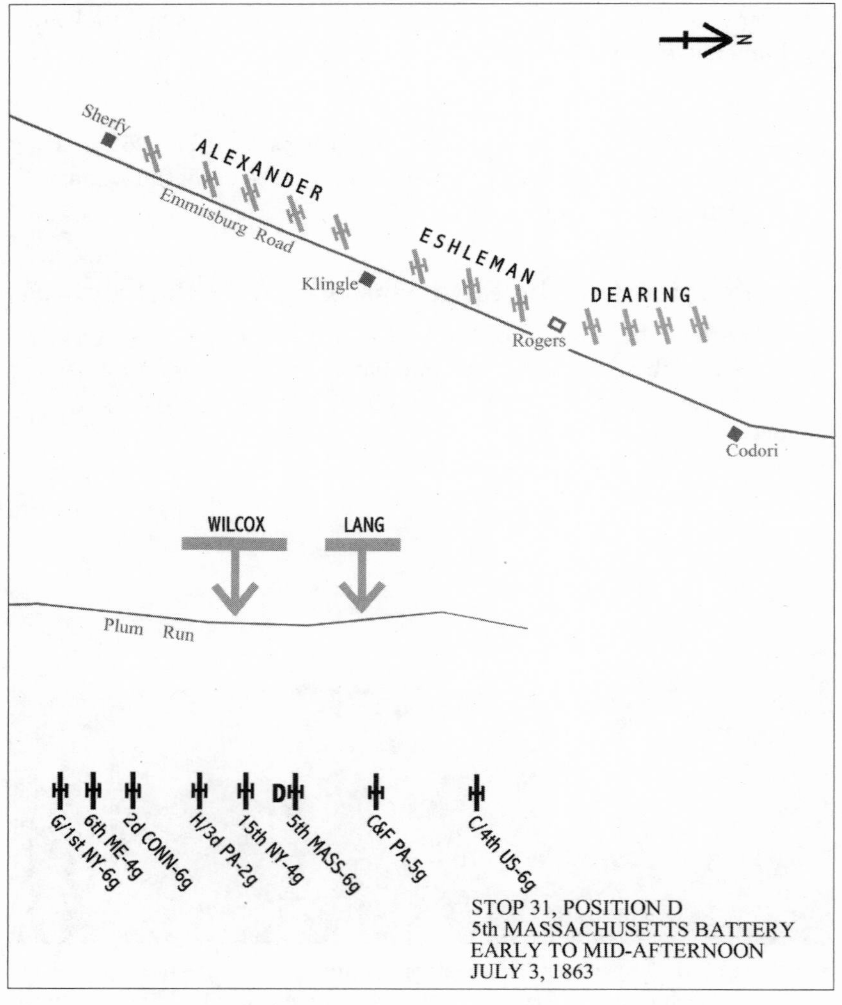

STOP 31, POSITION D
5th MASSACHUSETTS BATTERY
EARLY TO MID-AFTERNOON
JULY 3, 1863

ward, crossed the Emmitsburg Road, crossed the same ground they had on July 2, and attacked toward McGilvery's artillery.

McGilvery's batteries and even the batteries on the Second Corps left flank, after engaging *Pickett's* Division, redirected their fire to this new threat. *Wilcox's* and *Lang's* Brigades were turned back with heavy casualties along Plum Run.

Report of Capt. Charles A. Phillips, USA, Commanding Fifth Massachusetts Battery, First Volunteer Artillery Brigade, Artillery Reserve, Army of the Potomac

At daylight on the 3d, I was ordered to the front, and took position to the right and rear of the position of the day before, on the right of Captain Hart and left of Captain Thompson. The guns were protected by a slight parapet, which proved of very great service.

About 1 o'clock the enemy opened a heavy fire from a long line of batteries, which was kept up for an hour, but beyond the noise which was made no great harm was done. Having received orders from General Hunt and from Lieut. Col. McGilvery not to reply to their batteries, I remained silent for the first half hour, when General Hancock ordered us to open. We then opened fire on the enemy's batteries, but in the thick smoke probably did very little damage. By Lieut. Col. McGilvery's orders, we soon ceased firing. Soon after, a charge was made by [Pickett's Division], and from my position I was enabled to pour a heavy enfilading fire into the rebel infantry. After the repulse of this charge, another was made by [*Wilcox's* Brigade and *Lang's*] Florida brigade within range of my guns. During the charge, the rebels advanced a battery of 12-pounders on our left, whereupon the batteries of the First [Volunteer Artillery] Brigade were ordered to concentrate their fire on it, which was done with such good effect that the rebel cannoneers were driven from their posts almost immediately, and left their guns on the field. [*OR* 27, pt. 1, p. 885]

Captain Charles A. Phillips, USA. U.S. Army Military History Institute

Colonel *Lang* wrote a description of his brigade's attack against this position.

Report of Col. *David Lang,* CSA, Commanding *Perry's* Brigade, *Anderson's* Division, *Hill's* Corps, Army of Northern Virginia

Soon after General *Pickett's* troops retired behind our position, General *Wilcox* began to advance, and, in accordance with previous orders to conform to his movements, I moved forward also, under a heavy fire from artillery, but without encountering any infantry until coming to the skirt of woods at the foot of the heights. Just before entering the woods [along Plum Run], a heavy body of infantry advanced upon my left flank. [This infantry was the Sixteenth Vermont and part of the Fourteenth Vermont of Brigadier General George Stannard's Third Brigade, Third Division, First Corps.]

The noise of artillery and small arms was so deafening that it was impossible to make the voice heard above the din, and the men were by this time so badly scattered in the bushes and among the rocks that it was impossible to make any movement to meet or check the enemy's advance. To remain in this position, unsupported by either infantry or artillery, with infantry on both flanks and in front and artillery playing upon us with grape and canister, was certain annihilation. To advance was only to hasten that result, and, therefore, I ordered a retreat, which, however, was not in time to save a large number of the Second Florida Infantry, together with their colors, from being cut off and captured by the flanking force on the left. Owing to the noise and scattered condition of the men, it was impossible to have the order to retreat properly extended, and I am afraid that many men, while firing from behind rocks and trees, did not hear the order, and remained there until captured. [*OR* 27, pt. 2, p. 632]

Return to your car for the drive to Stop 32.

Continue driving north on Hancock Avenue for 0.1 mile to the Pennsylvania Monument. Park, leave your car, cross to the left, or west, side of the road, and walk to the guns and monument for Battery I, First Michigan Artillery (Ninth Michigan Battery). Stand beside the guns and monument, and look west.

Stop 32—Reinforcing Artillery Arrives

From this location you continue to have a good view of the Confederate artillery positions. To your left front at a distance of 1,500 yards is the Peach Orchard and the south, or right, flank of the Confederate artillery line. From the Peach Orchard look slightly right, and you can see the Sherfy Barn 1,400 yards from you. Farther right the Klingle House is 880 yards from you. Slightly right of the Klingle House and 700 yards from you is the site of the Roger's House, Stop 30. This is where you parked when you looked at *Longstreet's* artillery line. To your right front at a distance of 1,500 yards is the Virginia Monument; slightly right and at a shorter distance of 500 yards is the Codori Barn; and, again, looking farther right, at a distance of 1,600 yards is the North Carolina Monument.

Along the line from the Peach Orchard to the Sherfy Barn and then to the Klingle House were the guns of two of *Cabell's* batteries and *Alexander's* Battalion. From the Klingle House to the site of the Rogers House was *Eshleman's* Battalion. To the right of the Rogers House site was *Dearing's* Battalion. To Dearing's left, the right as you view it, was *Cabell's* two other batteries and then two batteries from *Pogue's* Battalion. Continuing on north, the rest of *Pogue's* artillery and the other battalions of *Hill's* Corps artillery began to the left of the North Carolina Monument and went north, to your right, to the Hagerstown Road. *Hill's* artillery positioned is marked by the thin tree line along West Confederate Avenue.

You are standing just to the right of McGilvery's right flank battery: Lieutenant Evan Thomas's Battery C, Fourth U.S. Artillery, armed with six Napoleons. To Thomas's left was Captain James Thompson's Batteries C & F (Combined), Pennsylvania Artillery, with five 3-inch rifles. During the artillery cannonade and counter-battery fire, Thompson's battery was badly damaged and ordered to the rear. Three hundred and twenty-five yards to your right was the left flank battery, Battery B, First New York Artillery, of the Second Corps artillery. Between where you are and that location were deployed infantry from the Major General Abner Doubleday's Second Division, First Corps. The new corps commander, Major General John Newton, had requested artillery to strengthen his defensive position.

As the artillery fight began, reinforcing artillery arrived in this vicinity. It did not arrive at once but over a short period of time. When the last unit deployed and opened fire, four batteries with a total of twenty-four guns (eighteen 3-inch rifles and six 10-pound Parrotts) had been added to the defense. Lieutenant Augustin Parsons's Battery A, First New Jersey Artillery, from the Fourth

Volunteer Artillery Brigade with six 10-pound Parrotts deployed to your left and replaced Thompson's badly damaged battery. When the other three batteries had deployed, the artillery line where you are and to your right consisted of Captain Jabez Daniels's Battery I, First Michigan Artillery (Ninth Michigan Battery) from the cavalry's First Horse Artillery Brigade with six 3-inch rifles; next to the right was Captain Robert Fitzhugh's Battery K, First New York Artillery, with the Eleventh New York Battery attached from the Fourth Volunteer Artillery Brigade with six 3-inch rifles; and farther right was Captain Andrew Cowan's First New York Battery from the Sixth Corps Artillery Brigade with six 3-inch rifles. A fifth

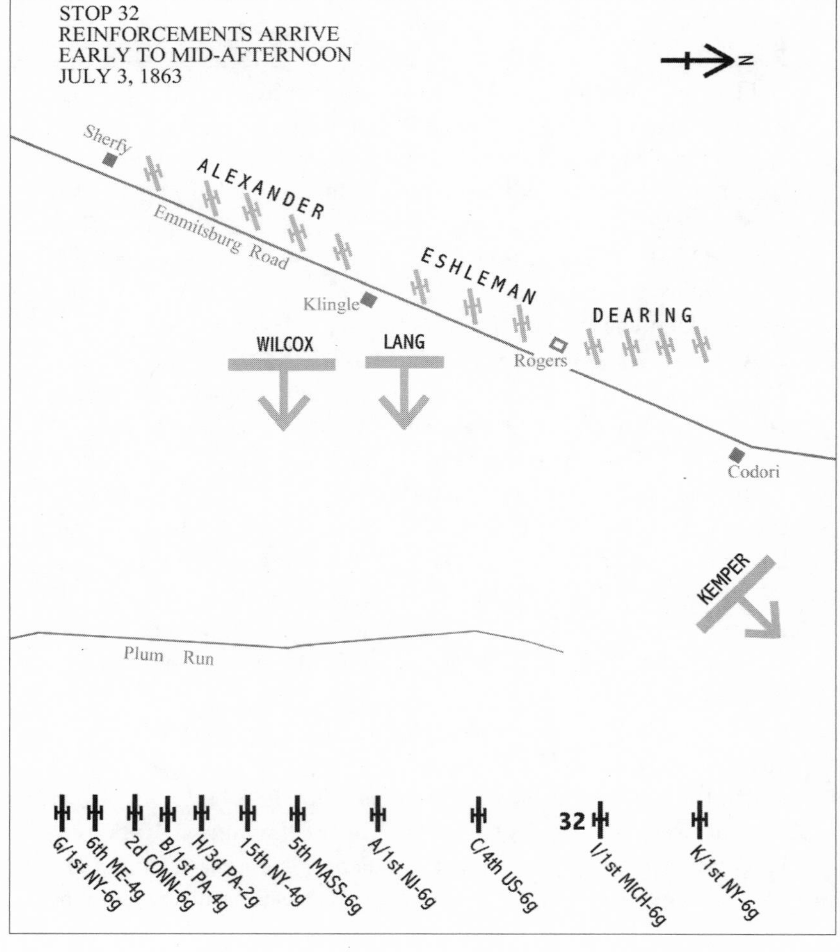

battery, Lieutenant Gulian V. Weir's, upon arriving in this vicinity was told a battery of Napoleons was not needed as the defenders wanted 3-inch rifles, probably for counterbattery fire. Weir then positioned his Battery C, Fifth U.S. Artillery, in defilade to your right rear on the east side of Cemetery Ridge. It was not destined to remain there long, and you will encounter this battery later on.

To your far left Captain James H. Cooper added four more 3-inch rifles to the defenses when his Battery B, First Pennsylvania, deployed between the Second Connecticut Battery and Battery H, Third Pennsylvania Heavy Artillery.

The deployment of batteries to reinforce here and at other critical locations along the defensive position before and during the Confederate attack continued to demonstrate the organizational effectiveness of the Army of the Potomac's artillery.

Report of Brig. Gen. Henry J. Hunt, USA, Chief of Artillery, Army of the Potomac

I had just finished my inspection, and was with Lieutenant Rittenhouse [Battery D, Fifth U.S.] on the top of Round Top, when the enemy opened, at about 1 p.m., along his whole right, a furious cannonade on the left of our line. I estimated the number of his guns bearing on our west front at from one hundred to one hundred and twenty. To oppose these we [initially] could not, from our restricted position, bring more than eighty to reply effectively. Our fire was well withheld until the first burst was over, excepting from the extreme right and left of our positions. It was then opened deliberately and with excellent effect. As soon as the nature of the enemy's attack was made clear, and I could form an opinion as to the number of his guns, for which my position afforded great facility, I went to the park of the Artillery Reserve, and ordered all the batteries to be ready to move at a moment's notice. . . . I then proceeded along the line, to observe the effects of the cannonade and to replace such batteries as should become disabled.

About 2.30 p.m., finding our ammunition running low and that it was very unsafe to bring up loads of it, a number of caissons and limbers having been exploded, I directed that the fire should be gradually stopped, which was done, and the enemy soon slackened his fire also. I then sent orders for such batteries as were necessary to replace exhausted ones, and all that were disposable were sent me.

About 3 p.m., and soon after the enemy's fire had ceased, he formed a column of attack in the edge of the woods in front of the Second Corps.

At this time Fitzhugh's (K, First New York, six 3-inch), Parsons' (A, First New Jersey, six 10-pounders), and Cowan's (First New York Independent, six 3-inch) batteries reached this point [where you are], and were put in position in front of the advancing enemy. I rode down to McGilvery's batteries, and directed them to take the enemy in flank as they approached. The enemy advanced magnificently, unshaken by the shot and shell, which tore through his ranks from his front and from our left. [*OR* 27, pt. 1, pp. 238–39]

Before *Lee's* artillery opened fire, Hunt had given instruction that the Union artillery was to fire slowly and deliberately so as to conserve ammunition for the expected infantry attack against their position. As the bombardment continued, the decision was made to have the Union artillery stop firing so as to give the impression that the Confederate artillery fire was being successful and to conserve ammunition. This slowing and then stopping the artillery fire, along with several of Hazard's batteries withdrawing from their positions, gave *Alexander* the impression that his fire was accurate and the infantry should move forward and attack.

As with many things at Gettysburg, there was controversy after the war as to who developed this idea. Both Hunt and Osborne each claimed it was theirs. As they were competent artillery officer and tacticians, it is possible that both of them independently came up with the idea. Regardless of who thought of it, it worked.

Most of the batteries that had been firing at the Confederate artillery came to a ceasefire. The exception was Hancock's Second Corps artillery. After they came to a ceasefire, Hancock order Hazard to have them recommence firing. This they did. When the Confederate infantry came forward, Hancock's artillery only had short-range canister ammunition available and could not engage the attackers until they were within close range.

When the infantry attack began, *Pettigrew's* and *Trimble's* troops advanced from the tree line in the vicinity of the North Carolina Monument across the open ground to your right front. Their objective was that portion of Cemetery Ridge between the "Copse of Tree" to your right and that part of the ridge farther to the right.

Pickett's three brigades were located in low ground behind *Eshleman's* and *Dearing's* artillery line. As mentioned before, any artillery fire from this location that went over the Confederate artillery hit among *Pickett's* troops.

Pickett's objective was the area marked by the "Copse of Trees." To get there, he had to have his brigades continually echelon to their left. *Pickett's* infantry came into view when they passed through the line of Confederate artillery on the low ridges in front of you. As they moved toward the "Copse of Trees," their right flank was exposed to the artillery located to your left and right. This allowed enfiladed fire to be placed down the lines of infantry. This fire was especially damaging to *Pickett's* right flank brigade, *Kemper's,* as it passed by about 250 yards to your front and right front.

Report of Lieut. Col. Freeman McGilvery, USA—Continued

[There] appeared three extended lines of battle advancing upon our center. These three lines of battle presented an oblique front to the guns under my command, and by training the whole line of guns obliquely to the right, we had a raking fire through all three of these lines. The execution of the fire must have been terrible, as it was over a level plain, and the effect was plain to be seen. In a few minutes, instead of a well-ordered line of battle, there were broken and confused masses, and fugitives fleeing in every direction. [*OR* 27, pt. 1, p. 884]

The first reinforcing battery to reach this position was Captain Jabez Daniels's.

Report of Capt. Jabez J. Daniels, USA, Commanding Ninth Michigan Battery (Battery I), First Brigade, Horse Artillery, Cavalry Corps, Army of the Potomac

I received orders from Captain Robertson, commanding this brigade, at 12 m. on the 3d instant, to report with my battery to Major-General Newton, commanding First Army Corps. After reporting to General Newton, received orders from him to take a position on the [ridge south] of the town, and engage the enemy's batteries. I proceeded at once and took position as directed, and opened fire at 12.30 p.m. I succeeded in silencing one of the enemy's batteries at 2 p.m. Another battery was then brought into the open field at a range of 700 yards. This battery was disabled before they could do me any damage. The enemy then formed a division of infantry, and charged desperately upon my battery, but were promptly repulsed and driven back from the field with great slaughter by our infantry and artillery. The enemy made a second attempt to form, but were broken and forced to retire.

Area west of Battery A, First New Jersey Artillery's position (Stop 32) on the right of McGilvery's July 3 artillery position.

I expended 322 rounds. The ammunition used was Hotchkiss shot and shell and canister.

My loss during the engagement was Private John W. Barber killed; Corpl. C. Hass, Privates T. P. Smith, Harvey Collins, and J. M. C. Forbes, all slightly wounded. I also lost 23 horses killed, and received slight damage to two ammunition chests. [*OR* 27, pt. 1, pp. 1022–23]

Soon after Daniels's battery went into firing position, Lieutenant Augustine N. Parsons's Battery A, First New Jersey Artillery, took up a firing position on the other side of Thomas's Battery C, Fourth U.S. Artillery. Parsons filled the gap created by the withdrawal of Thompson's heavily damaged battery.

Report of Lieut. Augustin N. Parsons, USA, Commanding Battery A, First New Jersey Artillery, Fourth Volunteer Artillery Brigade, Artillery Reserve, Army of the Potomac

I received orders from General Hunt to move the battery to the front as quickly as possible. I at once obeyed the order, and soon had the battery in position about one-fourth of a mile south of Gettysburg Cemetery and near the Second Division, Second Corps, Captain Fitzhugh's battery following immediately after me and taking position on my right. At this time the enemy's infantry were advancing very rapidly. I at once opened fire upon them with case shot, and fired about 120 rounds with good effect. As soon as they fell back, I opened fire upon one of the enemy's batteries (which by this time had gotten an exact range of my position) with shell, and used 80 rounds, when I received orders from General Hunt to cease firing.

During the action I lost 2 men killed and 7 wounded. I also lost 3 horses killed and 2 wounded, which have since died. [*OR* 27, pt. 1, pp. 899–900]

Lieutenant Augustin N. Parsons, USA. U.S. Army Military History Institute.

To your right was Battery K, First New York Artillery. The commander of the Fourth Volunteer Artillery Brigade, Captain Robert H. Fitzhugh, brought this battery and Parson's battery into position on the ridge.

Return to your car for the drive to Stop 33.

Continue driving north on Hancock Avenue for 0.3 mile to the "Copse of Trees" and "The Angle." Park on the right of the road, leave your car, stand just off the road, and face to the west.

Stop 33, Position A—Hazard's Artillery

Directly in front of you at a distance of 1,350 yards is the Virginia Monument. On a direct line from you to the Virginia Monument, 600 yards distant on the low ridge, on the other side of the Emmitsburg Road was the left flank of *Longstreet's* Artillery. Two batteries of *Cabell's* Battalion were the left flank. Look slightly left, and at a distance of 475 yards is the red Codori Barn. Five hundred and twenty-five yards beyond the Codori Barn, 1,000 yards from your position, is the site where the Rogers House was. *Dearing's* Battalion was deployed from *Cabell's* right to the Rogers House.

Again slightly to the left of the Codori Barn and 825 yards farther on, 1,300 yards from your position, is the Klingle House. The space between the site of the Roger House and the Klingle House was the area occupied by *Eshleman's* Battalion. Four hundred and fifty yards directly beyond the Klingle House and 1,750 yards from your position is the Sherfy Barn. *Alexander's* battalion was deployed on the ground from the Klingle House to the left, as you view it, to the Sherfy Barn. From the left of the Sherfy Barn to the Peach Orchard, 1,900 yards from where you are, were the remaining two batteries of *Cabell's* Battalion.

Pickett's Division was in the low ground to the left of the Virginia Monument. They could not be see from here, but any artillery at this location fired at *Cabell's* and *Dearing's* guns and aimed too high would strike *Pickett's* infantry.

Look back right to the Virginia Monument. To the right of the Virginia Monument was the right flank of *Hill's* Corps artillery. Deployed from there to your right, along today's West Confederate Avenue, was *Pogue's* Battalion, two batteries of *Lane's* Battalion (where the North Carolina Monument is), then *Pegram's* Battalion. The white house you see farther to your right at a distance of 1,500 yards is the McMillan House. It marks the center of *Garnett's* Battalion. To *Garnett's* left, your right, were guns of *Dance's* Battalion, then *McIntosh's* Battalion. *Pettigrew's* and *Trimble's* infantry were deployed behind the artillery on either side of the North Carolina Monument.

The five batteries of Captain John G. Hazard's Second Corps Artillery Brigade were deployed along a position that covered 650 yards of Cemetery Ridge. This position began 300 yards to your left and went 350 yards to your right. Forward of your present location was Lieutenant Alonzo H. Cushing's Battery A, Fourth U.S. Artillery, with six 3-inch rifles. To Cushing's left and on the other side of the "Copse of Trees" was the four Napoleons of Lieutenant T. Frederick Brown's Battery B, First Rhode Island Artillery, now commanded by Lieutenant Walter S. Perrin. To Perrin's left was Captain James M. Rorty's Battery B, First New York Artillery with four 10-pound Parrotts. Immediately to Cushing's right was Captain William A. Arnold's Battery A, First Rhode Island Artillery, armed with six 3-inch rifles. To Arnold's right and on the other side of the white building, Bryan's Barn, were the six Napoleons of Lieutenant George A. Woodruff's Battery I, First U.S. Artillery.

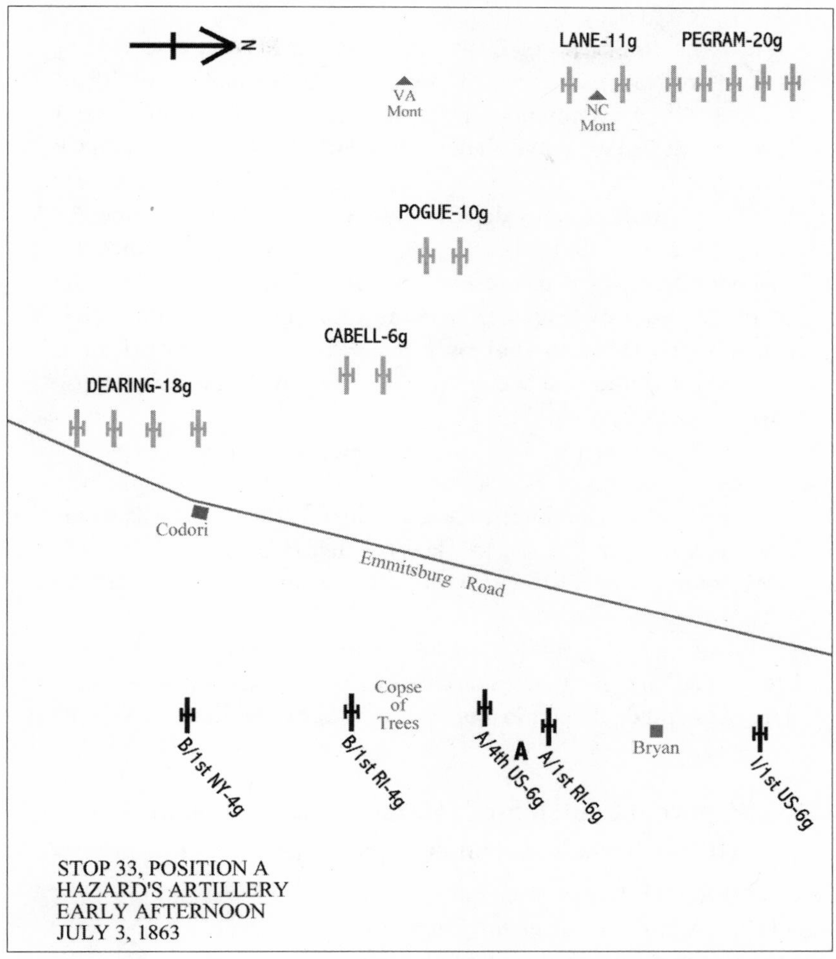

When the Confederate artillery bombardment began, Hazard had twenty-six guns: ten Napoleons, twelve 3-inch rifles, and four 10-pound Parrotts.

During the preattack bombardment and the infantry attack, some of Hazzard's artillery was so damaged as to render it ineffective or caused it to withdraw. This was probably what *Alexander* saw when he reported that Union batteries were being driven off the center part of Cemetery Ridge. However, during the attack Hazard was reinforced with the six 3-inch rifles of Cowan's First New York Battery. As the attack was repulsed, Hazard was reinforced with a section of two Napoleons from the Ninth Massachusetts Battery under the command of Lieutenant Richard Milton, a section of two more Napoleons from Batteries F and K (Combined), Third U.S. Artillery, commanded by Lieutenant John G. Turnbull, and Lieutenant Gulian V. Weir's Battery C, Fifth U. S Artillery, with six Napoleons.

The Union infantry deployed along this section of Cemetery Ridge were two divisions of Major General Winfield Hancock's Second Corps. At your present location and to your left were the three brigades of Brigadier General John Gibbon's Second Division. They were from your right to left the brigades of Brigadier General Alexander S. Webb, Colonel Norman J. Hall, and Brigadier General William Harrow.

On your right were two brigades of Brigadier General Alexander Hays's Third Division. To your immediate right was Colonel Thomas A. Smyth's brigade then farther right was Colonel Eliakim Sherrill's brigade. Hays's other brigade had been sent to reinforce East Cemetery Hill the evening before and had not returned.

During the preattack artillery bombardment, Hazard's batteries had engaged in counterbattery fire against the Confederate artillery and depleted most of their long-range ammunition.

Report of Capt. John G. Hazard, USA, Commanding Artillery Brigade, Second Corps, Army of the Potomac

The morning of July 3 was quiet until about 8 o'clock, when the enemy suddenly opened fire upon our position, exploding three limbers of Battery A, Fourth U.S. Artillery, but otherwise causing little loss. Little reply was made, save by [Battery] I, First U.S. Artillery, which battery during the forenoon had eight separate engagements with the enemy.

Captain John G. Hazard, USA. Roger D. Hunt and Jack R. Brown, *Brevet Brigadier Generals in Blue.*

At 1 p.m. the artillery of the enemy opened along the whole line, and for an hour and a quarter we were subjected to a very warm artillery fire. The batteries did not at first reply, till the fire of the enemy becoming too terrible, they returned it till all their ammunition, excepting canister, had been expended; they then waited for the anticipated infantry attack of the enemy. Battery B, First New York Artillery, was entirely exhausted; its ammunition expended; its horses and men killed and disabled; the commanding officer, Capt. J. M. Rorty, killed, and senior First Lieut. A. S. Sheldon severely wounded. The other batteries were in similar condition; still, they bided the attack. [*OR* 27, pt. 1, pp. 478–80]

Before the Confederate artillery had commenced firing, Hunt rode along the position and ordered the artillery commanders not to use up all their long-range ammunition with counterbattery fire, but to save it for the infantry attack that would follow. However, in the Second Corps area the corps commander, Major General Winfield S. Hancock, countermanded Hunt's order, and the artillery on this part of the ridge opened fire on the opposing guns. When *Lee's* infantry began their attack, which was centered on this location and to your right, most of the Second Corps artillery only had short-range ammunition available. They had to hold their fire until the attacking infantry came to within 400 yards or less. From your location that range would be in the vicinity of the Emmitsburg Road.

To your left front, in the direction of the Codori Barn, *Pickett's* infantry came into view as they passed over the small ridge occupied by *Dearing's* and *Eshleman's* Battalions. At that location they were brought under fire by the artillery on Cemetery Ridge to the left of the Second Corps. These were McGilvery's guns and the reinforcing batteries that had joined him.

Slightly to your right front, *Pettigrew's* and *Trimble's* infantry came into view as they passed through the line of artillery on Seminary Ridge. This part of the attack came under fire from the artillery on West Cemetery Hill. The guns to your left and right for the most part remained silent until the Confederate infantry closed to canister range. Two of Cushing's guns—Battery A, Fourth U.S.—were pushed to the rock wall in front of you.

Report of Capt. John G. Hazard, USA—Continued

The rebel lines advanced slowly but surely; half the valley had been passed over by them before the guns dared expend a round of the precious ammunition remaining on hand. The enemy steadily approached, and, when within deadly range, canister was thrown with terrible effect into their ranks. Battery A, First Rhode Island Light Artillery, had expended every round, and the lines of the enemy still advanced. Cushing was killed; Milne had fallen, mortally wounded; their battery was exhausted, their ammunition gone, and it was feared the guns would be lost if not withdrawn.

At this trying moment the two batteries were taken away [withdrawn]; but Woodruff still remained in the grove, and poured death and destruction into the rebel lines. They had gained the crest, and but few shots remained. All seemed lost, and the enemy, exultant, rushed on. But on reaching the crest they found our infantry, fresh and waiting. The tide turned; backward and downward rushed the rebel line, shattered and broken, and the victory was gained. Woodruff, who had gallantly commanded the battery through the action of July 2 and 3, fell, mortally wounded, at the very moment of victory. The command of the battery devolved upon Second Lieut. Tully McCrea.

Batteries from the Artillery Reserve of the army immediately occupied the positions vacated by the exhausted batteries of the brigade, and immediate efforts were made to recuperate and restore them to serviceable condition. So great was the loss in officers, men, and horses, that it was found necessary to consolidate [Battery] I, First U.S. Artillery [with] Battery A, Fourth U.S. Artillery, and Batteries A and B, First Rhode Island Light Artillery, thus reducing the five batteries that entered the fight to three. [*OR* 27, pt. 1, p. 480]

Walk forward for 30 yards to the guns representing Lieutenant Alonzo Cushing's Battery A, Fourth U.S. Artillery, stand in front of the guns, and look west toward Seminary Ridge.

Stop 33, Position B—The Angle (Battery A, Fourth U.S.)

Pickett's Division was rendered combat ineffective when the attack against the Union center was repulsed. A report by the surviving senior officer of *Garnett's* Brigade describes the movement from behind the Confederate artillery position to this location.

Report of Maj. *Charles S. Peyton,* CSA, Commanding *Garnett's* Brigade, *Pickett's* Division, *Longstreet's* Corps, Army of Northern Virginia

At about 12 m. we were ordered to take position behind the crest of the hill on which the artillery, under Colonel [*E. Porter*] *Alexander,* was planted,

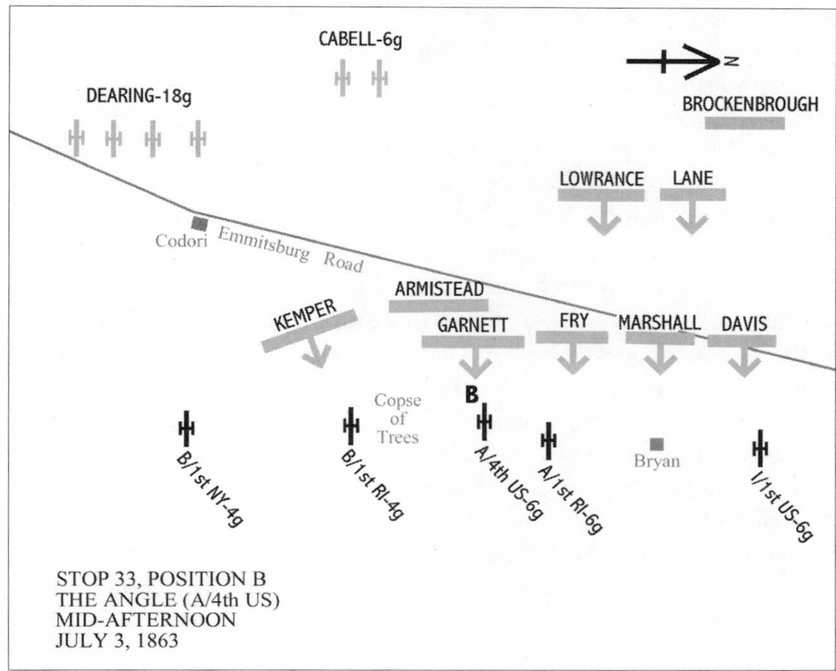

where we lay during a most terrific cannonading, which opened at 1.30 p.m., and was kept up without intermission for one hour.

During the shelling, we lost about 20 killed and wounded. Among the killed was Lieutenant-Colonel [*John T.*] *Ellis,* of the Nineteenth Virginia.

At 2.30 p.m., the artillery fire having to some extent abated, the order to advance was given, first by Major-General *Pickett* in person, and repeated by General *Garnett.* The brigade moved forward at quick time. The ground was open, but little broken, and from 800 to 1,000 yards from the crest whence we started to the enemy's line. The brigade moved in good order, keeping up its line almost perfectly, notwithstanding it had to climb three high post and rail fences, behind the last of which the enemy's skirmishers were first met and immediately driven in. Moving on, we soon met the advance line of the enemy, lying concealed in the grass on the slope, about 100 yards in front of his second line, which consisted of a stone wall, running nearly parallel to and about 30 paces from the crest of the hill, which was lined with their artillery.

The first line referred to above, after offering some resistance, was completely routed, and driven in confusion back to the stone wall. Here we captured some prisoners, which were ordered to the rear without a guard.

Having routed the enemy here, General *Garnett* ordered the brigade forward, which it promptly obeyed, loading and firing as it advanced.

Up to this time we had suffered but little from the enemy's batteries, which apparently had been much crippled previous to our advance, with the exception of one posted on the mountain [Little Round Top], about 1 mile to our right, which enfiladed nearly our entire line with fearful effect, sometimes as many as 10 men being killed and wounded by the bursting of a single shell. From the point it had first routed the enemy, the brigade moved rapidly forward toward the stone wall, under a galling fire both from artillery and infantry, the artillery using grape and canister. We were now within about 75 paces of the wall, General *Kemper* being some 50 or 60 yards behind and to the right, and General *Armistead* coming up in our rear.

Our line, much shattered, still kept up the advance until within about 20 paces of the wall, when, for a moment, it recoiled under the terrific fire that poured into our ranks both from their batteries and from their sheltered infantry. At this moment, General *Kemper* came up on the right and General *Armistead* in rear, when the three lines, joining in concert, rushed forward with unyielding determination and an apparent spirit of laudable rivalry to plant the Southern banner on the walls of the enemy. His stron-

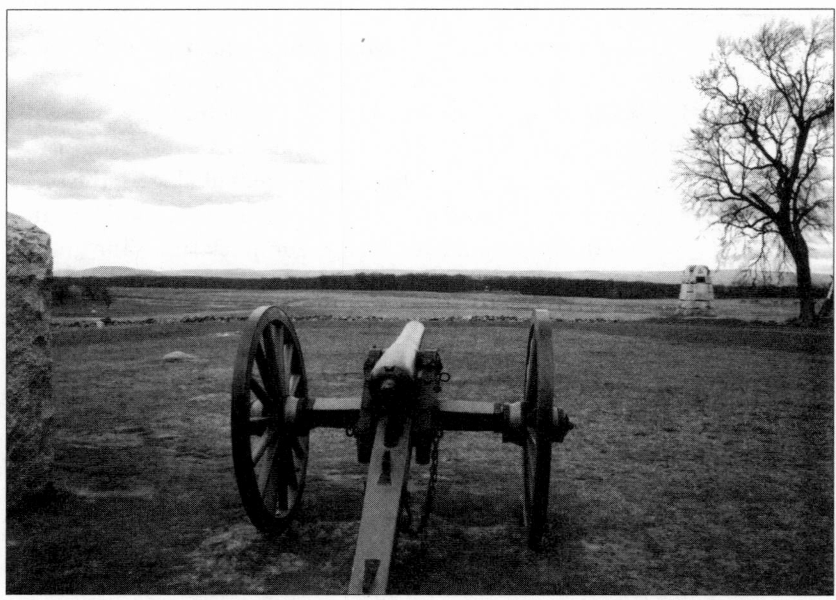

Seminary Ridge and the open approaches to Cemetery Ridge as seen from the position of Battery A, 4th U.S. Artillery (Stop 33B).

gest and last line was instantly gained; the Confederate battle-flag waved over his defenses, and the fighting over the wall became hand to hand, and of the most desperate character; but more than half having already fallen, our line was found too weak to rout the enemy. Yet a small remnant remained in desperate struggle, receiving a fire in front, on the right, and on the left, many even climbing over the wall, and fighting the enemy in his own [defenses] until entirely surrounded; and those who were not killed or wounded were captured, with the exception of about 300 who came off slowly, but greatly scattered, the identity of every regiment being entirely lost, and every regimental commander killed or wounded.

The brigade went into action with 1,287 men and about 140 officers and sustained a loss of 941 killed, wounded, and missing. [*OR* 27, pt. 2, pp. 385–87]

As the infantry of *Garnett's* Brigade and *Armistead's* supporting brigade crossed the Emmitsburg Road, the defending infantry in this vicinity and two of Cushing's guns opened fire. Initially Cushing used canister, then double canister, and finally triple canister. Gaps were torn in the attacking formation, but some of the infantry penetrated the defenses. Cushing, already wounded, was killed, and First Sergeant Frederick W. Fuger assumed command of the battery. *Armistead* led some of the attackers over the wall and into this area, and the guns were temporarily overrun. *Armistead* was mortally wounded, and the defenders and attackers engaged in hand-to-hand combat until the Confederates were killed, captured, or repulsed.

First Sergeant Frederick W. Fuger, USA. U.S. Army Military History Institute.

Turn around, walk back to the park road, face left, and walk north for 25 yards to the guns and monument to Battery A, First Rhode Island Artillery. When you reach the monument, face left, and look back to the west. The position of Cushing's battery will be to your left front.

Position C—Battery A, First Rhode Island Artillery

Look left and right along the line of the high point of Cemetery Ridge in this location. Notice that the top of the ridge is narrow. This gave the Union defenders a terrain advantage from the Confederate artillery fire. Any rounds fired at the defenders that did not strike in the narrow area on the west side of the ridge went over the ridge and hit the area to the east. Although considerable damage was done to the artillery along the ridge, the effectiveness of the Confederate fire was greatly lessened by the large number of rounds that went over the ridge.

Lee's preattack artillery bombardment did some damage in this area. However, overall the bombardment was relatively ineffective in suppressing Meade's artillery and softening up the infantry defenders. After the war one of *Hill's* artillery battalion commanders provided insight into the failure of *Lee's* artillery to accomplish what was expected.

Narrative of Maj. *David G. McIntosh,* CSA, Commanding *McIntosh's* Artillery Battalion, *Hill's* Corps, Army of Northern Virginia

The impression that any very serious effect had been produced upon the enemy's lines by the artillery fire proved to be a delusion; the aim of the Confederate gunners was accurate, and they did their work as well as could be, but the distance was too great to produce the results which they sanguinely hoped for. Previous experience should have taught them better. It is not a little surprising that General *Lee* should have reckoned so largely upon the result. Both sides had been pretty well taught that sheltered lines of infantry cannot be shattered or dislodged when behind breastworks, by field artillery, at the distance of one thousand yards and upwards.

The soldier who has been taught by experience to hug tight to his breastworks, and who knows that it is more dangerous to run than to lie still, comes to regard with stoical indifference the bursting missiles, which are mostly above or behind him. [David Gregg McIntosh, "Review of the Gettysburg Campaign: By One Who Participated Therein," *Southern Historical Society Papers* 37 (1909): 136–37]

The six brigades from *Hill's* Corps that participated in the attack came from the tree line to your front along Seminary Ridge. The angle of the rock wall makes an almost perfect dividing line between *Pickett's* troops and those of *Hill* Corps when they reached the area in front of you. Brigadier General *J. Johnston Pettigrew* commanded the four brigades of *Heth's* Division that were in the first line of the assault. Striking the defensive position where you are and just to your right was *Archer's* Brigade, commanded by Colonel *Birkett D. Fry,* who was wounded in the attack. To *Fry's* left, your right, was *Pettigrew's* Brigade, commanded by Colonel *John K. Marshall.* To *Marshall's* left, farther to your right, was Brigadier General *Joseph R. Davis's* brigade, which was attacking toward the white barn you can see 300 yards to your right. To *Davis's* left was Colonel *John M. Brockenbrough's* brigade. *Brockenbrough's* Brigade was the left flank of the attacking formation, but, as you will see later, it never reached the Emmitsburg Road. Following in the supporting line under the command of Major General *Isaac Trimble* were two brigades from *Pender's* Division. *Scales's* Brigade,

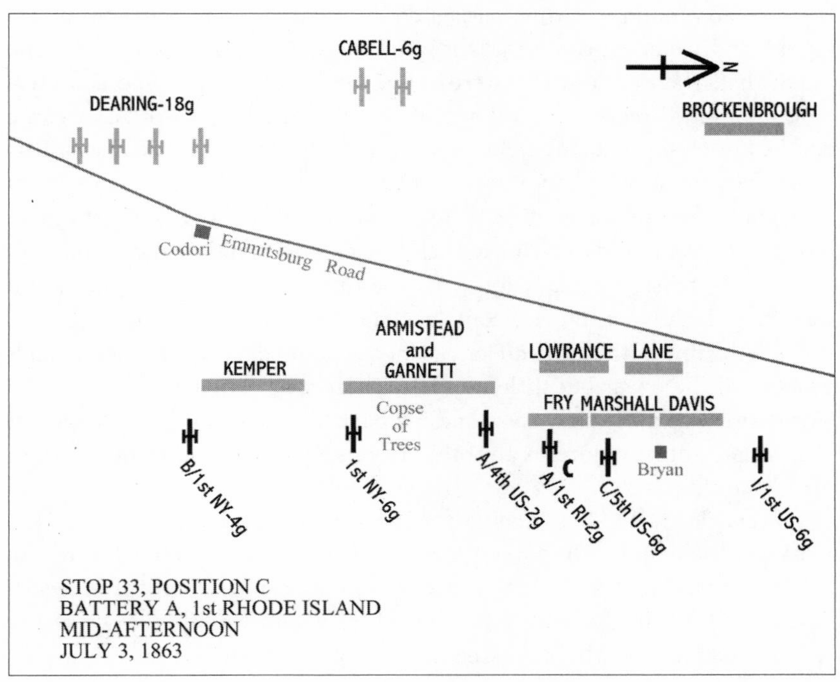

STOP 33, POSITION C
BATTERY A, 1st RHODE ISLAND
MID-AFTERNOON
JULY 3, 1863

commanded by Colonel *William Lee J. Lowrance,* followed *Fry,* and Brigadier General *James H. Lane's* brigade followed *Marshall.*

The senior surviving officer from *Archer's* (*Fry's*) Brigade recounted the attack from Seminary Ridge to this location.

Report of Lieut. Col. *Samuel G. Shepard,* CSA, Commanding *Archer's* Brigade, *Heth's* Division, *Hill's* Corps, Army of Northern Virginia

In the engagement of the 3d, the brigade was on the right of our division, in the following order: First Tennessee on the right, on its left, Thirteenth Alabama, next, Fourteenth Tennessee, on its left, Seventh Tennessee, and, on the left, Fifth Alabama Battalion. There was a space of a few hundred yards between the right of *Archer's* brigade and the left of General *Pickett's* division when we advanced, but, owing to the position of the lines (they not being an exact continuation of each other), as we advanced, the right of our brigade and the left of General *Pickett's* division gradually approached each other, so that by the time we had advanced a little over half of the way, the right of *Archer's* touched and connected with *Pickett's* left.

The command was then passed down the line by the officers, "Guide right;" and we advanced our right, guiding by General *Pickett's* left. The enemy held their fire until we were in fine range, and opened upon us a terrible and well-directed fire. Within 180 or 200 yards of his works, we came to [the Emmitsburg Road] inclosed by two stout post and plank fences. This was a very great obstruction to us, but the men rushed over as rapidly as they could, and advanced directly upon the enemy's works, the first line of which was composed of rough stones. The enemy abandoned this, but just in rear was massed a heavy force. By the time we had reached this work, our lines all along, as far as I could see, had become very much weakened; indeed, the line both right and left, as far as I could observe, seemed to melt away until there was but little of it left. Those who remained at the works saw that it was a hopeless case, and fell back. *Archer's* brigade remained at the works fighting as long as any other troops either on their right or left, so far as I could observe.

Every flag in the brigade excepting one was captured at or within the works of the enemy. The First Tennessee had 3 color-bearers shot down, the last of whom was at the works, and the flag captured. The Thirteenth Alabama lost 3 in the same way, the last of whom was shot down at the works. The Fourteenth Tennessee had 4 shot down, the last of whom was

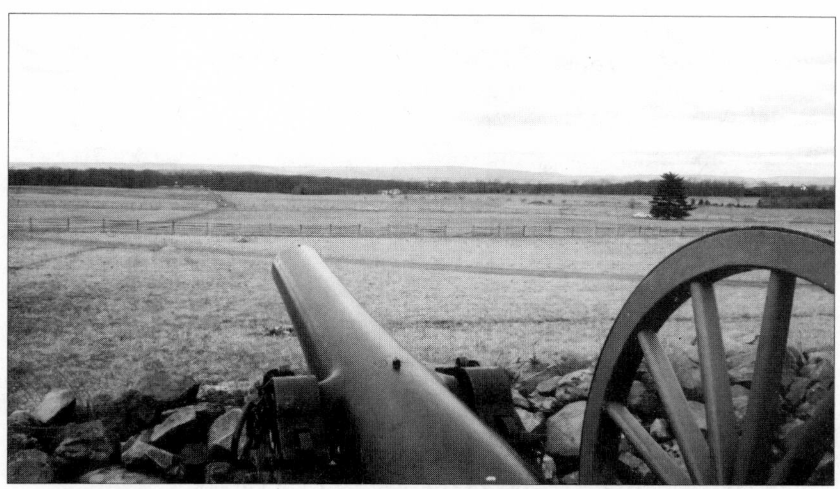

Seminary Ridge and the open approaches to Cemetery Ridge as seen from the position of Battery A, 1st Rhode Island Artillery

at the enemy's works. The Seventh Tennessee lost 3 color-bearers, the last of whom was at the enemy's works, and the flag was only saved by Captain [*Archibald D.*] *Norris* tearing it away from the staff and bringing it out beneath his coat. The Fifth Alabama Battalion also lost their flag at the enemy's works.

There were 7 field officers who went into the charge, only 2 of whom came out. The rest were all wounded and captured. The loss in company officers was nearly in the same proportion. [*OR* 27, pt. 2, p. 647]

As the Confederate attack came forward against this position, Captain Arnold's Battery A, First Rhode Island Artillery, out of ammunition, was withdrawn from the wall for a short distance. Lieutenant Weir's Battery C, Fifth U.S. Artillery, was deployed to this location. You last saw Weir's battery when you were on the right of McGilvery's artillery position. It had been placed in a defilade position on the east side of the ridge about 400 yards to your left rear. The battery moved to this vicinity and went into firing position to your right about the same time the Confederate infantry attack was repulsed and began to fall back. Weir's six Napoleons were brought forward, loaded with canister, and fired point blank at the attackers as they began their retreat. Loaded with canister each Napoleon discharged twenty-seven one-and-one-half-inch iron balls. Every time they fired, Weir's six Napoleons covered the area to their front with 162 iron balls, and when firing double canister, with 324 iron balls.

Face left, and walk south on the park road for 100 yards to the monument and guns for the First New York Battery, stop, and face right so that you are looking to the west. The "Copse of Trees" is on your right.

Position D—Double Canister (First New York Battery)

Initially this was the position Lieutenant T. Frederick Brown's Battery B, First Rhode Island Artillery, armed with the remaining four of six Napoleons and now commanded by Lieutenant Walter S. Perrin. Captain James M. Rorty's Battery B, First New York Artillery with four 10-pound Parrotts was to Perrin's left. The wall in front of this location and to the left marks the position of the infantry of Colonel Norman Hall's and Brigadier General Harrow's brigades of the Second Corps's Second (Gibbon's) Division.

The Confederate force attacking this section of the defensive position was the left of *Kemper's* Brigade and the right of *Garnett's* and *Armistead's* Brigades of *Pickett's* Division. *Kemper's* Brigade was the right flank brigade of *Pickett's* attack formation. It came into view as it passed by the Roger's House, which was 1,000 yards to your left front. After it crossed the Emmitsburg Road, *Kemper* began echeloning his brigade its left. This brought it along a line from the Rogers House to the right, left as you view it, of the Codori Barn and across the open fields to this location. As it passed by the Roger's House, it came under fire from McGilvery's artillery. Echeloning to the left marched the brigade in front of and across McGilvery's position and exposed its right flank to devastating enfilade fire from the artillery. As *Kemper's* infantry came closer to this location, the artillery here opened fire with canister.

During the Confederate preattack bombardment, Perrin's Battery B, First Rhode Island, was so damaged as to render it combat ineffective, and Perrin was ordered off the firing line. To your left Captain Rorty was killed and his Battery B, First New York, badly damaged, but its remaining guns were pushed forward to the wall to await the Confederate infantry. To reinforce this position, Hunt redeployed Cowan's First Battery New York Artillery from its ini-

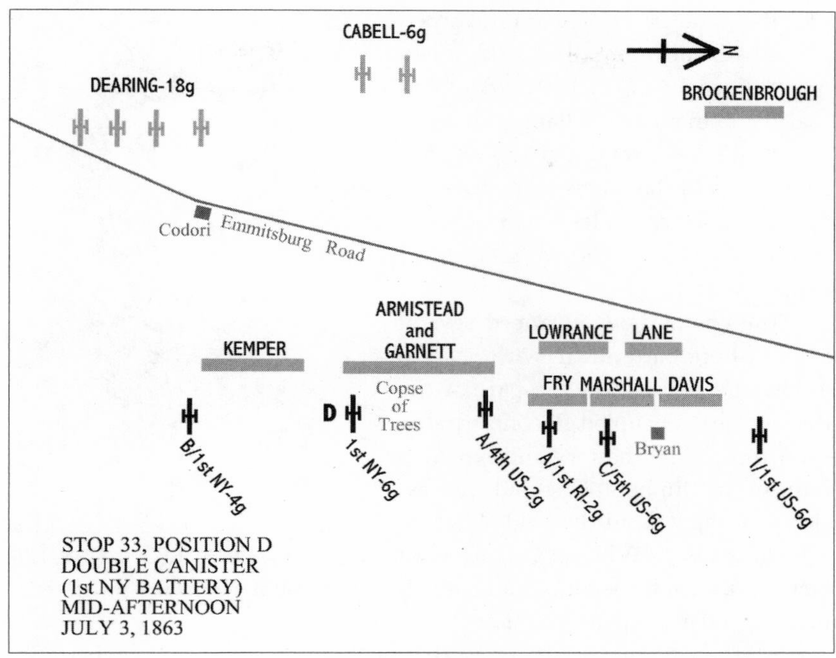

tial position on the right of McGilvery's line, just this side of the Pennsylvania Monument, to this location. When Cowan went into position, five of his 3-inch rifles were on this side of the trees while one was on the other side.

Report of Capt. Andrew Cowan, USA, Commanding First New York Battery, Artillery Brigade, Sixth Corps, Army of the Potomac

[I] received orders to move to the crest farther to my right, with General Webb's brigade, as the enemy was advancing. I moved up at a gallop, and came into position, several other batteries being on my right and left. The rebel skirmishers had just commenced firing, and their second line was advancing from the woods. [Our] artillery fire was quite accurate and did much execution; still, the rebel line advanced in a most splendid manner. I commenced firing canister at 200 yards, and the effect was greater than I could have anticipated. My last charge (a double-header) literally swept the enemy from my front, being fired at less than 20 yards. The [Union] infantry in front of five of my pieces, and posted behind a slight defense of rails, some 10 yards distant, turned and broke, but were rallied, and drawn off to the right of my battery by General Webb in a most gallant manner. It was then I fired my last charge of canister, many of the rebels being over the defenses and within less than 10 yards of my pieces. They broke and fled in confusion.

Captain Andrew Cowan, USA. U.S. Army Military History Institute.

The enemy now advanced several smooth-bore batteries to within 1,300 yards, and opened on the part of the line which I occupied. I concentrated my fire on a single battery, and exploded four of its limbers in rapid succession, driving it from the field. Another 3-inch battery [Wheeler's Thirteenth New York with three guns] came up on my left, and also opened on them.

After about an hour, there was but one section of the enemy's batteries firing, and it soon limbered up. As it was retiring at a gallop, a shell from my right piece exploded one of its limbers.

My loss was 4 privates killed instantly, and 1 soon after died of wounds: 4 enlisted men and 2 officers wounded. I also lost 14 horses, and 8 wheels were disabled. [*OR* 27, pt. 1, p. 690]

Walk 20 yards forward of Cowan's position, stop, turn around, and look back at the guns.

This is the distance some of *Kemper's* men were from the guns when the first charge of double canister was fired.

Now walk back half way from where you are to the guns.

This is where the infantry was when the second double charge of canister was fired. Depending on the manufacturer, a canister round for a 3-inch rifle contained approximately 100 one-half-inch-diameter balls. When Cowan's five guns fired double canister, they blanketed the area in front of their muzzles with 1,000 balls.

As you face Cowan's guns, turn right, and walk south for 150 yards to the marker for Battery B, First New York Artillery, stop, stand beside the marker, face to your right, and look to the west.

Position E—More Artillery Reinforcements

This is the position of Captain James Rorty's Battery B, First New York Artillery. During the fighting on the afternoon of July 3, Rorty was killed, and Lieutenant Robert E. Rogers assumed command of the battery. By the time the infantry attack crossed the Emmitsburg Road, Rogers was out of long-range ammunition and could only man two guns. Two of the battery's 10-pound Parrotts were loaded with canister and pushed down to the wall in front of you. When Lieutenant Perrin, on you right, pulled his heavily damaged battery out of position, Roger's two guns were the only artillery left in this area until Captain Cowan's battery arrived.

To your left in front of the Pennsylvania Monument (Stop 32), two reinforcing batteries, Captain Fitzhugh's Battery K, First New York Artillery, and Lieutenant Parson's Battery A, First New Jersey Artillery, had earlier taken up firing positions. From there they added their fire against *Pickett's* right flank.

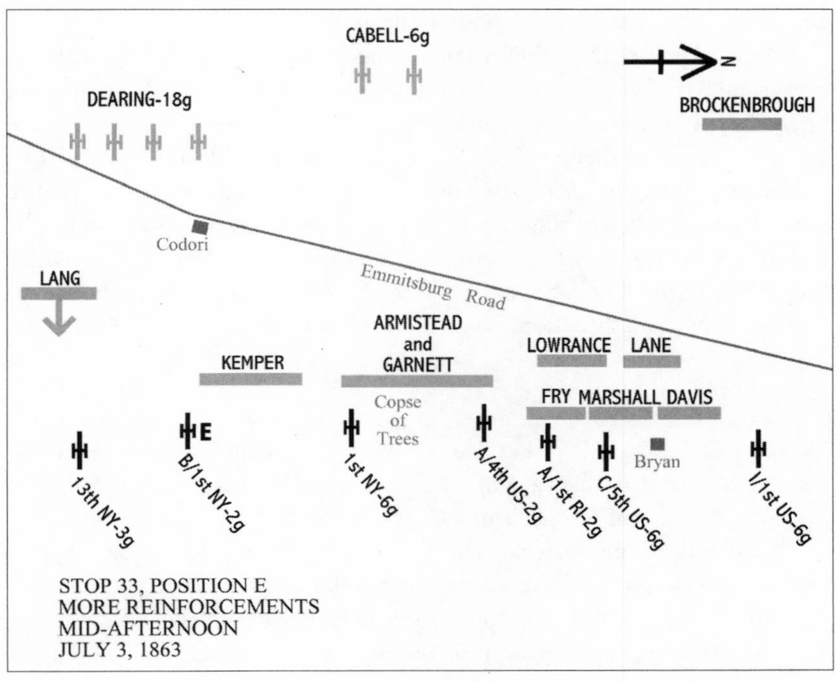

STOP 33, POSITION E
MORE REINFORCEMENTS
MID-AFTERNOON
JULY 3, 1863

Report of Capt. Robert H. Fitzhugh, USA, Commanding Fourth Volunteer Artillery Brigade, Artillery Reserve, Army of the Potomac

[Battery] A, First New Jersey Artillery, First Lieut. A. N. Parsons commanding, and [Battery] K, First New York Artillery remained unengaged until 1 p.m. of Friday, July 3, when, by order of General Hunt, I put them in position near the stone fence in front of General [Gibbon's] division of the Second Corps, Battery A, First New Jersey Artillery, on the left of K, First New York Artillery.

At this time the enemy were making a strong effort to break the Second Corps line, their infantry having charged up to the stone fence near a small wooded knoll about 75 yards on my right [the small knoll is to your left], while their artillery fire swept the ground occupied by the two batteries. Just then there were no other batteries at that point, and there seemed to be a good deal of confusion. The rebel artillery fire, from near [the Klingle] house and barn about 1,000 yards on my left and front, was especially severe, but soon materially slackened, and became very wild under a fire of percussion and time shell from Battery K. In the meantime, Lieutenant Parsons poured about 40 rounds of shrapnel into the flank of the rebel infantry charging the Second Corps, and in about half or three-quarters of an hour the enemy abandoned the attack on that point altogether.

After a pause, the rebel infantry began forming on the right of the house and barn before spoken of, while from the same quarter their artillery opened upon us a brisk but poorly directed and inefficient fire, to which, by direction of General Hunt, I made no reply, but awaited the attack of their infantry [*Lang's* and *Wilcox's* Brigades], who soon charged over the open field toward some broken ground about 500 yards on my left, as they did so giving the two batteries an opportunity to pour in an enfilading fire, which they did with great effect, for the enemy did not reach the point, but broke and gave way in all directions when about the middle of the field. [*OR* 27, pt. 1, p. 896]

As *Pickett's* Division closed with the defenders, the three 3-inch rifles of Lieutenant William Wheeler's Thirteenth New York Battery of the Eleventh Corps Artillery Brigade arrived on Cemetery Ridge. Wheeler's guns were place to the left of Battery B, 1st New York. Along with the other batteries, as the Confederate infantry approached, these guns opened fire. Wheeler's battery had participated in the fighting on July 1 and 2. Late on the second, it had fired all of its ammunition and had been sent to the Artillery Reserve area to resupply. Wheeler then returned his battery to the vicinity of Cemetery Hill.

Report of Lieut. William Wheeler, USA, Commanding Thirteenth New York Battery, Artillery Brigade, Eleventh Corps, Army of the Potomac

During the morning of July 3, I lay in reserve behind Cemetery Hill. During the heavy cannonade from 1 to 3 p.m., I lost some horses, but fortunately no men.

At about 4 p.m. I received an order to go to assist the Second Corps, upon which a very heavy attack was being made. I immediately reported to General Hancock, who showed me my position. Upon coming into battery, I found the enemy not more than 400 yards off, marching in heavy column by a flank to attack [Rorty's/Rogers's] battery, which was on my right and somewhat in advance of me. This gave me a fine opportunity to enfilade their column with canister, which threw them into great disorder, and brought them to a halt. The charge was finally repulsed, and most of the enemy taken prisoners. [*OR* 27, pt. 1, p. 753]

Return to your car for the drive to Stop 34.

Continue driving north on Hancock Avenue for just over 0.2 mile to the vicinity of a statue of an elderly gentleman seated on a bench. This is a monument to Albert Woolson, the last surviving member of the Grand Army of the Republic. Park in this area, leave your car, and walk north, the direction you were driving, for a few yards to the marker and guns for Battery I, First U.S. Artillery. At this location cross to the other side (west side) of the road, and stand so that you are looking to the west and southwest.

Stop 34—Hazard's Right Flank (Battery I, First U.S.)

The Bryan Barn is the white building to your left. You are standing in the vicinity of the right flank of Hazard's artillery position and also the right of Hancock's Second Corps. At your present location Lieutenant George A. Woodruff's Battery I, First U.S. Artillery, with six Napoleons was deployed. The infantry here was Brigadier General

Alexander Hays's Third Division of the Second Corps. Hays had two brigades deployed along this part of the defensive position. Where you are was his Third Brigade, commanded by Colonel Eliakim Sherrill. To your left was Colonel Thomas A. Smyth's Second Brigade. The artillery and infantry in this location was supported by batteries from Major Thomas Osborn's Eleventh Corps artillery positioned to your right rear on West Cemetery Hill.

Directly in front of you at a distance of 1,200 yards is Seminary Ridge. Look for the North Carolina Monument. This marks the vicinity of the right of *Hill's* Corps artillery. *Hill's* artillery was deployed on either side of where that monument is today. From there it extended north, to your right, to the Hagerstown Road. The position where you are was within the effective range of all of *Hill's* artillery.

To your right rear is West Cemetery Hill. This was the position of Major Thomas Osborn's Eleventh Corps Artillery Brigade and other reinforcing artillery. On the morning of July 3, Osborn had thirty-nine guns in position. Many of them could fire on *Hill's*

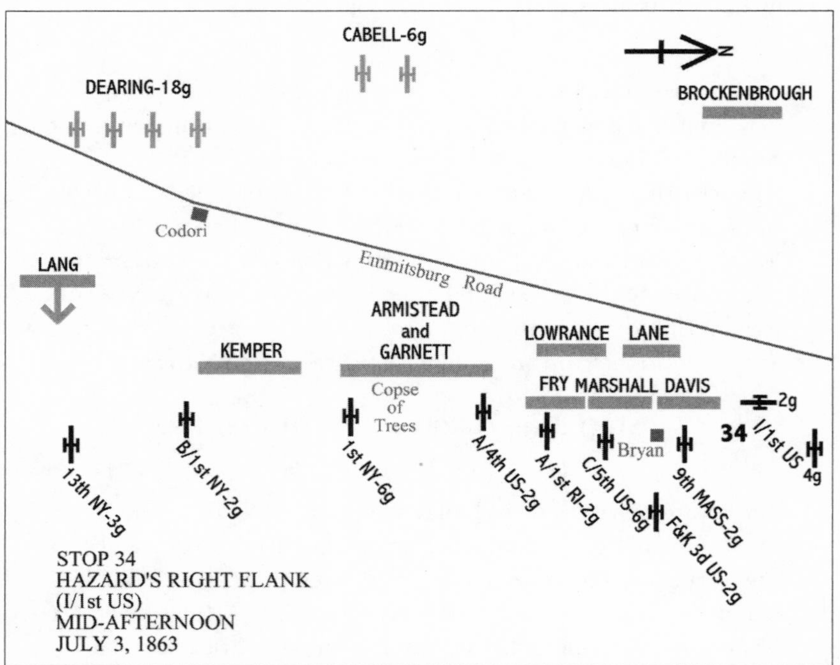

attacking infantry; others would be repositioned to allow them also to fire at the attackers.

Brockenbrough's Brigade was the left flank brigade of the attack. The objective for its attack was the position where you are and to your right. As it passed over Seminary Ridge, marched through the line of artillery, and came into view, it was brought under the concentrated fire of Osborn's guns, and then Woodruff's guns. The concentrated fire of these guns stopped *Brockenbrough's* infantry before it reached the Emmitsburg Road and drove it back. This exposed *Davis's* left flank.

Davis's Brigade, now the left flank of the attack, had as its objective the area of the ridge to your left. *Davis's* Brigade now began to feel the fire from Osborn's and Woodruff's guns. As his brigade came closer to the defenses, it was protected by the trees of Zeigler's Grove from Osborn's guns on Cemetery Hill. However, the fire from Woodruff became more of an enfilading fire. When *Davis's* Brigade crossed the Emmitsburg Road, a section of Woodruff's guns and defending infantry moved from your right and formed on a line from the rock wall to the Emmitsburg Road. This placed them on *Davis's* left flank, where they delivered punishing fire into the attackers.

Report of Brig. Gen. *Joseph R. Davis,* CSA, Commanding *Davis's* Brigade, *Heth's* Division, *Hill's* Corps, Army Northern of Virginia

About 1 p.m. the artillery along our entire line opened on the enemy, and was promptly replied to. For two hours the fire was heavy and incessant. Being immediately in the rear of our batteries, and having had no time to prepare means of protection, we suffered some losses. In *Davis'* brigade, 2 men were killed and 21 wounded. The order had been given that, when the artillery in our front ceased firing, the division would attack the enemy's batteries, keeping dressed to the right, and moving in line with Major-General *Pickett's* division, which was on our [division's] right, and marching obliquely to the left.

The artillery ceased firing, and the order to move forward was given and promptly obeyed. The [brigade] moved off in line, and, passing the wooded crest of the hill, descended to the open fields that lay between us and the enemy. Not a gun was fired at us until we reached a strong post and rail fence about three-quarters of a mile from the enemy's position, when we were met by a heavy fire of grape, canister, and shell, which told sadly upon our ranks. Under this destructive fire, which commanded our front and left with fatal effect, the troops displayed great coolness, were well in hand, and moved steadily forward, regularly closing up the gaps made in their ranks. Our advance across the fields was interrupted by other fences of a similar character, in crossing which the alignment became more or less deranged. This was in each case promptly rectified, and though its ranks were growing thinner at every step, this [brigade] moved steadily on in line with the troops on the right. When within musket-range, we encountered a heavy fire of small-arms, from which we suffered severely; but this did not for a moment check the advance.

The right owing to the conformation of the ridge on which the enemy was posted, having a shorter distance to pass over to reach his first line of defense, encountered him first in close conflict; but the whole division dashed up to his first line of defense—a stone wall—behind which the opposing infantry was strongly posted. Here we were subjected to a most galling fire of musketry and artillery, that so reduced the already thinned ranks that any further effort to carry the position was hopeless, and there was nothing left but to retire to the position originally held, which was done in more or less confusion. [*OR* 27, pt. 2, pp. 650–51]

With the repulse of *Davis's* Brigade the flank of the next attacking brigade was exposed and hit with heavy enfilade fire as well as frontal fire.

As the Confederate infantry attack was repulsed and the survivors were retreating to Seminary Ridge, four guns arrived to reinforce this section of the position. To your left was the surviving section of two Napoleons commanded by Lieutenant Richard S. Milton from Bigelow's Ninth Massachusetts Battery, First Volunteer Artillery Brigade. To Milton's left, but back from the wall, were two Napoleons of Lieutenant John G. Turnbull's Batteries F and K (Combined), Third U.S. Artillery, First Regular Artillery Brigade. As *Pettigrew's* and *Trimble's* surviving troops began to retreat, these guns and others subjected them to more artillery fire.

Return to your car for the drive to Stop 35.

Continue driving forward, to the north, on the park road for a short distance until you come to a T intersection with another park road. At the T intersection turn right, or east, drive into the parking area, and park. Leave your car, and walk east to the Taneytown Road. Be careful, as this is a busy road. At the Taneytown Road, turn left, and walk north beside the road for a short distance, then cross the road and enter the Cemetery where the gate is. Follow the walking path (DO NOT take the path to the left) for 160 yards to the guns and monument to Battery C, First West Virginia Artillery, stop, and face the direction the guns are pointed, northwest.

Stop 35, Position A—West Cemetery Hill (Osborn's Position)

You are standing in the left center of Major Thomas Osborn's artillery position on West Cemetery Hill. Osborn initially occupied this position late on the afternoon of July 1 with three batteries from his Eleventh Corps Artillery Brigade and one battery from Colonel Charles Wainwright's First Corps Artillery Brigade. One of Osborn's batteries was on East Cemetery Hill with Wainwright, and another had been sent to the rear for refit and resupply. On July 1 four of Osborn's five batteries had been supporting the Eleventh Corps infantry north of Gettysburg. With the collapse of the defenses there and along Seminary Ridge, they had retreated to this location. Initially Osborn had fifteen guns deployed on West Cemetery Hill. The next day Hunt reinforced him with five batteries from the Artillery Reserve. Concurrently part of Osborn's original force was sent to the rear for refit and resupply

On the morning of July 3, Osborn had seven batteries with a total of thirty-nine guns (twelve 3-inch rifles, four 10-pound Parrotts, seventeen Napoleons, and six 20-pound Parrotts) under his command on West Cemetery Hill.

At your location was Captain Wallace Hill's Battery C, First West Virginia Artillery, with four 10-pound Parrotts. To Hill's left was Battery H, First Ohio Artillery, commanded by Lieutenant George Norton, with six 3-inch rifles. Initially behind Hill and Norton was Captain Frederick M. Edgell's First New Hampshire Battery with six 3-inch rifles. Edgell's battery was brought forward during the fighting. All three of these batteries were from the Third Volunteer Artillery Brigade of the Artillery Reserve. To your right was Battery H, First U.S. Artillery, from the First Regular Artillery Brigade of the Artillery Reserve with six Napoleons commanded by Lieutenant Philip Mason. To Mason's right were Lieutenant Eugene A. Bancroft's Battery G, Fourth U.S. Artillery, with six Napoleons and then Captain Hubert Dilger's Battery I, First Ohio Artillery, with five Napoleons. Both Bancroft's and Dilger's batteries were from the Eleventh Corps Artillery Brigade. Completing Osborn's force was Captain Elijah Taft's Fifth New York Battery of the Second Volunteer Artillery Brigade of the Artillery Reserve with six 20-pound Parrotts. Taft's guns were initially rearward of Osborn's gun line, but two guns were brought forward during the infantry attack. All the batteries on West Cemetery Hill, regardless of their parent unit, were under Osborn's direct tactical command.

The four infantry brigades of Brigadier General Adolph von Steinwehr's and Major General Carl Schurz's divisions of the Eleventh Corps were deployed in multiple defensive lines at the base and on the lower part of the hill.

Across the Baltimore Pike, on East Cemetery Hill, were Wainwright's First Corps Artillery Brigade and other reinforcing artillery. Depending on the tactical situation, Wainwright's guns could be repositioned to reinforce Osborn or, in the event of a Confederate breakthrough, to fire across the open ground south of West Cemetery Hill.

Face slightly left, so that you are now looking directly west.

In front of you at a range of 1,500 yards is the section of Seminary Ridge that was occupied by the right of *Hill's* artillery, *Pogue's* and *Lane's* Battalions. To their left, your right, was *Pegram's* Battalion. Behind these artillery battalions were *Pettigrew's* and *Trimble's* infantry. To *Pegram's* left, your right, were *Garnett's, Dance's,* and *McIntosh's* artillery battalions. The cupola and steeple that mark the Lutheran Seminary are 1,900 yards to your right front. Five batteries from *Ewell's* Corps were in position north and south of there. Farther north on Oak Hill were the two Whitworth rifles of *Hurt's* Alabama Battery. West Cemetery Hill was within effective range of these guns. Conversely, from their positions on West Cemetery Hill, Osborn's guns could place counter battery fire on *Hill's* artillery.

Directly behind you at a range of 2,000 yards, just north of Benner's Hill, were five batteries from *Ewell's* Corps, a total of seventeen guns. Eleven of these guns were rifled artillery of various types, and, although firing at extreme range, these could place effective fire on West Cemetery Hill.

Ewell's artillery on Seminary Ridge and north of Benner's Hill in conjunction with *Hill's* artillery gave the Confederates the potential to place effective cross fire on the Union defenses on West Cemetery Hill and the northern part of Cemetery Ridge. However,

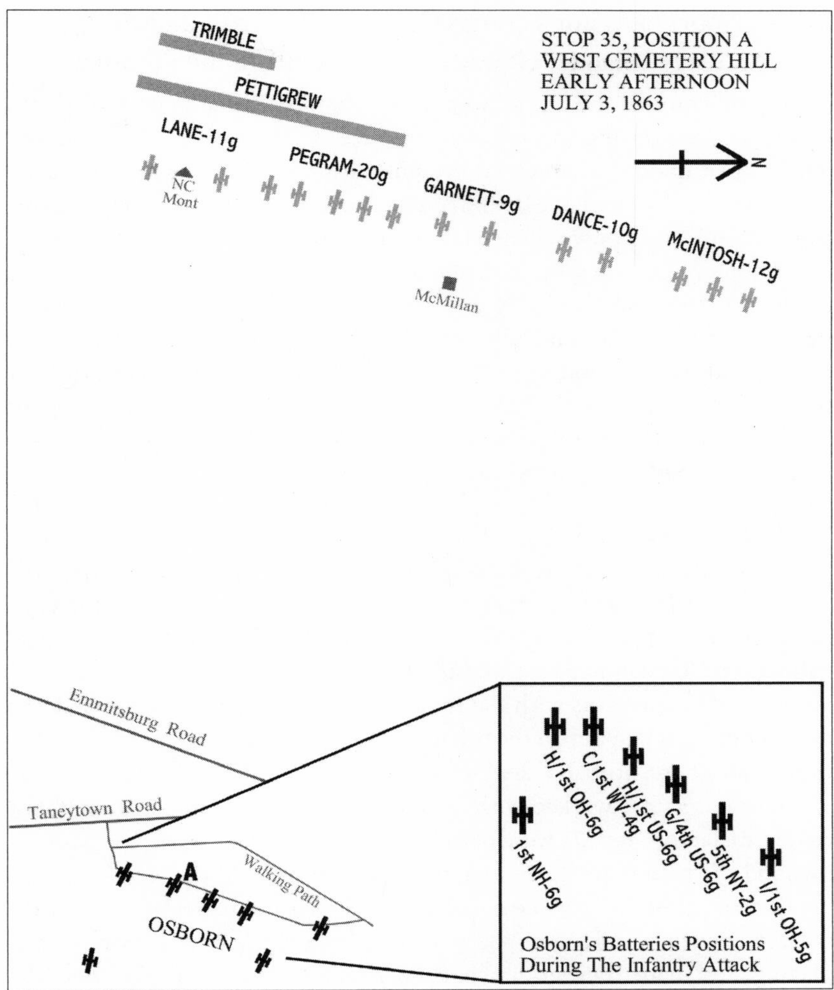

this was not effectively coordinated, and very few rounds were fired by *Ewell's* artillery. When this artillery did fire, Union defenders remarked on the damaging effect of the enfiladed fire.

When *Pettigrew's* and *Trimble's* infantry advanced across the open ground to attack the northern portion of Cemetery Ridge, Osborn moved the guns on his right forward and pointed them left. With his entire artillery facing west, he placed devastating fire on the attacking Confederate infantry. As the attackers came closer to Cemetery Ridge, the artillery fire from this position became oblique until blocked by Ziegler's Grove.

Report of Major Thomas Osborn, USA, Commanding Artillery Brigade, Eleventh Corps, Army of the Potomac

On the morning of the 3d, we were in position the same as on the 2d, but little was done during the a.m. by our corps. Occasionally a rebel battery would open upon the cemetery, evidently with a view to obtain the exact elevation and time to make their fire effective in the p.m.'s work on our position. At each attempt we silenced them, with but little loss to ourselves.

About 2 p.m. they opened along our whole front with an unbroken line of artillery, and also heavily on our right flank, apparently using every description of missiles and field artillery. The crest which the enemy occupied varied from 1,000 to 1,900 yards distance, and afforded an excellent protection. I judge that the guns of not less than one-half mile of this front were concentrated on our position, besides several batteries on our right, which enfiladed our position, excepting Captains Taft's and [Norton's] batteries.

Our artillery endured this fire with surprising coolness and determination. No battery even showed a disposition to retire, and several times during the cannonading we silenced several of their batteries, but at a moment's cessation on our part, they would reopen upon us. The fire was extremely galling, and by comparing the rapidity with which the shells fell among and passed by our guns with the rapidity with which our guns replied, the number of guns playing on the hill was very much greater than the number in position there; probably double.

Our guns were worked with great coolness, energy, and judgment, but as no satisfactory results were obtained, I ordered all our guns to cease firing, and the men to lie down to await developments. At the same time the artillery of our entire front ceased firing, and a few moments later the infantry of the enemy broke over the crest from where their artillery had been playing, and made their grand charge across the plain upon our lines. The left of the charging column rested on a line perpendicular to our front, then stretching away to [their] right beyond our view, thus offering an excellent front for our artillery fire. We used, according to distance, all descriptions of projectiles. The whole force of our artillery was brought to bear upon this column, and the havoc produced upon their ranks was truly surprising.

The enemy's advance was most splendid, and for a considerable distance the only hindrance offered it was by the artillery, which broke their lines fearfully, as every moment showed that their advance under this concentrated artillery fire was most difficult; and though they made desperate efforts to advance in good order, were unable to do so, and I am convinced that the fire from the hill was one of the main auxiliaries in breaking the force of this grand charge. But while the enemy was advancing, and after having been repulsed, I insisted that the artillery fire should be turned intensely upon the infantry, and no notice whatever was to be taken of their artillery. [*OR* 27, pt. 1, p. 750]

Face to your left, and retrace your steps on the walking path for 140 yards to where another walking path intersects from the right. Turn right on to this path, and walk for 50 yards to the guns and monument for First New Hampshire Battery. Stand beside the guns and monument, and look west and southwest, which was to your left as you walked along the intersecting path.

Position B—First New Hampshire Battery (Edgell's Position)

This is the position of Captain Frederick M. Edgell's First New Hampshire Battery, which was armed with six 3-inch rifles. Edgell's battery was one of the five batteries from the Artillery Reserve that

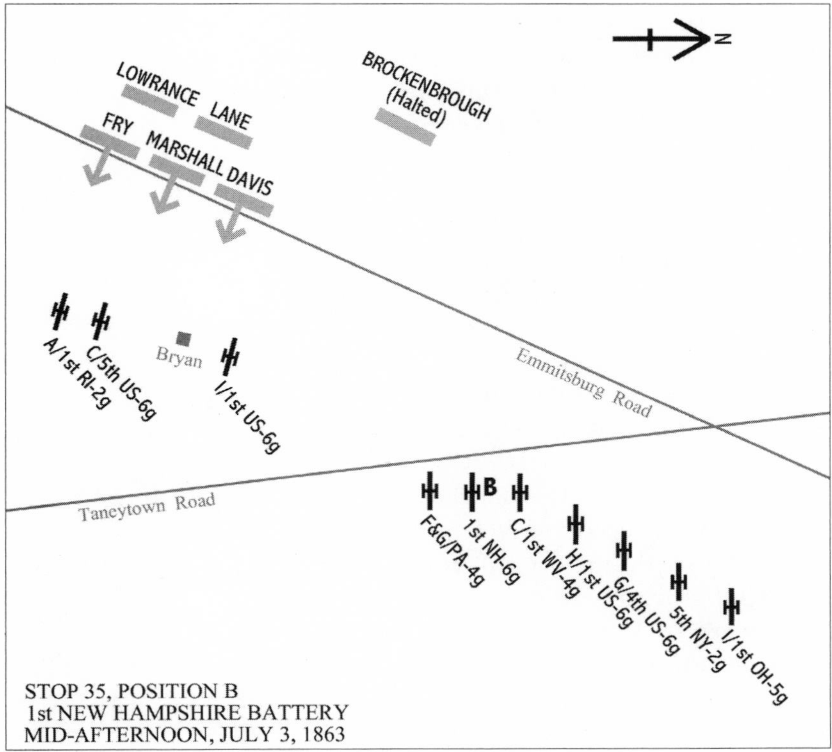

STOP 35, POSITION B
1st NEW HAMPSHIRE BATTERY
MID-AFTERNOON, JULY 3, 1863

had been sent to reinforce Osborn on July 2. Initially the battery had been in position on West Cemetery Hill, then it was redeployed east to the vicinity of the Baltimore Pike during the Confederate attempt to capture East Cemetery Hill. It remained there during the night, and, as the fighting developed on July 3, it was brought into position here to relieve Battery H, First Ohio Artillery, which had run out of long-range ammunition.

In 1863 the ground on the other side of the Taneytown Road all the way to Seminary Ridge was open and provided excellent fields of fire and observation. Like the other batteries on the hill, Edgell's gunners had immediate target acquisition as soon as the Confederate infantry moved forward from Seminary Ridge.

Report of Capt. Frederick M. Edgell, USA, Commanding First New Hampshire Battery, Third Volunteer Artillery Brigade, Artillery Reserve, Army of the Potomac

At about 1.30 p.m. [July 3] the enemy opened a rapid artillery fire on our center and left. Their batteries, in a semicircle about this point, swept the hill with a terrible cross-fire. The battery was now much exposed to the plunging shots of the enemy, which fell continually among my pieces, but fortunately without doing much damage.

At 2.30 p.m. I was ordered to take up my old position on Cemetery Hill, relieving Captain Huntington's [Lieutenant Norton's Battery H, First Ohio] battery. I commenced again to throw shell at the enemy's batteries, and also at some bodies of troops, apparently picket reserves, which caused them to break and retreat to the woods. The firing of the enemy's artillery was now very inaccurate, most of the shots being too high, and by the direction of General Meade the firing was discontinued by the batteries on the hill, and the men ordered to lie down.

Captain Frederick M. Edgell, USA. U.S. Army Military History Institute.

Soon after a grand attack was made by the enemy on our left, and I commenced a rapid fire of case shot on his advancing lines. I fired obliquely from my position upon the left of the attacking column with destructive effect, as that wing was broken and fled across the field to the woods. I next saw what appeared to be the remainder of the attacking force come into our lines as prisoners. There was no firing by my battery after this.

I expended this day 248 rounds of shell and case shot. The Hotchkiss time shell and Schenkl percussion worked well, but the Schenkl combination case seldom exploded. From what experience I have had with this fuse, I think it is not reliable.

The casualties in my battery were 3 men wounded (only 1 seriously). I also lost 3 horses killed, and a wheel and axle broken. [*OR* 27, pt. 1, pp. 892–93]

During the attack Osborn brought forward a section of two 20-pound Parrotts from Captain Elijah D. Taft's Fifth New York Battery and placed them in position to your right. Guns from Captain Bruce Ricketts's Batteries F & G (Combined), First Pennsylvania Artillery, that had been with Wainwright on East Cemetery Hill were also shifted to a position to your left.

As the Confederate infantry were repulsed and the survivors fell back to Seminary Ridge, four batteries from the Sixth Corps Artillery Brigade reinforced Osborn's position. Lieutenant Edward B. Williston's Battery D, Second U.S. Artillery, with six Napoleons; Lieutenant John H. Butler's Battery G, Second U.S. Artillery, with six Napoleons; and Lieutenant Leonard Martin's Battery F, Fifth U.S. Artillery, with six 10-pound Parrotts went into firing positions to your right front and right and fired upon the retreating Confederate infantry. The six Napoleons of Captain William H. McCartney's First Massachusetts Battey went into position behind you.

Although the participants may not have realized it, when the surviving Confederate infantry returned to Seminary Ridge and the artillery of both sides ceased firing, for all practical purposes, the Battle of Gettysburg ended.

Hunt summed up the status and condition of the Union artillery as night fell on July 3.

Report of Brig. Gen. Henry J. Hunt, USA—Continued

The losses of the artillery on this day, and especially in the assault on the Second Corps, were very large. The loss in officers was 3 killed, 2 mortally and 9 severely wounded. . . . The enemy's cannonade, in which he must have almost exhausted his ammunition, was well sustained, and cost us a great many horses and the explosion of an unusually large number of caissons and limbers. The whole slope behind our crest, although concealed from the enemy, was swept by his shot, and offered no protection to horses or carriages. The enemy's superiority in the number of guns was fully matched by the superior accuracy of ours, and a personal inspection of the line he occupied, made on the 5th, enables me to state with certainty that his losses in *materiel* in this artillery combat were equal to ours, while the marks of the shot in the trees on both crests bear conclusive evidence of the superiority of our practice.

This struggle closed the battle, and the night of the 3d, like the previous one, was devoted to repairs and reorganization. A large number of batteries had been so reduced in men and horses that many guns and carriages, after completing the outfit of those which remained with the army, were sent to the rear and turned in to the ordnance department.

Our losses in the three days' operations, as reported, were as follows:

Casualties, July 1, 2, and 3.

Organizations	**Killed**		**Wounded**		**Missing**	**Horses**
	Officers	Men	Officers	Men		
In the corps	5	57	18	361	52	565
Artillery Reserve	2	41	15	171	15	316
Total	7	98	33	532	67	881

The expenditure of ammunition in the three days amounted to 32,781 rounds, averaging over 100 rounds per gun. Many rounds were lost in the caissons and limbers by explosions and otherwise. The supply carried with the army being 270 rounds per gun, left sufficient to fill the ammunition chests and enable the army to fight another battle. There was for a short time during the battle a fear that the ammunition would give out. This fear was caused by the large and unreasonable demands made by corps commanders who had left their own trains or a portion of them behind, contrary to the orders of the commanding general. In this emergency, the train of the Artillery Reserve, as on so many other occasions, supplied all demands, and proved its great usefulness to the army. [*OR* 27, pt. 1, pp. 240–41]

In his report *Pendleton* indicated the Army of Northern Virginia's artillerymen's casualties as:

Command	Killed	Wounded	Missing	Total
Longstreet's Corps:				
Officers	2	9		11
Enlisted men	45	215	42	302
Ewell's Corps:				
Officers	2	8		10
Enlisted men	28	94	5	127
Hill's Corps:				
Officers	1	9	2	12
Enlisted men	16	102	28	146
Total	94	437	77	608

[*OR* 27, pt. 2, p. 354]

Lee began the campaign with 150 rounds for each gun. By the end of day on July 3 his artillery had fired 103 rounds per gun, leaving him critical short on artillery ammunition.

This completes your tour and study of the artillery at Gettysburg. You can read the "Aftermath" chapter while you are here in the Cemetery, return to your car and read it, or drive to the Visitors Center. Directions to the Visitors Center are at the end of chapter 5.

Chapter 5

THE AFTERMATH

The night of July 3 brought an end to the large-scale combat at Gettysburg. During the night *Lee* repositioned *Ewell's* Corps from north and east of Cemetery and Culp's Hills to the left, or north, of *Hill's* Corps along Seminary Ridge. The morning of July 4 brought a relative quite along the positions of both armies as both *Lee* and Meade considered their next course of action.

Lee had three possible courses of action. He could attack, defend, or redeploy/retreat his army to a new location. To continue to attack was not a viable option. Although its attack on July 1 had produced favorable results, in the following two days the Army of Northern Virginia's attacks were unsuccessful in obtaining decisive results. *Lee* did not believe that he could remain in defensive positions along Seminary Ridge as such a course of action could result in Meade gaining the initiative. Also, the longer his army remained static east of the passes in South Mountain, the more opportunity Meade had to position forces in those passes or move into the Cumberland Valley and block *Lee's* route back to Virginia. Included in *Lee's* decision process had to be his casualties, ammunition situation, and rations and forage available for his men and animals. In the three days of fighting his army had lost 28,063 men, 37 percent of its strength. Among the division, brigade, and regimental commanders, the casualties were equal to the leadership structure of an entire corps. The infantry had fired millions of small arms rounds and the artillery some 22,000 thousand rounds. The available ammunition was barely enough to sustain one more day of fighting, and then for all practical purposes *Lee's* army would be out of ammunition.

Lee's army had gathered large amounts of supplies, food, and forage while in Pennsylvania. However, there had been no opportunity to issue any of this in significant quantities to his troops; after combat began on July 1, the area east of South Mountain had been foraged out, and the troops had consumed much of the food they had available when the fighting began. Faced with this situation, *Lee* decided his only viable course of action was to retreat back through the passes in South Mountain into the Cumberland Valley and from there continue south to Virginia. *Lee's* army began its retreat on the night of July 4.

Meade also had the same courses of action as *Lee.* Having achieved a victory with a strong defensive position, Meade was in no hurry to attack *Lee's* in his defensive position on Seminary Ridge. Meade's losses were also high. Twenty-six percent, or 23,049 soldiers, were casualties. The highest percent of losses came from the First and Eleventh Corps, rendering them almost combat ineffective for offensive operations. As with the Confederates, there had been a significant loss among the army's leadership, including three corps, three division, twenty brigade, and eighty-three regimental commanders. Large amounts of small arms ammunition had been expended and the artillery had consumed more than 32,000 rounds of ammunition.

Meade opted to remain on the defense on July 4, to consolidate his position, and to conduct limited resupply. On July 5 a reconnaissance in force by the Sixth Corps revealed that *Lee's* army was retreating. This intelligence prompted Meade to march his army south then west through the South Mountain passes. On July 10 the Army of the Potomac was concentrating east of Hagerstown, Maryland. There it faced the Army of Northern Virginia in strong defensive positions. *Lee* arrived at the Potomac River on July 7, where he found the bridges destroyed and the river at flood stage. He was forced into a defensive posture until the water receded enough to allow a crossing. The armies faced each other at this location until the night of July 13, and the next morning *Lee* was able to cross the Potomac River into Virginia.

The artillery organizations of both armies had been tested during the three days of battle. In most cases the organization and tactics had proven good; however, there had been some deficiencies that decreased the combat power of *Lee's* artillery.

The Army of the Potomac had four critical elements that gave its artillery organization a high degree of effectiveness and combat power. First, part of the artillery was organized into brigades that were placed with each infantry corps and directly responsive through each artillery brigade commander to the corps commander. This was the ideal organization for fighting on the open and rolling terrain around Gettysburg. It provided the flexibility for the corps commander to assign a battery or batteries to one or more divisions for the march to the Gettysburg area while maintaining an artillery reserve that could be deployed as the situation required once the corps was committed to the fight. There was flexibility for the batteries attached to the infantry divisions to be withdrawn and placed back under command of the corps artillery brigade commander. This capability allowed artillery to be distributed across a corps front or rapidly brought together for concentrated fire support and counterbattery fire at one or two specific positions.

Examples of this organizational flexibility were seen on July 1 as the First and Eleventh Corps marched to Gettysburg. Colonel Charles Wainwright, commander of the First Corps Artillery Brigade, attached a battery each to two of the infantry divisions for the march to Gettysburg while keeping the other three under his command. Upon arriving in the vicinity of Seminary Ridge, Wainwright regained control of his two attached batteries and at the same time attached another battery to one of the other infantry divisions. Throughout the rest of the day, Wainwright deployed four of his batteries, fighting under his direct command, while a fifth battery remained under the control of the infantry division commander to which it was attached.

Similarly the Eleventh Corps artillery approached Gettysburg with part of its artillery attached to the infantry, while the rest remained under the control of Major Thomas W. Osborn, the artillery brigade commander. Osborn initially attached two of his batteries to two of the infantry divisions, while the remaining three remained with him. Upon reaching the battlefield, he sent one battery to reinforce a battery already in action, deployed another one just behind the center of the corps battle line, and held the remaining battery in reserve on Cemetery Hill.

As the First and Eleventh Corps were pushed off their initial defensive positions and retreated to the vicinity of Cemetery Hill, both artillery commanders brought all of their batteries back under their tactical control. As the artillery positions were consolidated on Cemetery Hill, it was discovered that the batteries of both corps were intermingled. Wainwright and Osborn solved this potentially disastrous command and control problem by deciding that Osborn would command all of the batteries on Cemetery Hill west of the Baltimore Pike while Wainwright commanded the batteries east of the pike, regardless of which corps they belonged to. As the fighting progressed into July 2 and 3, both Wainwright and Osborn, especially Osborn, were reinforced with additional artillery batteries. Again any artillery deploying on to West or East Cemetery Hill came under the tactical command of these two artillery officers. This resulted in a concentrate and coordinated use of artillery against Confederate offensive operations on those two days.

The second critical element of the Army of the Potomac's artillery was the Artillery Reserve. This army level organization grouped twenty-one batteries, with a total of 120 guns, into five artillery brigades under the command of Brigadier General Robert O. Tyler. These five artillery brigades provided the army commander through his chief of artillery or the commander of the reserve the capability to deploy large amount of artillery to critical points on the battlefield in order either to reinforce the corps artillery brigades or to act independently. During the fighting on the second and third day of the battle, this capability was a critical element in the successful defensive operations of Meade's army. Especially noteworthy was the deployment of Lieutenant Colonel Freeman McGilvery's artillery brigade to reinforce the Third Corps position along the Wheatfield Road and then McGilvery's establishment of a second defensive position along the southern part of Cemetery Ridge when the Third Corps was driven back by *Longstreet's* attack. The next day McGilvery was reinforced with additional batteries and turned this sector of Cemetery Ridge into a formidable defensive position that delivered devastating artillery fire into the flank of *Pickett's* Division as it attacked the center of the Union line. Another noteworthy example was the large reinforcement from the artillery reserve that Major Osborn on West Cemetery Hill received on the second and third day. Like McGilvery, Osborn created an artillery position on that dominant piece of terrain and placed deadly fire into the left flank and left front of *Trimble's* and *Pettigrew's* Divisions as they attacked with *Pickett* on July 3.

The third critical element was the army's chief of artillery, Brigadier General Henry J. Hunt. In this officer Meade had one of the premier prewar and wartime artillery officers. Hunt possessed an in-depth understanding of artillery command and control, organization, and tactics. As chief of the artillery, he was a staff officer for Meade and was tasked with staff supervision of the administration, supply, maintenance, and instruction of the army's artillery. Meade also gave Hunt wide latitude to use his capabilities to the utmost in the tactical deployment and coordination of the army's artillery. This gave Hunt the ability to assume tactical control over all of the army's artillery, which included giving tactical orders to the artillery brigade commanders of the various infantry corps. Hunt was at his finest on July 3. He replaced batteries that had become combat ineffective during *Lee's* artillery bombardment, and he reinforced the artillery on Cemetery Hill and along Cemetery Ridge prior to and during the Confederate infantry attack. Hunt issued the orders for the Union guns to largely ignore the Confederate artillery and save their ammunition for the attacking infantry so as to reduce the strength of the attack by the time it reached the center of Meade's defensive position.

The fourth critical element was the supply and maintenance organization for the artillery. Prior to the reorganization, artillery was assigned to the various infantry divisions. Because of this the artillery ammunition trains were integrated with the division trains. There were numerous occasions when batteries could not find their ammunition wagons, which slowed down ammunition resupply and effected battle readiness. With the reorganization each artillery brigade with the infantry corps was provided its own ammunition train, which was directly under the control of the brigade commander.

This simple organizational change greatly increased the effectiveness of ammunition resupply and returned batteries to action at a faster rate.

The reorganization also provided an ammunition supply train for the Army's Artillery Reserve, which was directly responsive to the Artillery Reserve commander, Brigadier General Tyler. During the battle this ammunition train issued seventy wagon loads, over 19,000 rounds of ammunition, 10,000 of which went to the batteries of the various corps artillery brigades. When he arrived at Gettysburg, Tyler established an artillery park in the rear of the army's center between the Taneytown Road and the Baltimore Pike. At this central support area, ammunition was issued, damaged batteries came back to repair their equipment and were returned to action, and the brigades of the artillery reserve were dispatched to reinforce various points on the battlefield. Maintaining the continued combat effectiveness of the artillery batteries was largely because of the support area—the artillery park.

The critical elements of organization, command and control, supply, and maintenance that affected Meade's artillery also had an impact on the effectiveness and combat power of the Army of Northern Virginia's artillery. In early 1863 *Lee's* artillery was organized into a two-battalion army artillery reserve and into six battalions for each of the two infantry corps. The corps artillery was further assigned with one battalion to each infantry division with the remaining battalions kept as corps reserves. In late May 1863, when *Lee* reorganized his army from two to three corps, he also reorganized the artillery. The artillery reserve was dissolved as a tactical organization and all of the army's batteries were organized into fifteen battalions. Each infantry corps was assigned five battalions of artillery each. This corps artillery was placed under the command of a corps chief of artillery who reported directly to the corps commander. Normally one battalion of artillery was assigned to each infantry division and two battalions were held in reserve. The cavalry continued to have a six-battery battalion of horse artillery. This was the tactical arrangement as the corps marched into Pennsylvania, but, as they approached Gettysburg and went into the fight, this configuration of artillery was change by each corps commander as the situation required. For example, in *Hill's* Corps on the morning of July 1, all of the artillery battalions were withdrawn from the infantry division and placed under command of the corps chief of artillery. Two of the battalions were sent forward along the Chambersburg Pike to support the infantry's movement to contact while the other three were held back to be used as the situation required. During the next two days, part of the artillery was reattached to the infantry with the remainder under command of the corps chief of artillery, *Colonel R. Lindsay Walker.*

On July 3 all of the artillery in *Longstreet's* Corps was placed under the tactical command of Colonel *E. Porter Alexander* for the preattack artillery bombardment. Essentially this decision detached the artillery battalion from the infantry divisions and placed them under *Porter,* who acted as the temporary corps chief of artillery.

The artillery organization at the corps level provided a good degree of flexibility for the artillery to be decentralized if required, for any battalions held in reserve to reinforce committed battalions, or for all of the battalions to be placed under central control at corps level to provide concentrated fire at a specific area on the battlefield. However, in the reorganization *Lee* eliminated the army's artillery reserve, which had consisted of two battalions, under command of the army's chief of artillery, Brigadier General *William N. Pendleton.* This decision disbanded the one army-level artillery organization that *Lee,* through his chief of artillery, had direct control over and that he could deploy to influence the battle. However, given *Lee's* command style, he may have thought the battalions that made up the army's reserve would be better used with the infantry corps.

Lee did not have as aggressive and tactically proficient chief of artillery with Brigadier General *Pendleton* as Meade did with Hunt. *Pendleton* seems to have preferred the administrative duties of his position to the tactical duties. This was evident on July 3, when he did not provide the coordinating instructions and orders necessary to ensure that all of the artillery of the three infantry corps was positioned to provide an effective concentrated cross fire on Meade's position prior to the infantry attack.

Although *Pendleton* was a staff officer and theoretically had no direct command over the artillery of the three infantry corps, he was *Lee's* chief of artillery. As such he had a duty to ensure that his commander's intentions were being carried out. He could have, in the name of *Lee,* issued whatever instructions were necessary to the three corps chiefs of artillery, and if necessary to the corps commanders, to ensure the most effective employment of the artillery for the preattack bombardment.

In *Hill's* Corps fifteen 12-pound howitzers were not used because their maximum effective range was only 1,000 yards, which was less than the distance from Seminary Ridge to Cemetery Ridge. However, they could have been displaced forward to the left flank of *Longstreet's* artillery, which would have put them within range of the center of the Union position.

A more glaring deficiency was the guns in *Ewell's* Corps that were not used in the bombardment. Fifty-one percent of his guns were not positioned to participate in the preparatory fire. Of those in position only the three batteries of *Nelson's* Battalion and one battery from *Dance's* Battalion, a total of fifteen guns, were positioned so as to take advantage of the Confederate position north and northeast of Cemetery Hill.

Meade's position with its interior lines had many advantages; conversely *Lee's* position with its exterior lines had many disadvantages. However, *Lee's* position had one potential advantage when it came to positioning the artillery. That part of the position north and northeast of Cemetery Hill, occupied by *Ewell's* Corps, could have been used to position guns that could place cross fire and enfilading fire on the Union position on Cemetery Hill and the north part of Cemetery Ridge.

When the preparatory strike began, some of *Nelson's* guns fired about twenty-five rounds then ceased. Major Osborn on Cemetery Hill later wrote, "a group of guns opened square upon our right flank so as to rake my entire line its entire length . . . the havoc among my guns, men, horses, and ammunition chest was fearful. Guns were hit and knocked off their carriages, ammunition chest were blown up and horses were going down by the half dozen. To meet this fire, I drew out from the line three batteries and swung then half around to face this new fire" [Herb S. Crumb, ed., *The Eleventh Corps Artillery at Gettysburg: The Papers Thomas W. Osborn* (Hamilton, NY: Edmonston Publishing, 1991), 34]. If these few guns had such an effect, one can imagine what the effect would have been of many more of *Ewell's* guns enfilading the right and right center of Meade's defensive position. How many guns would have been knocked out, how many more batteries would have had to divert their fire from the attacking Confederate infantry, and what would have been the effect on the northern part of the infantry line?

Lee's artillery also had problems with the availability of ammunition. In his memoir Colonel *Alexander* wrote that the army began the campaign with 150 rounds per gun. He estimated that the expenditure during the three days of battle was approximately 22,000 rounds, or 103 rounds per gun. This would leave only about 47 to 50 round per gun at the end of July 3. Ammunition consumption by an artillery piece during a fight was from one round every two minutes to two rounds per minute, depending on the range and the tactical situation. At best this meant that the artillery of the Army of Northern Virginia had sufficient ammunition for less than two hours of combat. Holding batteries in reserve then moving them forward as other batteries depleted their ammunition could have extended the combat time. The trade-off was that artillery firepower would be reduced by partial use of the available guns. But, no matter how its viewed, there was insufficient ammunition to support further army operations in Pennsylvania or Maryland.

In summation, the artillery organization of both armies had the potential, if commanded and coordinated effectively, to provide effective fire support to the infantry and to concentrate fire at critical areas on the battlefield. At the senior leadership level the Army of the Potomac clearly had the advantage with Hunt as the chief of artillery. In ammunition and resupply the Army of the Potomac again had the advantage. Hunt, in his article "The Third Day at Gettysburg," now published in *Battles and Leaders of the Civil War,* vol. 3, wrote that his batteries and ammunition trains carried 270 rounds for each gun. Even after firing more than 100 rounds per gun, there was more than enough ammunition left to support continued combat operations. And, as Meade's army moved south and then west into the Cumberland Valley, it was reducing the distance to its railroad-supplied ammunition dumps.

The Army of Northern Virginia began the campaign with 150 round per gun in the batteries and ammunition trains. After three days of combat the ammunition level was reduced to a critical shortage that could only sustain combat for a few hours at best. Unlike Meade, *Lee's* closest resupply of ammunition was across the Potomac River in Virginia. With the rise of the river, this ammunition was unavailable to his artillery.

Drive forward to the Taneytown Road. Turn right on to the Taneytown Road, and drive south for just over 0.1 mile. You will pass a park road on your left, and just after that will be the entrance to the Visitor's Center parking lot.

Appendix I

UNION ARTILLERY ORDER OF BATTLE

ARMY OF THE POTOMAC
Maj. Gen. George G. Meade

Chief of Artillery
Brig. Gen. Henry J. Hunt

FIRST ARMY CORPS
Maj. Gen. John F. Reynolds (k)
Maj. Gen. Abner Doubleday
Maj. Gen. John Newton

ARTILLERY BRIGADE
Col. Charles S. Wainwright

- 2d Maine Battery, six 3-inch Ordnance rifles
  - Capt. James A. Hall
- 5th Maine Battery, six Napoleons
  - Capt. Greenleaf T. Stevens (w)
  - Lieut. Edward N. Whittier
- Battery L, 1st New York (Battery E, 1st New York attached), six 3-inch Ordnance rifles
  - Capt. Gilbert H. Reynolds (w)
  - Lieut. George Breck
- Battery B, 1st Pennsylvania, four 3-inch Ordnance rifles
  - Capt. James H. Cooper
- Battery B, 4th United States, six Napoleons
  - Lieut. James Stewart

SECOND ARMY CORPS
Maj. Gen. Winfield S. Hancock (w)
Brig. Gen. John Gibbon

ARTILLERY BRIGADE
Capt. John G. Hazard

Battery B, 1st New York (14th New York Battery attached), four 10-pound Parrotts
Lieut. Albert S. Sheldon (w)
Capt. James M. Rorty (k)
Lieut. Robert E. Rogers

Battery A, 1st Rhode Island, six 3-inch Ordnance rifles
Capt. William A. Arnold

Battery B, 1st Rhode Island, six Napoleons
Lieut. T. Frederick Brown (w)
Lieut. Walter S. Perrin

Battery I, 1st United States, six Napoleons
Lieut. George A. Woodruff (mw)
Lieut. Tully McCrea

Battery A, 4th United States, six 3-inch Ordnance rifles
Lieut. Alonzo H. Cushing (k)
Sergt. Frederick Fuger

THIRD ARMY CORPS
Maj. Gen. Daniel E. Sickles (w)
Maj. Gen. David B. Birney

ARTILLERY BRIGADE
Capt. George E. Randolph (w)
Capt. A. Judson Clark

2d New Jersey Battery, six 10-pound Parrotts
Capt. A Judson Clark
Lieut. Robert Sims

Battery D, 1st New York, six Napoleons
Capt. George B. Winslow

4th New York Battery, six 10-pound Parrotts
Capt. James E. Smith

Battery E, 1st Rhode Island, six Napoleons
Lieut. John K. Bucklyn (w)
Lieut. Benjamin Freeborn

Battery K, 4th United States, six Napoleons
Lieut. Francis W. Seeley (w)
Lieut. Robert James

FIFTH ARMY CORPS
Maj. Gen. George Sykes

ARTILLERY BRIGADE
Capt. Augustus P. Martin
- 3d Massachusetts Battery, six Napoleons
  - Lieut. Aaron F. Walcott
- Battery C, 1st New York, four 3-inch Ordnance rifles
  - Capt. Almont Barnes
- Battery L, 1st Ohio, six Napoleons
  - Capt. Frank C. Gibbs
- Battery D, 5th United States, six 10-pound Parrotts
  - Lieut. Charles E. Hazlett (k)
  - Lieut. Benjamin F. Rittenhouse
- Battery I, 5th United States, four 3-inch Ordnance rifles
  - Lieut. Malbone F. Watson (w)
  - Lieut. Charles C. MacConnell

SIXTH ARMY CORPS
Maj. Gen. John Sedgwick

ARTILLERY BRIGADE
Col. Charles H. Tompkins
- 1st Massachusetts Battery, six Napoleons
  - Capt. William H. McCartney
- 1st New York Battery, six 3-inch Ordnance rifles
  - Capt. Andrew Cowan
- 3d New York Battery, six 10-pound Parrotts
  - Capt. William A. Harn
- Battery C, 1st Rhode Island, six 3-inch Ordnance rifles
  - Capt. Richard Waterman
- Battery G, 1st Rhode Island, six 10-pound Parrotts
  - Capt. George W. Adams
- Battery D, 2d United States, six Napoleons
  - Lieut. Edward B. Williston
- Battery G, 2d United States, six Napoleons
  - Lieut. John H. Butler
- Battery F, 5th United States, six 10-pound Parrotts
  - Lieut. Leonard Martin

ELEVENTH ARMY CORPS
Maj. Gen. Oliver O. Howard

ARTILLERY BRIGADE
Maj. Thomas W. Osborn
Battery I, 1st New York, six 3-inch Ordnance rifles
Capt. Michael Wiedrich
13th New York Battery, four 3-inch Ordnance rifles
Lieut. William Wheeler
Battery I, 1st Ohio, six Napoleons
Capt. Hubert Dilger
Battery K, 1st Ohio, four Napoleons
Capt. Lewis Heckman
Battery G, 4th United States, six Napoleons
Lieut. Bayard Wilkeson (mw)
Lieut. Eugene A. Bancroft

TWELFTH ARMY CORPS
Maj. Gen. Henry W. Slocum
Brig. Gen. Alpheus S. Williams

ARTILLERY BRIGADE
Lieut. Edward D. Muhlenberg
Battery M, 1st New York, four 10-pound Parrotts
Lieut. Charles Winegar
Battery E, Pennsylvania Light, six 10-pound Parrotts
Lieut. Charles A. Atwell
Battery F, 4th United States, six Napoleons
Lieut. Sylvanus T. Rugg
Battery K, 5th United States, four Napoleons
Lieut. David H. Kinzie

CAVALRY CORPS
Maj. Gen. Alfred Pleasonton

FIRST HORSE ARTILLERY BRIGADE
Capt. James M. Robertson
9th Michigan Battery, six 3-inch Ordnance rifles
Capt. Jabez J. Daniels

6th New York Battery, six 3-inch Ordnance rifles
Capt. Joseph W. Martin
Batteries B & L (Combined), 2d United States, six 3-inch Ordnance rifles
Lieut. Edward Heaton
Battery M, 2d United States, six 3-inch Ordnance rifles
Lieut. A. C. M. Pennington, Jr.
Battery E, 4th United States, four 3-inch Ordnance rifles
Lieut. Samuel S. Elder
Battery H, 3d Pennsylvania Heavy Artillery, two 3-inch Ordnance rifles
Capt. William D. Rank
(Attached to First Cavalry Brigade, Second Cavalry Division)

SECOND HORSE ARTILLERY BRIGADE
Capt John C. Tidball
Batteries E & G (Combined) 1st United States, four 3-inch Ordnance rifles
Capt. Alanson M. Randol
Battery K, 1st United States, six 3-inch Ordnance rifles
Capt. William M. Graham
Battery A, 2d United States, six 3-inch Ordnance rifles
Lieut. John H. Calef
Battery C, 3d United States, six 3-inch Ordnance rifles
Lieut. William D. Fuller
(Attached to Second Cavalry Brigade, Second Cavalry Division)

ARMY ARTILLERY RESERVE
Brig. Gen Robert O. Tyler
Capt. James M. Robertson

FIRST REGULAR RIGADE
Capt. Dunbar R. Ransom
Battery H, 1st United States, six Napoleons
Lieut. Chandler P. Eakin (w)
Lieut. Philip D. Mason
Batteries F & K (Combined), 3d United States, six Napoleons
Lieut. John G. Turnbull
Battery C, 4th United States, six Napoleons
Lieut. Evan Thomas

Battery C, 5th United States, six Napoleons
Lieut. Gulian V. Weir

FIRST VOLUNTEER BRIGADE
Lieut. Col. Freeman McGilvery
5th Massachusetts Battery (10th New York Battery attached), six 3-inch Ordnance rifles
Capt. Charles A. Phillips
9th Massachusetts Battery, six Napoleons
Capt. John Bigelow (w)
Lieut. Richard S. Milton
15th New York Battery, four Napoleons
Capt. Patrick Hart
Batteries C & F (Combined), Pennsylvania Light, six 3-inch Ordnance rifles
Capt. James Thompson

SECOND VOLUNTEER BRIGADE
Capt. Elijah D. Taft
Battery B, 1st Connecticut Heavy Artillery, six 4.5-inch rifles
Capt. Albert F. Brooker
(Guarding trains at Westminster, MD.)
Battery M, 1st Connecticut Heavy Artillery, six 4.5-inch rifles
Capt. Franklin A. Pratt
(Guarding trains at Westminster, MD.)
2d Connecticut Battery, four James rifles and two 12-pound howitzers
Capt. John W. Sterling
5th New York Battery, six 20-pound Parrotts
Capt. Elijah D. Taft

THIRD VOLUNTEER BRIGADE
Capt. James F. Huntington
1st New Hampshire Battery, six 3-inch Ordnance rifles
Capt. Frederick M. Edgell
Battery H, 1st Ohio, six 3-inch Ordnance rifles
Lieut. George W. Norton
Batteries F & G (Combined), 1st Pennsylvania, six 3-inch Ordnance rifles
Capt. R. Bruce Ricketts

Battery C, West Virginia Light, four 10-pound Parrotts
Capt. Wallace Hill

FOURTH VOLUNTEER BRIGADE
Capt. Robert H. Fitzhugh
6th Maine Battery, four Napoleons
Lieut. Edwin B. Dow
Battery A, Maryland Light, six 3-inch Ordnance rifles
Capt. James H. Rigby
Battery A,1st New Jersey Artillery, six 10-pound Parrotts
Lieut. Augustin N. Parsons
Battery G, 1st New York, six Napoleons
Capt. Nelson Ames
Battery K, 1st New York (11th New York Battery attached), six 3-inch Ordnance rifles
Capt. Robert H. Fitzhugh

(k) killed in action
(mw) mortally wounded
(w) wounded in action

[*OR* 27, pt. 1, pp. 155–68; "Composition of Federal Batteries by States," Gettysburg National Military Park Document]

Appendix II

CONFEDERATE ARTILLERY ORDER OF BATTLE

ARMY OF NORTHERN VIRGINIA
Gen. Robert E. Lee

Chief of Artillery
Brig. Gen. William N. Pendleton

LONGSTREET'S CORPS
Lieut. Gen. James Longstreet

McLAWS'S DIVISION
Maj. Gen. Lafayette McLaws

CABELL'S ARTILLERY BATTALION
Col. Henry C. Cabell

- Battery A, 1st North Carolina Artillery, two 10-pound Parrotts, two 12-pound howitzers
  - Capt. Basil C. Manly
- Pulaski (Georgia) Artillery, two 3-inch Ordnance rifles, two 10-pound Parrotts
  - Capt. John C. Fraser (w)
  - Lieut. William J. Furlong
- 1st Richmond Howitzers, two 3-inch Ordnance rifles, two Napoleons
  - Capt. Edward S. McCarthy
- Troup (Georgia) Artillery, two 10-pound Parrotts, two 12-pound howitzers
  - Capt. Henry H. Carlton (w)
  - Lieut. C. W. Motes

PICKETT'S DIVISION
Maj. Gen. George E. Pickett

DEARING'S ARTILLERY BATTALION

Maj. James Dearing

Fauquier (Virginia) Artillery, two 20-pound Parrotts, four Napoleons

Capt Robert M. Stribling

Hampden (Virginia) Artillery, one 3-inch Ordnance rifle, one 10-pound Parrott, two Napoleons

Capt. William H. Caskie

Richmond Fayette Artillery, two 10-pound Parrotts, two Napoleons

Capt. Miles C. Macon

Blount's (Virginia) Battery, four Napoleons

Capt. Joseph G. Blount

HOOD'S DIVISION

Maj. Gen. John B. Hood (w)

Brig. Gen. Evander M. Law

HENRY'S ARTILLERY BATTALION

Maj. Mathias W. Henry

Branch (North Carolina) Artillery, one 6-pound gun, one 12-pound howitzer, three Napoleons

Capt. Alexander C. Latham

German (South Carolina) Artillery, four Napoleons

Capt. William K. Bachman

Palmetto (South Carolina) Artillery, two 10-pound Parrotts, two Napoleons

Capt. Hugh R. Garden

Rowan (North Carolina) Artillery, two 3-inch Ordnance rifles, two Napoleons, two 10-pound Parrotts

Capt. James Reilly

CORPS ARTILLERY RESERVE

Col. James B. Walton

Col. E. Porter Alexander

ALEXANDER'S ARTILLERY BATTALION

Col. E. Porter Alexander

Maj. Frank Huger

Ashland (Virginia) Artillery, two 20-pound Parrotts, two Napoleons

Capt. Pichegru Woolfolk, Jr. (w)

Lieut. James Woolfolk

Bedford (Virginia) Artillery, four 3-inch Ordnance rifles
Capt. Tyler C. Jordan
Brooks (South Carolina) Artillery, four 12-pound howitzers
Lieut. S. Capers Gilbert
Madison (Louisiana) Artillery, four 24-pound howitzers
Capt. George V. Moody
Parker's (Virginia) Battery, three 3-inch Ordnance rifles, one 10-pound Parrott
Capt. William W. Parker
Taylor's (Virginia) Battery, four Napoleons
Capt. Osmond B. Taylor

WASHINGTON (LOUISIANA) ARTILLERY
Maj. Benjamin F. Eshleman
First Company, one Napoleon
Capt. Charles W. Squires
Second Company, two Napoleons, one 12-pound howitzer
Capt. John B. Richardson
Third Company, three Napoleons
Capt. Merritt B. Miller
Fourth Company, two Napoleons, one 12-pound howitzer
Capt. Joseph Norcom (w)
Lieut. H. A. Battles

EWELL'S CORPS
Lieut. Gen. Richard S. Ewell

EARLY'S DIVISION
Maj. Gen. Jubal Early

JONES'S ARTILLERY BATTALION
Lieut. Col. Hilary P. Jones
Charlottesville (Virginia) Artillery, four Napoleons
Capt. James McD. Carrington
Courtney (Virginia) Artillery, four 3-inch Ordnance rifles
Capt. William A. Tanner
Louisiana Guard Artillery, two 3-inch Ordnance rifles, two 10-pound Parrotts
Capt. Charles A. Green

Staunton (Virginia) Artillery, four Napoleons
Capt. Asher W. Garber

JOHNSON'S DIVISION
Maj. Gen. Edward Johnson

ANDREWS'S ARTILLERY BATTALION
Lieut. Col. R. Snowden Andrews (w)
Maj. Joseph W. Latimer (mw)
Capt. Charles I. Raine
1st Maryland Battery, four Napoleons
Capt. William F. Dement
Alleghany (Virginia) Artillery, two 3-inch Ordnance rifles, two Napoleons
Capt. John C. Carpenter
Chesapeake (Maryland) Artillery, four 10-pound Parrotts
Capt. William D. Brown (w)
Lee (Virginia) Battery, one 3-inch Ordnance rifles, two 20-pound Parrotts, one 10-pound Parrott
Capt. Charles I. Raine
Lieut. William W. Hardwicke

RODES'S DIVISION
Maj. Gen. Robert E. Rodes

CARTER'S ARTILLERY BATTALION
Lieut. Col. Thomas H. Carter
Jeff. Davis (Alabama) Artillery, four 3-inch Ordnance rifles
Capt. William J. Reese
King William (Virginia) Artillery, two 10-pound Parrotts, two Napoleons
Capt. William P. Carter
Morris (Virginia) Artillery, four Napoleons
Capt. Richard C. M. Page
Orange (Virginia) Artillery, two 3-inch Ordnance rifles, two 10-pound Parrotts
Capt. Charles W. Fry

CORPS ARTILLERY RESERVE
Col J. Thompson Brown

FIRST VIRGINIA ARTILLERY
Capt. Willis J. Dance
2d Richmond (Virginia) Howitzers, four 10-pound Parrotts
Capt. David Watson
3d Richmond (Virginia) Howitzers, four 3-inch Ordnance rifles
Capt. Benjamin H. Smith, Jr.
Powhatan (Virginia) Artillery, four 3-inch Ordnance rifles
Lieut. John M. Cunningham
Rockbridge (Virginia) Artillery, four 20-pound Parrotts
Captain Archibald Graham
Salem (Virginia) Artillery, two 3-inch Ordnance rifles, two Napoleons
Lieut. Charles B. Griffin

NELSON'S ARTILLERY BATTALION
Lieut. Col. William Nelson
Amherst (Virginia) Artillery, one 3-inch Ordnance rifle, three Napoleons
Capt. Thomas J. Kirkpatrick
Fluvanna (Virginia) Artillery, one 3-inch Ordnance rifle, three Napoleon
Capt. John L. Massie
Milledge's (Georgia) Battery, two 3-inch Ordnance rifles, one 10-pound Parrott
Capt. John Milledge

HILL'S CORPS
Lieut. Gen. Ambrose P. Hill

ANDERSON'S DIVISION
Maj. Gen. Richard H. Anderson

SUMTER ARTILLERY BATTALION
Maj. John Lane
Company A (Georgia), three10-pound Parrotts, one 12-pound howitzer, one Napoleon, one 3-inch naval rifle
Capt. Hugh Ross
Company B (Georgia), two Napoleons, four 12-pound howitzers
Capt. George M. Patterson
Company C (Georgia), three 3-inch naval rifles, two 10-pound Parrotts
Capt. John T. Wingfield

HETH'S DIVISION
Maj. Gen Henry Heth (w)
Brig. Gen. J. Johnston Pettigrew (k)

GARNETT'S ARTILLERY BATTALION
Lieut. Col. John J. Garnett
Donaldsonville (Louisiana) Artillery, two 3-inch Ordnance rifles, one 10 pound Parrott
Capt. Victor Maurin
Huger (Virginia) Artillery, one 3-inch Ordnance rifle, one 10-pound Parrott, two Napoleons
Capt. Joseph D. Moore
Lewis (Virginia) Artillery, two 3-inch Ordnance rifles, two Napoleons
Capt. John W. Lewis
Norfolk Light Artillery Blues, two 3-inch Ordnance rifles, two 12-pound howitzers
Capt. Charles R. Grandy

PENDER'S DIVISION
Maj. Gen. William D. Pender (mw)
Brig. Gen. James H. Lane
Maj. Gen. Isaac R. Trimble (w)
Brig. Gen. James H Lane

POAGUE'S ARTILLERY BATTALION
Maj. William T. Poague
Albermarle (Virginia) Artillery, two 3-inch Ordnance rifles, one 10-pound Parrott, one 12-pound howitzer
Capt. James W. Wyatt
Charlotte (North Carolina) Artillery, two Napoleons, two 12-pound howitzers
Capt. Joseph Graham
Madison (Mississippi) Artillery, three Napoleons, one 12-pound howitzer
Capt. George Ward
Brooke's (Virginia) Battery, two Napoleons, two 12-pound howitzers
Capt. James V. Brooke

CORPS ARTILLERY RESERVE
Col. R. Lindsay Walker

McINTOSH'S ARTILLERY BATTALION
Maj. David G. McIntosh
Danville (Virginia) Artillery, four Napoleons
Capt. R. Sidney Rice
Hardaway (Alabama) Artillery, two 3-inch Ordnance rifles, two Whitworth rifles
Capt. William B. Hurt
2d Rockbridge (Virginia) Artillery, two 3-inch Ordnance rifles, two Napoleons
Lieut. Samuel Wallace
Johnson's (Virginia) Battery, four 3-inch Ordnance rifles
Capt. Marmaduke Johnson

PEGRAM'S ARTILLERY BATTALION
Maj. William J. Pegram
Capt. Ervin B. Brunson
Crenshaw (Virginia) Battery, two 3-inch Ordnance rifles, two 12-pound howitzers
Lieut. Andrew B. Johnson
Fredericksburg (Virginia) Artillery, two 3-inch Ordnance rifles, two Napoleons
Capt. Edward A. Marye
Letcher (Virginia) Artillery, two 10-pound Parrotts, two Napoleons
Capt. Thomas A. Brander
Pee Dee (South Carolina) Artillery, four 3-inch Ordnance rifles
Lieut. William E. Zimmerman
Purcell (Virginia) Artillery, four Napoleons
Capt. Joseph McGraw

CAVALRY

STUART'S DIVISION
Maj. Gen J. E. B. Stuart

STUART HORSE ARTILLERY
Maj. Robert F. Beckham
Breathed's (Virginia) Battery, four 3-inch Ordnance rifles
Capt. James Breathed
Chew's (Virginia) Battery, one 3-inch Ordnance rifles, one 12-pound howitzer
Capt. R. Preston Chew

Griffin's (Maryland) Battery, four 10-pound Parrotts
Capt. William H. Griffin
Hart's (South Carolina) Battery, three Blakely rifles
Capt. James F. Hart
McGregor's (Virginia) Battery, two 3-inch Ordnance rifles, two Napoleons
Capt. William M. McGregor
Moorman's (Virginia) Battery, three rifles (type unknown), one Napoleon
Capt. Marcellus N. Moorman

IMBODEN'S COMMMAND
Brig. Gen. John D. Imboden

ARTILLERY
McClanahan's (Virginia) Battery, one 3-inch Ordnance rifles, four 12-pound howitzers
Capt. John H. McClanahan
Jackson's (Virginia) Battery, two 3-inch Ordnance rifles, two 12-pound howitzers
Capt. Thomas E. Jackson
(Attached to Jenkins's cavalry brigade)

(k) killed in action
(mw) mortally wounded
(w) wounded in action

[*OR* 27, pt. 2, pp. 283-91; "Composition of Confederate Batteries by Battalions," Gettysburg National Military Park Document]

Appendix III

ARMY OF THE POTOMAC WEAPONS DISTRIBUTION BY CORPS AND RESERVE

Weapon/Unit	3-inch Ordnance rifle	12-pound Napoleon	10-pound Parrott	20-pound Parrott	12-pound howitzer	James rifle	4.5-inch rifle	**Total guns**
Artillery with the Infantry Corps	**58**	**98**	**50**	—	—	—	—	**206**
First Corps Artillery Brigade	16	12	—	—	—	—	—	28
Second Corps Artillery Brigade	12	12	4	—	—	—	—	28
Third Corps Artillery Brigade	—	18	12	—	—	—	—	30
Fifth Corps Artillery Brigade	8	12	6	—	—	—	—	26
Sixth Corps Artillery Brigade	12	18	18	—	—	—	—	48
Eleventh Corps Artillery Brigade	10	16	—	—	—	—	—	26
Twelfth Corps Artillery Brigade	—	10	10	—	—	—	—	20
Cavalry Corps Artillery	**52**	—	—	—	—	—	—	**52**
First Horse Artillery Brigade	30	—	—	—	—	—	—	30
Second Horse Artillery Brigade	22	—	—	—	—	—	—	22
Army Artillery Reserve	**42**	**44**	**10**	**6**	**2**	**4**	**12**	**120**
First Regular Brigade	—	24	—	—	—	—	—	24
First Volunteer Brigade	12	10	—	—	—	—	—	22
Second Volunteer Brigade	—	—	—	6	2	4	12	24
Third Volunteer Brigade	18	—	4	—	—	—	—	22
Fourth Volunteer Brigade	12	10	6	—	—	—	—	28
Army of the Potomac Totals	**152**	**142**	**60**	**6**	**2**	**4**	**12**	**378**

Appendix IV

ARMY OF NORTHERN VIRGINIA WEAPONS DISTRIBUTION BY CORPS AND BATTALION

Weapon/Unit	3-inch Ordnance rifle	12-pound Napoleon	10-pound Parrott	20-pound Parrott	12-pound howitzer	24-pound howitzer	6-pound gun	3-inch naval rifle	Whitworth rifle	Blakely rifle	**Total guns**
Longstreet's Corps	**14**	**39**	**14**	**4**	**11**	**4**	**1**	**—**	**—**	**—**	**87**
Cabell's Battalion	4	2	6	—	4	—	—	—	—	—	16
Dearing's Battalion	1	12	3	2	—	—	—	—	—	—	18
Henry's Battalion	2	11	4	—	1	—	1	—	—	—	19
Alexander's Battalion	7	6	1	2	4	4	—	—	—	—	24
Washington Artillery	—	8	—	—	2	—	—	—	—	—	10
Ewell's Corps	**29**	**28**	**16**	**6**	**—**	**—**	**—**	**—**	**—**	**—**	**79**
Jones's Battalion	6	8	2	—	—	—	—	—	—	—	16
Andrews's Battalion	3	6	5	2	—	—	—	—	—	—	16
Carter's Battalion	6	6	4	—	—	—	—	—	—	—	16
First Virginia Artillery	10	2	4	4	—	—	—	—	—	—	20
Nelson's Battalion	4	6	1	—	—	—	—	—	—	—	11
Hill's Corps	**25**	**28**	**10**	**—**	**15**	**—**	**—**	**4**	**2**	**—**	**84**
Sumter Battalion	—	3	5	—	5	—	—	4	—	—	17
Garnett's Battalion	7	4	2	—	2	—	—	—	—	—	15
Poague's Battalion	2	7	1	—	6	—	—	—	—	—	16
McIntosh's Battalion	8	6	—	—	—	—	—	—	2	—	16
Pegram's Battalion	8	8	2	—	2	—	—	—	—	—	20
Cavalry's Artillery	**10**	**3**	**4**	**—**	**7**	**—**	**—**	**—**	**—**	**3**	**27***
Stuart's Horse Artillery	7	3	4	—	1	—	—	—	—	3	18*
Imboden's Artillery	3	—	—	—	6	—	—	—	—	—	9
Army of Northern Virginia Totals	**78**	**98**	**44**	**10**	**33**	**4**	**1**	**4**	**2**	**3**	**277***

* Does not include 3 unspecified "rifles" in Stuart's Horse Artillery

Appendix V

CANNONS AT GETTYSBURG

Ordnance rifle, 3-inch

3-inch Ordnance rifle, muzzle view.

3-inch Ordnance rifle, breech view.

Characteristics

Tube diameter	3 inches
Length of tube	69 inches
Tube weight	820 pounds
Tube composition	wrought iron
Projectile weight	9.5 pounds
Powder charge	1.0 pound
Effective range	1,830 yards (at 5° elevation)

At Gettysburg

Army of the Potomac	152
Army of Northern Virginia	78

Parrott Rifle, 10-pound

10-pound Parrott, muzzle view.

10-pound Parrott, breech view.

Characteristics

Tube diameter	2.9 or 3 inches
Length of tube	74 inches
Tube weight	890 pounds
Tube composition	cast and wrought iron
Projectile weight	9.5 pounds
Powder charge	1.0 pound
Effective range	1,850 yards (at 5° elevation)

At Gettysburg

Army of the Potomac	60
Army of Northern Virginia	44

Parrott Rifle, 20-pound

20-pound Parrott, muzzle view.

20-pound Parrott, breech view.

Characteristics

Tube diameter	3.67 inches
Length of tube	84 inches
Tube weight	1,750 pounds
Tube composition	cast and wrought iron
Projectile weight	20 pounds
Powder charge	2.0 pounds
Effective range	1,900 yards (at 5° elevation)

At Gettysburg

Army of the Potomac	6
Army of Northern Virginia	10

Whitworth Rifle, 12-pound (2.75-inch)

Whitworth rifle, muzzle view.

Whitworth rifle, breech view.

Characteristics

Tube diameter	2.75 inches
Length of tube	104 inches
Tube weight	1,092 pounds
Tube composition	iron
Projectile weight	12 pounds
Powder charge	1.75 pounds
Effective range	2,800 yards (at 5° elevation)

At Gettysburg

Army of the Potomac	0
Army of Northern Virginia	2

James Rifle, 14-pound

14-pound James rifle, muzzle view.

14-pound James rifle, breech view.

Characteristics

Tube diameter	3.8 inches
Length of tube	65 inches
Tube weight	918 pounds
Tube composition	bronze
Projectile weight	14 pounds
Powder charge	0.75 pound
Effective range	1,700 yards (at 5° elevation)

At Gettysburg

Army of the Potomac	4
Army of Northern Virginia	0

Blakely Rifle

Blakely rifle, muzzle view. Shiloh National Military Park.

Blakely rifle, breech view. Shiloh National Military Park.

Characteristics

Tube diameter	3.4 inches
Length of tube	59 inches
Tube weight	800 pounds
Tube composition	iron
Projectile weight	10 pounds
Powder charge	1.0 pound
Effective range	1,850 yards (at 5° elevation)

At Gettysburg

Army of the Potomac	0
Army of Northern Virginia	3

Napoleon 12-pound Field Gun

12-pound Napoleon, muzzle view.

12-pound Napoleon, breech view.

Characteristics

Tube diameter	4.62 inches
Length of tube	66 inches
Tube weight	1,227 pounds
Tube composition	bronze
Projectile weight	12 pounds
Powder charge	2.5 pounds
Effective range	1,619 yards (at 5° elevation)

At Gettysburg

Army of the Potomac	142
Army of Northern Virginia	98

Napoleon 12-pound Field Gun, Confederate Manufacture

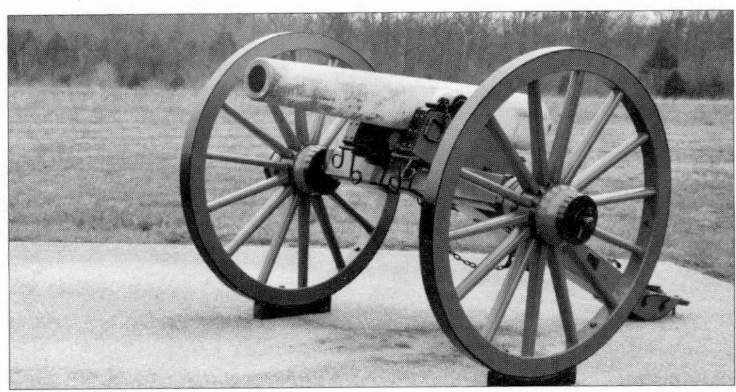

12-pound Napoleon, Confederate manufacture, muzzle view.

12-pound Napoleon, Confederate manufacture, breech view.

Characteristics

Tube diameter	4.62 inches
Length of tube	66 inches
Tube weight	1,227 pounds
Tube composition	bronze
Projectile weight	12 pounds
Powder charge	2.5 pounds
Effective range	1,619 yards (at 5° elevation)

Field Howitzer, 12-pound

12-pound howitzer, muzzle view.

12-pound howitzer, breech view.

Characteristics

Tube diameter	4.62 inches
Length of tube	53 inches
Tube weight	788 pounds
Tube composition	bronze
Projectile weight	8–12 pounds
Powder charge	1.0 pound
Effective range	1,072 yards (at 5° elevation)

At Gettysburg

Army of the Potomac	2
Army of Northern Virginia	33

Field Howitzer, 24-pound

24-pound howitzer, muzzle view.

24-pound howitzer, breech view.

Characteristics

Tube diameter	5.82 inches
Length of tube	64 inches
Tube weight	1,318 pounds
Tube composition	bronze
Projectile weight	18–24 pounds
Powder charge	2.0 pounds
Effective range	1,322 yards (at 5° elevation)

At Gettysburg

Army of the Potomac	0
Army of Northern Virginia	4

Field Gun, 6-pound

6-pound gun, muzzle view.

6-pound gun, breech view.

Characteristics

Tube diameter	3.67 inches
Length of tube	60 inches
Tube weight	882 pounds
Tube composition	bronze
Projectile weight	6 pounds
Powder charge	1.25 pounds
Effective range	1,523 yards (at 5° elevation)

At Gettysburg

Army of the Potomac	0
Army of Northern Virginia	1

Appendix VI

BENNER'S HILL, JULY 2, 1883

From Cemetery Hill, drive north into Gettysburg on the Baltimore Pike/Street for 0.5 miles to High Street. Turn right on to High Street, and drive east 1 block to Stratton Street. Turn left on to Stratton Street, and drive north 2 blocks to York Street. Turn right on to York Street, and drive east. In 1 block there is a Y in the road and York Street goes to the left. Do not go left, but take the right part of the Y by going straight ahead. You are now on Hanover Street/Road (Pennsylvania 116). Drive east on Hanover Street/Road for 0.7 miles to a National Park Service road on your right. Turn right on to this road and drive to the guns and marker for Brown's (Maryland) Battery. It is the second marker on your left. Park, get out of your car, stand beside the marker, and look in the direction the guns are pointed, which is southwest.

Position A—An Artillery Duel

When you were at Stop 27 on Cemetery Hill (chapter 3), you looked at the artillery duel between the Union guns there and the Confederate guns here. You will now look at that action from the Confederate perspective.

You are on the low ridge that goes north from Benner's Hill. The hill proper is 300 yards to your left. This low ridge comes north from the hill to where you are and then continues on to your right to the other side of the Hanover Road. Historians have traditionally called the hill and ridge Benner's Hill. Look in the direction the guns are pointed, southwest, and at a distance of 1,700 yards you can see Cemetery Hill. The U.S. flag that you see is on West Cemetery Hill, where the military cemetery is. To the left of Cemetery Hill, you can see Culp's Hill. Union artillery batteries were located on these two terrain features. There were five guns on Culp's Hill, twenty-three guns on East Cemetery Hill and Stevens's Knoll, and twelve guns on West Cemetery Hill that could bring

View from the center of *Latimer's* Battalion's position on Benner's Hill toward East Cemetery Hill. East Cemetery Hill is between the two trees in the center of the photo and at a greater distance.

this position under fire. Additional guns on West Cemetery Hill could be reoriented, if needed, so as to add their fire against this position. The closest battery on Cemetery Hill was at a range of 1,500 yards, the furthest 1,800 yards. The closest battery on Culp's Hill was at a range of 950 yards, the furthest 1,400 yards. The average elevation of the Benner's Hill position is 560 feet. The elevation where the Union artillery was on East Cemetery Hill is 600 feet and on Culp's Hill 610 feet.

Lee's tactical plan for July 2 was for *Longstreet's* Corps supported by *Anderson's* Division of *Hill's* Corps to conduct the main attack against the Union south flank, collapse the defenses, and capture Cemetery Hill. A supporting attack was to be conducted by elements of *Ewell's* Corps against Culp's Hill and East Cemetery Hill.

Report of Gen. *Robert E. Lee,* CSA, Commanding Army of Northern Virginia

General *Ewell's* corps constituted our left, *Johnson's* division being opposite the height [Culp's Hill] adjoining Cemetery Hill, *Early's* in the center, in front of the north face of the latter, and *Rodes* upon his right. *Hill's* corps [along

Seminary Ridge] faced the west side of Cemetery Hill, and extended nearly parallel to the Emmitsburg road, making an angle with *Ewell's*, *Pender's* division formed his left, *Anderson's* his right, *Heth's*, under Brigadier-General *Pettigrew*, being in reserve. His artillery, under Colonel *R. L. Walker*, was posted in eligible positions along his line.

It was determined to make the principal attack upon the enemy's left, and endeavor to gain a position from which it was thought that our artillery could be brought to bear with effect. *Longstreet* was directed to place the divisions of *McLaws* and *Hood* on the right of *Hill*, partially enveloping the enemy's left, which he was to drive in.

General *Hill* was ordered to threaten the enemy's center, to prevent re-enforcements being drawn to either wing, and co-operate with his right division [*Anderson's*] in *Longstreet's* attack.

General *Ewell* was instructed to make a simultaneous demonstration upon the enemy's right, to be converted into a real attack should opportunity offer. [*OR* 27, pt. 2, pp. 318–19]

Ewell's attack began as a demonstration (feint) to keep the Union defenders on Culp's Hill and East Cemetery Hill and prevent them from reinforcing the center or south sectors of Meade's defensive position. In addition, *Ewell* might have created confusion as to which attack was the main attack and thus caused Meade to commit reserve units to the wrong area. *Ewell* began his demonstration with artillery. The artillery mission was given to Major General *Edward Johnson.*

Report of Major General *Edward Johnson*, CSA, Commanding *Johnson's* Division, *Ewell's* Corps, Army of Northern Virginia

Early next morning, skirmishers from *Walker's* and *Jones'* brigades were advanced for the purpose of feeling the enemy, and desultory firing was maintained with their skirmishers until 4 p.m., at which hour I ordered Major *Latimer* to open fire with all of his pieces from the only eligible hill within range, *Jones'* brigade being properly disposed as a support. The hill [Benner's] was directly in front of the wooded mountain [Culp's Hill] and a little to the left of the Cemetery Hill; consequently exposed to the concentrated fire from both, and also to an enfilade fire from a battery near the Baltimore road. The unequal contest was maintained for two hours with considerable damage to the enemy, as will appear from the accompanying report of Lieutenant-Colonel *Andrews*. Major *Latimer* having reported to me that the exhausted condition of his horses and men, together with the terrible fire of the enemy's artillery, rendered his position untenable, he was ordered to cease firing and withdraw all of his pieces excepting four, which were left in position to cover the advance of my infantry. [*OR* 27, pt. 2, p. 504]

Johnson's divisional artillery battalion was Lieutenant Colonel *R. Snowden Andrews's* battalion. *Andrews* was wounded on June 13 in the fight for Winchester, Virginia, and Major *Joseph W. Latimer* temporarily commanded the battalion. *Andrews's* Battalion was composed of four batteries with a total of sixteen guns. The guns were three 3-inch rifles, two 20-pound Parrotts, five 10-pound Parrotts, and six Napoleons. These weapons occupied a frontage of 450 yards from Benner's Hill north along the ridge on the other side of the Hanover Road. Captain *Archibald Graham's* Rockbridge Artillery Battery with four 20-pound Parrotts from *Dance's* Battalion of the corps reserve artillery was ordered to reinforce *Andrew's* Battalion and went into position on the right flank.

Where you are was the position of Captain *William Brown's* Chesapeake (Maryland) Artillery Battery with four 10-pound Parrotts. To *Brown's* right were two 20-pound Parrotts from Captain *Charles I. Raine's* Lee (Virginia) Battery. To *Brown's* left were the two 3-inch rifles and two Napoleons of Captain *John C. Carpenter's* Alleghany (Virginia) Artillery Battery, to Carpenter's left was Captain *William F. Dement's* First Maryland Battery with four Napoleons. Next left and on the left flank of the position were the two remaining guns, one 3-inch rifle and one 10-pound Parrott, of *Raine's* Battery.

In late afternoon the battalion, under command of Major *Joseph W. Latimer,* deployed onto this position and opened fired on the Union artillery on East Cemetery Hill.

Report of Lieut. Col. *R. Snowden Andrews,* CSA, Commanding *Andrews's* Artillery Battalion, *Ewell's* Corps, Army of Northern Virginia

July 2, Major *Latimer,* having carefully examined the ground, had selected the only eligible position in his front. The ground offered very few advantages, and the major found great difficulty in sheltering his horses and caissons. The hill which he selected brought him directly in front of the wooded

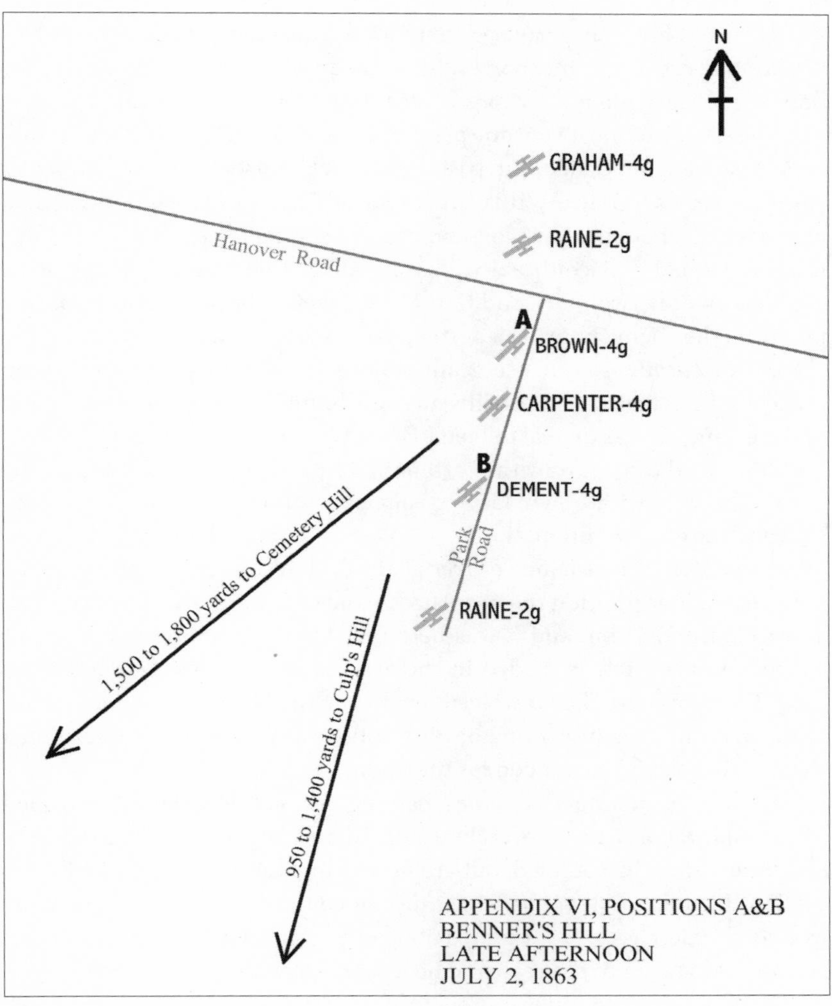

mountain [Culp's Hill] and a little to the left of the Cemetery Hill. All the guns excepting two long-range guns had to be crowded on this small hill, which was not in our favor.

About 4 o'clock, Major *Latimer* received orders to take position and open on the enemy. Fourteen guns of the battalion were then planted on this hill above mentioned. The two remaining guns (20-pounder Parrotts) were placed on an eminence [on the right] of the battalion. Captain *Brown's* battery occupied the right, Captain *Carpenter's* occupied the center, while Captain *Dement* and Captain *Raine,* the latter with one section of his battery, took the left. As soon as the major opened, the enemy replied with a well-directed fire from a superior number of guns, causing many casualties among officers, men, and horses. This unequal contest was sustained by both the officers and men with great fortitude until near night.

The enemy in the meantime planted some guns on the left [Culp's Hill], which partially enfiladed our batteries, which caused Captain *Carpenter* to suffer very severely. By this time, two of Captain *Dement's* pieces had expended all their ammunition and one caisson had been blown up. Captain *Brown* had a piece disabled, and his detachment so reduced that he could work only two guns, and Captain *Brown* had been shot down at this juncture, the enemy pouring a destructive fire on them.

Major *Latimer* sent his sergeant-major to General *Johnson* to say that, owing to the exhausted state of his men and ammunition and the severe fire of the enemy, he was unable to hold his position any longer. General *Johnson* sent him word to withdraw the battalion, if he thought proper. Most of the guns were then withdrawn, leaving four guns on the hill to repel any advance of the enemy's infantry.

Soon after this, Major *Latimer* again opened on the enemy with the four guns left in position to cover the advance of our infantry, which drew a terrible fire on him, and it was here that the accomplished and gallant *Latimer* was severely wounded in the arm, of which wound he has since died. The command then devolved upon Captain *Raine*, the senior captain of the battalion. Night coming on, Captain *Raine* withdrew the battalion a short distance, and encamped for the night.

Casualties in Captain *Raine's* battery: Second section, commanded by Captain *Raine* 1 man severely wounded and left in enemy's lines; several others slightly wounded, but are now doing duty; 3 horses killed. First section, Lieutenant *William W. Hardwicke* commanding—3 men severely wounded; axle-tree of No. 1 gun, damaged by solid shot. The horses of this section were taken to the rear, and hence did not suffer.

Casualties in Captain *Brown's* battery: Captain *Brown* severely wounded; Lieutenant *B. G. Roberts* wounded; 4 men killed and 10 wounded; 9 horses killed or permanently disabled.

Casualties in Captain *Dement's* battery: 1 corporal killed; 4 men wounded; 9 horses killed or permanently disabled; 1 caisson exploded and 1 disabled.

Casualties in Captain *Carpenter's* battery: 1 corporal killed; 4 men killed; 1 sergeant wounded; 1 corporal wounded; 17 enlisted men badly wounded; several others very slightly wounded, now on duty; 9 horses killed.

Summary: 1 major severely wounded; 1 captain severely wounded; 1 lieutenant wounded, 1 non-commissioned officer and 9 men killed; 2 non-commissioned [officers] and 30 men wounded; 30 horses killed. [*OR* 27, pt. 2, pp. 543–44]

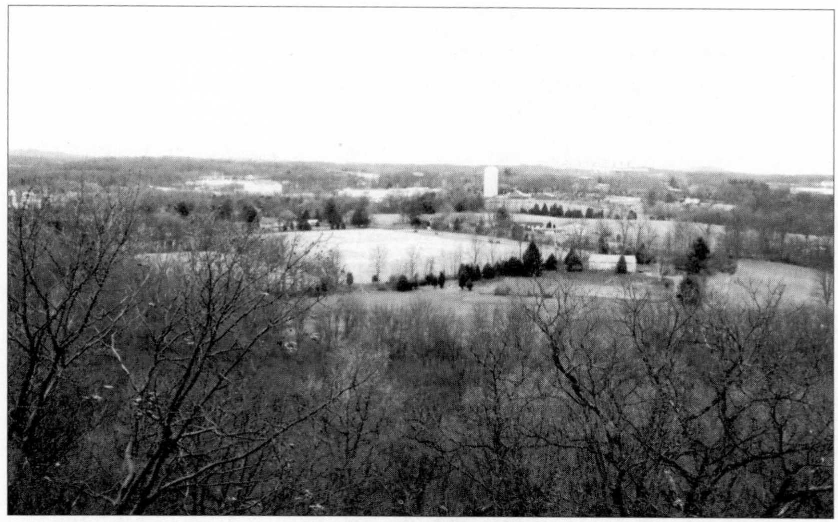

Benner's Hill and the position of *Latimer's* Battalion as seen from Culp's Hill. *Latimer's* guns were positioned on the far right side of the open field in the center of the photo.

Face left and walk or drive the 60 yards to the guns and marker for *Dement's* First Maryland Battery. Stand beside the marker and look in the direction the guns are pointed.

Position B – An Artilleryman Story

The four Napoleons of Captain *William F. Dement's* battery were deployed at this location. *John W. F. Hatton*, a member of the battery, left a graphic account of the fighting here from the view of a soldier under fire.

Narrative of *John W. F. Hatton*, CSA, *Dement's* First Maryland Battery, *Andrews's* Artillery Battalion, *Ewell's* Corps, Army of Northern Virginia

At 4 o'clock p.m. our battery advanced to the line of battle and rolled our guns in position on a hill . . . east of Gettysburg. Our whole artillery battalion opened fire as fast as the guns could be gotten into position, and a storm of shell greeted us the moment our first gun fired. It seemed the enemy had gotten [the] range of the hill even before we fired, and were expecting us to occupy the position and were watching for us. Solid shots were whistling by us, striking among a few scattering bunches of trees along the hill side and tearing up the ground in several places; and the shells were bursting over us, around us, and among us, keeping the air in a continuous vibration like a severe storm raging. Horses were killed in harness while others were plunging from fright and wounds. Men were struck, wounded and killed, while their comrades continued at their duties regardless of the cry's of agony and the moans of the dieing. Our guns were served as fast as could be with shot and shell. After a while both sides ceased firing as though both combatants were exhausted. During the lull we cleared away the fragments of shattered carriages and tangled up horses and the dead and made ready to renew the carnage. A short distance to my left Corp. *Thompson (Sam)* was engaged during the firing in detailing out ammunition from the caisson. He was rather careless as to closing the lid of the box immediately after extracting a round. He was warned by a comrade that he was running a great risk. His reply was, "Oh nothing's going to hurt *Sam*! *Sam's* going to Baltimore!" A few seconds after he uttered these words with a light and joyful heart, a shell exploded in close proximity to his caisson, scattering sparks in every direction, some of which fell into the open limber box, causing it to explode [in] a sheet of flame, a terrific report, and all was over in a flash of lightning. As the smoke drifted away, the caisson was revealed in a wrecked condition—spindles of the axel twisted, wheels shattered and warped, ammunition boxes reduced to splinters and whirled out of sight, a few black and burnt fragments scattered around, and the horses frantic, some wounded and tangled in the harness. A few yards away from the scene of destruction was a form lying prone upon the ground, clothes scorched, smoking and burnt, head divested of a cap and exposing a bald surface where use to be a full suit of hair, whiskers singed off to the skin, eye-brows and eye-lids denuded of their fringes and the eyes set with a popped gaze. Was he breathing? No! It was the body of *Sam Thompson*, the jovial soul.

A few minutes of preparation and rest had placed our artillery in readiness to renew the fight. The wreckage was cleared away; ammunition arranged; the guns loaded, and the word was given "fire!," and all the guns of the battalion were discharged at the same time; and the ground upon which we stood trembled from the jar. So promptly did the enemy reply that it seemed as though they caused our own shells [to] rebound against us, after the manner of a boomerang, after leaving the muzzles of our guns but a step or so. Doubtless, they had occupied the few minutes of respite, like ourselves, in a vigorous preparation for the renewal of the contest. Doubtless, they were watching our demonstrations, and fired at seeing the flash of our guns before our balls reached them. The enemy fired more furiously than before, having contrived to obtain a cross range [cross fire] of our position, as though they planned to annihilate us.

While the fight was raging in its fury, and the sun was suspended a few minutes above the Western horizon, Maj. *Latimer*, commanding our battalion of artillery, was riding upon the crest of the hill, directing and encouraging the men, [when] a shell burst close to him, killing his horse and wounding him severely. Both rider and horse fell, the latter partly upon the former so as to pin him to the ground. My brother *Joseph* seeing the accident ran to his assistance and helped to extricate the major from the perilous position. The major was wounded in the arm and did not long survive.

Major *Joseph W. Latimer*, CSA. National Archives.

About this time, we ceased firing; but the enemy continued a while longer. I took this as a bad omen. Had we gotten the better of them, they would have been the first to desist. I felt the day was decided against us.

About sundown, we had orders to retire from the field. We fixed up our shattered condition and slowly dragged ourselves to the rear. So shattered, indeed, was the battery to our right [*Carpenter's* Battery], that we had to lend them men to get their guns from [the] position. [Memoir of *John William Ford Hatton*, *Dement's* First Maryland Battery, Library of Congress Accession No. 9243, DLC]

After most of the artillery withdrew from this position, *Johnson's* Division moved across the ground to your rear and left rear and attacked Culp's Hill. Then Major General *Jubal Early* sent two of his brigade from the location to your right front to attack East Cemetery Hill.

Return to your car for the drive to Stop 28 and the beginning of July 3.

Continue to drive on the park road to the turn around area, then retrace your path and drive back north to the Hanover Road. Turn left on to the Hanover Road and drive for 0.8 miles to Stratton Street. Turn left on Stratton Street and drive south for 1 block to Middle Street. Turn right on to Middle Street and drive west for 0.8 miles to the intersection with West Confederate Avenue, which is on Seminary Ridge. Once you leave downtown Gettysburg, Middle Street becomes the Hagerstown Road. You will see the Lutheran Seminary on your right front as you approach Seminary Ridge. At the intersection with West Confederate Avenue, turn left and drive for 1.1 miles to the Virginia State Monument. Park in the area provided or alongside of the road, leave your car, and walk east for 250 yards on the walking path that goes past the monument and on to a rise of ground. As you walk east on the path there will be a woods to your right. When you reach the rise of ground stand so that you are facing east.

Turn to the first page of chapter 4, and continue your tour.

INDEX